Soulful Living

The Process of Personal Transformation

From *PERSONAL TRANSFORMATION* Magazine

Edited by

Rick NurrieStearns, Mary NurrieStearns
and Melissa West

Health Communications, Inc.
Deerfield Beach, Florida

www.hci-online.com

We would like to acknowledge the many publishers who granted us permission to reprint the cited material. (Note: Material written by Rick NurrieStearns, Mary NurrieStearns and Melissa West is not included in this listing.)

Permissions section begins on page 375.

Library of Congress Cataloging-in-Publication Data

Soulful Living: the process of personal transformation/edited by Rick NurrieStearns, Mary NurrieStearns, and Melissa West.

    p. cm.

Includes bibliographical references and index.

ISBN 1-55874-675-7 (trade paper)

    1. Spiritual life. 2. Self-realization—Religious aspects.

I. NurrieStearns, Rick, date.

291.4'4—dc21   98-52013

                                                   CIP

Publisher: Health Communications, Inc.
              3201 S.W. 15th Street
              Deerfield Beach, FL 33442-8190

Cover design by Lisa Camp
Cover image of bird by Richard Bates
Book design by Dawn Grove

Dedicated to the reader:
May you find meaning, energy and happiness

CONTENTS

v

FOREWORD

There are two main ways we become wiser, said Joseph Campbell, the great mythologist—through revelation and through suffering. For must of us, suffering is by far the most common process. Because suffering is a part of everyday life, this means that opportunities for cultivating wisdom, personal growth, and transformation are limitless. In fact, if we totally eliminated suffering in our quest for happiness, we would stunt our spiritual growth, because this would mean eradicating our major path to becoming wiser. If suffering is the price we pay for being human, wisdom is the dividend—that is, if we make proper use of the painful challenges we bump into, which is what this book is all about.

This book teaches us to *engage* the world. Our world needs an engaged spirituality as never before—a spirituality made up of warriors, not worriers, who are not afraid to roll up their sleeves and *risk* something. Too often, we imagine that spiritual work is something that happens in the rarefied atmosphere of weekend retreats, meditation chambers and cathedrals. It does, but it also occurs when we get our hands dirty—when we chop wood and carry water, as the Buddhists put it. We need to remind ourselves of this fact. Spirituality is always in danger of degenerating into passivity, morbid self-absorption, and fixed silence, turning the seeker into a "stone Buddha," as the Zen tradition warns. The other extreme also exists—frenetically trying to save the world without first saving ourselves, without attending to our own inner life. As in most things, balance is the key.

If our work toward personal transformation doesn't translate into our daily activities, we need to reexamine our direction. According to the Sufi tradition, it isn't sufficient to remain on the mountaintop following enlightenment. One must come down to the foothills, lowlands and the valleys of the world—and even into the gutters, if that's where our work takes us—and integrate so completely with our world that we can't be distinguished as someone special. This is literally what transformation means—"trans" form, beyond form, becoming a nobody.

An example of applied spirituality can be found, again, in the life of Joseph

Campbell. He once said that he found vacations to be rather irritating experiences. While sitting on a beach, doing nothing, his mind was always preoccupied with his beloved work, which was his passion in life. Why should he give this up for a few do-nothing days at the beach? Here we see a searing vision and a life on fire. This is the full-bore level of commitment often demonstrated in the lives of the great saints and mystics, who often transformed not just themselves but the world around them.

The following pages are a marvelous collection of inspiring insights into the process of personal transformation and how to apply these realizations to daily life. I have emphasized one aspect of this process—spiritual activism—because I find this sadly lacking today in so much spiritual work. Ultimately, there can be no self-healing which does not involve the healing of others. Want to jump start your personal process of transformation? Do something for someone else—putting yourself as completely out of the picture as possible, allowing empathy and caring to flow forth, setting aside all personal desires, *including the desire for personal transformation*.

But readers will respond differently to the different messages that follow, depending on where they are on their spiritual path. Yet, as we progress, the challenge is always to go beyond the initial stages of spiritual awakening, to *give* something of ourselves, to be of service to others and to our world, and to do so with love and compassion and without fanfare. In so doing, we invariably find that *personal* transformation is also about *mutual* and *collective* transformation. We're in this together. My task is yours, and yours mine. No one need bear her burden alone.

Shall we begin?

Larry Dossey, M.D.
executive editor, *Alternative Therapies in Health and Medicine*
author, *Healing Words, Prayer Is Good Medicine* and *Recovering the Soul*

ACKNOWLEDGMENTS

I would like to acknowledge the late Lina Psaltis for her encouragement in my first transformational steps. Since then, many spiritual teachers and healers have guided me and I thank each of them for their wisdom and insight.

In particular, I am grateful to Zen master Thich Nhat Hanh, a remarkable Buddhist teacher who simply states the essence of the human condition in a profound and inspiring way.

Professionally, I wish to acknowledge my literary agent, Barbara Neighbors Deal, for her enthusiasm and encouragement in the development of this book. I also am indebted to Melissa West for her help in bringing to life this book.

And to my wife, Mary, my deepest gratitude. I am grateful for and appreciative of her support in publishing PERSONAL TRANSFORMATION magazine.

INTRODUCTION

By its very nature, life is an ongoing transformation. As we grow from infant to adult our body and mind experience profound changes. Up to a certain level of maturity transformation naturally occurs, regardless of our strategies or efforts to resist. Beyond that level of maturation, transformation may continue, but it requires conscious effort.

This book is designed to inspire you on your conscious transformational journey. It contains a collection of articles from past issues of PERSONAL TRANSFORMATION magazine, a publication my wife and I developed eight years ago. We selected the following articles to communicate the process of personal transformation.

Personal transformation, in its higher aspects, is more than individual happiness or individual enlightenment. It's about becoming open to the evolutionary impulse within life itself, reaching full maturation and becoming whole. In its simpler aspects, personal transformation is about learning to live life fully. It's about reclaiming our lives in ways that bring renewed meaning, energy and happiness to ourselves and others.

We started publishing PERSONAL TRANSFORMATION magazine shortly after we married. It sprang forth from our desire to help and to share with others what we were learning. We published material that touched our hearts and taught us how to live more gently and fully. The magazine represented our distinct, but complementary approaches to life. Mary, a licensed psychotherapist, was trained in the Western psychological approach to life and healing. I had followed a less mainstream approach, studying the spiritual and philosophical paths of Buddhism and Hinduism. The combination of Eastern and Western taught us that both psychological and spiritual methods are needed to help us break free.

In a transformational life, we gradually learn how to truly live. We find what we are called to do and how to access our inner fire and joy. In the process of maturing, aspects of ourselves and our lifestyles that no longer serve our life are discarded. As we tap into our real selves—living our deepest values and ideals—we become connected with all of life.

To transform ourselves, we must become more conscious of who we are; we must develop self-awareness. Being aware helps us to merge with our essential nature. Self-observation helps us to discover and make conscious our unconscious, so we don't unconsciously sabotage our efforts to create the life we are meant to live. To transform our lives, we must reclaim our unowned parts so we can discover our social, mental and emotional imprints.

I remember being at a workshop for couples years ago and noticing that many of the arguments between the couples seemed absurd, not worth arguing about. Several months later Mary and I had an argument. Actually, I had an argument with Mary, as she really didn't say much. In preparing to go on vacation, Mary wanted to leave extra food out for our dogs. She put dog food in a bucket, a bucket that to me was special, the one I used for swimming pool maintenance.

I told her this was a special bucket and to use another. She looked at me in disbelief: to her a bucket was a bucket. I became angry; I felt she wasn't listening to me. As I continued to argue, I started to see the similarities between the absurd arguments of the couples at the workshop and mine. I was determined not to give in—not to Mary, and not to my realization that what I was saying was ridiculous. I stuck to my points, but my body would not cooperate. As I angrily argued my mouth started to smile. I turned my face from Mary so she couldn't see. Just then, the absurdity of my words really sank in and I burst out laughing. My anger had been transformed into laughter. Self-awareness helped me to discover an unconscious habit of wanting to win arguments more than wanting to be understanding in relationships. That was a transformational moment for me. Since then, I have had many more. I treasure them, as I know that is the way of transformation.

Transformation frees us from our own internal resistance, from the confines of our self-imposed constraints, enabling us to make radical shifts in the way we live. Over time, it aligns our body, heart and mind with our deeper spiritual nature, which gives us freedom from old, habituated living. With this freedom, we move closer to our highest self, essence, soul or "god self."

This is how we become the grand men and women we are meant to be. We ongoingly rebirth ourselves. Who we were yesteryear and who we are today die, so that we may breathe life into the possibilities of who we are becoming. We literally forsake old beliefs, visions and experiences of who we were, so that we may be molded into ever-finer expressions of our life essence.

It is my sincere hope this book will be a guide and companion on your journey of self discovery and help open your way to a richer, fuller, more rewarding life.

Rick NurrieStearns
Publisher
PERSONAL TRANSFORMATION magazine

1

Learning to Live

The process of personal transformation has many points of entry. Illness, the death of a loved one, divorce or other shocking event can shatter your sense of who you are and why you are here. This shattering thrusts you into a deep inner terrain that begins your journey of awakening. Other times, the journey begins in response to a disquieting yearning that insists there is more meaning to life than is reflected by the way you are living. For some, a spontaneous spiritual or mystical experience alters their awareness of who they truly are, and begins their journey of reconnecting with the depth of being that was opened to them spontaneously.

Once you intentionally begin a transformational journey, you come to know yourself more completely, open to mystery, and feel connected to life in general, and yours in particular. Along the way, you begin to reprioritize and recreate how you live. Your sense of inner peace, honesty and kindness grows, reflecting the psychological maturation and spiritual grounding that result from your efforts. These shifts also reflect the grace that accompanies transformational work.

The day comes when everyone asks, "How am I to live?" This chapter guides you through that question. It shows you how to quiet your mind and open your heart so your mind can be guided by the wisdom of your heart and you can truly learn to live.

The Wish to Grow

The wish to grow, to evolve and mature into the finest person we can possibly be, is one of the fundamental driving forces behind any extraordinary life—certainly any spiritual life. We only get out of life what we're willing to demand from ourselves, and if we want to attain our highest potential, growing will have to be our number one priority.

In its most intense and powerful form, this wish to grow does not include any personal agendas or desired outcomes. We understand that our minds are too limited to conceive of the greatness we might become or the ways in which that greatness might unfold in our lives. In fact, there is no finer wish because we are surrendering all of our desires and limitations into the hands of God.

The words themselves, "I wish to grow," when deeply felt, plant a seed in us which has within it the power to completely transform our lives. While this transformation is wonderful, it is also a challenge. Real growth brings us face to face with uncertainty, testing our strength, our commitment, our flexibility and our trust in Life itself. The alternative—staying the same—is unthinkable to a person who truly wants to know God.

—Swami Chetanananda

Living in the Fast Lane

EKNATH EASWARAN

Constant hurry and day-in, day-out pressure take a cumulative toll on the nervous system. When the hurry becomes chronic, the effects of this toll build up in the mind as well. What begins as nervous tension becomes rigid patterns in the way we think and act. The mind itself gets speeded up; and when the mind gets speeded up, it is easily subject to negative emotions like anger and fear. A racing mind is simply moving too fast for love, compassion, tenderness and similarly quiet states. Judgment is replaced by snap decisions. In a mad rush, in a frantic hurry, where is the time for making choices?

On the hairpin curves in the hills around the Bay Area there are signs warning "25 miles per hour." It reminds me of the Blue Mountain area of South India where I used to live. On those winding, narrow roads there was one dangerous hairpin curve after another. But since many drivers did not know how to read, instead of a sign saying "25 miles per hour" there was a grisly picture of a human skull. Most drivers immediately became cautious when they saw that skull, because a mistake on those roads could be fatal.

Every driver understands that if you go too fast, you can't control your car. But few of us understand that the mind is very much like a car. It drives us through life, and we go where it takes us. When we are in a hurry, the mind is moving too fast for us to absorb what is going on around us, heed the warning signs and make the judgment calls we need to avoid a potential accident. And when judgment is blurred by speed, we are in the greatest danger. It is no exaggeration to say that we are then on a mountain road taking blind hairpin bends at sixty miles an hour, barely holding the road.

"Living in the fast lane" has become a notorious phrase with reason. Nobody should travel in that fast lane. When your life and your mind are going faster and faster, there can be no decisions. There are only reflexes—and reflexes become compulsive. When the same thought—that is, the same emotional response, the same urge, the same craving—repeats itself over and over again without a break, it becomes compulsive. It can be a compulsive addiction to smoking or drugs, it can be a compulsive attachment to a particular person. Whatever it is, every compulsive cycle of thinking is dangerous because it means we are not free. The mind is as powerful as a Ferrari. We cannot get control of our behavior until we get a firm grip on the wheel. And that means we have to learn to slow down our pace of living.

Trying to get through life without control over your attention is a little like trying to reach a destination with no control over your car.

Suppose you get into your car at five o'clock as usual, ready to drive straight home after a long day at work. Unbeknownst to you, however, your car has taken on a life of its own. To outward appearance it is still your reliable old Ford station wagon, but under the hood it has been possessed by a ghost.

You get in and head for home—north, say, out of San Francisco, across the Golden Gate Bridge. It is a beautiful day, and you are enjoying the view and the unusually light traffic when suddenly, without warning, your car swerves into the right-hand lane. You grab the wheel sharply, but the car ignores the wheel and pulls off onto the exit to Sausalito. In horror, you realize that you are not driving your Ford any more; it is driving you.

You want to go home, but your car has other ideas. It finds Sausalito tempting. Even a ghost is susceptible to fine seascapes and good restaurants. You are in a panic. What is the matter with this car?

After a desperate struggle, your Ford begins to respond to the steering wheel again, and you manage to get back on the freeway. "Whew," you say to yourself. "That was a strange incident. But everything seems all right now. I just hope I can get home before anything else happens."

Your worries are well founded. As you pass Mill Valley, you again feel an irresistible tug on the wheel. The ghost takes over once more, pulling fiendishly to the right to get off the road. After fighting with you for a few exits, it gets its way and careens off at Paradise Drive. The malls on both sides of the highway are full of shops your ghost finds fascinating, but you hardly notice. All you want is to get back to Highway 101.

It's a fight like this all the way home. When you finally arrive, three or four excursions later, you're out of gas and it's almost morning—time to head back to San Francisco to go to work again.

This story belongs in the realm of science fiction but when it comes to our attention, we often have as little control over our lives as the driver of this ghost-driven car. With temptations and distractions on every side of us, we are used to the mind weaving all over the road, swerving from lane to lane and causing danger to ourselves and everyone around.

Fortunately, you don't have to put up with this. Attention can be trained, and no skill in life is greater than the capacity to direct your attention at will.

The benefits of this are numerous. If you have trained your mind to give complete attention to one thing at a time, you can achieve your goal in any walk of life. Whether it is science or the arts or sports or a profession, concentration is a basic requirement in every field. And complete concentration is genius.

I have a friend who is an excellent driver with a first-rate car. On a long distance trip, she glides smoothly into the through lane and cruises straight to her destination without even changing lanes. She never seems to exert herself, and she always manages to think a little ahead. Streams of traffic just part like the Red Sea before Moses to let her through. And her concentration is like that, too. When she is behind the wheel, her mind is steady and her attention never wavers.

This kind of one-pointed attention is helpful in whatever job you are doing. But perhaps the greatest benefit of a trained mind is the emotional stability it brings. In order to get angry, your concentration must be broken—your mind has to change lanes. In order to get afraid, your mind has to change lanes. In order to get upset, your mind has to change lanes. It is not that you choose to let your attention wander; your mind simply takes over and changes whether you want it to or not. If you can keep your mind in one lane, your concentration is unbroken; you are master of your attention. Whatever the circumstances, whatever the challenges, you will not lose your sovereignty over your thinking process.

A wandering mind is not just a modern problem. Even in the days of the Compassionate Buddha, more than twenty-five hundred years ago, people used to complain to him, "I have problems at home. I have problems at work. I can't sleep well; I can't eat well; I am always upset."

The Buddha would look at them with his wise eyes and say, "Nobody is upsetting you. Nothing is upsetting you. You get upset because you are upsettable."

Then he would add, "Don't you want to be un-upsettable?"

"Yes, Blessed One."

"Don't you want to be happy?"

"Of course, Blessed One."

"Then," he would say, "you have to train your mind."

That is what we all yearn for—a mind that cannot be upset by anything. And we can achieve it, too. But it calls for a lot of work in the training of attention.

The Buddha was perhaps the most acute psychologist the world has seen, because he understood the workings of the mind from the inside. When we have resentments or hostilities or ill will, he would say, not only our attention but our vital energy is caught in the past. When we learn to recall attention from the past and keep it completely in the present, we reclaim a tremendous reserve of vital energy that has been trapped in the past like a dinosaur. Every time we do this, we restore a little more of our vital wealth to the present moment.

Just as all of us carry the burden of resentments from the past, we all have fears and anxieties related to the future. This is part of our conditioning as human beings. But here, too, we can learn to prevent our energy from wandering into the future and keep it completely in the present.

In the long run—I am anticipating many years of training attention—you won't think about the past at all. It is not that you cannot remember the past; you just don't think about it. You won't think about the future, either; not that you don't plan for the future but you are not entangled in what it will bring. You live 100 percent in the present—which means you are 100 percent alive.•

Plant What You Love in the Garden of Your Life

W A Y N E   M U L L E R

W hen we plant a garden, we must first prepare the soil. We must take great care to clear the ground of rocks, twigs and weeds, removing anything that will prevent healthy growth. We work the soil, sifting the hard clumps, digging in essential nutrients. Then we might build a fence, an enclosure to keep out predatory animals—rabbits, deer, gophers—so that the garden will be safe from harm.

But what if we stop there? What if we spend all our time preparing the soil, moving rocks, pulling weeds and building fences? At the end of our work, what will we have? Only a clear, empty patch of ground. There will be no harvest, no flowers, no nourishment from this garden.

The second, indispensable question we must answer is this: What shall we plant in this garden? What harvest, when it comes, will bring us great joy? What seeds, when they blossom, will provide us with delight? It is not enough to keep clearing, sifting, removing obstacles, securing boundaries. While it is essential that we prepare the soil, this will not in itself produce a harvest.

In the same way, our various healing methods, our psychologies and therapies can help us clear the ground of our past and prepare us to receive a better life. But it is not enough simply to clear the debris of the past. We must plant what we love in the garden of our life. As the *Tao Te Ching* insists, our center will heal us. When we attend to what is loving and beautiful, we are brought forward into our most exquisite manifestation. "Correct handling of flowers," suggests Bokuyo Takeda, "redefines the personality."

This is the difference between a life repaired and a life well-lived. When we spend all our time clearing the ground of our life story, we are seeking only to repair what is broken, to fix what is defective. But even when we are successful, the best we can hope for is to climb all the way up to ground level, to "recover" some imagined state of being "normal." But what if we imagine something beyond a life repaired?

Our work in therapy, telling old stories and healing the old wounds, is necessary and important. This is the work of clearing the ground of our lives. But then there are seeds to plant. Thich Nhat Hanh writes:

> *There are many kinds of seeds in us, both good and bad. Some were planted during our lifetime, and some were transmitted by our parents, our ancestors and our society. Our ancestors and our parents have given us seeds of joy, peace and happiness, as well as seeds of sorrow, anger and so on.*

Every time we practice mindful living, we plant healthy seeds and strengthen the healthy seeds already in us. Healthy seeds function similarly to antibodies. When a virus enters our bloodstream, our body reacts and antibodies come and surround it, take care of it, and transform it. This is true with our psychological seeds as well. If we plant wholesome, healing, refreshing seeds, they will take care of the negative seeds, even without our asking them. To succeed, we must cultivate a good reserve of refreshing seeds.

Anne grew up with an alcoholic father. Now, with five children and a demanding career, she often feels overwhelmed and exhausted by her life. She is always taking care of something or someone, and she resents that she has to work so hard for so little emotional reward. Just as she did with her alcoholic father, she is always watching for what needs to be done, what tasks are required, how to make sure everything and everyone is taken care of.

Anne and I worked together for some time on her childhood and how the pain of her family alcoholism gave birth to her compulsions and her weariness. At the same time, I could see that Anne was also a very playful, creative woman who rarely allowed herself to nurture her artistic spirit. "My father was the artist in the family," she reported to me one day. "It was my job to clean up the messes he left behind." We discussed the possibility of her listening more closely to her creative impulses. She said she would try, but it would be hard. Where would she find the time?

A few weeks later, Anne proudly announced she had begun taking a watercolor class two evenings a week at the community college. When she told me about her painting, her eyes were bright and her face shone. She brought me some of her paintings. They were bright and playful, rich with passionate colors. "When I'm painting, I feel something deep in my body, a joy, a happiness.

These may not be great paintings—I just love doing them so much. I lock myself in my room for hours, and no one is allowed to bother me. I'm just letting myself go. I'm having so much fun."

The more Anne painted, the more she shifted her awareness. She no longer watched like the child of an alcoholic. Now she saw with the eyes of a painter. Instead of always watching for responsibilities, now she also watched for colors, lines, textures and shapes. She had shifted her inner language; she was now seeking what she loved.

Her family, her children and her marriage were still the same. But Anne could now see with eyes that were more in balance, eyes that could also uncover what was beautiful and rich in her daily, ordinary life.•

Finding Joy

DANNEL SCHWARTZ

Mystics understood the simple truth of human existence: Happiness is to be treasured and welcomed into every life. The key to this thinking is found in the Talmud, which tells us that upon death every person will be asked the following questions to determine their eternal fate:

Were you honest in business?

Did you set aside time for study?

Did you have hope?

Did you enjoy all the permitted pleasures of life? Or, why weren't you happy with those pleasures you did experience?

For many of us, the problem is as simple as not understanding what true happiness is and not recognizing that the cloth of contentment and joy is woven with the threads of spirituality. Happiness results from a frequency of positive emotions and a minimizing of life's pain. It is the sum total of all the positive emotions we can muster. By concentrating on the positive, we can create happiness, which can help put the painful, problematic parts of our lives into perspective.

I had a professor in college who, at the first class in each semester of his beginning-level psychology course, before even introducing himself or telling his students what they'd learn, would draw a large dot in the center of a sheet of white paper. He then held the paper over his head and asked his curious students: "What do you see?"

Dozens of answers came from every corner of the lecture hall. Many of the professor's more clever students who thought the dot was a Rorschach test let their minds wander: a butterfly, the earth, the tip of a very red rose. Others were more literal. They saw a black dot or a maybe a black dot with tiny white specks in it.

When the students became quiet, the professor lowered the drawing, looked at it as if he were trying to assess each answer he'd received, and said: "I see a sheet of paper with a dot in its center, eight and a half by eleven inches with a spot that perhaps covers 20 percent of the total writing surface available on this one side. I could write the Declaration of Independence, the Magna Carta, the entire Bill of Rights on this one sheet of paper. Yet, all you saw was the black dot."

He paused, allowing his point to penetrate. Then he drove that point home: "That is how most people view their lives. Let that be your first lesson in psychology."

My professor's point is that most of us are so busy studying the black dots that mar our lives that we lose sight of the bold whiteness of possibility that surrounds those dots. We don't see our accomplishments and how we touched the world in a positive way because of those insignificant dots, the problems, the troubles large and small over which we have no control. We just know we'll never be happy. And, if we're not happy, something must be wrong.

HAPPINESS COMES WITH THE RIGHT ATTITUDE UNDER ANY CIRCUMSTANCE

We don't partake of what the Talmud calls "the permissible pleasures," because we let the black spots block our view. Minimizing those obstacles and maximizing the possibilities that surround them is the goal of practical spirituality.

It's not that easy, though. Even mystics and spiritual people throughout history realized that the world conspires to make the average person unhappy. It is not a plot devised by some evil genie or a cosmic joke or a test created by a divinity eager to grade us on our grace under pressure. Things happen, pain happens, problems happen, sometimes for no apparent reason. There are times when we will be exposed to the worst that life has to offer. Even barring that, none of us is immune from the scrapes and crises of everyday life, no matter how rich or well-known we may be. The fancy new car *will* squeak. It *will* get dirty. It might even break down.

The black dot that makes a day miserable is frequently a small problem. A tiny hole in an otherwise unconsidered tooth. Thousands of our body parts may be working perfectly, but one small sprain of an obscure tendon and our well-exercised machine can become an utter wreck that seems to demand our full attention and energy. Once we're miserable, we seek out like company and spread gloom to others.

Think of all the ways a day can be ruined in the first hour after awakening. The toast can burn; the milk can be sour. Your spouse can be a bit surly. The school bus may come too early or your child may get out the door too late. Good mornings are hard to come by if you let the pain of living get you down.

Jewish mystics teach that a happy person is not someone who has just the right set of circumstances. Instead, the happy person is someone who has the right attitude about any circumstance and is able to communicate that attitude to his or her soul, and then do something either to heighten a positive experience or lessen a negative one. It is crucial, mystics say, to realize that the sharpest stones beneath our bare feet can be diamonds, if we just recognize them as such. In other words, a happy person can bounce back from failure or defeat not only by looking at the bright side, but also by learning from the dark side.

Remember that Albert Einstein flunked math in grade school. Edgar Allan Poe and Salvador Dali were expelled from college. Thomas Edison was at the bottom of his class. Every genius and every true talent has a way of finally blossoming.

JOY MUST BE PRACTICED

The mystics advise a simple strategy to avoid losing it. Because holiness, they say, is wrapped in very ordinary clothing, we just need to be focused enough to see what's special in the familiar things around us. Like muscles that have to be used to avoid atrophy, the soul must be constantly aware and interact with the physical side of life or it will lose its ability to buoy us when we are down or temper our emotions when we are up. This strategy is what the mystics call the daily exercise of the soul: practice.

So, like an athlete, we practice, but still we're troubled. What is the goal of our practice? When do we know whether we've succeeded?

Jewish tradition gives us a goal: we should say one hundred blessings each day. When we try it, we discover that it's quite difficult to find one hundred things each day for which to be thankful. So difficult, in fact, that we spend most of our time looking.

In the course of looking, we find many things worth noting that might have otherwise passed us by. That's the goal. The practiced eye sees far more than the lazy one. As a result, the more we look for happiness, the more we can see it. Happiness then becomes not a final state to be achieved, but a process, a way of life and of living it in a spiritual way. It's something that we can do day in and day out.

This process of searching for one hundred blessings also creates an important awareness—that it is impossible to be happy all the time. We may never reach one hundred blessings, but there's still plenty to be happy about. Many things bring us joy, no matter what our struggles or misfortunes.

There's a wonderful story, popularized by the writer Robert Fulghum, about a man who felt discouraged because he was only happy half the time. He went to his rabbi in tears, moaning that he felt like a failure. The rabbi stroked his beard (all rabbis in stories seem to have beards), nodded his head wisely and suggested cryptically that the man refer to a specific page of the current *World Almanac of Facts*.

The surprised fellow dutifully followed the rabbi's instruction and came back, confused. "I don't understand," said the troubled man, showing the rabbi the book. "All I can find on that page is a list of baseball batting statistics."

The rabbi pointed at a line on the page. The man read it aloud: "Highest lifetime batting averages."

"And who is at the top of that list?" the rabbi asked.

The man answered: "Ty Cobb, with a lifetime average of .367."

The rabbi looked deeply into the man's disconsolate eyes and said: "So?"

The man was disturbed. "I don't understand," he said.

"Listen, my friend," the rabbi answered. "Ty Cobb only got a base hit once every three times, but still he was the best, still he made the Hall of Fame."

The man, in despair, twisted his hands together anxiously. "I'm not a base-ball fan," he said. "I don't understand."

The rabbi rose from behind his desk, frustrated. "If one out of three got Ty Cobb into the Hall of Fame, then you are a superstar, because you told me you were happy one of every two days," the rabbi said. "You're batting .500. So don't complain."

What the rabbi didn't say is that, with a little practice, who knows what heights the man might have reached. With a little practice, when asked that fateful question upon his death, "Why didn't you enjoy all the permitted pleasures?" he could answer, "But I did." •

Heart Lessons:
Peace, Joy and Happiness

BERNIE SIEGEL, M. D.

This is the essence of how I help myself remain aware of my feelings: I write a poem whenever something moves me. This one came after watching a story on television about Lassie. "I love Lassie, Lassie loves me. Lassie is love. A dog, a dog, a dog teaches love. I'm going to set my sights on becoming a dog. I have a role model now." So that's how I manage. Whenever I wonder how to be more loving, I behave as if I were Lassie. Love is so important. When we're in pain, if someone is there for us, loving us, we receive the greatest gift in the world, and we ultimately hurt a lot less. I hope that someday we shall reach a point where it is normal for people to love well and fully. It's certainly not that we don't have enough information about how to love, but many of us don't have the ability, because we weren't loved ourselves. The best way around this problem is to practice and rehearse loving behavior daily.

Years ago, I asked the anthropologist Ashley Montagu how I could be a more loving human being. I said, "For example, if my mother-in-law moves into my house and I want to have a better relationship with her, be more loving with her, what can I do?" And he said, "When your mother-in-law comes in the room, behave as if you love her." I thought this advice sounded superficial, but then I realized that I really wanted to achieve this mindset. I wasn't trying to fool my mother-in-law or my wife or my children or anyone else. I only wanted to love them more. So I began to stop and think when somebody entered the room: "If I love this person, how would I behave toward him or her?" And, of course, what I found was that the more I acted this way, the more loving and sensitive I became. And the other people are changed by simply being loved; it really becomes easier to love them. With this basic approach, over time I changed myself, my body, my state of health, my relationships and many other aspects of my life.

Learning to love more effectively merely involves performing and practicing like a movie star or an athlete. When someone says to actors or athletes, "Oh, you're such a lucky person to be born with this skill," they look at the person as if to say, "Wait a minute, I am a wonderful performer or athlete not because I was born with this skill, but because I spent a lot of time practicing and rehearsing and working my way up." So becoming a lover works exactly the same way—rehearsing and practicing. Find role models. A person could say, "What would the Buddha or Jesus do in this situation? Or Moses, Confucius, Gandhi, the Dalai Lama, Mother Teresa, Martin Luther King Jr.?" Or just imagine how a loving mother would act. And if that's too hard, then you can always go back to "What would Lassie do?" A dog will lick your face even if you ignore it. Unless repeatedly abused, a dog will lick your face, even when a vet has amputated a limb or is about to put it to death. It simply doesn't hold onto hostility. It is here to love, be loved and, along the way, teach us a few things.

All the world's a theater, and we can choose how to act. We're given a lifetime to practice and can become as good as we want to be. But we must remember that we cannot perform well all the time. Therefore, we need to be forgiving of ourselves and others, recognizing that we're doing the best we can at any moment.

As a physician, I have found that being good at loving has nothing to do with physical health. There are plenty of wonderful lovers out there who are missing parts of their bodies or the ability to move. I call these "the healthy people," but it has nothing to do with the state of their bodies or their physical health. Sometimes, in fact, it takes the threat of death for people to pay attention to love and to make it a priority. Our mortality can be a great teacher.

It's hard for people who don't know how to play, who have lost that childlike quality, to be lovers because they are more likely to be hostile. Love and play go together. People who have studied pathological killers say that many of them just don't know how to play. They can't kid around. Everything is serious.

Laughter brings out the child in everybody. It diffuses much of the fear and resentment people have of one another, making it easier to be loving. Just look at your baby picture, and you'll know how easy it is to love that child. Now look in the mirror. Do you have the same feelings? Why not?

To encourage love at the hospital (this can also be done in any office), I give out rainbow pins with people's names that say, "You make a difference." If I saw people acting in a loving way, I would get their names and give them pins and thank them. Just think, if everybody who was dedicated to love wore a symbol, you would behave differently toward them when you saw them.

I was lucky to be brought up loved. Not that everything I did was liked, but I knew that I was loved—and knowing this gave me the ability and freedom to be who I wanted to be. Because I had my parents' support, I didn't need everybody else's approval, and I could be loving and free. The benefit of this kind of support is that when you want to be different, you can, because you know you will always be accepted. When I married, I always knew that I could come home to a loving person who accepted me. So, if I were a little bizarre, crazy, or whatever, I had a place to go. Even when disturbing things happened to me, I knew I could go home, where I was still number one.

Sadly, others are not so fortunate. People who have not been loved as children are often in a great deal of pain, even if they do not show it outwardly. We need to communicate about the pain we suffer and listen to one another in order to heal. We can't assume that everyone thinks or feels like we do.

I suggest that we have an American Society for the Prevention of Cruelty to Humans, like the ASPCA. Basically, I want people to love themselves and others as they would a pet. Some people feed themselves things they would never feed their pets. They'll take drugs they wouldn't give their pets. People exercise their pets, while they themselves just sit around. They hug their pets, but not their own families. People need to be as kind to themselves as they are to their pets. We have the information but not the inspiration.

In my practice, I've often seen that people wouldn't take the necessary steps to stay healthy. I learned that for most people wellness becomes a spiritual journey. So in trying to inspire people, I ask them, "Why are you here? Why were you born? Why is the world the way it is? What is all this about?" And my answer is that we're here to learn to love more fully, to be God or angels in disguise for one another, to show our love, to show our compassion, to be active in creation. That is the reason and the meaning behind our lives. Each of us has a choice about how to love the world in our unique way.

Wherever I lecture, I hear people complaining about how other people act at work or at home. They often let their irritations ruin their lives. To have a happy life, we have to practice loving people, including their imperfections, which means learning and practicing tolerance and compassion. If you are here for a limited time, would you rather spend it being irritated or being loving?

Here's a story about how I once handled a disagreement with my wife,

Bobbie. The handles broke off some cups because of the way I put them in the dishwasher. My wife wanted to throw them out. I didn't. I thought they were still useful. So I just put the cups in a bag to hide them and prevent divorce proceedings. I took them to our vacation house where my wife wouldn't see them as often. One morning while we were on Cape Cod, I went out jogging as usual with a plastic bag to pick up either things that God leaves me along the way or recyclables. I was running along and saw a cup with a broken handle lying in the road. I knew it was a message from God. So I ran over, picked it up, turned it over, and saw a drawing of two fat elephants hugging under mistletoe. Inscribed on the cup was "I love you just the way you are." I brought the cup home and showed it to Bobbie. Now the cup sits on a shelf in our house, reminding us every day of the real message of life. (The other cups are now accepted and used by my wife.)

When you're a lover, you don't destroy—whether it's nature, society or an individual. Children who have plants and animals learn to care and nurture a reverence for life.

At any given time, our five children used to have up to a hundred creatures in our home, including three dozen turtles in kiddy pools, lizards, dogs, skunks and crickets. I tried to teach my kids that if they had a life in their hands, they cared for it and eventually became an expert in its care. I think a child brought up this way is going to be a lot different as an adult from one who learns that suffering is meaningless and it's okay to kill a neighbor or torture animals or that a neighbor isn't the right color, shape or whatever. As our son Jeff said, "The animals get along because they're all the same color inside." So are we.

I suggest that people keep a journal or write a poem every day, like the one I wrote about Lassie. It helps them get in touch with all aspects of life, including the painful ones. It's important to write not only about the tough stuff, which we tend to remember, but also about the good and funny events. If people can see the humor in a tense situation, then they can laugh and diffuse the anger.

It's great when parents can act childlike, because their kids notice and then feel free to behave that way. Making others laugh is such a loving act, because if love didn't exist between people, they wouldn't be interested in laughing or in making another person laugh. Perhaps if we can all become a little less serious, laugh more often, and act more loving toward ourselves and others, we can live in a more loving world, and we can all fill our lives with love.•

Joy Is Your Natural Birthright

CHARLOTTE   DAVIS   KASL

Joy has the power to open our hearts, remove fear, instill hope and foster healing. Joy leads us to wisdom because it connects us to all we are—our mind, heart, power and spirit. Joy stimulates our immune system, increases our energy and gives us mental clarity. It helps us heighten our level of consciousness so we can more readily tap our inner wisdom. Instead of agonizing over decisions, we become more able to simply listen within and know what to do.

As we open ourselves to joy we experience the breadth of human emotions, realize our connection to all life, feel compassion and dance lightly with the dramas of our lives. As our joy expands we feel deeply connected to ourselves and to something bigger than ourselves.

When we have the ability to access joy, we are more able to stay centered in the midst of life's difficulties and tap our creativity. This helps our creativity pour forth uncensored by our rational minds. We become able to recapture the spontaneity of childhood before we were taught to stop our wild scribbling and start coloring within the lines. Creativity that springs from joy also helps us reach beyond the boundaries of traditional thought for new, original, compassionate solutions to the problems and challenges of our lives and our society.

Joy is not about getting high, or prolonged indulgence in sense pleasures. While enjoying our senses in a balanced way helps us touch the experience of joy, ultimately joy comes from moving beyond our senses to a deeper experience of stillness and inner knowing. Once we touch this place, even momentarily, our lives are altered because we become aware of the vast resources of our intricately interwoven body, mind and spirit in shaping the course of our lives. When we develop our capacity for joy, it lives within us like a wellspring of awareness that heightens our ability to be intimate with others without fear.

We are all born with a capacity for love and joy. Yet many of us feel uneasy at the thought of seeking more joy in our lives. That is not surprising because we have been taught repeatedly that growth comes through struggle and suffering. Joy and happiness are suspect in our culture, often regarded as childlike, indulgent or immature. Our culture is focused on competition, control, activity, striving, and productivity.

While you may not have been taught directly that quietness or idleness are to be feared, it is an undercurrent that pervades our culture. An echo of the old phrase—"Idle brains are the devil's workshop"—still lingers in many people's minds, creating uneasiness, guilt or discomfort at the idea of relaxing or doing things solely for pleasure and delight. Yet the journey to joy includes allowing ourselves time to do nothing, be idle and let our inner world be known. An idle mind helps us to slip beneath the activities of our daily lives into the quiet knowing place that resides in each of us, a place at once secure, peaceful and vast. Our culture may fear joy, because joy empowers people to feel alive, exuberant, self-respecting and unlikely to tolerate being exploited or harmed. Thus becoming a joyful, happy person can feel like a crime against the powers that be, an act of arrogance or willfulness that is somehow wrong. But it is not wrong. An inner sense of joy is our spirit coming alive.

Our culture also emphasizes control and obedience, which are based on fear—fear that people allowed free expression of emotions and thoughts will go out of control, rebel, be lazy or deceitful. Thus, people become divided inside, their passion, anger and tears constricted like an unseen enemy that could attack if not closely guarded. People fear they will cry forever if they let themselves feel sad, become violent if they allow themselves to vent their rage or gain one hundred pounds if they allow themselves pleasure with food. For many, constant external striving and control of our natural joys lead to a point where our inner child or spirit rebels, yelling, "Enough of all this work, let's go outside and play."

When we don't listen to this healthy rebellion we are likely to experience anxiety, depression or lack of energy. When we deny ourselves natural joys we tend to substitute counterfeit joys—substances, sex, food, status, activity, new cars, new hairdos, fewer wrinkles and snazzy clothes. It's the right search at the wrong door because true joy is not something we buy off a shelf, but rather it is a richness of spirit that dwells within and is expressed through our relationships to others.

I believe we are born blessed as an integral part of all creation. We all have the potential to access our inner world that leads to joy and peace. Sometimes we encounter this quiet resting place much more easily than we expect. Other times it is illusive, something just outside our grasp. But it is always there.

Awaken Your Inner Fire

Joy is a source of personal power. Joy awakens as we open ourselves to the wonder of the universe, both inside us and around us. As we allow the expansive power of joy to flow through ourselves, our awareness expands and we see beyond the concrete world to a world of love, intimacy, creativity and wisdom.

We create room for joy as we move beyond "shoulds" and "musts" to an expansive state where we accept our capacity to be both powerful and gentle, expansive and reclusive, delighted and bored, wise and confused, passive and assertive, giving and receptive, generous and withholding, frightened and adventuresome, angry and loving. As we become accepting of ourselves we are more able to reach inside and speak our truths: Yes, No, I want, I can, I feel, I believe, I see, I love. This is a form of self love that creates unity and peacefulness within because we are living at one with our wisest self.

Joy leads us to the heart of our spiritual journey because it ignites the fire of transformation that enables us to change our thoughts, perceptions and feelings. In doing so we are able to transcend an empty, humdrum existence and infuse our lives with vitality, awareness and the ability to move beyond the limited boundaries of self. Finding joy doesn't mean life will always be easy; rather life becomes rich because we live near the pulse of possibility. To open the door you can start by saying, I am willing. I am willing to feel, to know, to love and to expand. I am willing to let the concrete walls of my beliefs slip away and move into a new level of awareness.

In his "Ode to Joy," the German poet Friedrich Schiller wrote, "By that holy fire impassioned, to thy sanctuary we come." When we allow ourselves to feel joy, we create an inner sanctuary, a home for the soul that allows us to feel safe to laugh, cry, be angry, question and think for ourselves. When we create this home for truth and delight, we feel a sense of inner strength. Unkind remarks and difficult situations lose their ability to singe our souls or tear at our hearts because we are no longer candles in the wind. Rather, we become the fire of life itself—a being, an identity that cannot be blown about or extinguished by external events because we accept all of who we are.

REMEMBER JOY AND FIND HOPE

Joy brings hope and hope brings joy. Imagine joy as a memory dwelling within you—a bird perched on your soul singing a song of hope. Let yourself know it is always there. Sometimes we lose contact with that voice and feel despair. In those times if we can remember that the potential for joy lives within us, we may regain hope and find the strength to take steps to improve our lives.

If you feel down, blue, depressed or tend to be hard on yourself, take time to remember the good things you have done for yourself, the risks you have taken, the ways you have survived. Remember times when you experienced contentment or joy. Then hold these images in your heart and tell yourself you can re-create them. You have the power to create happiness in your life; the potential for joy is within you. You might ask yourself what in your life right now blocks you from feeling joy, and consider what you need to do to get on a path toward greater happiness.

The bird of joy that "perches in the soul" never stops singing—we just stop listening. When we can hear the promise of joy within us, we have more power to come alive to our desire for life.

PREPARE FOR JOY

Joy may seem illusive or fleeting, yet there is a path we can walk that brings the delight, passion and sweetness of joy into our lives, sweeping over us, filling us, transporting us, making life feel worth the trouble. Joy may appear to come suddenly, but in reality we prepare for joy every time we speak our truths, care for ourselves, expand our knowledge, nurture our friendships, let people love us, take on new adventures and go where our hearts lead us.

REMEMBER THE MIRACLE OF YOUR BODY

We have been given a miraculous body to live in. Many religions and spiritual philosophies have made a separation between body and spirit. At worst people have been told to beat on their lowly flesh because it was of the devil. I believe our body is a blessing of creation, a wondrous home intertwined with our spirit, something to enjoy and care for. When our body is well and alive, it is easier to feel our spirit and experience joy.

So ponder your amazing body. Your brain can store vast amounts of information. Your heart has been pumping blood every minute of every day of your life and your liver works day and night to detoxify all the toxins or junk food that get into your body. Your immune system, which works to clear out anything that doesn't belong in the body, has about a hundred million trillion molecules or antibodies, and in the time it took you to read the last two sentences your body has produced a million billion new antibody molecules. Just imagine! And now it has done it again.

When you run, talk, walk, see, move, a million billion things are working together in your body, like an information system more vast and intricately interwoven than all the phone lines in the world. Intelligence literally circulates throughout your body. If you injure yourself, your body immediately responds to the situation with adrenaline, blood movement, heart rate change and so on. I remember going into shock and within seconds my heart rate dropped to 54, my temperature to 94. It was my body's amazing instantaneous survival response to a sudden trauma.

To help you ponder this marvelous body you live in, I suggest you watch the video *The Incredible Human Machine*, produced by National Geographic. It's available at many video stores and it's one of the best deals for ninety-nine cents I've found in a long time. Although the body is much more than the video title suggests, the show is inspiring and inspiriting.

Listen to Your Heart, Always Beating for You

One of the first sounds you ever heard was the beating of your mother's heart. As it was an echo in a cave, you heard it beating, beating, beating as you developed in her womb.

When you were only a few months old—womb time—your own heart started beating. And unless you have suffered a heart attack, it has never stopped. No matter whether you've been happy, angry, lonely, sad, tired, joyful or just muddling through every minute of every day, your heart has been working, like a loyal friend, carrying blood through your body, transporting oxygen and other nutrients, keeping you alive. At a heart rate of 70, it will beat over one hundred thousand times today!

Find your pulse. Listen to the beat. Imagine your heart sending blood, flowing out into your body, renewing you. The Sanskrit word for heart is *Anahata*. You might say it out loud: Anahata. Anahata. Hear the rhythm as you say it. It sounds a lot like your heart, always beating, never stopping.

As you listen to your pulse, think of your heart as more than a muscle that pumps blood. There is an exquisite link between your heart, your brain and every cell in your body—a constant feedback loop. The cells of your heart have intelligence similar to the brain. They respond to signals that you are being loved, cared for and are experiencing happiness. That's why there are endearing terms such as sweetheart, honey and sugar for people we love. Loved ones nourish our heart. Love is sweet. Part of our journey toward joy involves nurturing our heart with love so we can hear the calling of our heart.•

Choosing Happiness

VERONICA RAY

Our personal identity and self-image affect all that we think, feel and do. What we believe of ourselves is fundamental to our perspective on everything. If we see ourselves as merely bodies and conscious minds, we are likely to remain unhappily searching for perfection in these areas. If we see ourselves as incapable of love, peace, joy, cooperation and forgiveness, we won't be able to see the opportunities for them in our lives.

Human beings have struggled with the question of identity since the beginning of time. We have turned to philosophy, religion and science for the answers, and countless theories, ideas and possibilities have evolved. But we often become disillusioned and even angry when these answers prove to be imperfect or incomplete. The truth is, at this point in history, we just don't know the meaning of life with absolute certainty.

We all want to find a clear, simple understanding of ourselves and our world. But just as no one can control everything, no one can know everything. Once we accept it, we can live with this limitation quite fully and happily. We don't have to have all the answers, and even more, we can't have all the answers. This acceptance frees us to be more open to hearing the truths already whispering in our hearts. Acknowledging our confusion can be the first step toward letting go of our old, self-defeating beliefs and behaviors.

When we give up our desire for indisputable evidence of absolute truths, we can begin to accept some comforting, helpful, guiding ideas. Once we accept that there may always be some unanswered questions, we can choose our beliefs about being human based on whether they enhance our lives and the contributions we make to others. We can choose to view life and ourselves in ways that help us live better, healthier, happier lives.

To each of us, "truth" is made up of our own perceptions. Whether or not we realize it, we are always choosing our perceptions, beliefs, attitudes and behaviors. When we begin choosing consciously, we can learn to avoid those that cause our unhappiness and self-defeating actions. We can pragmatically choose those perceptions that help us instead of those that hurt us.

MAN OR BUTTERFLY?

There is an ancient Chinese legend about a man who dreamt he was a butterfly. It was the loveliest dream imaginable. He felt himself floating about through the air, light and free. He felt completely, blissfully happy. Everything in this dream was beautiful, peaceful and joyous. According to the legend, when the man awoke from this dream, he was never again certain whether he was really a man who had dreamt he was a butterfly or a butterfly who now dreamt he was a man. This story illustrates the split we feel as human beings. We are uncertain of our identity—are we body, mind, emotions or spirit? Are we naturally loving, peaceful, happy, angry, afraid, aggressive or cooperative? All of these things and more seem to be part of being human, but some get more attention than others—they're noisier. It's hard to ignore a feeling of rage within us and easy to miss the quiet voice of peacefulness, gentleness and love. But that doesn't mean the loving part isn't there.

To simplify this whole confusing picture, let's stick with the idea of the man/butterfly. Let's call all of those noisy feelings, thoughts, beliefs and actions our ego. This is the "man" part of us—fearful, defensive, angry, territorial and worried. This part of us keenly feels the needs and desires of survival and pleasure and in fact, feels nothing else. In his book, *Good-Bye to Guilt*, Jerry Jampolsky defines our ego as "our body/personality or lower self."

But also within each of us lives a higher self, a *butterfly:* a purely loving, peaceful, joyous spirit untouched by anything in the outer world. This part of us is quiet, gentle, peaceful, forgiving, accepting and fearless. From Plato to Spinoza to Thornton Wilder, humans have always expressed a feeling that we are somehow eternal. This butterfly, or *spirit*, is the eternal part of us, the part that is free of the cares and concerns of the world and is connected to our Higher Power and to the spirits of all other people.

USING OUR MINDS

John Milton wrote, "The mind is its own place, and in itself can make a heaven of hell, a hell of heaven." Our mind chooses which viewpoint to see—our ego's or our spirit's. It can live in a self-imposed hell of fearful, angry thoughts or a heaven of loving, peaceful thoughts. But we can choose how to use our mind.

For example, if someone says something unkind to us, our ego will probably immediately perceive this as an attack against which it must defend itself. It will fill us with anger, hostility and fear. It may prompt us to attack the other person verbally or in some other way. But if we understand our ego and its frightened, defensive viewpoint, we can turn to our other way of seeing—the way of our spirit. Our mind can see our spirit's loving, forgiving, understanding perspective, and help our ego to calm down and temper its response.

Since we are both ego and spirit, we can't always behave in a perfectly loving way. But we can take control of our actions before our ego gets carried away and causes harm. If we've already caused harm, we can still find our spirit's perspective after we've calmed down and then make appropriate amends.

As we become more accustomed to seeing ourselves as responding either from our ego or our spirit, we can learn to recognize our ego's feelings and reactions more quickly and let our spirit take over sooner. Our unhappy, self-defeating feelings and behaviors can become less intense and long-lasting.

Simplifying our view of our reactions, beliefs, feelings and behaviors by identifying them as either belonging to our ego or spirit can help us accept ourselves and improve our lives. We don't have to be angry or impatient with ourselves. That would only be our ego fighting against itself. Instead, we can accept that we have these two parts or viewpoints within us and learn to work with them to produce the best results.

Our Ego

In his play, *Our Town,* Thornton Wilder wrote, "Whenever you come near the human race, there's layers and layers of nonsense." Our ego is the part of us that creates these layers and layers of nonsense. Egos are not inherently *bad,* they simply have certain capabilities, limitations and a specific viewpoint. It is not our goal to eradicate our ego, even if that were possible. But rather, we can learn to understand it, accept it and use it for our highest well-being.

Our ego can be thought of as a level of consciousness that includes much of what we think of as ourselves, including our bodies and personalities. It is convinced that it is us, complete in itself. It misinterprets everything and creates our self-defeating behaviors and beliefs. It convinces us that it can make us safe and happy, but it never does.

Our ego is the part of us that always needs to be right, to have the last word. It values conflict and always feels threatened. Its only modes of communication are attack and defend. But it often disguises these with elaborate rationalizations and justifications. It denies, lies, tricks, confuses, hurts, blames, hates and fears. And all the while, it is certain that it is acting only in our best interests.

Our ego will never change of itself. It's like a child who is incapable of growing up. This is why we so often react and behave in self-defeating ways even long after we feel we know better. But our ego does not have to rule us. We can learn to recognize its confusion, mistakes, its fear and its pain. We can learn to choose love over fear, and joy over pain.

OUR SPIRIT

Our spirit is our ego's direct opposite in many ways. It's incapable of feeling anger, pain, worry, fear or sorrow. It never feels threatened in any way, because it is absolutely certain of its invulnerability. It knows itself to be eternal, at one with all other spirits and connected to a Higher Power.

Our spirit is only capable of unlimited love and joy. It has no interest in who is right or wrong. It has no use for conflict. It values peace, love and sharing above all else. It recognizes the abundance of the universe as infinite and available to all of us, always. It only offers unconditional love, acceptance and forgiveness. It is purely joyful, generous, content and gentle, and always knows our true best interests.

OTHERS' SPIRITS

Recognizing our own spirituality can transform our self-image, behavior and lives. Likewise, recognizing the spirit in others can transform our outlook and all of our relationships. But it's sometimes difficult to see the good, spiritual part of another person, especially when he or she has done harmful things or expresses a callous, self-centered attitude.

We can begin by recognizing that everyone has an ego that is always afraid and acting out self-defeating beliefs. We can think, with understanding, *Look at what their egos did*, instead of thinking, with condemnation, *Look at what they did*. If we take a moment to let our initial ego reaction pass, and to overlook the ego reactions of others, we can move beyond them to more peaceful, happy relations with other people. This can help us stop defining people as their egos and we can begin overlooking and forgiving their faults and mistakes. Then instead of searching for what we can judge as good in them (which can sometimes be very hard to find), we can simply know that they also have within them a perfect, loving spirit, even if we can't see it beneath all those layers and layers of ego-nonsense.

SPIRITUAL GROWTH

I don't believe our spirits need to grow or evolve at all. I believe they are already perfect. What spiritual growth or evolution means to me is that we human beings need to grow in our awareness of this spiritual aspect of ourselves and get to know it. We need to learn to see its viewpoint and hear its guidance. Then we can learn to extend its qualities out into our lives and the world. This way our spirit grows in the sense of expanding, touching the spirits in others and growing together with them.

Every day, situations and relationships contain opportunities to open up to our spirit's viewpoint and guidance. Everywhere there are chances for us to extend the highest, best, spiritual part of ourselves out into the world. No matter who we are or what our particular circumstances might be, we can all discover the power and peace of our spirituality.

We have to take the time needed for spiritual growth and not allow ourselves to become impatient. There is no end to the wondrous discoveries we can make on this journey. But we have to allow them to unfold in their own time. It may take many months, or even years, for us to see that we have turned a corner in our spiritual evolution. As the meditation book, *God Calling*, reminds us, "When climbing a steep hill, a man is often more conscious of the weakness of his stumbling feet than of the view, the grandeur, or even of his upward progress."

Faith, hope and persistence will keep us growing spiritually.

OUR INNER TRUTH

Because our egos are so noisy and demanding, they often obscure our awareness of our spirituality. But since we can never experience true happiness through our ego, we feel a nagging sense of dissatisfaction until we turn to our spirit. When we are in conflict within ourselves, that conflict is reflected in our outer lives. It's a kind of self-betrayal to place our center of personal energy outside our true selves, as we do when we define ourselves as our egos. It makes us sick, tired and unhappy to go against our own inner truth.

We must each experience our spirituality for ourselves. Reading, thinking, talking or writing about it doesn't give us the experience of it. These things may help us move in the direction needed to open ourselves up to our own spirituality, but eventually we must turn inward.

Deep inside, we all know that we are spiritual beings. As long as we ignore this part of ourselves, we may feel a kind of gnawing ache, like a vague memory, a yearning for something we can't quite name. We may feel a sort of home-sickness for our spirits whenever we recognize great beauty or experience moments of unconditional love. We may experience brief flashes of inspiration or perfect peace when we know we are something more than our egos.

There is a sense of familiarity, of coming home, in discovering—or rather rediscovering—our spirituality. It's like hearing an old song, suddenly remembering where you were when you first heard it and who you were with and recalling the feelings you had then. Think of an old love song that reminds you of a special person you once knew. How much more powerful, more beautiful, more moving is the recognition of our spirituality than even this fond memory!

Only when we rediscover our spirit and begin letting it grow into our conscious awareness can we experience the peace of harmony and balance between our bodies, minds and spirits. For some of us, this begins with a transformational experience—a spiritual awakening.

SPIRITUAL AWAKENING

In *The Varieties of Religious Experience*, William James identified the following characteristics of a spiritual experience:
- It defies description; it must be experienced first-hand to be understood.
- It brings a sense of certainty, of knowledge or profound insight into truth unreachable by the usual sensory or intellectual means.
- It doesn't last long.
- It feels as if one is not willing or controlling the experience; it includes a sense of a superior presence or power.
- It is a deeply memorable experience, leaving a sense of its importance.
- It changes the inner life of the person who experiences it.
- It changes the outer behavior, attitudes, character and outlook of the person experiencing it.

We've all had some spiritual experiences of varying intensity and effects. Déjà vu, creative inspiration, intuitive knowledge and deep love are the everyday experiences of our spirituality. Intense, even overwhelming feelings of wonder and appreciation of the beauty of nature; a sudden jolt of recognition or understanding; a momentary sense of oneness with humanity and the universe—these are all spiritual experiences.

But these common experiences don't necessarily affect us in a dramatic or long-lasting way. They can be thought of as flashes or sneak previews of a more profound and transformational spiritual awakening. For some of us, a deeply painful experience—some form of "hitting bottom"—provides the necessary openness to experiencing a true spiritual awakening.

OUT OF THE DARKNESS

Like the man who dreamt he was a butterfly, once we awaken to our spirituality we can never again be quite sure of ourselves as mere egos. Having opened a window to the light of our spiritual selves, the darkness in our minds can never be quite so dark again.

For most of us, coming to our true spiritual identity doesn't happen suddenly. We have to persist in being open to it and take advantage of all our opportunities for spiritual growth. We do this by patient awareness of the lesson each present moment brings. We do it by accepting where we are right now, today, without anxiety over where we have been or where we are going.

We can help ourselves experience our spirituality through prayer, meditation and acting "as-if"—trying to discover the loving part of ourselves by behaving in a loving manner. We can recognize our ego and spirit by their manifestations in our thoughts, actions and lives. We can use our mind to choose our spirit's viewpoint.

Our deep inner happiness and ability to withstand all the problems and experiences of human life depend on recognizing our true spiritual identity. We are far more than our bodies, desires, mistakes and behaviors. We are capable of living spiritually, lovingly, peacefully and happily even in the world as it is. All we have to change is our minds.•

Free to Be Present

D E L O R A   C I A C C I O   W A R D

I watched the edges of the pages curl as the fire engulfed the journal I had
kept for the past five years. My husband had just driven away, leaving behind
empty hangers and out-of-season clothes. What had begun as the love of a lifetime fourteen years earlier seemed to be crumbling. I had asked my husband
for a separation with hopes of freeing the tortured soul within me. I blamed
him for stifling my personal growth, my creativity that never seemed to find its
voice. I felt sad, trapped, empty, lonely. He had not brought me the happiness
and fulfillment for which I had so desperately longed. I reread some of my journal entries. I was struck by the thinly veiled descent into darkness, disappointment, despair. I wanted no one to read my journal, so burning it would put the
journal and the past behind me. Or so I thought. But as I watched it burn, it was
like watching my home burn to the ground. Everything I was, everything I felt,
and my only connection to my inner self were in that journal. I sat in silence,
mourning its loss for a long time.

The days passed with my husband and me living apart. Instead of feeling
free and exhilarated as I had imagined, I felt scared, more alone and confused.
A few months earlier, I had cut out a newspaper ad for a counselor and kept it
on my desk, as if for the inevitable emergency. It seemed the time was right to
make the call.

The therapist welcomed me into her office. Her warmth and gentle manner were immediately comforting. She asked enough questions quickly to
uncover what I had feared most. The demons were back. I had been treated for
depression before I was married. I had thought it was behind me and confirmed
it with my happy new marriage, the birth of my daughter and all the years of
contentment that had followed. I had known on some level that it was happening again. I struggled and fought against entering treatment again because I
considered it a personal failure. I should be able to snap myself out of it, stop
feeling sorry for myself. I had tried many things and drifted in and out of
various interests to fill the void I felt inside: self-directed vitamin therapy,

vegetarian diet, self-help books, feminism, radical politics. All worthwhile pursuits perhaps, but none a panacea. I then found myself turning to self-medication with drugs and alcohol. My substance abuse in time intensified my problems even while numbing me to the pain of being myself. I was confused and so very tired of running.

With the help of my therapist, I began to sort out my thoughts, my priorities and my needs. I asked my husband to come home. With his support, I broke my chemical dependencies. We had long talks about our personal needs and our hopes for our marriage. I began treatment with Prozac. Prozac works by restoring the patient's brain chemistry to normal levels. Clinical depression in many cases is believed to be caused by biochemical imbalances in the brain, specifically, in my case, abnormalities in serotonin levels. Stress and trauma may play a causal role in the altered brain function, tying together experiential and biochemical culprits. It also speaks directly to the body-mind-spirit connection.

I saw my therapist weekly. We had no insurance coverage, and it meant sacrificing for the whole family. I began to visit the little country church in town. I met people there who asked me to join their volunteer work in the church and the community. I had always been very shy, and I found great satisfaction in having friends of my own. I began art classes, and I toyed with writing about my experiences. I submitted a short essay to the readers' section of a small literary magazine, and it was chosen for publication!

Subtly and slowly, I began to sense a change. I began to notice how lovely my little girl was, how soft my cat felt when he rubbed against my legs, how warm the sunshine was that shone in the window. I finally began to understand the concept of living in the moment, mindful living. I took pleasure in the creative expression of cooking a meal, planting a garden, writing to a friend, painting my daughter's room. I could struggle with the sadness of my past and the darkness of my childhood without sliding back down into the pit of depression. I realized that my happiness was my responsibility, not my husband's nor anyone's. The power to change and direct my life toward fulfillment of my needs and dreams is within me. When we look outside ourselves for our identity and our self-esteem, we are missing the point and are invariably disappointed.

I savor the peace of mind, the glad-to-be-alive feeling with which I awake each morning. My success is that in daring to confront my demons and put them to rest, I am now free to be totally present in each moment of my life.•

L E A R N I N G   T O   L I V E

Soul Practice

Each of the chapters in this collection concludes with "Soul Practice," helping you to apply the material to your own life. We at Personal Transformation believe that the work of personal transformation happens in the details of our everyday lives: our relationships, our work, our creative pursuits, self-care and spiritual practice. Reading inspirational material is wonderful; putting it to work in our lives is exciting, challenging and very rewarding. Included in each of these sections will be thought questions, meditations and tips for engaging the chapter material in your life. If you are already keeping a journal, you can work with this material there. If you don't have a journal, you might set aside a notebook or journal to record your responses to the thought questions, and record how you put the material to work in your life.

Q U E S T I O N S

1. What gives you real joy and pleasure in your life?
2. What stops you from allowing more joy into your life? What negative messages did you receive growing up, from family, church, school and culture, about pleasure? How do those messages still affect you?
3. What concrete steps can you take today to allow more joy in?
3. What are you grateful for in your life, right now?
4. If your whole life were like the circle in Dannel Schwartz's article, how big would the black dot of all your current difficulties be? How much energy and attention do you devote to that black dot, and how much to the space of your life surrounding it?

PRACTICES

1. Keep a gratitude log: every night before sleep, list three things that you
   noticed or that happened today that you are grateful for.
2. Think of a current challenge in your life. Ask yourself, what are the hidden blessings in this challenge? What am I learning that is healing for me?
   What am I grateful for in this challenge? Even if you can't think of any
   immediately, continue to gently ask yourself these questions until, over
   time, answers emerge.
3. Begin a running list of everything that brings you joy, from small joys like
   watching leaves shimmer in the breeze to big ones like great vacations.
   Include things from childhood: squishing mud between bare toes, bubble
   baths, watching clouds. Post the list on your refrigerator or other conspicuous place, and add to it as you remember things. Be on the active
   lookout for what brings you joy; when you find something, write it down.
   Commit to consciously doing one thing on your list each day.
4. Begin to notice when your mind wanders to the past or to the future. If
   that is not where you consciously want it to go at that moment, take a
   deep breath and say compassionately to yourself, "Present," or your own
   name, calling yourself back. Notice the room, the sounds around you.
   Come back to your own body and soul. What may happen at first is that
   you become aware of how often you are not in the present moment. Be
   gentle with yourself; as Eknath Easwaran and others have said, this is a
   lifetime practice!
5. Play with acting "as-if." Each day, do one small gesture of love and caring
   for yourself "as-if" you were your own best friend. Experiment, when you
   are feeling stressed, with acting "as-if" you feel loving and do something
   small and spontaneous for someone else. Check out how you feel after
   your "as-if" gesture to yourself or someone else.

2

Opening to Love

Everyone is touched by the difficulties of life; no one escapes. It may at times seem preferable to close your heart or to be half-hearted about life. It is even understandable, if your heart was crushed or if you were not loved enough, to shut down your heart, to withdraw your love from life.

If we are to survive as a species, it is because, one by one, more hearts open fully to life. Deep in your heart is the wellspring of your spiritual essence. That is the place in you that knows you are interconnected with all of life. From the depths of your heart arises the intelligence that will inform you of your life's purpose, how you are to serve life.

Your heart can reveal itself to you only when you allow it to open. Opening your heart and keeping it open can be challenging, even though the rewards are extraordinary.

This chapter will help to open your heart with its touching stories and encourage you to stay open as you live your life.

A B R O T H E R   L I K E   T H A T

A friend of mine named Paul received an automobile from his brother as a Christmas present. On Christmas Eve when Paul came out of his office, a street urchin was walking around the shiny new car, admiring it. "Is this your car, Mister?" he asked.

Paul nodded. "My brother gave it to me for Christmas." The boy was astounded. "You mean your brother gave it to you and it didn't cost you nothing? Boy, I wish . . ." He hesitated.

Paul knew what he was going to wish for. He was going to wish he had a brother like that. But what the lad said jarred Paul clear down to his heels.

"I wish," the boy went on, "that I could be a brother like that."

Paul looked at the boy in astonishment, then impulsively he added, "Would you like to take a ride in my automobile?" "Oh yes, I'd love that."

After a short ride, the boy turned and, with his eyes aglow, said, "Mister, would you mind driving in front of my house?"

Paul smiled a little. He thought he knew what the lad wanted. He wanted to show his neighbors that he could ride home in a big automobile. But Paul was wrong again. "Will you stop where those two steps are?" the boy asked.

He ran up the steps. In a little while Paul heard him coming back, but he was not coming fast. He was carrying his little crippled brother. He sat him down on the bottom step, then squeezed against him and pointed to the car.

"There she is, Buddy, just like I told you upstairs. His brother gave it to him for Christmas and it didn't cost him a cent. And some day I'm gonna give you one just like it . . . then you can see for yourself all the pretty things in the Christmas windows that I've been trying to tell you about."

Paul got out and lifted the lad into the front seat of his car. The shining-eyed older brother climbed in beside him and the three of them began a memorable holiday ride.

That Christmas Eve, Paul learned what Jesus meant when he had said, "It is more blessed to give . . ."

—*Dan Clark*

The Awakened Heart

GERALD G. MAY, M.D.

There is a desire within each of us, in the deep center of ourselves that we call our heart. We were born with it; it is never completely satisfied; and it never dies. We are often unaware of it, but it is always awake. It is the human desire for love. Every person on this earth yearns to love, to be loved, to know love. Our true identity, our reason for being, is to be found in this desire.

I think William Blake was right about the purpose of humanity; we are here to learn to bear the beams of love. There are three meanings of bearing love: to endure it, to carry it and to bring it forth. In the first, we are meant to grow in our capacity to endure love's beauty and pain. In the second, we are meant to carry love and spread it around, as children carry laughter and measles. And in the third we are meant to bring new love into the world, to be birthers of love. This is the threefold nature of our longing.

You can find evidence of the longing in great art, music, literature and religions; a common universal passion for love runs through them all. Psychology offers evidence as well. The passion for love can be found at the core of human motivation. There is even evidence in neurology. The researcher Paul MacLean says the highly developed human cerebral cortex "makes possible the insight required to plan for the needs of others" and gives us "a concern for all living things."

But for real proof you must look at your own longings and aspirations; you must listen to the deep themes of your own life story. In most of us the desire for love has often been distorted or buried, but if you look at your own life with honest and gentle eyes, you can discern it in yourself as a deep seeking of connectedness, healing, creation and joy. This is your true identity; it is who you really are and what you exist for. You have your own unique experience of desiring love, but there is something universal about it as well. It connects you with all other human beings and with all of creation.

You probably already know your longing very well. You have felt it as hope for relationship, meaning, fulfillment, perhaps even a sense of destiny. Think for a moment about what has prompted you to do what you have done in life. When you have tried to be successful in your studies or work, what have you been seeking? When you have wanted to be pleasing, attractive or helpful to others, what have you really been hoping for? Remember some moments in your life when you felt most complete and fulfilled; what did you taste there? Recall also feeling very bad, alone, worthless; what were you missing?

If you pause and look quietly inside, you may be able to sense something of your desire for love right now in this moment. Sometimes it is wonderful to touch this deep longing. It can seem expansive and joyful. At other times it can be painful, lonely and even a little frightening. Whether it feels good or bad, its power and depth are awesome. When the desire is too much to bear, we often bury it beneath frenzied thoughts and activities or escape it by dulling our immediate consciousness of living. It is possible to run away from the desire for years, even decades, at a time but we cannot eradicate it entirely. It keeps touching us in little glimpses and hints in our dreams, our hopes, our unguarded moments. We may go to sleep, but our desire for love does not. It is who we are.

Sometimes, in moments of quiet wonder, it is possible just to be with our desire. We can sense its power and beauty even when it aches for fulfillment. In truth it is an utterly simple thing. I can remember experiencing it in childhood, standing in a field and looking at the sky and just *being* in love. It wasn't love for any particular thing or person. It was more like being immersed in an atmosphere of love, feeling very alive, very present in the moment, intimately connected with everything around me.

Now and then we experience the same simplicity as adults. But for most of us it does not last very long. We have difficulty just being; we think we must get on with more important things. We have to be efficient. In becoming adults, we have been conditioned to believe that efficiency is more important than love.

EFFICIENCY AND LOVE

Efficiency is the "how" of life: how we meet and handle the demands of daily living, how we survive, grow and create, how we deal with stress, how effective we are in our functional roles and activities.

In contrast, love is the "why" of life: why we are functioning at all, what we want to be efficient *for*. I cannot specifically define love, but I am convinced it is the fundamental energy of the human spirit, the fuel on which we run, the wellspring of our vitality. And grace, which is the flowing, creative activity of love itself, is what makes all goodness possible.

Love should come first. It should be the beginning of and the reason for everything. Efficiency should be "how" love expresses its "why." But it gets mixed up so easily. When I was a young parent, I wanted to take good care *of* my children (efficiency) because I cared so much *for* them (love). This was the way it should be. But soon I became preoccupied with efficiency. What were my kids eating? Were they getting enough sleep? Would we be on time for the car pool? My concerns about efficiency began to eclipse the love they were meant to serve. Getting to the car pool on time became more important than attending to a small fear or a hurt feeling. Too often the report card—the preeminent symbol of childhood efficiency—was more significant than the hopes and fears of the little one who brought it home.

It happens to all of us. Some people are so caught up in striving for efficiency that love seems like a luxury or even an obstacle to efficient functioning. Taken far enough, this makes for the ominous prospect of people who are very unloving and very efficient at what they do. For nearly a decade, Adolf Hitler was extremely efficient at expanding the Third Reich. A medical school professor I remember told his students that he found it more worthwhile to love his surgical successes than to love his patients. "As soon as you start feeling your patients' pain," he said, "you start losing your skill." He was only trying to help.

WHERE YOUR TREASURE IS

In most cases, thank God, love and efficiency are not mutually exclusive. It is entirely possible to use your money charitably and still balance your checkbook, though I have not yet achieved either. It should be possible for your work to contribute to the welfare of others and for you to receive adequate recompense for it, though most homemakers have yet to achieve it. We should be able to educate our children well while we are loving them, though in practice it sometimes feels impossible.

The problem is not whether we want love or efficiency; it is which we want *more*. Which do we give the higher priority? On the surface it seems natural to value love more highly. Nearly all the great institutions of our culture—religion, philosophy, art, even politics—give lip service at least to love as the supreme virtue. Most say that efficiency should exist only to serve the cause of love. The common sense of our human hearts says the same thing.

It is easy to say, but very difficult to put into practice. Individually and corporately, no matter how noble our words about love may sound, we are conditioned to believe efficiency is everything. Efficiency is the standard by which every person and enterprise is judged in our modern, developed culture. We weigh people's worth by how well they function. The value of blue-collar workers is determined by their productivity. The worth of executives and professionals is based on their success. The merit of entertainers depends upon their draw at the box office. With such standards, the person disappears behind the product. We have even come to refer to children as "products" of their home environments.

We measure ourselves not by beginnings but by ends, not by what is in our hearts but by what we are able to accomplish. Even in marriages and families where we might most easily say, "I love you for who you are, not for how you look or what you do," we seldom act according to our words. Too often we disparage the spouse who fails to meet our expectations for attractiveness, entertainment and affirmation of ourselves. Too often we scorn the child who does something wrong and says, "I didn't mean to."

But there is a worse thing. Our society encourages us to believe that love is just another function, an ability to be learned and refined. There are techniques for love, we are told, and if we love efficiently we will have something to show for it: well-managed, smoothly functioning relationships; social popularity; emotional security; sexual fulfillment. Seen in this light, expressions of love become commodities, loved ones become objects, and the pains of love become problems to be solved. In therapy, people have told me, "I don't know how to love," or "I think I am incapable of loving." What sadness! No one is incapable of loving. We all have difficulty expressing love. It would not be love if it didn't cause us trouble. To some extent we are all afraid of love; we do not want to be hurt. Sometimes people become so afraid or embittered that they are indeed paralyzed in expressing or perceiving love. But everyone loves. No matter how much trouble we have expressing or appreciating it, love is inescapable; it is what causes us to care. "Was it not love," I asked my patients, "that wounded you in the first place? And is it not your love that makes you care enough to miss it now?"

Let me say it again. No one is incapable of loving. When it comes to love, *capability* is the wrong word entirely. Capability is competence at performing a function. There is much I do not know about love, but of this I am certain: love is not a function. It is a quality of being that exists beneath and before all our functions. The word we must use is *capacity*. Capacity implies space; it refers to how much we can hold, perhaps how much we can bear. This has much to do with love. Machines have capabilities. Vessels have capacity. Love is always with us, seeking to fill us to our capacity.

If we give love primacy, if we claim it as our true treasure, there will still be plenty of room to develop our capabilities, our efficiency. But with efficiency as the ruling standard there is little or no space for love. We are led to doubt the value of love and our capacity for it.

When we hold efficiency as our primary value, we expect to achieve control, success, and security on our own terms. Even when our expectations are not met, we still believe we will come out secure and satisfied if we just do things differently, learn more, or make ourselves better in some way. Thus, we make a god of efficiency, an idol of success, a deity of achievement. These are the false gods that tell us we should be gods ourselves, in charge of our lives.

By worshipping efficiency, the human race has achieved the highest level of efficiency in history, but how much have we grown in love? Are we really any more graceful than our forebears were? The nations of our world have taken some significant steps toward freedom and justice, but at the same time technology has made us more destructive to one another and our planet. I do not know how the balance works out, whether we are really becoming more loving. But it is clear that our love has not kept up with our efficiency. We have too often sacrificed love for progress.

THE INVITATION OF LOVE

If we want to set the relationship between efficiency and love in its rightful order, we must go beyond laws and proclamations. If we desire a more loving society, we individual persons must return to the deepest common sense of our hearts. We must claim love as our true treasure. Then comes the difficult part: we must try to live according to our desire in the moment-by-moment experiences of our lives.

There is nothing more beautiful and freeing than living with conscious dedication to love. The way of love invites us to become vessels of love, sharers in grace rather than controllers of achievement. It invites us toward increasing freedom from all our slaveries and addictions. It encourages us to ease our grasping and striving for false security. It asks for vulnerability rather than self-protection, willingness instead of mastery. It beckons us toward participation in the great unfolding of creation, toward becoming one with it rather than standing apart and trying to overcome it.

But the invitation of love is as challenging as it is beautiful. Whether you have in mind such wide goals as reshaping human rights and world values or something as intimate as simple gratitude for the grace in your own life, saying yes to the invitation of love will hurt you. Living for love requires openness to love itself, a radical vulnerability to consciously being in love. To claim this is to enter a gentle warfare against immense internal and external forces. The enemy is that which would stifle your love: your fear of being hurt, the addictions that restrict your passion, and the efficiency worship of the world that makes you doubt the value of love. It is warfare because these forces are very real and very threatened by love. They will fight to keep their power. But the warfare must be gentle on your part; your only weapon is love itself. It feels more vulnerable than David facing Goliath. David had a sling and knew how to use it, but love can never be used. It can only be embraced and trusted. Love does not conquer all, because *conquer* is the wrong word entirely.

I am not exaggerating. Choosing love will open spaces of immense beauty and joy for you, but you will be hurt. You already know this. You have retreated from love countless times in your life because of it. We all have. We have been and will be hurt by the loss of loved ones, by what they have done to us and we to them. Even in the bliss of love there is a certain exquisite pain: the pain of too much beauty, of overwhelming magnificence. Further, no matter how perfect a love may be, it is never really satisfied. The very fulfillment of a desire sparks our passion for more. Sooner or later we discover a deepened yearning within what felt like satisfaction. Even in their beauty, the beams of love can often seem too much to bear.

In both joy and pain, love is boundless. Love is open, allowing our hearts to be touched and moved by what exists. Love is honest, willing to be present to life just as it is, in all its beauty and ugliness. True love is not blind at all; it sees what is and feels it as it is with no rose-colored glasses and no anesthesia.•

The Power of Love

SRI CHINMOY

Love is a pure and radiant flame. When we follow the path of love, we find our spiritual life, our inner life, most fulfilling. Nothing can be greater than love. Love is life, and life itself is spontaneous nectar and delight. If love means possessing someone or something, then that is not real love; that is not pure love. If love means giving and becoming one with everything, with humanity and Divinity, then that is real love. Real love is our total oneness with the object loved and with the possessor of love. Who is the possessor of love? God.

Whom are we loving? We are loving the Supreme in each individual. When we love the body, we bind ourselves; when we love the soul, we free ourselves. It is the soul in the individual, the Supreme in each human being, that we have to love.

You can consciously give pure love to others if you feel that you are giving a portion of your life-breath when you talk to them or think of them. This life-breath you are offering just because you feel that you and the rest of the world are totally and inseparably one. When there is oneness, it is all pure love.

THE PATH OF THE HEART

Divine love is the quickest way to realize the Highest. The mind has played its role. Now the world is crying for the wealth of the heart, which is love. If we follow the path of the heart, we will see that deep within the heart the soul abides. True, the light of the soul permeates the whole body, but there is a specific place where the soul resides most of the time, and that is in the heart. The spiritual heart is located in the center of the chest. If we want to establish a free access to our soul, we have to focus our attention, our concentration, on the heart. This is the center of pure love and oneness.

You can reach the spiritual heart through concentration and meditation. If you want to do this, every day for a few minutes you should concentrate on the heart and nowhere else. You have to feel that you do not have a head, you do not have legs, you do not have arms; you have only the heart. When you stay in the mind, life can seem like a dry piece of wood. But when you stay in the heart, life can be turned into a sea of pure love and bliss. If you can keep your consciousness in the heart, you will gradually begin to experience a spontaneous feeling of oneness. When you cultivate the spiritual soil of the heart, you will find growing there spontaneous love for God and spontaneous oneness with God's creation.

Ramesh and Gopal

Once there was a young boy named Ramesh, who was a very good student. His parents were not only rich, but also extremely kind.

At school, the students used to bring food from home to eat during lunch hour. One day Ramesh realized that his friend Gopal had not eaten anything for lunch for a few days. Ramesh went to his friend and asked why he had not brought anything to eat with him. Gopal said, "My mother could not give me anything. She said we had nothing at home."

Ramesh said, "Do not worry. I will share with you."

"No, I cannot take your food," replied Gopal.

"Of course you can," insisted Ramesh. "My parents give me much more food than I need." Finally, Gopal agreed, and for a few weeks the two boys shared Ramesh's lunch.

One day, Gopal stopped coming to school. Ramesh was concerned. When he asked the teacher why his friend was not coming anymore, the teacher told him, "He comes from a poor family. His parents cannot afford to pay the school fees. Therefore, he can no longer come to school."

Ramesh felt sad for his friend. When school was over, he took down Gopal's address from his teacher and went to Gopal's house. Ramesh begged his friend to come back to school, saying that he would ask his parents to pay the fee. Gopal's parents were deeply moved by his kindness, and Gopal again started going to school.

Gopal's father was an old man. In a few years' time, he died. The family became totally poverty-stricken, and Ramesh supported them with his own money. When Gopal's sister was stricken with a serious disease, the family could not afford the hospital bills. Again, Ramesh helped them out. In every way, he was the friend and guardian of Gopal's family.

Both Ramesh and Gopal completed high school and went to college. One day, Gopal said to Ramesh, "To say that my heart is all gratitude to you is an understatement. I love you more than I love my own life."

Ramesh answered him, "My friend, if you love me, that is more than enough for me. You do not have to love me more than your own life."

Gopal said, "But I do, and I want to prove it." Then he opened his penknife and cut his own arm. Naturally, he began bleeding. Gopal placed a few drops of blood at the feet of Ramesh.

Ramesh cried, "What are you doing, what are you doing?" He touched the cut on Gopal's arm and placed a few drops of blood on his own heart, saying: "This is the right place for your life-blood. I give you my earthly treasure in the form of material wealth. You give me your heart's love, which is Heavenly wealth beyond all measure."•

Finding Your Heart of Love

C H A R L O T T E   D A V I S   K A S L

L ove is the energy at the center of all life. It is the reality beneath our fears, the breath within the breath, the seed of all that grows. Loving ourselves, loving others, and loving spirit/God are inseparable, for all life is inter-connected and sacred. Love is an energy force like the air you breathe; if you withdraw your love from anyone, you take your breath away.

We become increasingly able to love as we integrate ourselves and become whole. Our wholeness is expressed in a lust for life and a capacity for joy, delight and adventure. Our wholeness gives birth to compassion, which Ram Dass describes in *Compassion in Action* as "the tender opening of our hearts to pain and suffering." For most people, the journey toward love requires that we penetrate the armor around our hearts, feel our grief and open ourselves to all our feelings. In doing so, we become more truly alive, deepen our self-acceptance and become less and less dependent on others to validate our worth. This frees us to stand in the center of our power and to give gener-ously of ourselves from a sense of inner safety, potency and vitality. The ability to give generously of ourselves without feeling we are giving up some-thing or being controlled is at the heart of intimacy because it reflects our individual strength and development.

We reach for words to describe love, but, ultimately, love is an experience of unity, peace or ecstasy that goes beyond words. Too often people mistake love for fancy presents, sentimental greeting cards or lavish praise. But love is not sen-timental; love takes discipline, awareness and a willingness to step into the fire of transformation. It is born of the minute-to-minute choices we make throughout our days as we bring honesty, integrity and compassion to all we do and say.

People often treat love like a commodity that you can turn on for some people and off for others. But you can't truly love your partner and hate your neighbor, or exploit the people who work for you. Love can't be compartmentalized because it is central to your being. You can't turn on half a light bulb. You can dim it or make it brighter, but when it's on, the light shines equally in all directions.

Disconnection and separateness, nearly always stemming from fear, are the opposite of love. To be disconnected can be a dull anxious feeling of inner detachment that makes life seem mundane, superficial and routine. We feel controlled by external events and lack an inner core that allows us to be spontaneous, fluid and flexible. We see people as bodies, but not as souls—they have form and shape and even beauty, but we don't feel their essence. When we are disconnected from our inner core, we are unable to absorb and be moved by beauty, wonder and kindness. We hear music, but it doesn't make our heart sing. We see flowers, but they might as well be plastic. We touch someone, but there is no connection. When we feel separated, it's hard to trust that anyone cares, or could possibly love us if they were to see our hidden, shameful side.

We can bring ourselves back to love—to the home of our heart—by remembering that we are all children of our Creator, sacred because we are alive. If we accept our intrinsic worth, we can give up the futile search for external validation and put our energy into developing our ability to develop our talents and strengths. We can also remember that we have free will. Because we are pure potential, we are not locked into our past, but have the ability to re-create ourselves moment to moment by our thoughts, actions and willingness to experiment with new behavior and give up old rigid patterns that no longer serve our growth. We also become willing to dive deep below the surface into our buried wounds. We have an amazing ability to heal and transform as we tap the powerful energy source underlying all our feelings and emotions. Instead of labeling our feelings as good or bad, we see them as energy that can be redirected for our growth. The inward journey becomes easier as we tap into our heart's capacity for humor, compassion and mercy. We become able to take ourselves into our heart, embracing all that we are and all that we have been. It becomes a mystical, humorous, fascinating show as we learn to observe ourselves, yet immerse ourselves in life.

From this point of self-acceptance and compassion, we develop the willingness to share our feelings in their raw, vulnerable state, not after we've figured them out or gotten them under control. This doesn't mean that we unload our emotions on others; it means that we stop hiding, faking a smile or presenting ourselves as we wish to be seen. We accept our humanness and allow it to be seen.

One of my favorite phrases from one of the dances of universal peace is "God is love, lover and beloved." If we break "beloved" in two, we have "be loved": be loved by spirit, be loved by yourself, be loved by others. If we remove the last letter of "beloved," we have "be love." Don't seek love or lover; simply *be love*. Be at peace with All That Is, and know you *are* the beloved. And when you find a lover, know that the journey is to dance together in the circle of love, growing, playing, struggling and accepting with a smile the incredible predicament of being human. When we can do this, even for a few moments, we will feel a flow of energy like the current of a river dissolving our separateness and bringing us to greater unity.

To become love, lover and beloved means making love your highest priority. It doesn't necessarily mean you quit your job or change the external situation of your life, although that might be part of the process. It means giving yourself to the daily practice of bringing love and awareness to everything you do. It also means stretching, reaching, growing and stepping through fear again and again. This usually involves some form of daily spiritual practice or a daily plan to go deeper into yourself and break old patterns that sit like ice jams inside, blocking your ability to reach out and love generously or be reached by those who would love you.

Love involves a fundamental change in consciousness of realizing there are no "others" out there; rather, we are all intertwined in a single web that is the miracle of life, a cosmic energy field. On a concrete level, this means internalizing in the deepest part of yourself the thought, "There but for the grace of God go I," or, more accurately, "There go I." When you feel scorn or contempt for someone, a part of you can remember that given different circumstances, you could be like that person or in that person's situation. Likewise, when you see someone show greatness, you can know that you too have a great nature within you.

In Nepal, where many religions and customs meet, it is customary to greet people by saying "*Namaste,*" which can be translated as "I salute the divinity in you," or, "To the light in you," or, "To the God in you." It is like taking a breath of life and combining it with the knowledge that we are all children of creation and are sending this energy out to everyone we meet. *Namaste.* I salute the divinity in you. This is where we begin.

ALLOW YOURSELF YOUR LONGING

Reach down inside, past the worries of the day, the thoughts of tomorrow, and listen to the deepest part of yourself. Tap into your longing for love, connection and understanding. Can you hear it? What does it say? When I listen deeply, I think of the relationships and community I have, and I feel good. Then, as I listen longer, I crack open to a deeper layer that longs for closer connections with more honesty, passion, consciousness and a greater ability to give and receive love. I want to know love in all of my being, to feel free to experience a deeper sense of unity with people, animals and the earth.

Many of us bury our longing for greater love and intimacy because we believe it is out of reach—it is not for ordinary people. We might tell ourselves it is too painful to long for passionate, intimate connections because we have been hurt, rejected or betrayed. Maybe it's hard to have faith in our worthiness because we have internalized the notion of a judgmental, fearsome God, or have been taught that we are inferior. Maybe we've hid out so long in a role, it seems unimaginable to let it slip away and feel the nakedness of our longing. So we put on a protective coating that keeps us from ourselves and others. We dissociate from our true selves in a myriad of ways. We put on a mask, we drink, smoke, eat too much or get busy and productive. Yet what do we produce? Even if we rush through the day obsessed with tasks to accomplish, read a ton of books or exercise compulsively, we can only mask the longing for connection because it is natural to human existence. We are all tribal people and our health, joy and happiness are intricately tied to interconnecting with others and with spirit.

Take a look at the motivation underlying all the things you do. If you look deep enough, you will realize that many of your actions are motivated by a desire for love and connection—to find it, maintain it or keep from losing it. Remember the miles you have traveled, the money you have spent, the heartaches you have survived, the times you stayed up all night, worried about your looks, or sought wealth, status and fame. Wasn't much of that all about a great longing to feel special so that someone would love you or say, "Good for you"?

Think for a moment of how you spend your time. What are you truly seeking? What do you want to have accomplished when you finish this life? Go as deep as you can. Is there a place that simply wants to slow down, tune into life, know yourself and feel close to others? A turning point in my life came at the age of forty-four when I saw my father die a very lonely man. He had waited until retirement at age sixty-eight to travel, but it was too late; he had Alzheimer's disease. He had written books, been admired and had received numerous awards, yet he was profoundly lonely. It jolted my complacency about work and relationships. I resolved to make a priority of friendships and spiritual growth, along with doing work I loved.

If you are seeking greater love and intimacy in your life, you might ask yourself how much time you give to growing, reaching out to others and nurturing your relationships. How deep is your capacity for stillness and quiet, which allows the wisdom within you to emerge? How honest are you with yourself and others?

Your longing is your connection to your soul, the part of you that cries out for spirit and for love. To hear this inner cry is to touch the earth, reach for the sky and open yourself to your awakening heart, the source of compassion and understanding. To feel your longing creates a thirst and hunger for the true nourishment of life. Dare to feel it and immerse yourself in a passionate journey for all that will truly fill you and bring peace.

MAKE FRIENDS WITH YOUR EMPTY PLACES

When we allow ourselves our longing, we sometimes find a big, empty place inside. It makes us uncomfortable and anxious. We want to run. If this is your experience, instead of running away, you might take a few deep breaths and slide down into that scary place inside. Stay with it. The empty place won't swallow you up. Notice how you feel—sweaty, jumpy, scared, or fascinated, excited and curious? If it's frightening, breathe, soften your belly and elicit compassion for this wounded part of you that has been ignored for so long. Feel it. Embrace this part of you. Remember, it is out of the womb, the emptiness, that life is created. In this place of anxiety or emptiness, you will come to know your rejected self and your fears. It is from this scary place that you will free yourself and open the door to love and intimacy.

One way people become more at peace with their empty place is to visit it daily. Every time you want to detach, numb out or run away, stop, go inside and make friends with your fears. Stay with the terror of silence, of nothingness. One woman I knew drew her empty place. It started as a frightening dark hole. Then a day or so later, she drew the hole with herself sitting at the bottom with a ray of light shining in. Over time, as she drew pictures of her empty place, she added flowers and books and a comfortable chair. She was increasingly able to breathe and relax in her empty place without wanting to eat or get busy—her usual escapes. Then she drew a ladder on the wall of the empty place and saw someone peering over the rim. She invited him to come sit with her. They both talked about their empty places, and as they did, they felt a sense of happiness and warmth coming over them. Like everything, the empty place is energy. When we meet it with consciousness and simply breathe into it and stop labeling it as bad, it begins to dissolve into a peaceful stillness.

Denying our empty place creates fear and anxiety. So long as we run away, the dark hole seems bigger and bigger, scarier and scarier, like a villain or a big dragon chasing us in a bad dream. If we stop and face the dragon, we begin the process of knowing and integrating ourselves. When we hide from parts of ourselves—our fears, anger, grief, power and joy—we feel split inside. It's like locking up parts of ourselves in little boxes and using a lot of energy to keep the boxes from flying open. The distance we keep from our buried selves is reflected in the distance we keep from others. In a hundred ways we transmit the message, "Stay away, you might see me." Stay away, I might see myself. In this state of self-absorption, we have little ability to see or empathize with others.

The more we heal the split-off places within us, the more our fears dissolve and the more we feel centered in ourselves. This allows us to take the armor off our heart and say, "Come close, I want to know you and be known by you." Another way to start the process of making friends with your empty places is to talk with a friend about the parts of you that seem shameful and unlovable. You might find that your friend understands you very well.•

Stirring-the-Oatmeal Love

ROBERT A. JOHNSON

Many years ago a wise friend gave me a name for human love. She called it "stirring-the-oatmeal" love. She was right. Within this phrase, if we will humble ourselves enough to look, is the very essence of what human love is, and it shows us the principal differences between human love and romance. Stirring oatmeal is a humble act—not exciting or thrilling. But it symbolizes a relatedness that brings love down to earth. It represents a willingness to share ordinary human life, to find meaning in the simple, unromantic tasks: earning a living, living within a budget, putting out the garbage, feeding the baby in the middle of the night. To "stir the oatmeal" means to find the relatedness, the value, even the beauty, in simple and ordinary things, not to eternally demand a cosmic drama, an entertainment or an extraordinary intensity in everything. Like the rice hulling of the Zen monks, the spinning wheel of Gandhi, the tent making of Saint Paul, it represents the discovery of the sacred in the midst of the humble and ordinary.

Jung once said that feeling is a matter of the small. And in human love, we can see that it is true. The real relatedness between two people is experienced in the small tasks they do together: the quiet conversation when the day's upheavals are at rest, the soft word of understanding, the daily companionship, the encouragement offered in a difficult moment, the small gift when least expected, the spontaneous gesture of love.

When a couple are genuinely related to each other, they are willing to enter into the whole spectrum of human life together. They transform even the unexciting, difficult, and mundane things into a joyful and fulfilling component of life. By contrast, romantic love can only last so long as a couple are "high" on one another, so long as the money lasts and the entertainments are exciting. "Stirring the oatmeal" means that two people take their love off the airy level of exciting fantasy and convert it into earthy, practical immediacy.

Love is content to do many things that ego is bored with. Love is willing to work with the other person's moods and unreasonableness. Love is willing to fix breakfast and balance the checkbook. Love is willing to do these "oatmeal" things of life because it is related to a person, not a projection.

Human love sees another person as an individual and makes an individualized relationship to him or her. Romantic love sees the other person only as a role player in the drama.

A man's human love desires that a woman become a complete and independent person and encourages her to be herself. Romantic love only affirms what he would like her to be, so that she could be identical to anima. So long as romance rules a man, he affirms a woman only insofar as she is willing to change, so that she may reflect his projected ideal. Romance is never happy with the other person just as he or she is.

Human love necessarily includes friendship: friendship within relationship, within marriage, between husband and wife. When a man and a woman are truly friends, they know each other's difficult points and weaknesses, but they are not inclined to stand in judgment on them. They are more concerned with helping each other and enjoying each other than they are with finding fault.

Friends, genuine friends, are like Kaherdin: They want to affirm rather than to judge; they don't coddle, but neither do they dwell on our inadequacies. Friends back each other up in the tough times, help each other with the sordid and ordinary tasks of life. They don't impose impossible standards on each other; they don't ask for perfection; and they help each other rather than grind each other down with demands.

In romantic love there is no friendship. Romance and friendship are utterly opposed energies, natural enemies with completely opposing motives. Sometimes people say, "I don't want to be friends with my husband [or wife]; it would take all the romance out of our marriage." It is true. Friendship does take the artificial drama and intensity out of a relationship, but it also takes away the egocentricity and the impossibility and replaces the drama with something human and real.

If a man and woman are friends to each other, then they are "neighbors" as well as lovers; their relationship is suddenly subject to Christ's dictum, "Love thy neighbor as thyself." One of the glaring contradictions in romantic love is that so many couples treat their friends with so much more kindness, consideration, generosity and forgiveness than they ever give to one another! When people are with their friends, they are charming, helpful and courteous. But when they come home, they often vent all their anger, resentments, moods and frustrations on each other. Strangely, they treat their friends better than they do each other.

When two people are "in love," people commonly say that they are "more than just friends." But in the long run, they seem to treat each other as less than friends. Most people think that being "in love" is a much more intimate, much more "meaningful" relationship than "mere" friendship. Why, then, do couples refuse each other the selfless love, the kindness and good will, that they readily give to their friends? People can't ask of their friends that they carry all their projections, be scapegoats for all their moods, keep them feeling happy and make life complete for them. Why do couples impose these demands on each other? Because the cult of romance teaches us that we have the right to expect that all our projections will be borne—all our desires satisfied and all our fantasies made to come true—in the person we are "in love" with. In one of the Hindu rites of marriage, the bride and groom make to each other a solemn statement, "You will be my best friend." Western couples need to learn to be friends, to live with each other in a spirit of friendship, to take the quality of friendship as a guide through the tangles we have made of love.•

The Human Heart

JOHN O'DONOHUE

Though the human body is born complete in one moment, the human heart is never finally born. It is being birthed in every experience of your life. Everything that happens to you has the potential to deepen you. It brings to birth within you new territories of the heart. Patrick Kavanagh captures this sense of the benediction of happening: "Praise, praise, praise/The way it happened and the way it is." In the Christian tradition, one of the most beautiful sacraments is baptism. It includes a special anointing of the baby's heart. Baptism comes from the Jewish tradition. For the Jewish people, the heart was the center of all the emotions. The heart is anointed as a main organ of the baby's health, but also as the place where all its feelings will nest.

The prayer intends that the new child will never become trapped, caught or entangled in false inner networks of negativity, resentment or destruction toward itself. The blessings also intend that the child will have a fluency of feeling in its life, that its feelings may flow freely and carry its soul out to the world and gather from the world delight and peace.

Against the infinity of the cosmos and the silent depths of nature, the human face shines out as the icon of intimacy. It is here, in this icon of human presence, that divinity in creation comes nearest to itself. The human face is the icon of creation. Each person also has an inner face, which is always sensed but never seen. The heart is the inner face of your life. The human journey strives to make this inner face beautiful. It is here that love gathers within you. Love is absolutely vital for a human life. For love alone can awaken what is divine within you. In love, you grow and come home to your self. When you learn to love and to let yourself be loved, you come home to the hearth of your own spirit. You are warm and sheltered. You are completely at one in the house of your own longing and belonging. In that growth and homecoming is the unlooked-for bonus in the act of loving another. Love begins in paying attention to others, in an act of gracious self-forgetting. Paradoxically, this is the condition in which we grow.

Once the soul awakens, the search begins, and you can never go back again. From then on, you are inflamed with a special longing that will never again let you linger in the lowlands of complacency and partial fulfillment. The eternal makes you urgent. You are loath to let compromise or the threat of danger hold you back from striving toward the summit of fulfillment. When this spiritual path opens, you can bring an incredible generosity to the world and to the lives of others. Sometimes, it is easy to be generous outwards, to give and give and give, and yet remain ungenerous to yourself. You lose the balance of your soul if you are a generous giver but a mean receiver. You need to be generous to yourself in order to receive the love that surrounds you. You can suffer from a desperate hunger to be loved. You can search long years in lonely places, far outside yourself. Yet the whole time, this love is but a few inches away from you. It is at the edge of your soul, but you have been blind to its presence. Through some hurt, a door has slammed shut within the heart, and you are powerless to unlock it and receive the love. We must remain attentive in order to be able to receive. Boris Pasternak said, "When a great moment knocks on the door of your life, it is often no louder than the beating of your heart, and it is very easy to miss it."

It is strangely ironic that the world loves power and possessions. You can be very successful in this world, be admired by everyone, have endless possessions, a lovely family, success in your work and have everything the world can give, but behind it all you can be completely lost and miserable. If you have everything the world has to offer you, but you do not have love, then you are the poorest of the poorest of the poor. Every human heart hungers for love. If you do not have the warmth of love in your heart, there is no possibility of real celebration and enjoyment. No matter how hard, competent, self-assured or respected you are, no matter what you think of yourself or what others think of you, the one thing you deeply long for is love. No matter where we are, who we are or what we are, or what kind of journey we are on, we all need love.•

Letting in Love

B R A D F O R D   K E E N E Y,   P H. D.

An awakened heart is a necessary condition for being able to receive the light. Consider choosing three days where you pay special attention to any appropriate living creature, whether it be your spouse, parent, child, friend, pet or plant. Imagine that these are the last three days you will be with them. Tell them that you are taking three days to conduct a spiritual experiment and that they are not to have any unnecessary concern about your actions. Repeat this every other month until it is a bimonthly holy day for you. Watch how the practice of love's actions helps deepen your preparation to encounter the light and enrich your every day.

The value of practicing the love that opens your heart is illustrated by the story of a solitary dog who spent the last three days of his life being awakened by the generosity of a lonely man.

One day while walking through a park, an old crippled dog came up to an old man who had never experienced love in his entire life. The dog caught his attention by speaking these words, "I am old and crippled. Children don't like to look at me because I look so sick and pitiful. I only have three days left to live, and more than anything else in the world, I long to have the experience of being loved by my master. I want this so much that I have learned how to speak so someone could hear my request. I have searched the world for a person who would understand my situation, and I think you understand what it is like not to have love in your life. Would you please grant me my wish that you be a good master to me in my last three days? You don't have to really love me. It would be fine for you to pretend that you love me."

The old man was moved by the sincerity of the dog's request. Without deliberation he told that dog that he would give him the best three days of his life. Off they went on a great three-day adventure. The old man took him to a restaurant and fed him a delicious steak, showed him all the beautiful places in the park, and took him to the spots that had unique odors and smells. The old creature was permitted to sleep on his master's bed, and throughout the night the man rubbed his belly and sang him soothing songs.

At the end of the three days, the dog said to the old man, "You have truly cared for me, and I am most grateful. You have enabled me to open my heart. For the first time, I know what it feels like to love someone." The old man began weeping and replied, "I, too, have learned to love and have never felt more alive." At that moment a shaft of bright white light entered the old man's apartment window and transformed itself into a staircase to the sky. A voice from above was heard by all the neighbors, "Come, both of you, unto my house. You have prepared the ground for your hearts to enter the kingdom of light." The old man with the dog by his side walked all the way up that staircase of light and disappeared into the clouds.

It is said that all dogs know this story and to this day they look to the sky when they howl their song. They haven't forgotten that it requires a heart filled with longing and love to enter the light of the heavens.

Sultan Walad, son of Rumi, speaks to us about this new life in soul:

"A human being must be born twice. Once from his mother, and again from his own body and his own existence. The body is like an egg, and the essence of man must become a bird in that egg through the warmth of love, and then he can escape from his body and fly in the eternal world of the soul beyond time and space."

You enter the soulful flight to bring spirited life into your daily action. You earn your wings through the heartfelt practice of love. This is how your life is illumined by spirit and how you become a midwife to the birth of everyday soul.•

Taking the Step of Unconditional Self-Love

A L I N E   C O O K

My odyssey began in May of 1988, with a separation—culminating in divorce by December—from my twenty-three year marriage. As individuals are endowed with uniqueness, so was this divorce—not the legalities, but the horrific desolation of my spirit. By nature, I am a learner and a tenacious overcomer; from this remnant of vitality, my reconstruction began.

I applied and was accepted in a service position in a religious community associated with a local university. Soon, I had many resources available to assist me to walk again, one of which was a women's group. This group was a safe environment for me to gain an understanding of myself in relationship. I was blessed with a friend in this meeting ground, and we jointly declared our journey as having brought us to the crossroads, choosing to be "victors rather than victims."

Within the next year, I had an insight, a shift in perception, brought about by a wonderfully simple dream. In the dream, I am swimming in a river with a good, intimate friend. We are enjoying ourselves, laughing, moving along with the current of the river. The river narrows, becoming a concrete-lined ditch. It takes two turns and becomes an even shallower ditch. Now, it is about eight or ten inches deep, with enough water for moving along, as on a slide. My mate is no longer with me: I am alone. The ditch ends abruptly, and the water falls over a ledge into a pool thirty feet below. There are two friends in the pool below, beckoning to me to let go and enter the pool. I am uncertain/fearful about just "jumping" in, and look to either side of the ditch for a trail that leads down to the edge of the pool. There are only insurmountable rocky cliffs on either side. One choice is to turn away and go back upstream. After consideration, I let go and enter the pool.

When I shared the dream with my friend, we laughed and cried about choosing life and "jumping in." After the laughter subsided, I clearly understood my message. It was time to embrace life and get in the swim.

The next few years were seasons of baby steps and giant steps, intermingled. One blessing was a spiritual counselor of immense focus and humility. His compassion and clarity illuminated my spiritual journey through days of spiritual storms and muck. A gentle angel in the form of a priest, he was as supportive and encouraging as a personal therapist.

The ending of my employment, which had been so promising and was work that I loved, was a setback. My spirit during this process was again bruised and stretched. I decided to rigorously examine my needs and talents regarding employment. I composed and recomposed this profile. I defined questions, such as, what expresses my creativity. These became helpful guidelines.

I worked three jobs simultaneously, fearful of not having enough money. Financially I was afloat, emotionally I was buoyed up with support I was drawing to me, spiritually I was going along with the flow and physically I was beginning to sink. Just as I felt myself submerging, I found new employment that met most of the criteria I had laid out for myself, salary and use of my talents among them.

Another dream came to me: I am alone on a winding path and descending some hills. The hills are pleasant and grassy, but somewhat sparse with no trees. As I descend to the base of the hills, the path turns sharply "right" and ahead of me, across a sizable pond in the distance, is the Emerald City. This time, the impediments to the left and right are the steep, impassable hillside and a marshy wood. The only way to the city is through the pond. I awoke from the dream with no solution.

I decided to meditate on the dream. In meditation, many choices revealed themselves, with one wonderful option that I've continued to use since. During meditation, I saw that I could walk on the water as if there were special stepping stones, unseen but there. One particular stone was as precious as gold. When I asked what it meant, the answer was, "It is the step of unconditional self-love!" I have returned many times to ask, "What is unconditional self-love?" Answers that have come to me are Allow, Accept, Nonjudgment, Be, Love, and Cease the Struggle.

Many synchronistic blessings have flowed my way that line up with unconditional self-love. They include Dan Millman's Courage Training and graduate studies in Organizational Leadership. Transformation is a process I have come to invite and appreciate.

Spirit has stood with me in the form of many treasured relationships—work associates, family, and friends. Recently a friend called to say hello after returning from a spiritual renewal. I listened to his insights and heard his restored spiritual vigor. As a caring friend and skilled listener, he invited me to share my spiritual state as well, which was stuck and in need of reorienting. Within moments, he reflected back to me that I had been giving up "thrival for survival." Without a revealing dream, once again I stood at the edge of the pool/pond with a choice to move ahead or not. Moving ahead was easy this time. My creativity engaged, and after ending my evening meditation, answers and solutions flooded in so quickly that I was challenged to document them.

Thrival means expanding spirituality, nurturing creativity, declaring my passions, fulfilling my purpose, and celebrating the abundance of God. These past eight years of transformation have been amazing. I am very aware of the enjoyment and the abundance I am living. •

Opening to Love

Soul Practice

QUESTIONS

1. How has the longing for love influenced what you have done in your life—work, relationships, spiritual practice—and how you have done it? How deeply buried has been the awareness of that need?

2. Think about efficiency, the "how" of your life, and love, the "why" of your life. How do they get mixed up in your life? Which do you want more? How can you make love more of a priority, if that's what you choose?

3. Whom do you need to tell that you love them? When, and how can you do it?

4. What blocks the commitment to loving yourself and others more fully and deeply, such as fears, addictions, efficiency?

5. What would it be like to approach your feelings as life energy, rather than labeling them as "good" or "bad"?

6. With whom can you take a chance and allow them to see yourself vulnerable and open-hearted in your feelings?

7. What is the difference for you between showing someone your vulnerability in your feelings vs. unloading your feelings on others?

8. What is the difference between romance and love? How willing are you to allow "stirring-the-oatmeal" love into your life? How may you embrace it more fully?

9. What does it mean to be "a generous giver but a mean receiver"? Does this fit for you? If so, how can you be a more generous receiver?

P R A C T I C E S

1. Give yourself five minutes of quiet and solitude. Take a deep breath and bring your attention inward to your heart. Open to your deep longing for love. What does it feel like: joyful, painful, a little of both? Simply notice your feelings as you acknowledge them. Cherish this longing: it is what connects you to the deepest part of your own soul.

2. Practice the path of the heart: every day, if only for a couple of minutes, get quiet and imagine that you are only your heart: breathe into it, allow it to soften and open. Make space for yourself, all of you, in your own heart. Make space for others. At the end of a couple of minutes, imagine how a particular aspect of your life might be different if you approached it with this soft and open heart.

3. Try this when standing in a grocery store line or when caught in traffic: imagine seeing all those around you as souls, rather than as bodies. How does this change your perception of them? How does it change you?

4. Try going through an afternoon silently saying "Namaste" ("I salute the divinity in you") to everyone you meet. What happens to your heart? How does it change the interaction?

5. Imagine this is the last day you'll ever be with someone you love. What do you want to say to them that has been left unsaid? How do you want to be with them?

3

Healing the Body

Life longs for us to be healed, that is, for us to experience the unity that our body, mind and spirit is. The words healing *and* wholeness *come from the same Latin root word. Accordingly, healing and wholeness share the same meaning. To be cured means to be restored to a previous level of functioning, to have eliminated the contaminants from the body. This happens, for instance, when antibiotics or a strong white cell count free a person from infection. Healing is more than a return to a prior state of health.*

Healing implies an integration of body, mind and spirit that did not exist prior to illness or accident. Powerful healing can occur even if the person is dying or is unable to regain a previous level of health, as may occur when the person has cancer or arthritis. Serious illness is an opening for the spirit. It's an opportunity for the voice of the spirit to be heard, which prompts people to move into more fulfilling work and to reconnect with loved ones during a healing process. The pain accompanying illness reveals our attitudes about life and how we relate to it. Healing often requires us to understand and correct the life-limiting thinking that contributed to the illness. Astounding research verifies that love heals the body, which demonstrates the powerful interplay of body, mind, spirit in healing.

This chapter focuses specifically on the influences of mind, heart and spirit in physical healing. In that sense, this is a chapter about becoming whole.

Your Natural Healing Ability

Crying is the body's innate way of dealing with pain. When children fall and hurt themselves, they have a short period of crying, then are up and playing again. They wail and then are okay. A woman in labor may have periods of yelling; it is her body's emotional cleansing system. Anne Wilson Schaef says that sounds are like a grappling hook; they detox the toxins in our bodies. We are naturally created to make sounds of joy, ecstasy and anguish. Sounds are part of the internal guidance healing system. When we cry and go all the way into an emotion, making the sounds associated with it, we heal ourselves while making sound. When we squelch and choke back tears, our guidance system has no choice but to come back as disease at a later time to get our attention. If we do not listen the first time, we get hit with a bigger hammer the second time.

A child naturally does a quick cry and goes on. When you are taught not to make your sounds in order to be a good girl or boy, you spend years pushing down your natural healing ability. When people become sick and hit this bedrock of pain, they cry tears that have been unshed for years. They are not just tears about the current situation, they are tears unshed from a lifetime.

—Christiane Northrup, M.D.

Illness and the Search for Meaning

AN INTERVIEW WITH JEAN SHINODA BOLEN, M. D.

In this interview, we discuss the essence of Jean Shinoda Bolen's book, *Close to the Bone.* Her compassionate work guides individuals and their loved ones through the realm of life-threatening illness. Jean offers hope and perspective for navigating through the "crisis of the soul" that accompanies serious illness.

Life-threatening illness visits us all, either in our own lives or in the lives of dear ones. At some point, descending into the depths of the soul is inevitable.

PERSONAL TRANSFORMATION: *Life-threatening illness as a crisis for the soul is a central theme in your book. What does that mean?*

JEAN SHINODA BOLEN: Life-threatening illnesses are usually viewed as crisis. Crisis, in ancient Chinese language, is comprised of two elements, danger and opportunity. In medicine, it used to be that crisis occurred when a patient's temperature went up and up and up and then broke. Crisis was the place where one was in danger, and yet there was opportunity for major change. Life-threatening illness has that effect on people. The focus often is entirely on the danger to the body, without awareness that the danger offers a major possibility of transformation of relationships and of the psyche, as well as the body.

PT: *We are never the same after life-threatening illness.*

JSB: In hospitals and doctors' offices, often everything is ignored except the part of the body that has something wrong with it. People are discouraged from being conscious and expressing what is happening at a deep level, at the soul level. Patients get the message to be just the terrain or the body where the doctor and modern medicine will fight the illness.

PT: *You use the term* liminal time, *meaning threshold. What is this threshold that life-threatening illness takes us to?*

JSB: When you are in between, you are in a threshold time, or a liminal time. When you are between the potential of life and death, you are in liminal time, on the threshold of crossing over from the visible material world to the invisible one. Life-threatening illness puts you there because you know that your illness could result in your death. You are straddling the possibility of living or dying. During that in-between time, different elements can tip the scales one direction or the other. You can be hexed by the people around you. If your doctor emphasizes the negative potential of what you have, and if you accept the message that this is going to kill you, the probability increases that it will. However, when you are in between, in that liminal place, it is also possible that you will deepen your connection with others who believe in the possibility that you can make it through. You can challenge authority, you can seek alternative possibilities to add to what modern medicine offers that can increase the possibility of surviving.

In my work, I often draw upon myth, because the language of myth touches the soul. The soul listens to metaphor, stories, poetic expression and music. The soul is moved by emotion-laden expressions. In the myth of Persephone, she is burying flowers in a meadow and all is well one moment, and the next moment the earth opens up in front of her and Hades, the Lord of the underworld, comes and abducts her and she is pulled, terrified and screaming, into the underworld. Acute onset of a diagnosis or of symptoms can be like that. One moment you are fine, living ordinary everyday life in the upperworld, where the sun is shining. And then, the sudden onset of serious symptoms, the pain of a major heart attack, a test result that says you're HIV positive, or the appearance of cancer in the breast, requires much more definitive medicine, and you have to enter the hospital. The shift between everything being fine one moment, and you and the people who love you being in the underworld the next moment, is mythic. The myth helps express what your own experience is like. In the myth, Persephone is not given up on. Hermes, the messenger God, comes down to the underworld to bring her back. At that point, Persephone realizes that it is possible that she will not stay in the underworld forever. It is possible that she actually might return to life.

The story that you believe about the possibility of recovery goes into the depths of yourself. In your bones, there is a response that says, it is possible for me to recover. Then the equivalent of Hermes goes through your entire body in the form of neuropeptides and every cell of your body shifts from a depressed state to actively responding to the possibility of recovery. At that point, there is an infusion of a life-force energy conveyed to your body. When that happens, in this liminal time, the potential of pointing toward life makes the tilt.

PT: *This liminal time is also the time of soul questions. What are these soul questions?*

JSB: We are spiritual beings essentially. We are spiritual beings on a human path, rather than human beings who may or may not be on a spiritual path. We know this in our bones. An illness that brings us close to the bone brings us into the realm of soul, where we know things, not with our intellectual minds, but at a soul level. I think that we do know that we have a soul. When I say that we are spiritual beings on a human path, I don't have to prove it; this is not an intellectual debate. The words describe what we deeply know. As spiritual beings on a human path, we come into a material existence in our bodies, where suffering and limitation is essentially part of the human path. We cannot get through life without our particular encounter with suffering, in whatever form it may take. All of us are limited by our life spans. Life itself is a terminal condition.

If we let this sink in, that we are spiritual beings on a human path, the questions are: What did we come to do? What did we come to learn? Who did we come to love? What did we come to hear? What are we here for? These are questions whose answers come from within, so that only we truly know when we are authentically living from our deepest self. When life-threatening illness comes, a lot of what we are doing with our lives is revealed to us as being superficial or inauthentic. After realizing how precious life is and how potentially short it is, many people, especially women, become empowered by that knowledge to make major changes in their relationship life, and many men and women make changes in their work life.

PT: *You discuss Procrustes' myth in your book. What are its implications for illness and recovery?*

JSB: The myth is that if you were on the road to Athens, you had to pass Procrustes' bed. He would put you on his bed, and whatever part of you did not fit, he cut off. If you were too short for the bed, you were stretched, like on a medieval rack, until you fit. This story applies to us all. Every person has expectations placed on him or her as to what success means. It might be work success, or it might be to marry well. Your particular family expects its members to be a certain way. Whatever parts of who you really are don't fit expectations, or are unacceptable to the successful world you are expected to enter, you cut yourself off from. We lose that part of ourselves that stays buried in our underworld.

Facing the realization that life is limited is a midlife issue. Life-threatening illness raises all of the major questions of midlife because midlife, whenever that might be, is a state of mind when we understand how short life is. We have lived as many years as we have to that point, and life has gone by really fast. We have a sense of the limitations of time and of our active energies for life. An illness is an acute form of the crisis that many people have at midlife, as they realize they may be wasting this experience, and become depressed. This might precipitate a crisis in relationship and work and life. When this happens, we are plunged into an underworld, where we find all of the human fears that none of us want to look at, but all of us have to.

When it is a life-threatening illness, the fears are of death and dismemberment, of losing our essential womanhood or manhood, of pain, and also that we are going through something, and we will never be the same again. Going into the underworld also brings us into the realm of all the possibilities that we cut ourselves off from, our particular depths of talent and inclinations of joy that we stopped along the way. It is a time of remembering and reconnecting with that which we cut ourselves off from, as well.

PT: *We often fear the underworld as this place of fear and vulnerability, yet if we are willing to, or are forced to descend there, we can discover great richness and the realm of the soul.*

JSB: That's right. And that can make the experience a major turning point.

PT: *How can illness be a turning point for us?*

JSB: In psychological work, people make a descent, often precipitated by depression or anxiety. They begin to listen to their dreams and to connect with feelings that they have buried. In the underworld, there is a reconnecting with sources of mortality, and sources of meaning, and the potential of living authentically. Jung would describe it as the potential of individuation, of following your own personal myth, of living from the inside out, rather than shaping yourself to meet or fulfill other people's expectations. When you descend into the psychological process, the turning point is when the potential of getting on a heart-and-soul track can grow.

I was very taken with the parallels between that which I do with depth analysis and Dr. Lawrence LeShan's work with terminal cancer patients. He initially found that even though people seemed to appreciate their sessions with him, they died at the same rate as people who were not doing psychotherapy. Then, he changed his focus in his work with apparently terminal people and began to address what was right with these people. He has a wonderful series of questions that people were encouraged to find the answers to. They were questions such as: What would make you happy to get up in the morning, looking forward to what you would be doing during the day? What would you be doing if at the end of every day you would go to bed tired, but good tired? What would you be doing if your life were physically, spiritually and emotionally in harmony? What would your life be like if you could imagine the world adjusting to you, rather that you adjusting to it?

His questions assumed that we have our own particular song to sing. Those are poetic ways of asking individuation questions. People found answers to these questions by going deep inside of themselves to remember and reconnect with their own sources of meaning and joy and service. He found that when people discovered what really would give their lives meaning, invariably, service to others was involved. People who were expected to die went into long-term remissions. Half of the people he worked with lived on. Their cancers became a turning point in their lives.

PT: *Recovery literally can be dependent upon this discovery.*

JSB: Yes. Life-threatening illness puts us on a soul path that may well lead to recovery on a physical level.

PT: *Suffering and illness can be the pathway that brings into our awareness what our talents and purpose are. For some of us, this may be impossible to discover without suffering. In this sense, suffering has great meaning.*

JSB: That's true. Our suffering and how we react to it has a possibility of really shaping and strengthening our purpose, or not. If people are able to grow through their experiences of suffering, the suffering is redeemed. They understand that their suffering was meaningful. One of my colleagues gave me Albert Schweitzer's description of "the fellowship of those who bear the mark of pain." Schweitzer had his health restored through a series of operations. After he went through those painful experiences and was restored to health, he knew suffering firsthand, and out of that, he responded to a need to help alleviate the suffering of others.

My colleague, an exceptionally fine psychiatrist for very disturbed patients, went through a descent into the mental realm of suffering when she was a medical student, and spent some time on a locked psychiatric ward. That descent into mental suffering provided her with insights and awareness of what it is like to be there, and she has grown to be a guide for others.

Creative work also grows out of the suffering of life. The depths that music takes us to may echo the experience of the depth the composer lived. Our potential for poetic expression is tapped when we go through periods of anguish and suffering. Essentially, life happens with its potential for joy and suffering, and how we react to it is soul shaping. The person who insists on identifying with the victim may get stuck there, while the person who learns compassion for others as well as themselves may grow and find motivation for their work.

PT: *Let's focus on healing and what helps. Begin by discussing the myth of Psyche and her two tools.*

JSB: When you find yourself in the dark, and become aware that you are not conscious of the reality of your situation, you enter the realm of Psyche. In her myth, Psyche took a lamp and a knife to see the man who came to her every night. She wanted to know who her unseen bridegroom was. Was he a monster, which an earlier prediction seemed to indicate? She took the lamp and the knife and hid. In the darkness, after he went to sleep, she took the lamp to see who he was and the knife so that she could sever his head if he turned out to be a monster.

We need those symbols to look at what might be destructive in our lives. The lamp is a symbol of consciousness, of illumination. The knife is the symbol of discrimination and the power to sever the bonds with those people or addictions that, if we were to see clearly, we would know are bad for us. It is not enough to have some conscious awareness of a destructive situation, because without the capacity to sever the bond, the consciousness dims. Many people are in codependent relationships that are destructive to them. They need to be able to look at the situation holding both the lamp and the knife, so they have the power to sever those relationships or those addictions, if needed.

PT: *Or those attitudes within ourselves that are destructive or negative.*

JSB: I've heard women say that their diagnosis of cancer was both the worst thing and the best thing that happened to them, because for many, it allowed them to put themselves first or to take care of themselves. It's as if the cancer gave them permission to say no.

PT: *What about the usefulness of rituals in healing?*

JSB: Ritual is a deeply creative process that re-enacts and draws up qualities of participants into consciousness. Ritual brings elements of energy or power to life situations. For example, one of my friends wanted to gather her friends, to be with her on her journey, which was an encounter with chemotherapy for her recurrent cancer. She was told to expect that her hair would fall out in clumps. She heard about a women who cut her hair off before chemotherapy, and she decided to have a ritual in which we would witness her having her head shorn. It was a powerful experience to be present and to watch her go through this major change in front of us. Her hair was beautiful. It was a symbolic, as well as a real act, to have it cut and shaved. She was transformed physically before us. The courage it took to do that reflected the courage it took to go through the realm of cancer and treatment, which is a major heroic ordeal. That ritual was an archetypal experience.

Some rituals touch on patterns that humans have engaged in for thousands of years. Having your hair shaved is a major initiatory act from marine boot camp to the ordination of Buddhist priests. Women who marry in an orthodox Jewish tradition shave their heads, and Catholic nuns used to shave their heads as part of their initiatory experience. Another ritual that some women have done is to take either a symbol of or the actual pathology specimen that was surgically removed from them and ritually bury it in the ground, as a symbol of returning to the earth. I recall a woman who buried the uterus that was removed from her, that it might become part of the earth, and then planted a tree that her uterus might contribute to new life.

PT: *Let's move to the power of relationship. When we are in relationship with someone who is going through a life-threatening illness, how can we help?*

JSB: Companions on the journey make a tremendous difference. An I/thou experience with soul connection is essential, and often makes the difference as to whether a person comes through the underworld descent into which illness takes them. At a research level, participating in cancer support groups results in living twice as long and maybe even surviving a terminal prognosis. This finding contributes to the scientific validation of what we know at a soul level, which is that who and how others are with us influences whether we come through. People have extraordinary capacity to give support to each other. The support is partly emotional and spiritual, and partly energetic. A healthy person has an excess of life force, and through physical touch conveys energy to a person who is sick and may have a deficit of it. When you love the person that you are supporting through the journey, you might want to be a conduit for the energy of love and compassion, which are words that describe energy that is healing. The combination of energy and supportive belief helps

significant others to endure and to come through. In most cases where unexpected remarkable recoveries or spontaneous recoveries have happened, a significant relationship has contributed. A connection between people is
significant on a healing journey, and a relationship to the invisible world
through prayer is significant.

People's prayers make a major difference in recovery. We know this at a soul
level, and research studies verify the effectiveness of prayer. I quote the study
done at San Francisco General Hospital on patients who were in the cardiac
care unit. One half of them were prayed for and the other half were not, in a
research project in which no one knew who was being prayed for and who was
not prayed for. The results were dramatic. The prayed-for group did much better. Studies like this help us, for we can minimize that which we know on a soul
level until the scientific feedback confirms that what we innately want to do is
right. Healing touch, prayer or other alternative or complementary choices,
such as affirmations or rituals, aid healing. Without scientific backing, there is
a tendency to not want to appear foolish or do something that others might say
is silly. What we innately know to do, that which arises in the moment, is right
to do. Outside authority, especially skeptics and cynical people, are toxic to
healing processes.

PT: *In healing, it is important for us to turn to people and to stories that
give hope and that nourish us deep inside.*

JSB: It is so important, for example, if you are expected to go through
chemotherapy that has serious and difficult side effects, and you have a disin-
terested, impersonal oncologist who says, "This is what I am prescribing for
you; it has a 40 percent chance of helping you," and you already feel bad; you
will think the odds are against you. As you get weak and throw up and feel
awful, when you receive this treatment, chances are that your psyche is
depressed and has little hope that this experience is going to result in something good. On the other hand, you might have an oncologist who says, "I've
chosen this particular chemotherapy because I think that it will help you. It has
a 40 percent record for your particular kind of cancer, but I've chosen it feeling
that it is going to help." Next, you talk to somebody who was helped by
chemotherapy, who describes its positive effect. As you take chemotherapy,
your belief is "this is an ordeal, and it's making me sick now, but it's going to
help me." The messages from the doctor and from the anecdotal story, the witness who says it helped her, have the effect of giving every cell in the body the

message "this is going to help." The body is much more likely to respond to that belief system and to the chemotherapy.

PT: *How does life-threatening illness impact relationships?*

JSB: When there is a life-threatening illness, especially if the person who has it is a woman, her relationships are tested, and some of them don't make it. If the people in the woman's life are self-absorbed and draining of her, and she has been codependent to them prior to this, she may need to and finally be empowered to sever those relationships. With her primary relationship, the husband may grow in his capacity to be a loving person, and find inside himself the ability to be a caretaker at a level that he never knew was in him. The woman and the man discover their barriers to emotional intimacy, and take down what has been erected. The potential of death makes both risk loving more. Others do the opposite. The risk of losing this person makes them draw away. It is a true test of relationships. When you come through such an ordeal, the people who helped you through the descent are the ones that you then proceed on with. With AIDS, it is remarkable seeing men who were, up until then, living an eternal youthful side of themselves be able to be caretakers at a profound level for their significant other.

PT: *In closing, if you were to give a statement of hope to someone with a life-threatening illness, what would you offer?*

JSB: Wherever we are, on the journey that is our particular life, encounter with a life-threatening illness is a major time of transformation. It is part of the great adventure that is life. Remembering that we are spiritual beings on a human path, how we react to this illness is critical and crucial. It is at a soul level that the journey is significant. The quality of the life we have remaining, and our capacity to recover from whatever it is that we are suffering from is enhanced when we act as if what we do can make all the difference, while at the same time knowing that there is a great mystery. When it is our time to go, it is our time to go. We need the capacity to hold both in consciousness. It is a paradox, holding the opposites, and yet to live with both is to live a very meaningful life. My observation is that when we are ready to go, and many life-threatening illnesses provide a preparation time to go inside and to come to some deep understanding about who we are, that however much we have struggled, when we approach death and there is a sense that we are now ready to go, a sense of serenity and peace is usually present at the moment that we do go.

PT: *Fear subsides.*

JSB: I think that the soul makes the transition out of the body when we die, and that is a major moment. My realization of the soul being in the body and going on after the body is no longer was the great lesson of being present when my father's soul left his body. I saw his face light up with joy at that moment, then saw an instant later the body that he was no longer in was worn and discarded; clothes no longer needed to be worn. That experience helped me profoundly know that we are spiritual beings, who for a time come into the material body, go through a life that has potential for suffering and potential for joy. We make choices as to how we respond to the unchosen circumstances that are part of all of our lives. There is something soul shaping about experiencing and reacting to what happens to us in life. That is what the journey is about.•

Follow Your Bliss

BERNIE SIEGEL, M. D.

The more I see the workings of the universe, the more mystical I become. I'm not mystical in spite of being a surgeon; I'm mystical because I am a surgeon. As a surgeon, I watch miracles daily. The body knows much more than I do. In fact, every time I perform surgery I rely on its wisdom, because I don't know why a wound heals or how anesthesia works (nor does anyone else). Neither do I understand how a fertilized egg grows to be a human being. But I do know that each cell, organ, system of organs and person is directed by what I call the loving intelligence of energy. We all started out life as fertilized eggs the instant a particular sperm and egg met to become us. Somewhere within that fertilized egg was a set of instructions—a blueprint, a path laid out to guide and show us how to achieve our full potential and uniqueness before we let go of the tree of life. Carl Jung liked to refer to a person's blueprint as her or his individual myth. All of us need to discover our own myth.

Biologically, it is your destiny to be similar to every other human being on this earth in your basic composition at the same time that your DNA makes you as unique as your fingerprints. God gave us all certain gifts, but it is up to us to decide how to use them in such a way that even the Being who gave them to us will look down one day in admiration and say, "Hmmm, I never thought of it that way before."

I believe that if you stick to your path, you will achieve your full growth and potential as a human being before you let go of the tree of life—whether you die at two or at 102. If you don't, you will become psychologically or spiritually troubled. And if that doesn't call your attention back to your path, your body will become physically ill. The sculptor Louise Nevelson, who loved her work and kept at it right until her death at age eighty-eight, knew that sculpting was the work she was put on this earth to do. She once told an interviewer: "I stopped working for a little while and got abscesses and boils. If you're a Rolls-Royce, you can't be walking, you've just got to be riding. . . ."

Few of us live up to the potential of our own uniqueness. In fact, for many people it takes an illness to put them on the path to self-realization. Their bodies have to get sick in order for their lives to heal.

Discovering the ways in which you are exceptional, the particular path you are meant to follow, is your business on this earth, whether you are afflicted with an illness or not. It's just that the search takes on a special urgency when you realize you are mortal. Carl Jung said, "It was only after my illness that I understood how important it is to affirm one's own destiny." And it was after his illness that his most creative work was done, by his own admission.

As a woman in one of my workshops told me, some of the most exciting opportunities of our lives come cleverly disguised as insoluble difficulties.

COMMITTING YOURSELF TO LIFE AND LOVE

Instead of judging the events in our lives as good or bad, right or wrong, we must recognize that, of itself, nothing is good or bad, and everything has the potential to help us get back on the universe's schedule. This does not mean that we have to like what happens, but simply that we must remain open to the uses even of adversity. A crisis, be it a health problem or something else, may serve as a redirection—or, as I often describe it, a reset button—that starts you up again.

When you learn to live your life with a "we'll see" attitude, you will understand how it is that disease can be considered a blessing. You will know why it is that people asked to describe their illness have called it a beauty mark, a wake-up call, a challenge and a new beginning. The beauty mark was a malignant melanoma, the wake-up call was breast cancer, the challenge and new beginning can be anything from amyotrophic lateral sclerosis to lupus.

People with life-threatening illnesses who have dared to defy the statistical odds against them all tell some version of the same story. If their stories had nothing in common, then maybe we would say that these people were just lucky or had errors in diagnosis, spontaneous remissions, weak AIDS viruses, well-behaved cancers and all the other euphemisms that doctors use when they don't understand something and simply refuse to see it because it confronts their belief system. But these people do share something: peace of mind, the capacity for unconditional love, the courage to be themselves, a feeling of control over their own lives, independence, an acceptance of responsibility for whatever happens to them, and the ability to express their feelings.

A young medical student whom I had worked with was in an automobile accident that left her paraplegic. She said in a letter to me that she now knows her paraplegia is a gift to her, but "I can't believe I'm really writing this." And yet it's the message I hear all the time. Why? Because the greatest lesson people learn from life-threatening illnesses is the difference between what is and is not important.

Love is high on everyone's list of important things. In the face of illness, this can sometimes mean healing a marriage gone bad; at other times letting go of one that is beyond repair and going on to new things. A woman who had cancer wrote me a letter describing how she arrived at the decision to seek a divorce after her diagnosis: "I felt, at the time I came down with breast cancer, that I could not live another moment without the love I had so craved my entire life. I felt that love was more important than my next breath of air."

After her surgery, as she records in a diary she sent me, she committed herself to life and love: "I am going to regain my positive attitude toward life, enjoy every day as if it were my last, and have a beautiful love affair. Human love is the most important thing in life."

Within the year this woman had a new husband and a new horse—the latter "a present I have waited for every Christmas of my life since childhood."

On the other hand, physiological disease can be the catalyst that enables some couples to find the life and love they need within their marriage. A man and a woman came to my office, and when I asked them each to describe the disease he had, the wife said she saw it as a blossom, an opportunity for growth; the husband said it was eating him up alive. Now, when for one it was a blossom and for the other it was a destroyer, you know these were two people who needed to communicate better—and the miracle was that from the time they left the office together, they did.

He had been a man who never expressed his needs but kept everything inside of him, where, as he had said, it was devouring him. But after they had that conversation in my office things were different. As his wife explained when she told her story several years later at a workshop, this previously quiet, unassertive man started speaking up about his needs as they had left my office that day and headed down to the parking lot—and he didn't stop.

That night they had stayed up all night talking about their life together. The days they shared after they had finally learned to listen to each other were a gift to both of them, one that they might have never had without his illness. A successful life is not about not dying; it is about living well.

You Know More Than You Think

Today many scientists think we should not talk about a central nervous system and an endocrine system and an immune system, but rather one healing system, which constitutes a sort of super-intelligence within us. Just as that healing system can be set in motion by self-affirming beliefs, self-negating or repressive emotional patterns can do the reverse: as Woody Allen said in one of his movies, "I can't express anger. I internalize it and grow a tumor instead."

People like Russell Lockhart and Arnold Mindell have theorized about cancer: that the cancer, being a kind of growth gone wild, lives something of the life that is unlived by those with repressed, constricted personalities. It is almost as if the absence of growth and excitement externally leads to the cancer's internal expression. All the energy kept inside seems to fuel the cancer, for it has no place else to go.

It's important to express all your feelings, including the unpleasant ones, because once they're out they lose their power over you; they can't tie you up in knots anymore. Letting them out is a call for help and a "live" message to your body. My own family tries to live like this, and as a result one of our daughter's friends, who spent some time with us on the Cape, told me there was something wrong with us. "What's that?" I asked her. "You don't know how to fight," she said. "In my family when we get mad we really get mad and sometimes don't speak to each other for days. But in your family you all yell and scream at each other, and five minutes later that's the end of it." I took that as a great compliment.

When you value yourself you express all your feelings, and then you let them go. Letting people know who you are and where you are in life means fewer conflicts will occur. Your relationships will improve—even your business may improve. Trying to find love within yourself can be an incredibly painful journey. But don't think it can't be done; it can. You are capable of changing and finding your true self.

If you are sick, participating in your own medical care can be the first expression of yourself and your energy. Form a team with your physician and play an active, responsible role in your health care: get second opinions, make choices, and become the expert only you can be about your life and health. Don't let your doctor be the only expert on your case. It isn't his or her life, and experts don't know everything.

At an intuitive level, there is in each of us knowledge of what is therapeutic.

While I do know, for example, that some diets are healthier than others, I also think you have to do what feels right for your life. A man with cancer who attended one of my workshops took issue with my having said that vegetarians get cancer less often. "For eighteen years I was a vegetarian and natural hygienist and lived such a pure life—raw foods, exercise, meditation—and this should happen to me."

When he asked me what was the point of being a vegetarian if you could still get cancer, I told him that he'd eaten vegetables for the wrong reasons.

The vegetables may have prevented him from getting cancer ten years earlier—I don't know. But I do know that joggers and vegetarians die, too. If you eat vegetables and get up at 5:00 A.M. to go jogging because you feel better when you do, that's terrific. If you're just trying not to die, however, you're going to be damned angry when you discover that you're going to die anyway. That's when you wish you had slept late and eaten a lot of ice-cream cones.

Within each of us is the knowledge that we all must die someday. Our bodies know it, even if our minds do not. The point is to find a life that's enjoyable to you and live that life. It may be longer or it may be shorter than someone else's life, but if it's not a life you enjoy, you can be sure it will seem longer. Better to feel that our lives are "over much too quickly."

A woman with multiple sclerosis came into my office one day. Her accomplishment was that she had taught herself to walk again: she had an infant at home and had wanted to learn to walk before her child did. What courage and beauty. I've known so many incredibly inspiring and awesome people; each was someone who had found her or his own way of being exceptional, of being strong at the broken places. If you simply accept yourself, you will find yours, too. The varieties of exceptional behavior are endless.

To be exceptional doesn't always mean having to perform extraordinary feats, however. It's your attitude about living and loving that makes you exceptional, not whether you can ski one-legged, create mouthstick paintings, or heal yourself through visualization and meditation. What we're talking about is taking on the challenges of life.

The truly heroic know that heroism lies in living, fully and joyously, in each moment given to us. The important thing, as mythologist Joseph Campbell said, is to follow your bliss.•

Miracle Makers

P A U L   P E A R S A L L ,   P H. D.

I see the balloons!" screamed little Patsy. "I see the balloons! They're blow-ing them all up right there for the parade. But that little balloon won't stay up. It just can't hold air. It can't keep the air inside it. It must feel like me."

Patsy was a miracle maker. She was only eight years old but she had wis-dom that many don't have even after decades of living. Her favorite statement was, "That's just the way." All of her games followed the rules of "the way." She was undergoing a bone marrow transplant as treatment for leukemia. She was in the hospital room next to mine, and on this Thanksgiving morning, her screams were of excitement and not from the pain of the needles that usually began our mornings.

Patsy often sat with the nurses at their station. They needed her to boost their courage on one of the most stress-inducing units of any hospital. The entire floor is sealed off from the rest of the hospital and has its own air cir-culation to save us patients from contracting infections. Our immunity was down to zero because of chemotherapy and radiation, and our blood counts would have signaled death under normal circumstances. A common cold could kill dozens of us within days. Masks, gowns and sterile gloves were worn by everyone, including the limited number of visitors who always seemed so afraid when they came to see us. Once on this unit, we patients seldom felt the touch of another person's skin against our own. There were many "almost hugs" that stopped short of contact for fear of contamination. We learned to signal our hugging by wrapping our arms around ourselves while our loved ones hugged themselves.

All of us were on the verge of death. Almost half of us would die. Most of us would be exposed to more radiation than the workers in the nuclear accident in Chernobyl. In fact, lessons learned from treating the victims of nuclear acci-dents were applied to the treatment of bone marrow transplant patients.

We were all in terrible pain, constantly vomiting and losing control of our bowels at the same time. We were sick with repeated infections, and festering oral sores from the chemotherapy grew so large that they almost sealed off our mouths and made swallowing nearly impossible. We were all losing weight and had to be fed through our veins because radiation treatments had burned our appetites away. We ached where needles had drilled into our bones to withdraw marrow samples. I have never known such pain as the sensation of my own marrow being sucked from deep within me.

A bone marrow transplant typically requires about two months of hospitalization in almost total isolation. Prior to this time, the most rigorous tests are conducted and, ironically, the candidates for a transplant must be in "good health" even though they are dying. A "donor transplant" is a process through which the patient receives bone marrow provided by someone who perfectly matches the patient's own. An autologous transplant, as in my case, requires the removal of the patient's own marrow, sometimes "purging" or treating it with intense chemotherapy and then placing the marrow back inside the body after the patient has had days of near-lethal whole-body radiation and/or chemotherapy. Including the diagnosis, evaluation, numerous tests, chemotherapy and radiation therapy, transfusions, and lengthy recuperation during which the immunity of the patient is so low that every cough and sneeze causes a fear of death, the patient and his or her family surrenders any semblance of a normal life for about two years.

All of us looked like walking ghosts. "I have an idea for a new diet," said Patsy one morning when we all were getting weighed. "Everyone who wants to look skinny can come here to get chemicals and rays. Then they will look like us. They could go on our cancer diet."

We could hear each other retching during the night and crying all day, but Patsy would cry only for a little while. Then she would hop onto her metal stand, which held the IV bags and tubes that always dangled beside each of us. Each stand was hung with several different colored bags that ballooned out in fullness with toxic chemicals designed to burn away any growing cell in our body, the latest drugs to treat the many infections we all contracted, and nutrients to keep us alive while we were unable to eat and digest food. The chemotherapy medications were equal-opportunity killers. They attacked any fast-growing cell in the body, whether or not that cell was a normal hair or stomach-lining cell or a killer cancer cell. The contents stung and destroyed our veins so completely that the multiple daily blood tests we received had to be taken from a plastic catheter surgically implanted in our chests.

In the middle of the night, the nurses would come to pop out the heparin seals that served as chemical corks to hold back the blood in our chest tubes. The blood would spurt out, sometimes soaking the patient, nurse and the bed. Hundreds of blood tests were necessary to determine when transfusions would be needed to save our lives. We sometimes tried to pretend we were not awake when the blood was taken, but the smell of heparin and our own blood would nauseate us. We patients called this catheter the "Dracula Drain," but our feeble attempt at humor could not mask our terror.

When we were given platelets to increase our blood count, we would feel freezing cold. I shook so hard that I still have soreness in my joints and muscles. A sudden fever would result, followed by tremors, headache and nausea. All of this was overwhelming for a grown man, but Patsy weathered each torturing procedure with humor and strength. Her presence permeated the entire unit.

Patsy loved to ride her IV stand, crouched so low that the nurses saw only what seemed to be an unguided stand moving past their high counter. Patsy sneaked by the nurses' station and rode what she called her Christmas-tree IV stand every day, and we all laughed at this daily joke. She would often drag along dolls in her parade and demanded that patients who were out for a wobbly walk join her. We had to keep in line, because that was Patsy's way. The nurses and doctors came to rely on Patsy's procession as a boost to their morale and energy, and we patients came to see her parade as a form of protest against the overwhelming urge to give up.

Now, however, Patsy was losing her physical battle. The transplant had taken just too much from her, and although she had pulled through countless crises that should have killed her, this time she would not survive. A virus so small and so weak that almost any person would never be bothered by it eventually would take advantage of Patsy's lowered immunity and kill her. First, there would be a slight fever and then, within hours, Patsy would be gone. Still, she continued to humble all of us with her strength and the making of her miracles.

On this Thanksgiving morning just before the crisis that all of us feared could happen to any of us at any time, her cries were of excitement about preparations for the Detroit Thanksgiving Day parade that were taking place (by coincidence) right underneath her window in the hospital courtyard. She hollered with glee at the big, multicolored balloons, and we all clustered to Patsy's room, dragging our own Christmas-tree IVs. Like prisoners pressed up against the bars of our cell, we looked down on the impending holiday celebration.

"But that one little balloon can't hold air," said Patsy. She had been unusually pensive the last several days, and we all noticed that Patsy's parade was not taking place as regularly as it once did. She became somber now as she pressed her nose to the hospital window. We pretended we could not hear her murmur, "That's just the way."

Suddenly, the little balloon inflated and floated away from its handler and up into the sky. "There it goes" yelled Patsy. "It's going to heaven, but the parade is still going to go on, isn't it? There are lots of balloons and air is everywhere. That's the way it will be." With her words, the little balloon's journey seemed to be a meaningful coincidence for Patsy and for us all.

THE TIMELESSNESS OF MIRACLES

After my own bone marrow transplant, I almost died from suffocation. A simple virus not unlike the one that took Patsy's life attacked my lungs. As the nurses rushed me to surgery and I gasped for air, my nurse Carolyn said, "Remember Patsy and her parades. Think of your lungs as balloons and try to fill them up with air. Find the way." That's all she said, but it was all she had to say. She knew I needed Patsy's spirit then. I could barely breathe, but I relaxed as I felt comfort in Patsy's principle of "the way."

I survived what was supposed to be an "always fatal virus" to bone marrow transplant patients, and I began to breathe again. I had been given strength from Patsy. I knew her to be a miracle maker. I knew her spirit was still making miracles for all of us. Patsy had not survived her own illness, but miracles are not measured individually and in linear time. The measure of miracles is not living to an old age but of living life with the confidence that there is much more to life than just a local living. Miracles are not measured as successes but as celebrations of the strength and eternity of the human spirit.

The healing energy of Patsy's living provides clues for what it takes to be a miracle maker. Patsy's life must be measured in the depth and meaning she brought to it, not in the number of her years and birthdays. The science principles of nonlocality and nonlinearity are proven through the power, pervasiveness and permanence of who Patsy always will be. Patsy lives forever in her enduring relationship with all of us. The temple of miracles is in our relationships and in our connectedness to others, not in our body or our skills. I will never see a balloon or a parade without feeling Patsy's power.

If we use long life, heroic survival, and the conquering of disease as the exclusive criteria of a miracle, we are trapped into believing that miracles "happen" only to a chosen few. We seem to think that if we are very lucky, very good or try very hard, a miracle will happen "to" us and we will achieve victory over time, space, disease and grief. But miracles are not payoffs for earned cosmic points. Miracles occur when we perceive life from the perspective of the cosmic laws or the "way it is" in the universe.

If we are impressed only by the misguided miracles of levitation or by dramatic stories of heroic patients conquering disease, we fail to see the simple miracles of a cloud moving at just the right time, a silver lunar rainbow, or the glory of a Christmas-tree IV protest parade in support of healing. We can copy and learn from miracle makers such as Patsy. They know how to do everyday miracles.

Miracle makers like Patsy have found the way. As philosopher Sengtsan writes, "For the unified mind in accord with the Way all self-centered striving ceases." In other words, miracles have little to do with the survival of the self unless that self is all of us. Miracle makers are aware of their nonlocality, as when Patsy saw herself as one with the little balloon that escaped the confines of earth. They know that their chosen view of their world designs that world, as when Patsy made joyful parades in a place where funeral processions were more likely. They know of the principle of complementarity, as when Patsy saw our potential for marching in her parade even as we wobbled down the hospital hall. They know the hope that comes with the uncertainty of life, as Patsy seemed to know when she pensively looked out of her hospital window and said that the parade would always go on even though some balloons escaped. After twenty-five years of clinical work with my seventeen miracle makers and after my own near-death experiences, I now know that we don't have to go to gurus or channelers to find our role models for miracle making; we just have to look for people like Patsy.•

Love and Healing

L A R R Y   D O S S E Y ,   M. D.

If scientists suddenly discovered a drug that was as powerful as love in creating health, it would be heralded as a medical breakthrough and marketed overnight—especially if it had as few side effects and was as inexpensive as love. Love is intimately related with health. This is not sentimental exaggeration. One survey of ten thousand men with heart disease found a 50 percent reduction in frequency of chest pain (angina) in men who perceived their wives as supportive and loving.

The power of love to change bodies is legendary, built into folklore, common sense and everyday experience. Love moves the flesh; it pushes matter around—as the blushing and palpitations experienced by lovers attest. Throughout history "tender, loving care" has uniformly been recognized as a valuable element in healing.

David McClelland, Ph.D., of Harvard Medical School, has demonstrated the power of love to make the body healthier through what he calls the "Mother Teresa effect." He showed a group of Harvard students a documentary of Mother Teresa ministering lovingly to the sick and measured the levels of immunoglobulin A (IgA) in their saliva before and after seeing the film. (IgA is an antibody active against viral infections such as colds.) IgA levels rose significantly in the students, even in many of those who considered Mother Teresa "too religious" or a fake. In order to achieve this effect in another way, McClelland later discarded the film and asked his graduate students simply to think about two things: past moments when they felt deeply loved and cared for by someone else and a time when they loved another person. In his own experience, McClelland had been able to abort colds with this technique. As a result of his personal experiences and research, he became an advocate for the role of love in modern healing. He once told a group of his medical colleagues,

I can dream a little about changing hospital environments, one that relaxes you, gives you loving care and relieves you of the incessant desire to control and

run everything. A healthful environment. Certain doctors, nurses, social workers—all of us—can learn . . . that being loving to people is really good for their health. And probably good for yours too.

But can love and caring do more than act *within* a person? Is it powerful enough to act at a distance *between* individuals, overcoming separation in space and possibly in time? Can love unite people over geographical distances even when the "receiver" is unaware that love is being offered? This is a way of asking if prayer works, because when one person prays for the welfare of another, the person who prays is extending compassion, empathy and love. Can these qualities genuinely "reach out"?

One of the greatest scholars and researchers in the history of parapsychology, F. W. H. Myers, was struck by the fact that people who were "telepathic" with each other—people who could share thoughts at great distances—were frequently connected emotionally with one another deeply and lovingly. Meyers concluded that love, empathy and compassion somehow made it possible for the mind to transcend the limitations of the body. Love was so important in this process that Meyers honored it by giving it a place in a natural "law." As he put it, "Love is a kind of exalted but unspecialized telepathy—the simplest and most universal expression of that mutual gravitation or kinship of spirits which is the foundation of the telepathic law."

Virtually all psychic healers who use prayer agree. They claim uniformly that distance is not a factor in the healing power of prayer, and most of them state emphatically that love is the power that makes it possible for them to reach out to heal at a distance. During attempts at healing, healers generally feel infused by love and transformed by caring. This feeling is so pronounced that they typically describe "becoming one" with the person being prayed for. In his landmark study of psychic healing, *The Medium, The Mystic, and the Physicist,* psychologist Lawrence LeShan—who is perhaps the greatest living authority on the subject—reported the observations of several famous healers:

> *In Agnes Sanford's words, "Only love can generate the healing fire." Ambrose and Olga Worrall have said, "We must care. We must care for others deeply and urgently, wholly, and immediately; our minds, our spirits must reach out to them." Stewart Grayson, a serious healer from the First Church of Religious Science, said, "If this understanding is just mental it is empty and sterile" and "the feeling is the fuel behind the healing." Sanford wrote, "When we pray in accordance with the law of love, we pray in accordance with the will of God."*

In addition to the beliefs of healers that love is vital if prayer is to "get through" and facilitate healing, considerable evidence, both laboratory-based and anecdotal, suggests that empathy somehow connects distant organisms. These entities are of a vastly different variety, ranging from microorganisms to human beings. This fact is important. If empathy indeed connects a vast range of living things, it may be a built-in feature of the natural world, not just a human quirk or perhaps an erroneous observation.

EMPATHIC CONNECTIONS

Empathy, compassion and love seem to form a literal bond—a resonance or "glue"—between living things. The following observations suggest that when empathic connections are present, feelings experienced by one entity may be felt also by another, in spite of considerable spatial separation.

J. B. Rhine and Sara Feather of the Parapsychology Laboratory at Duke University collected fifty-four "returning animal" cases. Some of them are quite astonishing because there is no obvious way the animal could have known the way back home. Thus these are not "homing" events as demonstrated by pigeons. An example is the case of Bobbie, a young female collie. She was traveling with her family from Ohio to Oregon, the site of their new home. Although the family had made the trip previously, Bobbie had not. During a stop in Indiana, Bobbie wandered, became lost and could not be found. Finally giving up the search, the family proceeded. Almost three months later, Bobbie appeared at the doorstep of the new home in Oregon. She was not a "look-alike" dog; she still had her name on her collar in addition to several identifying marks and scars.

In another case, a young boy named Hugh Brady who kept homing pigeons as pets found a wounded pigeon in the garden of his home and befriended him. He nursed the bird back to health and gave him an identification tag marked #167. The next winter Hugh suddenly became ill, was rushed to a hospital two hundred miles away and underwent surgery. While he was still recovering, on a bitterly cold, snowy night he heard a tapping at the window. Hugh summoned a nurse and asked her to open it. In flew a pigeon, which landed with a flutter on Hugh's chest. He identified his bird immediately by sight, which was confirmed by the tag number. Pigeons are well known of course for their homing ability; but #167 was not homing. He was traveling to a place he had never been.

Not only does empathy influence relationships between living things, it is apparently involved in human-machine interactions. In a series of experiments extending over the past decade, researchers at the Princeton Engineering Anomalies Research (PEAR) Laboratory at Princeton University have studied the ability of people to influence the behavior of random physical events occurring in different mechanical devices, such as a microelectronic random event generator (REG). This device produces a string of binary samples, or bits, at a rate of one thousand per second, in trials of two hundred bits each, and counts the number that conform to a regular positive or negative alternation. A human operator sits in front of this device, views on a display the sequence of numbers, and tries to influence the output distribution in either a positive or negative direction—in other words, trying to will the machine's output up or down. In addition to the REG, many other mechanical devices are employed in the PEAR Lab experiments. Over the years fifteen pairs of individuals have been tested in 256,000 attempts to influence the REG. Their results have been compared to those of ninety-one individual operators, who have generated 2,520,000 trials on the same device. The results indicate overwhelmingly that both individuals and couples working in concert can influence the REG, steering its output from sheer randomness toward a particular pattern. The most successful pairs are couples who are deeply attached emotionally and empathically to each other—so-called "bonded" couples.

This database, the largest of its kind ever collected, is impressive evidence that empathy and emotional closeness allow the emergence of a power that is capable of shaping physical events "out there" in the world. This is supportive evidence for the claims of the prayer healers above. "Love [empathy, compassion, caring, bonding] is the fuel behind the healing."

Does empathy help prayer "get through"? "Getting through" presumes that there is such a thing as a separate person fundamentally isolated and distinct from every other. This concept may be flawed. As the eminent researcher in parapsychology Stanley Krippner has stated:

> *Another posture could be taken, namely, that all consciousness is basically "group consciousness." An individual's awareness, attention, memory, etc. is socially constructed. Without group interaction, an individual would never achieve "identification" with anyone or anything. From this viewpoint, "group consciousness" is the fundamental matrix from which "individual consciousness" emerges.*

We have for so long defined ourselves as separate personalities that we have fallen into the hypnotic spell of believing that separation, not unity, is the underlying reality. But if *unity, not separation, is fundamental,* then at some level of the psyche, *nothing* may be "getting through" because there are no separate parts for something to get through to.

If this is so, the connections we feel with others during prayer are "nothing special." We do not have to establish or invent these connections because they already exist. Prayer is not an innovation; it is a process of remembering who we really are and how we are related. From this point of view, there is good reason to rid prayer of its aura that it is some rare state we enter only on certain occasions. If the unity it connotes is not the exception but the rule, there should be no celestial halo surrounding prayer.

This also implies that at certain levels of the psyche, there is no such thing as "understanding" healing because there is no distance separating people that must be overcome. This means that healing of another is in some sense self-healing, for the spatial distinctions between "self" and "other" are not fundamental. Perhaps that is why it always feels good to love another and why our prayers for others are also good for us.

LOVE'S PARADOXES

Of all the trivialized concepts in this so-called New Age, perhaps the greatest involves love. Books pour from the pens of well-meaning patients and doctors alike, attesting to its phenomenal power in healing. Love melts away tumors, cures addictions, banishes fear, catalyzes miracles, transforms lives— all this we are told *ad infinitum.* If we could only learn to love and forgive ourselves and others and let go of all our fears, grudges and hatreds, our health would be better. Paracelsus's dictum, "The main reason for healing is love," frequently becomes distorted into "The only reason for healing is love." The frenzied enthusiasm surrounding love has led to one of the greatest ironies of the New Age, namely that significant numbers of sick people are made to feel guilty in the name of love for not being well.

About ten years ago, a patient of mine developed a breast lump and had a mammogram and breast biopsy that revealed cancer. Considerably shaken, she sought help from a psychological counselor well known for dealing with newly diagnosed cancer patients. This man was deeply convinced that all physical ailments reflected emotional and spiritual shortcomings. On my patient's first visit, the counselor, without bothering to inquire deeply about her history and psychological makeup, stated abruptly, "There are only three possibilities for why you have cancer. You either don't *love* yourself enough, you have some deep-seated *fear* you're not in touch with or you are not *trusting* enough of yourself and others!" Deeply introspective, my patient felt the counselor's observations were simply wrong. "Having cancer is difficult enough without the guilt trip," she said. She rejected his analysis and found help elsewhere. Ten years later, after using orthodox cancer therapy as well as continued inner psychological work, she has no trace of illness.

This is not to suggest that I do not believe in the role of love in healing. As I have explained, I believe it is vastly important, particularly in prayer-based healing. I only want to point out that love should not be enshrined as some magical, monolithic principles in health and healing. When it is, the sick person often pays.

At some point one wants to stand up and demand of all the love merchants, what do you *mean* by love? There is a tendency in holistic health circles to regard it simply as an emotion that has something to do with unconditional caring, compassion and empathy. This is fine as far as it goes, but it is only a partial picture. The ancient Greeks, for example, believed that love was the domain of Eros—and Eros was above all mysterious and paradoxical. As Jung explained, "In classical times when such things were properly understood, Eros was considered a god whose divinity transcended our human limits and who therefore could neither be comprehended nor represented in any way." In contrast to most New Agers, the Greeks recognized that many of Eros's qualities were decidedly not nice. Jung agreed. As a result of observing the actions of Eros in the lives and dreams of thousands of his patients, he concluded that Eros was a "daimon whose range of activity extends from the endless spaces of the heavens to the dark abysses of hell . . . [and which contains] . . . incalculable paradoxes. . . ."

A lot of New Age literature has stripped love of its complexity and sanitized it into something nice that can be made into a simplified formula everybody can understand. Love's mysterious, darker qualities are relegated to the shadows or completely ignored.

The Old Testament story of Job is about the shadow side of love and how one can be victimized by a loving God. Job's story should be required reading for those who today insist on linking spiritual perfection and health, for it shows that horrible things can happen to blameless people and that the currently popular love formulas for health are sadly incomplete.

We are told at the outset that Job was "perfect and upright" (Job 1:1). In other words he did nothing to deserve his fate. But in spite of his perfection, God allowed terrible things to be done to him—his ten children were killed, his wealth destroyed, his health replaced by disfiguring, painful disease. If we believe that "God is love," then we are forced to conclude that love must be an extremely complex phenomenon—Jung's "daimon" in action.

Things haven't changed much since Job's time. People who are highly spiritual, God-realized and "enlightened" still become ill. In order to "keep God's skirts clean," as Alan Watts once put it, we hear various rationales for these troubling events. Some say that the sick person only appears loving, trusting and free of fear but deep down, real problems exist that he or she isn't "in touch" with. Or that the sick are living out their karma and "paying back" for transgressions in past lives, or that they "chose" this illness in a previous life, and so on. One gets the feeling that these are desperate, ad hoc attempts to preserve the love-model of health rather than confront the obvious: the model is flawed; love is no guarantee of health, longevity or anything else but paradox and deep mystery.

What do we really know about the place of love in healing? What can we say without undue fear of contradiction? We can demonstrate experimentally that love, compassion, caring and empathy catalyze healing events and that this power operates at a distance and outside of time. But we know also that love is compatible with illness—in the same sense in which Jesus said, "Love your enemies," not "Don't have any."

Love occupies a majestic place in healing. Lying outside space and time, it is a living tissue of reality, a bond that unites us all. •

Healing with Love

An Interview with Dean Ornish, M. D.

For the past twenty years, Dean Ornish, M.D., has directed clinical research demonstrating—for the first time—that comprehensive lifestyle changes may begin to reverse even severe coronary heart disease, without drugs or surgery.

PERSONAL TRANSFORMATION: *You are known as the diet doctor. You have recommended diet, along with lifestyle changes, for the treatment of heart disease. Yet, your latest book,* Love and Survival, *is on love, intimacy and healing. Do you think the power of relationship is more significant than these other lifestyle changes you advocate in the treatment of heart disease?*

DEAN ORNISH: I have always talked about the importance of love and intimacy; however, people tend to focus on diet. Certainly, diet is important; I haven't changed my views on that. But I don't know of anything in medicine, not drugs, not diet, that has greater impact on our health and well-being, as well as premature death and disease from virtually all causes, than the healing power of love and intimacy. I decided that if I wrote a whole book about it, people would tend to pay more attention to that.

PT: *So, this book is an emphasis on this aspect of your work, not a shift in your orientation.*

DO: This has always been part of my work, but over time I have developed a greater appreciation, in both my personal life and in the lives of the patients with whom I work, of how important love and intimacy are.

PT: *Early in the book, you gave an introduction to the ways that loneliness and isolation affect our health, and I am going to quote you. You wrote, "It increases the likelihood of disease and premature death from all causes by 200–500 percent—independent of behaviors—through different mechanisms, many of which are not fully understood." That was astounding to me.*

DO: Yes. It is to most people. Isolation and loneliness impact our behaviors as well. People who are depressed, lonely, unhappy and/or isolated are much more likely to smoke, overeat, eat too much fat and cholesterol, drink excessively, abuse drugs, work too hard and so on. I find it interesting, however, that even when those factors are controlled, these studies show the effect of loneliness and isolation.

PT: *In the book, you describe numerous studies that demonstrate the healing power of love and intimacy. This compilation of studies is a helpful resource for people like me, not in the medical field, who are interested in health and wellness. Would you highlight a couple of studies that are particularly revealing in documenting the healing power of support?*

DO: Yes, I reviewed hundreds of studies in the book, and a few are particularly meaningful for me. One study, conducted by Dr. Thomas Oxman, at the University of Texas Medical School, was with men and women before they had open heart surgery. The study examined the relationships of social support and religion to mortality in men and women six months after undergoing elective open heart surgery. The researcher asked them two questions: "Do you draw strength from your religious faith or spiritual faith, whatever that might be? Are you a member of any group that meets regularly, a civic group, a church group, a synagogue, support group, a bingo game, etc.?" The results were astonishing. Six months after open heart surgery, of those who answered no to both questions, 20 percent were dead, compared to only 3 percent who answered yes to both questions. There was a seven-fold difference in mortality, six months after open heart surgery, between those who answered yes to both questions and those who answered no to both questions. I don't know of anything in medicine that causes such a dramatic difference in fatality rates; yet these are not questions that most surgeons ask their patients, or that physicians even value.

PT: *In that particular study, they were talking about involvement in civic groups; they weren't necessarily talking about intimacy. Even casual contact with people is apparently good for our health.*

DO: I think that the real epidemic in our culture is what I call emotional and spiritual heart disease, not physical heart disease. The loneliness, isolation, alienation and depression that are so common in our culture are caused in part because of the breakdown of the social networks that used to give people a sense of connection and community. This study indicates how powerful these issues are and how deprived people are in these areas since something as simple as attending a civic group meeting regularly can make such a difference.

PT: *You are talking about emotional heart disease and spiritual heart disease. Are love and intimacy at the root of not only what makes us ill, but what makes us well?*

DO: Love and intimacy are certainly root cause of health and well-being on the one hand, and premature death and disease on the other hand, for many people. Certainly, genetic diseases are a primary determinant of health, but that's not the norm for most people. For most people, I think love and intimacy play an important and compelling role, not only of quality in our lives, but even of quantity of our lives. We've always known that people who feel loved are happy, but what we may not have known is what a powerful difference this makes in our survival. I am hoping that this book can raise the level of awareness of how much these things matter. It is easy to make fun of the need for support or not take intimacy seriously, as we tend to do in our culture. If we understand what an important difference love and intimacy make, we may have the courage to begin taking them more seriously.

PT: *In the last few days, since reading the book, I've had heightened awareness of not only my intimate, but particularly my social and casual relationships. Knowing that how I related was making a difference for both of us, in terms of our well-being, created a more authentic interchange on my behalf.*

DO: That makes me feel good because that is what I hope the book will foster. When people realize that relationships really matter, they might be more courageous. Vulnerability requires courage because you can get hurt, but if people understand what a powerful difference this can make, they may be more willing to risk—to learn to open their hearts, which is what it means to be vulnerable, because it's worth it.

A study I found particularly interesting, in addition to the one I mentioned already, was the study of Harvard undergraduates from the 1950s. The study shows how loving relationships may affect susceptibility to disease in general. The graduates were asked, "Were you close to your mother, and were you close to your father?" A follow-up study was done thirty-five years later. One hundred percent of those graduates who answered no to both questions had major illnesses in midlife, compared to only 40 percent who answered yes to both questions and 60 percent to those who answered yes to one of the questions.

This doesn't mean that you are doomed to get sick later in life if you weren't close to your parents when you were growing up, but we tend to relate as adults much as we did when we were children growing up. If we grew up in a family where we weren't rewarded for learning to be intimate, or even worse, if we were abused by our parents, then intimacy is dangerous. When we are older, we tend to relate to people or unconsciously choose relationships with people who have the same limited capacity for intimacy that we do.

Other studies show that we *can* change. The study by Dr. Spiegel at Stanford Medical School of women with metastatic breast cancer, and the study by Dr. Fauzy at UCLA, with men and women with malignant melanoma, found that a six-week support group in the melanoma study, and a year-long support group in the breast cancer study, caused significant reduction in premature death, extended survival, and in the melanoma patients prevented recurrence. Even a six-week support group made a difference! Five years later, these people had less recurrence and lived longer. It is almost mind-boggling to think that a six-week support group could have such a major impact on survival. I think the reason that it did is not because the six-week support group per se had such an important impact, but for many people, it was the first time that they were encouraged to be intimate and open. They learned to be open, and they began to experience how good it feels to be intimate, and then carried these skills beyond the six weeks.

PT: *Those studies are encouraging and motivating. This information can reassure people that changes can be made, that support does make a difference, and that we are not doomed. What would a new model of medicine be like that incorporated these findings?*

DO: It's a model that is more caring and compassionate, as well as more cost-effective and competent. That's what we are trying to create in our work.

PT: *Are the shifts more in the quality of relationships than in medical technology?*

DO: They are not mutually exclusive, but I don't think anyone needs to worry that we do not have enough technology in medicine. It's the other aspects that are lacking and people are voting with their feet by choosing alternative practitioners, because alternative practitioners respond more to basic human needs, which are to feel listened to, cared for, nurtured, nourished and loved. When people don't get that from their traditional doctors, they go elsewhere, even if elsewhere may not have the scientific basis or technology that a Western practice might have. It is always better to incorporate everything that works. I am a founder of the new Center for Integrative Medicine at the University of California, San Francisco, where we're trying to incorporate the best of allopathic and alternative approaches and to pay attention to these psychological issues as well.

PT: *Throughout the book, you use the term an "open heart." What does an "open heart" mean?*

DO: An "open heart" is the willingness to make oneself vulnerable. We've all been hurt at various times in our lives, and there is, metaphorically speaking, a wall around our hearts that protects us from pain. It's not that we shouldn't have our emotional defenses, but if we have no one with whom we feel safe enough to be vulnerable, those defenses that protect us also isolate us because they are always up. The goal is to have one person in your life, preferably more, but at least one person, with whom you can make a commitment to open your heart. By that, I mean to let down your emotional defenses and to make yourself vulnerable as a way of being more intimate with that person.

PT: *If we have one or two persons with whom we are intimate, do we also need quantity? You talk about quality and quantity of relationships in your book.*

DO: Some studies show that both may be important, but I believe that quality is the more important. If you have even one person in your life with whom you can truly be yourself, where you can be so vulnerable that they know your dark sides, as well as your social sides you show to other people, that relationship is healing. One person in your life who really knows you and loves you is healing. Many people don't have one person, not even their spouse, with whom they can be completely authentic, because they fear that if others knew that they weren't perfect and had dark sides, they would be unloved and abandoned. People often create an image of who they want other people to think they are that exposes just their good sides. Unfortunately, when you do that, if you don't get love and respect, you lose, and if you get it, you lose because it's not for you—it's for this image of you. When you can be authentic, when you have the courage to show all of yourself to someone else and to make yourself vulnerable, it often allows the other to do the same, and the level of intimacy can be much more powerful, even though the fear is often that you'll be more alone.

PT: *What's the importance of intimacy with oneself?*

DO: Intimacy is not just with other people, but also with oneself and with something spiritual. On one level, we are separate, and on another level, we are part of something larger that connects us all. By spiritual, I mean that direct experience of interconnectedness that is so healing. Intimacy can be with parts of oneself, as well. As we talked about a moment ago, many people feel as if parts of themselves are not lovable. They fear they wouldn't be loved if others knew about these fantasies or wishes or parts of themselves that they don't like very much, and so they hide them from other people. Often, these are hidden even from oneself. They are split off, and sometimes projected onto other groups of people. If you think you are not lovable or if you feel anger or hate and don't acknowledge that as an aspect of being human, there is a tendency to project that onto other groups of people. That is an underlying quality of racism or anti-Semitism or other forms of hatred of groups of people. Hatred is projected onto other people so that we don't have to deal with those under-lying issues in ourselves. Part of healing is to re-own and reintegrate those aspects, so that we realize they are a part of being human, too. Elisabeth Kübler-Ross used to say, "We have a Mother Teresa in us, and we have a Hitler in us as well, and when we can have compassion for that in ourselves, we can then have more compassion when we see that manifested in other people as well."

PT: *One of the people you interviewed for your book made the point that if we don't have intimacy with ourselves, when we are in a group—due to our projections and our defenses—we might not experience the support of the group, and in that sense, becoming intimate with oneself is also central to the healing process.*

DO: I don't know that I would put it quite like that. What makes a group experience powerful for many people is that it enables them to disclose those parts of self to the group. If the group is an effective group, you can say, "You know, I may look like I have it all together, but my kids are on drugs," or "I may look wealthy, but I am really bankrupt," or "I may look like I am success-ful, but I have a lot of doubts about myself." When people can say those kinds of things, just to use a few examples, they find that the group doesn't abandon or reject them, but just listens compassionately. Other group members say, "You know, I have similar kinds of feelings, too," and they find that they are more connected. The group process itself can help them become more integrated, accepting and compassionate to those parts within themselves. Becoming inti-mate with self and with others in a group can go hand in hand.

PT: *You mentioned relationship with spirituality or God. What's the sig-nificance of spirituality in healing?*

DO: You can be alone on a mountaintop or in your room and feel the direct experience of interconnectiveness and oneness with God or whatever religious term you put that experience into. Feeling a oneness with God is an ineffable experience, a limitless experience. You can be walking down Fifth Avenue, surrounded by thousands of people in New York City, and feel terribly alone. It is not necessarily the quantity of people you are with, but the inner experience that is the most important.

PT: *How do love, intimacy and social support get inside the body?*

DO: One of the things that I found interesting in interviewing these people about healing was that although most healing systems—Chinese, Indian, Japanese, African medicine—had different vocabularies and paradigms to describe these issues, there is a recognition of a vital life force, whether it is called Kundalini or Chi or Prana. In Western medicine we tend not to acknowledge the validity of these kinds of concepts because we don't have the technology to measure it. We tend not to believe what we can't measure. Every healing system, besides traditional American or Western medicine, talks about this life force. The idea is that when you close yourself off from another person or close yourself off from parts of yourself, you also close yourself off from that source of life and energy. Health consequences derive from doing that. When you open yourself up to that life force, you are less likely to get sick, and healing is facilitated. When you close yourself off from it, the opposite is more likely to occur. The sun still shines whether you open your window or not. Our choices in every moment, in every action, lead us more toward intimacy and healing or more toward isolation and suffering and often premature death and disease.

PT: *What you are discussing reflects a certain mystery in the energy of love and the energetics of healing.*

DO: Yes, there is an element of mystery to all of this. We don't have all the answers; yet because we don't understand the mechanisms of why these things matter, it doesn't mean that we can't benefit from them. There are many things in medicine that we don't fully understand, but we know that they make a difference, and this is one of them.

PT: *What about the relationship of meditation and intimacy?*

DO: Meditation helps you quiet down your mind and body so you become more aware of what you are feeling, which can be used to enhance intimacy. Once you know what you feel, you can express those feelings to another person, which can bring you closer together. Even more than that, when you quiet down enough, you can have a direct experience of transcendence. Whether it's through meditation or prayer, any system that helps you quiet your mind and body is useful. As Swami Satchidananda said, "When you tune your radio better, you can hear the music." The music is there, whether or not you turn your radio on. Meditation or prayer can help you find the right station and tune your radio more clearly.

PT: *Is there anything that you would like to share about your own journey with our readers?*

DO: I talked about myself in the book in a self-disclosing and personal way. I felt a little anxious writing about myself because, like everybody, I want people to think well of me. I talked about some personal struggles I have had in my life that most people don't talk about. I did that as a way to try to be an example of what I am writing about, with the hope that what I learned from my own struggles might be of benefit to other people.

PT: *Reading study after study that verified the significance of intimacy in relationships and well-being was the most impactful part of the book for me. I also enjoyed the pictures. Where did you get those photographs?*

DO: I took them. I was a photographer before I became a doctor, and I took thousands of pictures. I notice, looking back on that period of my life, how often the pictures were of people who were together, but weren't *together*. They embodied the loneliness that I was feeling at that time.

PT: *Is there anything you would like to say in closing?*

DO: Having seen the powerful difference these issues have made in my own life and in the lives of so many other people, I am grateful for the opportunity to share this with your readers.•

A Clear Voice Rising

NANCY PASTERNACK

For much of the past decade, the most difficult question anyone could ask me was, "And what do you do, Nancy?" It is a question that most in society answer by filling in the blank with their job title or career aspirations; it is what they do, and perhaps who they believe they are.

I have felt terrorized by this question, as people tend to want to hear a short, nonthreatening answer—not necessarily the truth. How could I explain in comfortable words that the healthy-looking person in front of them has been so desperately ill that she thought about suicide?

The difficulty in answering that question is reflective of the enormous challenge my life has been for the past eleven years. Answering it is my biggest lesson. What I do is heal.

In 1984, my life as I knew it began to disintegrate. I experienced pain and fatigue that would not go away, plus a host of other maladies not readily qualified. As a critical care nurse, I took care of others in seemingly worse shape than I. Without an acceptable diagnosis to validate my decline, I pushed myself through daily existence, depleting my final reserves of strength and energy, onward into total physical collapse. I had plummeted downward into a dark, isolated and silent place. I received vague diagnoses and various pills to take for a myriad of complaints. Coming from a conventional medical background, I was unprepared to know what type of help I needed, and in 1984 "alternative" health care was neither a buzzword, nor was it readily available. I became immobilized with a condition that eluded standard laboratory tests and appeared invisible, except for subjective symptoms.

It was two or three years before I was diagnosed with fibromyalgia, a debilitating muscle condition, and nearly six years before hearing a diagnosis of chronic fatigue syndrome (CFS). By that time, the physical symptoms and emotional traumas and patterns of chronic illness were deeply embedded.

I sometimes wonder how I survived the confusion, humiliation and physical suffering of those very dark years. But I know now that I was well-honed to living in a survival mode; I had done it most of my childhood and believed that is how life was supposed to feel. I have come to see my illness as a healing of my false life; my conscious healing now involves uncovering my true self.

I lost myself a very long time ago, early in childhood. I did not live in a home with physical abuse, alcoholism or incest, but I lived in numbed pain.

I lost my father at age six by way of divorce, after which he ventured in and out of my life irregularly and swiftly, leaving no forwarding address. A hit-and-run father. My mother remarried and divorced the same man twice when I was ages ten and fourteen. This man emotionally abused my mother, my sister and me with words and ambiguous violations of sexual boundaries. We moved five times in six years. There were many losses in my life of people, places and dearly loved pets.

I learned to be good and to be quiet, never to make a fuss. I became my mother's emotional caretaker. I grew up responsible and sensible. The clear message I received was that there was no reason to feel whatever feelings I was experiencing, that it was not okay. Feelings were "explained away" to me or "swept under the rug," out of sight. I learned to say nothing and to hide or stuff all my emotions. I did this very well until as an adult my body began screaming with pain for me to listen to what it had been trying to tell me my whole life. Not allowing my feelings even to exist, it has taken me a long time to understand this new type of message.

The "House of Cards" I lived in looked respectable and secure. The damaging messages came disguised, subtle and covert. Perhaps, if I had been bruised and beaten, I would have known something was wrong. So the little girl who loved music, loved to sing and dance and draw, and who organized plays and wrote poetry became very quiet, scared and numbed by her life.

The ironies of my life are in the fallout of my illness. I was taught to be independent (I have been financially dependent on my husband), there's no reason to have feelings (my suppressed feelings scream out through physical pain), to pick myself up from all situations (I have been, at times, physically unable to sit in a chair or brush my teeth), to be quiet and say nothing (I have been too tired to speak and too emotionally confused to know my own voice).

Over the years, I have put myself in a bubble for long periods of healing and rest. A self-imposed "bubble" is necessary when the pain of uncovering your past is overwhelming, and your physical vulnerability exposed. I realize that I am in the midst of generational healing; I am transforming a legacy of noble suffering.

Over the last several years of illness, I have had sparks of awareness that healing could be found in that creative child who never expected anyone to hurt her. I began to gain glimpses into that soul, but had no tools or strength or will to try.

In the spring of 1993, there came a turning point that stays with me still. I "found" a group of persons with CFS led by a therapist who had CFS. She used Expressive Art Therapy. When I walked in the building, I knew I was "home." After being ill for nine years, I finally met other women with CFS! I began to tap back into the creative side to access my "voice." I began to allow myself to do the things I loved as a child, to express in all ways. That expression has come out in violent floods of tears, and in drawings and written words, by dancing about the living room, and lately in scenic design for the theater. The creation of my artistic work in the theater has flowed, joyful and easy, showing me how life can feel when freed from painful emotional attachments.

Perhaps more important than any type of therapy I have used is the finding of my own voice. Keeping silent seems painful for me now, for it drives my soul, my true self, back into darkness. I am learning to listen to my body messages. I make choices by how I feel, and by what that still, small voice whispers to me.

I actively seek my spiritual connection to God and the energy of the universe. What a revelation when I found validation that spirituality has nothing necessarily to do with religion! It's something I've always known, as I am much more comfortable in the quiet of nature than in a building full of people.

I do not believe illness or disease is random, but rather crafted to bring our attention to whatever aspect of our soul needs attending to, and thus healing. I believe my illness and its particular qualities and symptoms are reflective of my lies—core beliefs and patterns that are untrue for me. Lies manifest.

Truth and lies cannot live together comfortably. Reactive emotions now tell me that a truth is pushing through, and a lie is being exposed. But that lie fights hard for control—knowing that its adversary has the real power.

The poet, Anne Sexton, wrote, "There is nothing in your body that lies. All that is new is telling the truth." There is particular meaning for me here, as my body has so tenaciously dramatized the struggle of my soul. So it's time to come clean, to tell the truth.

My long-ago necessary survival mode is breaking down. The armor is cracking and falling away. I am healing. It is the most difficult, painful, amazing and joyful thing I have ever done. And absolutely necessary.

Some people experience amazing miracles—I seem to have every stepping stone to feel. My miracle is to be where I am, just now, freeing myself from my numbed existence and happier and more at peace than I have ever been. I am usually able to make no judgments or comparisons concerning my own transformation, my own path and process.

Recently I was saddened to hear someone whom I care about say that her life has been wasted. She is only forty-two years old. If I were able to award myself a Medal of Honor for some particular aspect of my own transformation, it would be for honoring my pathway and knowing my life. My steps have not been wasted. They are just what they have been—my life, my steps, my path of transformation. There is no right or wrong way to heal and no timetable.

Perhaps I can tell my story and say there wasn't one life-changing "miracle" therapy; there were many little turning points. There wasn't one path, but many. I feel certain that it's okay to be where and who I am: a Transformation in Progress.

These days, if someone asks me what I do, I easily say, "I'm remodeling my life." It feels good to say—it's the truth.•

HEALING THE BODY

Soul Practice

QUESTIONS

1. If you are seriously ill, what is the story you tell yourself about the possibility of recovery? If it is negative, how might you change it into a more healing story?

2. What are some big soul questions that your illness is inviting you to ask, and to live into? For instance:
   - What did I come here to do, to learn?
   - Whom did I come here to love?
   - What is the meaning of my particular life? What am I here for?
   - What makes me truly happy? What—great or small—gives me joy?
   - If I had unlimited time/resources/good health, what would I now choose to do with my life?

3. How can you open to your illness as a gift, a teacher, a wakeup call?

4. What does it mean for you to love and cherish yourself as someone with an illness, rather than guilting yourself for "causing" it? How can you extend yourself compassion from an open heart?

5. If you are ill, how can you reach out more for love, support and intimacy?

6. If you love someone who is seriously ill, how can you be a carrier of healing and love for them? How can you allow your loved one's illness to be a transformative and healing event in your own life?

7. If you are in a committed relationship, how is the illness asking the two of you to grow?

8. If you love someone who is ill, how can you show your love and support in tangible ways?

P R A C T I C E S

1. Write out a list of your big soul questions. Spend some time each day contemplating one of them. You may journal about it (try writing with your nondominant hand), draw images as they come to you, make collages from magazine pictures. It is less important to come up with specific answers than to live into, and love, the questions themselves.

2. If someone you love is ill, practice sending them love every day for a short time, whether by praying, visualizing surrounding them with healing light, or speaking to them silently from the depth of your heart and soul. Remember, study after study has definitively concluded that distance makes no difference in prayer; your loved one could be in the same room or thousands of miles away.

4

Soulful Healing

Soulful healing involves a particular kind of life review. It is an intentional investigation of personality and motivation. A personality that operates mostly out of the unconscious never really evolves beyond the ways it developed in childhood, when personality was first formed. Without a conscientious examination of how we relate to life, how we attempt to control life and seek safety and approval, we remain trapped in an immature personality. The mechanisms we use for relating to life, along with our definitions of who we are and the basic nature of other people, help form personality in childhood.

Soulful healing assists us in evolving into a mature personality that is free to be loving, responsible and less self-serving. Along the way, old wounds surface, so they may be healed, and so that forgiveness may occur. These wounds are shown to us in many ways. They are revealed through our bodies, as well as in our hearts and minds. Soulful healing brings wholeness and integration. As the old and repressed is cleared away, space is made for spiritual essence to be made known throughout our being.

Through this process, we mature spiritually and psychologically. This chapter discusses the steps of soulful healing.

AWARENESS

We all have certain ideas, attitudes, core beliefs and emotional patterns that limit our experience of well-being. Deep feelings of unworthiness, a sense of scarcity, fear of failure or success, conflicting feelings and beliefs about money, and many other issues can block our growth and fulfillment.

The dawning awareness about what doesn't work in how we are living is by far the most powerful step in our growth. It is also the most difficult and uncomfortable. As soon as we recognize a problem, we are on the road to healing it. However, that healing takes time. Meanwhile, we may have to watch ourselves repeat the same old self-defeating patterns a few more times.

It's difficult to do this without getting frustrated and self-critical. We need to understand how important this step of awareness is. When you are unconscious, you can repeat a behavior endlessly without gaining much benefit. Once you have some awareness and can catch yourself repeating the same behavior, you learn an enormous amount. You really feel the pain of it. Then you are able to explore other possible ways of handling the same situation. It's not long before things start to change. You don't have to make change. Focus on gaining awareness, and change will follow.

—Shakti Gawain

Profound
Personal Healing

J A C K   K O R N F I E L D

Almost everyone who undertakes a true spiritual path will discover that a profound personal healing is a necessary part of his or her spiritual process. When this need is acknowledged, spiritual practice can be directed to bring such healing to body, heart and mind. This is not a new notion. Since ancient times, spiritual practice has been described as a process of healing. The Buddha and Jesus were both known as healers of the body, as well as great physicians of the spirit.

Wise spiritual practice requires that we actively address the pain and conflict of our life in order to come to inner integration and harmony. Through the guidance of a skillful teacher, meditation can help bring this healing. Without including the essential step of healing, students will find that they are blocked from deeper levels of meditation or are unable to integrate them into their lives.

Many people first come to spiritual practice hoping to skip over their sorrows and wounds, the difficult areas of their lives. They hope to rise above them and enter a spiritual realm full of divine grace, free from all conflict. Some spiritual practices actually do encourage this and teach ways of accomplishing this through intense concentration and ardor that bring about states of rapture and peace. Some powerful yogic practices can transform the mind. While such practices have their value, an inevitable disappointment occurs when they end, for as soon as practitioners relax in their discipline, they again encounter all the unfinished business of the body and heart that they had hoped to leave behind.

True maturation on the spiritual path requires that we discover the depth of our wounds: our grief from the past, unfulfilled longing, the sorrow that we have stored up during the course of our lives. As Achaan Chah put it, "If you haven't cried deeply a number of times, your meditation hasn't really begun."

This healing is necessary if we are to embody spiritual life lovingly and wisely. Unhealed pain and rage, unhealed traumas from childhood abuse or abandonment become powerful unconscious forces in our lives. Until we are able to bring awareness and understanding to our old wounds, we will find ourselves repeating their patterns of unfulfilled desire, anger and confusion over and over again. While many kinds of healing can come through spiritual life in the form of grace, charismatic revivals, prayer or ritual, two of the most significant kinds develop naturally through a systematic spiritual practice.

The first area of healing comes when we develop a relationship of trust with a teacher. The image of the statues of Jesus and Buddha in the midst of the Vietnam War reminds us that even in great difficulties, healing is possible. It also reminds us that healing cannot come from ourselves alone. The process of inner healing inevitably requires developing a committed relationship with a teacher or guide. Because many of our greatest pains come from past relationships, it is through our experience of a wise and conscious relationship that these pains are healed. This relationship itself becomes the ground for our opening to compassion and freedom of the spirit. Where the pain and disappointment of the past have left us isolated and closed, with a wise teacher we can learn to trust again. When we allow our darkest fears and worst dimensions to be witnessed and compassionately accepted by another, we learn to accept them ourselves.

A healthy relationship with a teacher serves as a model for trust in others, in ourselves, in our bodies, in our intuitions, our own direct experience. It gives us a trust in life itself. Teachings and teacher become a sacred container to support our awakening.

Another kind of healing takes place when we begin to bring the power of awareness and loving attention to each area of our life with the systematic practice of mindfulness.

HEALING THE BODY

Meditation practice often begins with techniques for bringing ourselves to an awareness of our bodies. This is especially important in a culture such as ours, which has neglected physical and instinctual life. James Joyce wrote of one character, "Mr. Duffy lived a short distance from his body." So many of us do. In meditation, we can slow down and sit quietly, truly staying with whatever arises. With awareness, we can cultivate a willingness to open to physical experiences without struggling against them, actually to live in our bodies. As we do so, we feel more clearly its pleasures and its pains. Because our acculturation teaches us to avoid or run from pain, we do not know much about it. To heal the body we must study pain. When we bring close attention to our physical pains, we will notice several kinds. We see that sometimes pain arises as we adjust to an unaccustomed sitting posture. Other times, pains arise as signals that we're sick or have a genuine physical problem. These pains call for a direct response and healing action from us.

However, most often the kinds of pains we encounter in meditative attention are not indications of physical problems. They are the painful, physical manifestations of our emotional, psychological and spiritual holdings and contractions. Wilhelm Reich called these pains our muscular armor, the areas of our body that we have tightened over and over in painful situations as a way to protect ourselves from life's inevitable difficulties. Even a healthy person who sits somewhat comfortably to meditate will probably become aware of pains in his or her body. As we sit still, our shoulders, our backs, our jaws or our necks may hurt. Accumulated knots in the fabric of our body, previously undetected, begin to reveal themselves as we open. As we become conscious of the pain they have held, we may also notice feelings, memories or images connected specifically to each area of tension.

As we gradually include in our awareness all that we have previously shut out and neglected, our body heals. Learning to work with this opening is part of the art of meditation. We can bring an open and respectful attention to the sensations that make up our bodily experience. In this process, we must work to develop a feeling awareness of what is actually going on in the body. We can direct our attention to notice the patterns of our breathing, our posture, the way we hold our back, our chest, our belly, our pelvis. In all these areas we can carefully sense the free movement of energy or the contraction and holding that prevents it.

When you meditate, try to allow whatever arises to move through you as it will. Let your attention be very kind. Layers of tension will gradually release, and energy will begin to move. Places in your body where you have held the patterns of old illness and trauma will open. Then a deeper physical purification and opening of the energy channels will occur as the knots release and dissolve. Sometimes with this opening we will experience a powerful movement of the breath, sometimes a spontaneous vibration and other physical sensations.

Let your attention drop beneath the superficial level that just notices "pleasure," "tension" or "pain." Examine the pain and unpleasant sensations you usually block out. With careful mindfulness, you will allow "pain" to show itself to have many layers. As a first step, we can learn to be aware of pain without creating further tension, to experience and observe pain physically as pressure, tightness, pinpricks, needles, throbbing or burning. Then we can notice all the layers around the "pain." Inside are the strong elements of fire, vibration and pressure. Outside is often a layer of physical tightness and contraction. Beyond this may be an emotional layer of aversion, anger, or fear and a layer of thoughts and attitudes such as, "I hope this will go away soon," or "If I feel pain, I must be doing something wrong," or "Life is always painful." To heal, we must become aware of all these layers.

Bringing systematic attention to our body can change our whole relationship to our physical life. We can notice more clearly the rhythms and needs of our bodies. Without mindful attending to our bodies, we may become so busy in our daily lives that we lose touch with a sense of appropriate diet, movement and physical enjoyment. Meditation can help us find out in what ways we are neglecting the physical aspects of our lives and what our body asks of us.

A mistaken disregard for the body is illustrated in a story of Mullah Nasrudin, the Sufi wise and holy fool. Nasrudin had bought a donkey, but it was costing him a lot to keep it fed, so he hatched a plan. As the weeks went on, he gradually fed the donkey less and less. Finally, he was only feeding it one small cupful of grain throughout the day. The plan seemed to be succeeding, and Nasrudin was saving a lot of money. Then, unfortunately, the donkey died. Nasrudin went to see his friends in the tea shop and told them about his experiment. "It's such a shame. If that donkey had been around a little longer, maybe I could have gotten him used to eating nothing!"

To ignore or abuse the body is mistaken spirituality. When we honor the body with our attention, we begin to reclaim our feelings, our instincts, our life. Out of this developing attention, we can then experience a healing of the senses. The eyes, the tongue, the ears and the sense of touch are rejuvenated. Many people experience this after some period of meditation. Colors are pure, flavors fresh, we can feel our feet on the earth as if we were children again. This cleansing of the senses allows us to experience the joy of being alive and a growing intimacy with life here and now.

HEALING THE HEART

Just as we open and heal the body by sensing its rhythms and touching it with a deep and kind attention, so we can open and heal other dimensions of our being. The heart and the feelings go through a similar process of healing through the offering of our attention to their rhythms, nature and needs. Most often, opening the heart begins by opening to a lifetime's accumulation of unacknowledged sorrow, both our personal sorrows and the universal sorrows of warfare, hunger, old age, illness and death. At times we may experience this sorrow physically, as contractions and barriers around our heart, but more often we feel the depth of our wounds, our abandonment, our pain, as unshed tears.

As we develop a meditative attention, the heart presents itself naturally for healing. The grief we have carried for so long, from pains and dashed expectations and hopes, arises. We grieve for our past traumas and present fears, for all of the feelings we never dared experience consciously. Whatever shame or unworthiness we have within us arises—much of our early childhood and family pain, the mother and father wounds we hold, the isolation, any past abuse (physical or sexual) are all stored in the heart.

Many of us are taught that we shouldn't be affected by grief and loss, but no one is exempt. One of the most experienced hospice directors in the country was surprised when he came to a retreat and grieved for his mother who had died the year before. "This grief," he said, "is different from all the others I work with. It's my mother."

Oscar Wilde wrote, "Hearts are meant to be broken." As we heal through meditation, our hearts break open to feel fully. Powerful feelings, deep unspoken parts of ourselves arise, and our task in meditation is first to let them move through us, then to recognize them and allow them to sing their songs. A poem by Wendell Berry illustrates this beautifully.

> *I go among trees and sit still. All my stirring becomes quiet*
> *around me like circles on water. My tasks lie in their places*
> *Where I left them, asleep like cattle . . .*
> *Then what I am afraid of comes. I live for a while in its sight.*
> *What I fear in it leaves it, And the fear of it leaves me.*
> *It sings, and I hear its song.*

What we find as we listen to the songs of our rage or fear, loneliness or longing is that they do not stay forever. Rage turns into sorrow; sorrow turns into tears; tears may fall for a long time, but then the sun comes out. A memory of old loss sings to us; our body shakes and relives the moment of loss; then the armoring around that loss gradually softens; and in the midst of the song of tremendous grieving, the pain of that loss finally finds release.

In truly listening to our most painful songs, we can learn the divine art of forgiveness. While there is a whole systematic practice of forgiveness that can be cultivated, both forgiveness and compassion arise spontaneously with the opening of the heart. Somehow, in feeling our own pain and sorrow, our own ocean of tears, we come to know that ours is a shared pain and that the mystery and beauty and pain of life cannot be separated. This universal pain, too, is part of our connection with one another, and in the face of it we cannot withhold our love any longer.

We can learn to forgive others, ourselves and life for its physical pain. We can learn to open our heart to all of it, to the pain, to the pleasures we have feared. In this, we discover a remarkable truth. Much of spiritual life is self-acceptance, maybe all of it. Indeed, in accepting the songs of our life, we can begin to create for ourselves a much deeper and greater identity in which our heart holds all within a space of boundless compassion.

Most often this healing work is so difficult we need another person as an ally, a guide to hold our hand and inspire our courage as we go through it. Then miracles happen.

Naomi Remen, a physician who uses art, meditation and other spiritual practices in the healing of cancer patients, told me a moving story that illustrates the process of healing the heart, which accompanies a healing of the body. She described a young man who was twenty-four years old when he came to her after one of his legs had been amputated at the hip in order to save his life from bone cancer. When she began her work with him, he had a great sense of injustice and a hatred for all "healthy" people. It seemed bitterly unfair to him that he had suffered this terrible loss so early in his life. His grief and rage were so great that it took several years of continuous work for him to begin to come out of himself and to heal. He had to heal not simply his body, but also his broken heart and wounded spirit.

He worked hard and deeply, telling his story, painting it, meditating, bringing his entire life into awareness. As he slowly healed, he developed a profound compassion for others in similar situations. He began to visit people in the hospital who had also suffered severe physical losses. On one occasion, he told his physician, he visited a young singer who was so depressed about the loss of her breasts that she would not even look at him. The nurses had the radio playing, probably hoping to cheer her up. It was a hot day, and the young man had come in running shorts. Finally, desperate to get her attention, he unstrapped his artificial leg and began dancing around the room on his one leg, snapping his fingers to the music. She looked at him in amazement, and then she burst out laughing and said, "Man, if you can dance, I can sing."

When this young man first began working with drawing, he made a crayon sketch of his own body in the form of a vase with a deep black crack running through it. He redrew the crack over and over and over, grinding his teeth with rage. Several years later, to encourage him to complete his process, my friend showed him his early pictures again. He saw the vase and said, "Oh, this one isn't finished." When she suggested that he finish it then, he did. He ran his finger along the crack, saying, "You see here, this is where the light comes through." With a yellow crayon, he drew light streaming through the crack into the body of the vase and said, "Our hearts can grow strong at the broken places."

This young man's story profoundly illustrates the way in which sorrow or a wound can heal, allowing us to grow into our fullest, most compassionate identity, our greatness of heart. When we truly come to terms with sorrow, a great and unshakable joy is born in our heart.

DEVELOPING A HEALING ATTENTION

Sit comfortably and quietly. Let your body rest easily. Breathe gently. Let go of your thoughts, past and future, memories and plans. Just be present. Begin to let your own precious body reveal the places that most need healing. Allow the physical pains, tensions, diseases or wounds to show themselves. Bring a careful and kind attention to these painful places. Slowly and carefully feel their physical energy. Notice what is deep inside them, the pulsations, throbbing, tension, needles, heat, contraction, aching that make up what we call pain. Allow these all to be felt fully, to be held in a receptive and kind attention. Then be aware of the surrounding area of your body. If there is contraction and holding, notice this gently. Breathe softly and let it open. Then, in the same way, be aware of any aversion or resistance in your mind. Notice this, too, with a soft attention, without resisting, allowing it to be as it is, allowing it to open in its own time. Now notice the thoughts and fears that accompany the pain you are exploring: "It will never go away." "I can't stand it." "I don't deserve this." "It is too hard, too much trouble, too deep," etc.

Let these thoughts rest in your kind attention for a time. Then gently return to your physical body. Let your awareness be deeper and more allowing now. Again, feel the layers of the place of pain, and allow each layer that opens to move, to intensify or dissolve in its own time. Bring your attention to the pain as if you were gently comforting a child, holding it all in a loving and soothing attention. Breathe softly into it, accepting all that is present with a healing kindness. Continue this meditation until you feel reconnected with whatever part of your body calls you, until you feel at peace.

As your healing attention develops, you can direct it regularly to significant areas of illness or pain in your body. You can then scan your body for additional areas that call for your caring attention. In the same way, you can direct a healing attention to deep emotional wounds you carry. Grief, longing, rage, loneliness and sorrow can all first be felt in your body. With careful and kind attention, you can feel deep inside them. Stay with them. After some time you can breathe softly and open your attention to each of the layers of contraction, emotions and thoughts that are carried with them. Finally, you can let these, too, rest, as if you were gently comforting a child, accepting all that is present, until you feel at peace. You can work with the heart in this way as often as you wish. Remember, the healing of our body and heart is always here. It simply awaits our compassionate attention.•

The Healing Power of Humor

CONNIE GOLDMAN
AND RICHARD MAHLER

Everyone has heard the truism that laughter is the best medicine, but the late Norman Cousins actually lived it. At the relatively early age of fifty, the noted critic and *Saturday Review* editor was stricken with a crippling form of spinal arthritis that bears the difficult name of ankylosing spondylitis. Once hospitalized, Cousins was told there was no known cure for the disease and that it was impossible to predict how long he'd remain bedridden. His physician told him to get his affairs in order, and an attending doctor passed a note to another that said, "I'm afraid we may be losing Norman."

Under the shadow of that grim prognosis, Cousins fell into a deep depression. As he grew more and more depressed, his disease worsened. Doctors told their morose patient that he could use some cheering up. "So I called up my friend Alan Funt, producer of the old *Candid Camera* TV show," Cousins told us in a subsequent interview. "He shipped me copies of several episodes and I also sent out for some old Marx Brothers movies." A film projector was set up in the hospital room and a nurse trained to run it. When they were barely into the first reel, Cousins was laughing so hard that his sides ached and his eyes watered. "I discovered that ten minutes of genuine belly laughs had an anesthetic effect and would give me at least two hours of pain-free sleep," Cousins later wrote in *Anatomy of an Illness*, a best-selling book about his experience.

On the second day, Cousins watched more comedies, along with some vintage Laurel and Hardy clips. He laughed so loudly that patients down the hall complained about all the noise he was making. "But the more I laughed, the better I got," said Cousins.

Within a few weeks, Cousins left the hospital, which seemed to him unnecessarily gloomy and stressful. He checked into a nearby hotel, where he found he could "laugh twice as hard at half the price." When he wasn't viewing his favorite sitcoms, Cousins read about the relationship between laughter and sickness and followed up on a related interest, the connection between stress and certain vitamins. With the consent of his physician, he began supplementing his laughing sessions with massive doses of vitamin C. These self-administered therapies, plus continuing prescribed medical treatments, apparently contributed to Cousins's complete recovery.

At the time of our conversation, four years before his sudden death from a heart attack, the author was leading a full and active life that included frequent lectures to medical students on the subject of positive emotions and healing. "You can't 'ha ha' your way out of a serious illness," advised Cousins, who was seventy-one when we met in his office at the Medical School of the University of California at Los Angeles. "Laughter is no substitute for competent medical attention, and humor should be part of an overall treatment plan. I always emphasize that I never abandoned what my doctors prescribed." Cousins referred to laughter as "internal jogging," a kind of inner aerobics that gets the body's positive juices flowing. He cited scientific evidence suggesting that a deep, hearty laugh can improve lung respiration, oxygenate the blood and promote the body's production of endorphins, natural painkillers that enhance our general sense of well-being.

Today the once-theoretical correlations between mood and health are accepted widely in the medical community, and many of the nation's most respected hospitals employ some variation of Cousins's "humor therapy." Psychiatrist William Fry, who has for more than thirty years studied the physiological effects of laughter, estimates that three minutes of knee-slapping guffaws are equivalent in health benefits to about ten minutes of mechanical rowing. Measurable side effects include a temporary reduction in blood pressure, pulse rate and muscle tension. "More important," said Cousins, "laughter can block the despair, panic and depression that figure in the onset or intensification of disease." Without laughter, he said, we are often cut off from a whole range of life-affirming feelings, including faith, love, determination and creativity. "A lot of us, it seems, are starved for joy."

The man who laughed his way back to robust health contended that "joyousness is as much a biological need as food is." Long after his recovery, Cousins continued to nourish himself with regular doses of funny movies and TV shows, along with plenty of practical jokes and wry stories. "I've never felt more engaged with life than I do now," said Cousins, who, at the time of our visit, was happily writing four books, teaching at UCLA, and playing both tennis and golf regularly. "Without question," he assured us, "I'm in my most productive phase ever."

What Cousins discovered was something each of us knows instinctively: the mind is a mysterious, powerful thing, and we seldom take full advantage of its potential. Just as we can learn to manipulate our thinking in order to see a glass of water as being either half empty or half full, so can we choose to focus on either the *benefits* of aging or its *disadvantages*. Our outlook can be dominated either by a fear of future unknowns and upsets or by excitement about undiscovered challenges and opportunities.

This insight brings to mind an anecdote about the late *Power of Positive Thinking* author Norman Vincent Peale, who remained on the lecture circuit into his mid-nineties. Peale had just finished delivering a motivational speech at a convention of the National Speakers Association. As the sharp-witted senior descended from the podium, a phalanx of dark-suited ushers rushed forward, intending to guide him gently back to his seat. "My gosh," Peale called out as they approached, "you all look like pallbearers coming to get me!" The crowded ballroom rocked with laughter. With that quick, casual remark, Peale displayed a vital ingredient of late-life humor: he showed that he refused to take his advanced age seriously, thus revealing a balanced perspective on a world in which our mortality is assured.

"The best laugh is always on yourself," reminds Dr. Clifford Kuhn, a practicing psychiatrist and researcher at the University of Louisville School of Medicine, who conducts humor-sensitivity sessions for patients with chronic diseases. "And for something to be truly funny," he adds, "it must have a grain of truth in it." Peale's spontaneous quip acknowledged the audience's unspoken awareness of reality; for at age ninety-two, he was closer to the end of his life than most of us. He died about three years later, still an active motivational speaker at age ninety-five.

Once comedian George Burns, making public appearances well into his nineties, was asked if a man his age could find happiness with a thirty-year-old woman. "No, not often," Burns dead-panned, clenching a cigar between his teeth. "Only once or twice a night."

Celebrities who are around for as long as George Burns and Norman Vincent Peale know the importance of peppering their remarks with clever and even risqué observations. Their one-liners can relax members of an audience who may not think growing older is particularly amusing. Such humor generates empathy—the feeling that "we're all in this together." Yet it isn't always easy for us to laugh at the truths of our later years. The painful reality is that by the time we're sixty, seventy or older, our lives sometimes start to feel like an unending succession of losses through illness, death, impairment of physical abilities and so on. How is it possible to remain lighthearted in the face of mortality? When is it helpful and appropriate to laugh at our own misfortune?

To a great extent, we already know the answers to these questions. We've proven that merely by surviving the trials and tribulations of daily life with our sanity more or less intact. As comic actress Carol Burnett has observed, "Humor is tragedy plus time." Some might argue that if you're over sixty and can still wake up with a smile, you already know the healing power of laughter.

"[Humor] is simply in the way we look at the world," suggests Robert Fulton, a sixty-five-year-old sociologist who founded the University of Minnesota's Center for the Study of Death, Dying, and Bereavement. "It's a matter of laughing *with* yourself, not *at* yourself." Fulton can't recall a time when he wasn't able to see at least some irony in every situation, no matter how unsettling. He tells the poignant story of the way his much-younger wife, after a long battle with cancer, died quietly at home in their bed as he sat clutching her hand. When she'd breathed her last, Fulton placed a bandanna over the top of his wife's head, which had gone completely bald during chemotherapy treatments. Sobbing and trembling with grief, he reached out his palm to close her lifeless eyes, still open and staring into space. "As I drew my hand away, one of her eyelids suddenly popped back open," Fulton remembered. "No peeking!" he exclaimed, before he could stop himself. Then, stunned that he had responded in a manner that seemed so inappropriate, Fulton quickly pulled his dead wife's eyelid shut again.

Reflecting later on this bizarre, spontaneous remark, Fulton realized that even though he was completely overcome with sadness, part of him had been able to find some levity in the situation. "I knew my wife would have understood my reaction," he added. "She had a way of always keeping things in their proper perspective."

Fulton believes this ability to laugh at ourselves and our dilemmas is essential if we are to endure successfully the slings and arrows of modern life. "You find your humanity this way," he said. "You acknowledge the world's seeming randomness, unpredictability and downright absurdity."

Unlike Fulton, many of us take a fair amount of time before we can laugh at a particularly painful experience. We need to be gentle and consoling with ourselves after a loss. In time, however, laughter often proves to be a balm that soothes our wounds.

This is a truth that our friend Eve Blake came to understand more fully after her seventieth birthday. A writer with a long list of literary credits, she's written scores of TV scripts (including many episodes of *The Lone Ranger* series) and had articles published in *Collier's* and *The New Yorker*. Yet the source of her greatest satisfaction is a short book full of homespun humor and heartfelt advice that she wrote and self-published a few years ago.

"I did show-biz work for many years and got utterly sick of it," Eve recalled, as we relaxed on the deck of her home in the Hollywood hills, overlooking the blinking lights of Los Angeles. "I said to myself, 'I'd like to do something worthwhile before I shuffle off this mortal coil.' It took me another eighteen months to figure out that what I wanted to do to make my mark was creative writing and public speaking."

A long-time Democratic Party activist who has kept abreast of local politics for many years, Eve first considered the suggestion that she run for public office. She speaks in the sort of deep, animated voice that commands instant attention. Although flattered by the positive feedback that greeted her tentative campaign feelers, Eve decided she'd be much happier putting together a collection of her own thoughts about aging, which she believes her peers approach much too pessimistically. "The title of my book, *Old Age Is Contagious but You Don't Have to Catch It*, simply came to me one day," Eve explained. "Everybody treats 'old age' as if it were an infectious disease, but that doesn't mean you automatically have to come down with it."

Eve takes a joking approach to her subject. She warns older people against becoming "a misery to themselves and a damned nuisance to others," but her underlying message is very serious. "You have a choice in almost any situation you'll ever find yourself," said Eve, "and old age is no exception. You can be depressed and upset or optimistic and hopeful. It's all up to you. That's why keeping a sense of humor is so important as you get older, because most people seem to find more to feel gloomy about. It's as if the calendar gives them an excuse to feel sorry for themselves."

Our friend wrote *Old Age Is Contagious* after her infirm mother asked Eve to help her find a suitable nursing home, anticipating that she'd soon be unable to take care of herself. "Mom and I looked at various places," Eve recalled. "I was very much surprised by what we found." Appalled by the lethargy and boredom she observed in many institutions, Eve saw no justification for allowing older people to settle for less than they were capable and worthy of. "It's not that I disapprove of nursing homes," Eve stressed. "I must tell you that Mother and I found one that we were both very happy with. What bothers me is the idea that people in these situations are so often conditioned to accept a dull, listless existence as all they deserve."

Eve wanted to demonstrate that growing older doesn't have to be dull and dreary. She collected an assortment of humorous thoughts, quotations and anecdotes about aging, then wove them into an inspirational speech. It wasn't long before she was invited to deliver her upbeat message to retirement centers, bridge clubs and community groups. After each presentation, Eve was surrounded by admirers who asked if she'd written anything else on the subject. "Although I was tired of writing, I decided I'd better put something on paper, if for no other reason than to be able to respond to these constant requests."

The practical wisdom in Eve's book is drawn from a life that, like almost everyone's, has seen its share of tragedy. When Eve was fifty-two, her husband died suddenly of a heart ailment. Eve's own health began to falter a few years ago when a bad back threatened to confine her to bed. Chronic insomnia sometimes keeps her awake all night, but she doesn't let it get her down. "What little disability I have is not worth talking about," she insists. "Griping about 'poor me' is not calculated to win hearts. When I encounter self-pity face to face, it provokes in me a desperate desire for a quick getaway."

Eve's conclusion is that we must apply the same skills to "learning humor" that we've used throughout life to master anything new. "A sense of humor is like anything else: you have to work on it if you don't come by it naturally," she explained. "You have to think about it, develop it and keep it honed by constant use. You do this by making light of your drawbacks or trying to see the funny aspect of something. Unfortunately, once they're past fifty, most people don't think about changing. They stick to the same old routines and think the same old ways. It takes a lot of work to take a different approach, but it really pays off."

Eve fosters flexibility in her own life by traveling the world as an inspirational speaker. This gives her the chance to meet interesting people and experience new ways of living in places like South Africa and New Zealand. The speaking engagements she sets up are deliberately scheduled in countries Eve is intrigued by so that they can also be part of a memorable vacation.

"If there's one word of advice that I could offer in connection with retirement," Eve summed up, "that word would be 'don't.' In nine out of ten instances, you don't really have to retire in the stereotypic sense. If you leave one thing, move on to something else, whether or not you're getting paid for it. To be forever interested in the possibilities of one's future is a major youthful trait. In fact, it's basic to the life process."•

Find True Healing

AN INTERVIEW WITH
JEAN SHINODA BOLEN, M. D.

In order for us to truly live, we have to heal our body and mind so that we unfold our whole potential as loving human beings. Jean Shinoda Bolen is a gifted healer of the psyche. The metaphors and love in her books provide a healing context for readers. When we decided to explore healing in this issue, we knew that Dr. Bolen could contribute a depth of understanding about healing in general and about healing of the psyche in particular.

PERSONAL TRANSFORMATION: *Let's begin by discussing the nature of healing.*

JEAN SHINODA BOLEN: What comes to mind are the similarities between healing a broken bone and healing a broken heart. In healing a broken heart, the need is to recover and love again, and the need of a broken bone is for it to become strong enough to support you again. Healing is about the capacity to function again. Something had to happen to get in the way of a natural functioning, whether it is the ability to walk or an ability to love. We come into the world with these capacities. When something goes wrong, people go to physicians or healers of all kinds. I don't consider myself as healing anyone, any more than I consider the orthopedic surgeon as healing a broken bone. Nature or God or something beyond the physician is the healer. The healer helps clear the way for what is natural to occur. The things in the way are the problems that people come with. One of the tasks in psychological healing is to remove the contaminants. You can't heal any part of the body when there is an infected foreign object in it, such as a splinter. Psychologically, the contamination is often an attitude that has been imposed on the psyche of the person, either a condemnation, a belittlement, an action that implied that this person is worthless.

PT: *So healing is a restoration of functioning, and the process includes removing some type of contamination.*

JSB: Yes, some contamination or some kind of limitation. Many people who come to see me had a natural growth impeded. Each person has their own seed of what they are supposed to develop into. The strength or the shape of that quality will be distorted, as a plant is affected if it does not receive sunshine, water and good soil. In a healing relationship, the person who provides the environment doesn't fix the person, but provides the equivalent of a green thumb. We attend to the person just as we attend to a plant. We give it energy and love. We notice whether there is enough food and water. It is natural for a healthy person, psyche, plant or bone to grow if the conditions allow it to happen.

PT: *In healing the physical body, many times we do nothing and the natural healing process occurs. While sometimes we need a bone set or something to be surgically removed, often our body heals itself. Is that also true in psychological healing?*

JSB: Time has a positive effect on most broken hearts. Time heals loss and pain. Though time and nature may heal the wound in the body and the wound in the psyche, sometimes body and psyche grow a layer over a festering wound that becomes toxic to the person. Childhood abuse or grief that is never expressed, or secrets that made you feel like you didn't deserve to be part of the human race, contain elements that are like a covering over a big infected boil. The body makes an effort to ward it off, yet the infection saps the person until it is opened and drained. A lot of emotional dysfunction needs to have the equivalent of opening the wound and letting it drain so that the person remembers the pain and experiences the feelings of grief and betrayal and shame. The wound is cleansed by the accepting presence of that other person who doesn't recoil.

PT: *How important is desire to heal to the healing process?*

JSB: It varies a lot. In physical illness the body's physiology has the capacity to respond in a positive way, to heal itself. The working of a healthy immune system is a natural response of the body to heal itself. If the person's body and psyche have been depleted over time, if the psyche is depressed and the person feels hopeless or wants to die, the body's response is affected. There is a psyche-soma connection.

PT: *Doesn't it take a certain amount of willingness to engage these processes, to seek out support and to undergo potentially uncomfortable experiences that can be aspects of the healing journey?*

JSB: A more old-fashioned term would be the will to live or the desire to survive. When people are lost in the wilderness or are going through a physical or psychological process, a positive commitment to stay the course does matter. Courage and conviction and desire have something to do with the hope that you can affect your personal fate. Sometimes, that is the missing quality that needs to be sparked before the rest can happen.

PT: *That quality can be provided through the presence of someone else. The physician or healer can hold that courage and faith when the person isn't able to.*

JSB: That is a major quality determining the effectiveness of a physician or psychotherapist. Of course, at certain places in the journey, the patient is going to get discouraged. The hope that something can be effective has a major effect on the psyche and in turn on the body. Andrew Weil described the power of doctors to encourage people or to hex them. What the person in authority says about the likelihood of your recovery makes an enormous difference to most people. Bernie Siegel speaks about exceptional patients, the ones who say, "I am not going to let authority tell me what my fate is going to be; I have something to do with my own fate." Exceptional patients have a survival quality that people have who make it through difficult situations.

PT: *They have the capacity to stay connected with courage and faith.*

JSB: It also makes a tremendous difference whether or not you are supported on that journey. People who run marathons talk about running into the wall, that place where it seems too painful to keep on going, and yet you only have a couple more miles to go. Knowledge about the wall helps, being aware that this is a natural part of the journey. During labor, women know that the most painful part is just before the baby comes out. Fortunately for most women, the process is beyond willpower. The baby is going to come out. The marathon racer facing more pain can give up and say "I quit." There isn't an instinct that is going to deliver the runner to the end of the line. That is true of the physical and psychological healing journey most of the time. The body can pull the person through, in spite of the person, sometimes. But most of the time, giving up and feeling hopeless affects what the body will do. People who believe in them and love them, who say whatever helps that person keep on keeping on, for as long as it takes to make it to this particular destination, make a large difference.

PT: *Does fear accompany chronic or potentially fatal conditions and does addressing fear turn the tide in healing?*

JSB: It varies a great deal. Some people don't feel much fear under circumstances where most others would. There is a psychological type who deals with what is in the present and doesn't have the intuition, imagination or worrywart element that anticipates the worst. The more you get out of the present moment and into the dire-what-can-happen-next, the more you are not present to deal with what is right now. Feeling overwhelmed by fear of what is coming is a real problem across the board. A person who has stage fright may avoid giving the performance that would allow them to really express some major gift, for example.

PT: *In your book* Close to the Bone, *you talked about the impact of potentially terminal illnesses. It seemed that people who came through those illnesses faced the fears of death and loss such that fear no longer had the power it can have over those of us who haven't faced a potentially terminal illness. Does something happen in that process that changes people's relationship with fear, rendering it less powerful?*

JSB: There is a considerable range of responses to approaching death. A great number of people who approach death do come to some sense of peace about it being a transition. Sometimes, people live a lot longer than expected because they are not ready to cross over yet. Will keeps them on this side until something shifts. Often, something is going on with people who take a long time, when doctors expect they wouldn't be around long. Great spiritual and psychological work is done in the last phase of the body being alive.

PT: *In that sense, death is a time of healing.*

JSB: The period before dying can be an enormous time of healing for people who felt they were not loved as infants and children, *if* they die with people around who love them. If they grew up with a sense people liked them only if they were productive or attractive, to find at the end of life when they aren't productive or attractive and are helpless that they are loved heals something that goes back to the beginning of their lives. Also, people who realize they are going to die soon make amends, forgive others and try to heal relationships that have been estranged.

Jane Wheelwright, a Jungian analyst, wrote a book, *Death of a Woman*, about twenty years ago. She describes an analysis that took place over the last year or so of a woman's life. The dying woman was relatively young. The question is why anyone would want to do an analysis if they know they are dying. Jane went to her house for sessions after the woman was no longer able to come to Jane's office. It was clear that she was working on deep psychological issues and that her psyche was engaged in resolving things until the end. I believe that we

are spiritual beings on a human path and that we come into life as a stage where
things can be encountered. There is a relevancy to doing this kind of work up
until the very end.

PT: *You mentioned that forgiveness is an aspect of deep psychological or
spiritual healing. Talk about forgiveness as an aspect of healing.*

JSB: Forgiveness and compassion are essential elements in psychological
healing, although the profession of psychiatry and psychology rarely uses these
words. When you go into the painful places, in childhood and adulthood,
where you were disappointed or betrayed or incested, and express it to someone who receives it compassionately, you begin to be compassionate with yourself. Most people who have been treated badly have an attitude toward
themselves which is not compassionate. It is as if a part of the person holds
onto the misguided notion that if she were treated badly, she must have
deserved it, or something irrational like that. When you tell your story and it
is received with compassion and understanding for you the sufferer, you start
to shift your own attitude toward yourself as you realize you didn't deserve
this, but it happened. In talking, you begin to understand who these people
were, what was happening and what their limitations were. That awareness
leads to compassion and forgiveness.

You need to let go of the wounds of your childhood in order to grow into
your own life. People who dwell on their less-than-happy childhoods are stuck
there. An old energy has a hold on them. They define themselves in terms of
what happened in the past, and they haven't grown in some crucial way. A
mature person doesn't deny the rough spots and the bad things that happened,
and in fact, because of it usually has compassion for other people. But a mature
person doesn't feel entitled because of their suffering. They go on. Things happen, they get slighted, somebody does something intrusive or whatever, but it
isn't amplified by the past. It is just what it is. They deal with it and go on.

PT: *Fear causes us to miss the present because of the influence of an imaginary future. Here is influence from another direction, from the past which is
contaminating to living in the present. Can we facilitate healing so that we
feel whole and live in the present? Can we communicate with or be guided by
this healing process?*

JSB: Because I am a Jungian analyst I think in terms of the archetypal.
Archetypes are a way of saying that there are elements inherent in us that we
come with. One of the things I like about the Jungian psychological framework

is that there is an assumption that we each have a center of meaning or an archetypal Self and that we are inherently a species for whom meaning matters. Meaning has to do with why we are here. There is a spiritual or divine element in us and in the universe. Archetypes don't just *exist* in us. They are *shared* with all human beings. Healing involves being in relationship with this archetypal Self, which provides us with a sense of interconnectedness and wholeness. It is in us all. It varies, but most people have an inherent sense that I am here for a reason, my life has some purpose, and I need to discover what it is. That is the individuation journey. One way to define psychological impairment is that depression or anxiety is getting in the way of a person's sense of having a purpose and of being on course.

PT: *How do you define a true healer?*

JSB: My comments are restricted to what I know, which is about health professionals who are also healers. I think of such people as needing to be skilled and proficient at what they do professionally, and beyond that, have a love for their patients, an attitude of service and a personal sense of the sacred. Such people are not arrogant. A healer is someone who can help the patient receive the invisible but real energies of healing. There is trust, an infusion of love, an absence of fear.

PT: *How do we find a true healer when we need one?*

JSB: Begin with seeking referrals to someone who is very competent as a physician or therapist, and then ask what he or she is like personally. Go to someone who will treat you as a person who matters. Remember that you are a choice-maker. Trust your intuition. Do the equivalent of shopping around until you feel that you are with someone who is excellent, both as a person and as a professional. If you intend some combination of regular (or allopathic) medicine and complementary (or alternative) regimes, you need a physician who will treat your intentions or experience with respect. Since I believe that healing has to do with love, a healing physician or professional is someone who loves the work and the patients, who cares what happens to them, and who also knows that there is a healer in the patient and a healing energy in the universe.

PT: *If someone enters the healing process in an acute condition, they might not be conscious and, at least for a while, they are unable to be an advocate for themselves.*

JSB: If I or a member of my family were unconscious, seriously injured, had a raging temperature, or massive burns—anything of this nature that is acute and needs immediate attention, the best place to be is at the nearest and best general hospital or medical center around. This is what allopathic medicine does best. And mobilize a prayer group as soon as you can.

PT: *What are you currently exploring about healing at this point?*

JSB: I'm working on *Goddesses in Older Women: The Third Phase of Our Lives.* In a way, it's "Goddesses in Every Woman: The Sequel" or "Goddesses in Every Woman—Growing Older and Wiser." I'm describing the archetypes in older women based on goddesses of wisdom, of transitions, of wrath and of laughter and sexuality.

PT: *Because of where the culture is in relationship to women and aging, I am happy to see that you are writing a book on growing older. There are not many positive role models or cultural perspectives to prepare baby-boomers to go through that phase.*

JSB: About forty million baby-boomer generation women will turn fifty or become menopausal coinciding with a new millennium. There has never been such a potential force for change as this number of women whose lives were influenced by the women's movement. This is the most empowered and educated significant-sized group of women in history. What the planet and humanity needs is an infusion of the wisdom women have. Maybe it is now or never for us as a species in an ecological system that is Earth. Maybe if individual women in sufficient numbers draw upon personal and collective wisdom and strength, and act to make things better, healing on a community and planetary scale will come about. Because I know that individuals can grow and be transformed, I believe that transformation is possible on this larger scale. In writing *Goddesses in Older Women*, I will be encouraging older women to become activists, to take stands where they are, to draw upon what they know in their bones, believing that the world changes one person at a time.•

Healing Through Forgiveness

MARY NURRIESTEARNS

Forgiveness is love's way of healing us. Forgiveness is an intimate relation-ship with mercy that soothes pain, dissolves anger and releases attitudes that don't serve our own life potential or humanity. Forgiveness is a journey that develops and requires the kind of courage that changes our lives in won-derful ways. This courage compels us increasingly to seek truth and compas-sion. Along the way, love's presence sustains us when our effort is great. As we deepen in our forgiveness practice, we come to know how we are to express ourselves in the world.

With forgiveness promising so much, why do we often hesitate to actively engage it? Even when we desire to face long-held feelings and let go of painful wounds, we shy away from the depths of what forgiveness would have us expe-rience. We may be reluctant to join hands with forgiveness because we lack the know-how, the tools of forgiveness. Or at some level, we may misunderstand forgiveness and decide it is not appropriate for us or that we are not ready.

Myths about forgiveness, such as forgive and forget, misinform us. Forgive-ness is not amnesia. We forgive and remember. Remembering helps us to break harmful cycles and reduces the likelihood that we will be hurt, or hurt others, in the same old ways. Forgiveness does not dull pain. It is not an escape route from intense emotions trapped within—or from the work required to under-stand and release those feelings. Forgiveness does not condone; we forgive the doer, not the doing. Forgiveness is letting go of intense emotions with the full knowledge that the behavior was cruel and that all parties involved were hurt by it. Treating pain with kindness produces insight and we come to realize the ignorance and history that fueled the event. We can then examine our rela-tionships through the eyes of mercy. Understanding human frailty, we are also more able to forgive ourselves.

Healing happens over time. We heal at one level, then another. We make the decision to forgive, again and again. Saying words of forgiveness is the first step. Reciting the words creates an opening and willingness, and moves us into a body, heart, mind, spirit process of remembering and releasing. According to Rumer Godden, in *A House With Four Rooms*, "There is an Indian proverb or axiom that says that everyone is a house with four rooms, a physical, a mental, an emotional and a spiritual. Most of us tend to live in one room most of the time, but unless we go into every room every day, even if only to keep it aired, we are not a complete person." Our bodies hold the imprints of unforgiven hurt and anger, and we must forgive with our entire being. Forgiveness literally becomes a healing way of life that enhances well-being, a lifestyle that keeps our inner rooms healthy.

How then do we forgive? There is no religiously correct or universally agreed-upon approach to forgiveness. Yet, there are tools that support and even accelerate the process. We begin by letting go of our unforgiving stance. We acknowledge the events and feelings that really happened. We admit that the past cannot be changed. However, through healing, we can leave those yesterdays in the past and create a better tomorrow. Realizing that forgiveness is our own personal journey, we release expectations that others will respond to our work, even though each person's healing has positive rippling effects. While journaling, drawing, dancing, breathing and talking, we face whatever our body, heart, spirit and mind present next for our healing. Through these processes, we begin relating differently to our suffering. We don't hold back. We gently swathe our pain with love. We allow thoughts and feelings to rise into awareness where they are recognized and permitted to pass on through. Setting aside sacred time daily, we pray and meditate on forgiveness, and we commune with the divine. And we trust—knowing that grace and a great wisdom are embracing our efforts.

The forgiveness meditation below, when practiced regularly, can take you deep into the heart of forgiveness.

FORGIVENESS MEDITATION
BY STEPHEN AND ONDREA LEVINE

Begin by centering the mind, as in meditation. Become quiet, soften the belly.

Slowly bring into your mind, into your heart, the image of someone for whom you have resentment. Gently allow a picture, a feeling, a sense of that person to gather there. Invite them into your heart for just this moment, noticing any fear or anger or sensation that arises. Soften around whatever arises.

Silently say in your heart, "I forgive you. I forgive you for whatever pain you may have caused me in the past, intentionally or unintentionally, through your words, your thoughts, your actions. However you may have caused me pain in the past, I forgive you."

Open to the possibility of forgiveness so that resentment may pass, so that your heart may be free and your life lighter. "I forgive you." It is so painful to hold someone out of your heart. "I forgive you."

Allow that being to go on their way touched by the blessing, the possibility of your forgiveness.

Now gently allow into your mind, your heart, the image of someone who holds resentment for you. Invite them into your heart and say, "I ask your forgiveness. I ask to be let back into your heart. Forgive me for whatever I may have done in the past that caused you pain, intentionally or unintentionally, through my words, my actions, even through my thoughts. However I may have hurt or injured you, whatever confusion, whatever fear of mine caused you pain, I ask your forgiveness."

Allow yourself to be touched by forgiveness, to be forgiven, to be allowed back into their heart. Allow forgiveness to fill your heart. Allow yourself to be forgiven. If your mind jumps forward with recriminations and judgments against you, just notice how merciless we are to ourselves. Let your heart meet this other heart in forgiveness.

Allow that being to go on their way touched by the blessing of forgiveness.

Now gently allow yourself into your mind, into your heart. It is so painful to hold yourself out of your heart. Say "I forgive you" to yourself. Using your own first name, say "I forgive you" to yourself.

Whatever hard thoughts arise against yourself from your mind, hold them with softness. Let softness touch your judgments with forgiveness. Allow yourself into your heart, into forgiveness. Let forgiveness fill your body with warmth and care. Bathe yourself in its mercy and kindness. Let yourself be loved. Return yourself to your heart.•

Healing and Moving On

JACQUELYN SMALL

The soul once turned toward matter, fell in love with it, and burning with desire to experience earthly pleasures, could no longer hold herself away from it. And so the world was born.

—From an ancient Russian text

We are both an ego and a soul, a species whose nature, according to Teilhard de Chardin, is made of "spirit-matter." Psyche is the mirrored reflection of our soul, and functions as the mediator between the spiritual and earthly dimensions, which we must somehow learn to blend. Our psyches are the battlefield where all our dualities play out. When our higher and lower selves are in misalignment, we suffer, for this is a violation of our nature. All human disease is the soul's inability to express through us.

Psyche is our perceiver. In order to be healthy, our bodies must have a healthy psyche to wrap themselves around. We must have a strong intention to live, and to know that our lives matter—to sense that there is a purpose and a plan for our incarnation here. Otherwise, no matter how much we exercise, how well we sleep or eat the proper foods, our physical health will run amuck. With no reason to live, we'll eventually break down. All disease is the soul's inability to express through us. So we must all learn to release anything that's in the way of living a soulful life.

Several authors today are telling us it's time now to "get over it." And it is indeed time that we all stop focusing on our wounded parts and get on with creating our whole self. It's time to turn away from the past and start creating our longed-for future. But "getting over it" is not an intellectual declaration! It's a process that truly must be honored, with compassion, right timing, patience and understanding. We didn't get wounded all at once, and our healing doesn't happen just like that. We must commit to the necessary inner work of making conscious all that we've repressed, so that we can truly focus on what we intend to be as more of our ideal. No one can do this work for us. We are self-creative organisms!

Your soul and its counterpart, your ego, have had a long history here, and have taken on many wounds. If we try to jump past any unfinished business in our biographies without bringing the issue out of denial and healing it, our bodies will tell the tale. We can sicken, and even die. We call it stress. The wear and tear of our unprocessed distant or immediate past cause us to suffer an emergency that was intended to be a spiritual emergence, a lesson we were to learn about being a loving human. We transform our lives through making our ways of being completely conscious.

Your psyche seeks completion, not perfection. We are to know and claim it all, both the dark and the light—for this is how we are made. It's in this willingness to live authentically within the tension of all the contrary opposites that plague us that we ultimately find that "something" that brings us fulfillment. We've given it many names: We find our balancing point, our center, the archetypal self, the jewel in the lotus. We complete our grand design. We come whole, or home. Whatever we call it, this is the purpose of our incarnation—to remember that we are divine.

So, in this crazy world of stacks of e-mail and overloaded appointment books, where do we go to find ourselves? How do we proceed for the advancement of our soul? Is there a map, or are there certain stepping stones along the path? There are.

In our work at our company Eupsychia, we've been guiding people directly through processes of personal transformation for over twenty years now, hundreds of people just like you. And we've found some "seeds of wisdom" along our way. For home is simply the remembrance of our divine heritage, the full awareness of who we really are. Psyche dove into matter, remember? She decided to take on this life, to experience it all. In the doing, she forgot that she was divine. Then, she had several impossible tasks to complete in order to return to Mt. Olympus from whence she came. She had to remember, while in human form, that she was divine. And this, too, is our story. This remembrance is our true healing.

To get back home again, the following may serve to comfort you, and help to remind you that you're not alone.

Step One. We realize we are dying to our old ways. The first step we take upon this path is one of complete upheaval. Your old life begins to fall away. And it seems to "just happen" while you were looking the other way. This process will usually start with some event that shatters some strong belief you hold. A spark must be bright enough to blast open the doors of our psyche, so she can release her divine/human treasures from the collective unconscious mind. Either an outer crisis, like your house burning down, a cherished relationship ending, or a critical medical diagnosis may come along. Or it can be an inner crisis, such as a complete loss of faith in life or in one's self, a serious depression or loss of life force. Nothing turns you on anymore. Life is no longer interesting. And you lose hope. This can be the beginning of your journey. The mystics call it the "dark night of the soul."

At this stage, we're required to remember: the self is greater than its conditions! Then we can pass through this stage more gracefully, being "in the world but not of it." Faith is the quality our soul brings us at this stage, if we make it through. Then, we must practice being a faithful servant to this process itself, and allow it to fully take hold. We consciously surrender to a power greater than ourselves, and voluntarily enter "the mystery."

Step Two. An uncomfortable confusion sets in, and you know you're no longer in charge; something's now in charge of you. So for a while, you'll go this way and that, trying first one thing, then another, hoping to regain control. At this stage, you at least become active, but not to much avail. Your energy is too scattered. Back and forth you go between opposing forces inside you. You may crave a geographical move, feel that you're in love with two people at once and having to make a hard decision, or you might desperately yearn to have a different profession, anything to get away from your unhappiness or ambivalence. Whatever the opposition, you feel stuck. But you simply must wait. Now, the keynote that will aid us is: it's not *out* but *through* that we heal.

Patience is the quality our soul is bringing forth. We are now to learn about cycles and rhythms, the natural seasons of change. Like the farmer who kept pulling up his new crops to see if they were growing, we are tested to the extent we need the lesson about how to stay faithful to our process and remain open to whatever's happening. We watch; we study; we journal and document our experiences. We are willing to know ourselves. We commit to not act until destiny truly moves us onward. And this, too, will seem to happen while we're looking the other way.

Step Three. We see how our shadow, the dark side of our personality, defeats us until we own it. The human shadow is our "holy grit" that keeps forcing us to move toward the realization of our ideal. We all detest our dark side. And we're even more resistant to owning it! We'd much rather project it out onto others and call them the problem. We've gone into denial about the parts of ourselves we're ashamed of, so we can do just that. But the shadow will act out and cause us a great humiliation until we finally face it. This means we are willing to see our faults and make the shadow conscious so it can heal. Anything still unconscious in us has the power to ruin us. We keep an ongoing dialogue in place with this unlived, unloved part of ourselves until it's fully known. Then, it loses its power. We can watch our emotional reactivities as clues to where we're still "charged" with some unprocessed stuff from our past. And we'll see the story we tell ourselves that's holding all this in place. Because we've repressed it, it's never had a chance to be conscious. So it's had to act out when our guard was down, to get our attention. The shadow is your unconsciousness—your anger, your fears, your pettiness, your unhealed or undeveloped aspect. It's not evil; it's just uncivilized.

If we'll do our shadow work, we'll start to become more transparent—so the winds of change can blow through us more readily. Knowing this is the dawning of our awakening. The keynote here is this: the shadow has a sacred function. Owning our shadows gives us compassion for others when their dark sides are acting out. In shadow work, we learn the quality of spiritual discrimination. This is the ability to separate the essentials and nonessentials in our lives and the willingness to heal or walk away from what's blocking our advancement.

Step Four. We begin to forgive ourselves, and others. We see how it's all been for our good—no matter how great the cost at times. We see our mistakes in the light of understanding, and this changes our past—how we view ourselves and others who have harmed us. We'll see that all our mistakes were for a sacred purpose of refining our personalities for the work of spirit. How else can we learn about human life and love? We now feel a part of a greater plan, and are beginning to see our purpose here, though we still have many unanswered questions. We've discovered by now that there are no outside "experts" on us; we see that the self is our only true teacher, that all is learned from within. The keynote to remember now is this: the open heart is the bridge to a higher consciousness.

We develop the quality of compassion. Our old judgments begin to fall away, and we become more broad-minded. After all, who can we blame when we once see that it's all a part of the plan?

Step Five. Our higher and lower minds come into rapport. Now we walk through life simultaneously gathering knowledge from our experiences while the wisdom of our inner and greater self brings us more enlightenment. We are growing in spiritual stature. Insights and revelations we've had begin to integrate into our daily lives. During this stage we become fascinated with the study of the self, of the universe and of the divine from whence we've come. We will seek out a spiritual practice or way of life that fits and feeds our deepest yearnings. Questions about our true life's purpose or life's work begin to preoccupy us. We want to find "our group."

Our creative imagination awakens, and we see that we can cocreate our future by imaging our own ideals. We take responsibility for being cocreators. The creative imagination is our higher cognition that fills in the gap between who we are today with who we long to become. This is how all manifestations come to be. We can never have what we cannot imagine.

Here, we learn the power of creative intelligence. And your keynote will be the recognition that "whatever you say 'I am' to has a way of claiming you." As conscious cocreators, we are learning to "think like gods." Having the courage of our convictions and the willingness to own the responsibility for what we create becomes our new ideal.

Step Six. Our aspiration to serve awakens. And we learn to follow our bliss. No longer so preoccupied with "what's in it for me?" we actually feel how connected we are to the whole. We are becoming soul-dominated human beings. And our true service to humanity is really quite simple: it's our willingness to be our authentic selves and to bring forward our true talents and passion to serve this greater whole. In this manner, both our egos and our souls are gratified all at once.

Integrated egos are an essential aspect of our transformational process. A healthy ego learns to sacrifice itself to a greater good. The ego feels high when being a faithful servant to something bigger than itself. It's the grandest "ego trip" of all! At this stage we experience the marriage of the ego and the soul. Without our personal egos we cannot function on this planet. Egos are masters of the material world. The soul would have no way to embody here on earth— no one to take care of it—without this healthy partner.

The soul quality we access here is the courage to be free. And the keynote that holds this step in place is this: service is doing our being. Most of the stress leaves our lives completely when we become free of so much egoistic need so our souls can shine through. All human disease is the soul's inability to express!

Step Seven. Our biographies become a small piece of our greater story. Now we've faced our shadow, forgiven ourselves and others, and stepped out of our limited past as being our only identity. We see that we've grown into a larger skin, now containing all the "goods" from our past, but no longer limited by believing we are our conditions. The self we've now become is no longer fixated on the same old needs. We are now a different and greater identity who walks upon a higher plane.

The quality we develop at this final stage of our human transformation is that of nonattachment. And the keynote here is "Our spiritual intention guides us home." We see that we are the journey itself, with nothing to prove, no place to go, only someone to be. We can relax now, and even know moments of enlightenment—which can only come when we are no longer attached to being enlightened. Psyche's task is to remember that she is divine. She is the feminine principle who lives within each one of us, whether man or woman in gender. It's time we all remember that it takes a healthy psyche to create a true and viable spiritual life. For psyche is our divine and earthly perceiver, who can "look both ways." She is the bridge between spirit and matter, our consciousness who makes us whole.•

Death of My Son

CAROLE SCHRAMM

My beloved Stephen died quietly and peacefully in my arms on August 27, 1993, exactly three months after his twenty-seventh birthday. Moments before, I told him how happy I was that he would soon see our Honey (our family's favorite aunt, who, at age eighty-seven, had passed away months before). We all knew that Stephen was the favorite person in Honey's world, and now she would be there to welcome him into a new one. I saw a faint smile, a long sigh, and then my Stephen let go of his last painful breath and lay quiescent at last.

At that moment, I felt a sadness deeper than tears. Yet with a heart full of gratitude and love, I let go of his hand and turned him over to God's care and keeping—and sent Stephen on to the light. I thanked God for this gift of Stephen's presence in my life and for the blessings he brought to our family. Whatever God's purpose for Stephen's life had been, he had fulfilled it perfectly and completely, and it was time for him to move on away from us.

The grieving cycle for me had begun four years earlier when we learned that our Stephen was infected with HIV, the virus that causes AIDS. During that first bout with pneumocystis pneumonia, he lay in the intensive care unit for two weeks, and we feared he would not survive. I begged, pleaded and bargained with God for just a little more time with my son, desperately wanting to show him how much we all loved him. My wish was granted, and we were all given that opportunity.

It wasn't until much later that I came to the realization that the painful "long good-bye" can be a doubled-edged sword. Letting go—and doing it slowly—is the most pain, I believe, that a parent can endure. For although our children can send us to great heights of happiness and joy, that unconditional love and closeness we feel for them contains the seeds of our deepest sorrow and despair. Their triumphs and disappointments are felt so deeply within our own being that it's as if they are our own.

There is nothing extraordinary about our family. We have had our share of divorces, separations, alienations, misunderstandings, petty jealousies and more than a few skeletons in our closets. What was remarkable, however, was how in facing the reality of what fate awaited one of our own, we all put aside our differences and pulled together to weave a fabric of love and compassion to embrace and cradle our Stephen. We encircled him, cared for him and tried our best to nurture and protect him.

Most of this reaction was due to the kind of person Stephen was. Stephen was not a saint. He had many of the same faults we all succumb to, and if he had lived for one hundred years, he would never have had a full-time job! But my young son was kind, sensitive and caring, always slow to judge others, and he treated everyone with gentleness and respect. He taught all of us how to connect to each other, and that what is truly important in this world is love. He taught me that to appreciate beauty in nature is God speaking to our souls. He radiated light like a candle expending itself.

My son's legacy to me is that I live life on a different, more intense level today than before. Life is truly beautiful, a miracle, and we must not waste a single moment. Time with our loved ones is to be cherished above all else. Because, inevitably, someday we must all say good-bye.

Now as I write this, one year after Stephen's death, I realize that what is conveyed in these words might serve as inspiration and hope for those in similar circumstances. People are not alone in their feelings of fear, isolation and devastation in facing the consequences of this disease that regrettably some people have not fully accepted as any other form of dying. But I have been there. I have felt these emotions. And I have triumphed to pick up the pieces.

Yes, this is a story about Stephen, and about a mother's struggle to cope. But in a way, it is a story about all of us. We are all on a journey called life. Change and challenge can either destroy our peace and happiness, or they can become vehicles enkindling our growth. The choice is always ours.

This experience has crystallized a few observations about life that others have made. Some are simple, and we've all heard them many times before. Through meditation and prayer, they have become a part of me.

When I first learned that Stephen had this disease called AIDS, I realized suddenly that what only happens to *them* was happening to us. It was my first vague awareness of the fact that we are all in this together. What happens to *another* human being in some way happens to *all* of us. If we are open to it, we will see that we are all unique children of God, each with our own special spirit.

Some people learn life's lessons easily. Stephen, for example, conducted his entire life by not judging others indiscriminately, and knowing that what happened to his neighbor also affected him. My son once confided in me that he felt he had been on this earth many times before, and this was the reason people were so drawn to him—as if they knew and latched on to his wisdom and experience. For me, I needed the equivalent of an atomic bomb dropped on me to hear this wake-up call!

It is true: we are our brother's keeper. In the Bible, it was Jesus who commanded us, "Love one another as I have loved you." Love isn't merely a feeling, but the actions of sharing, understanding and compassion. True love doesn't care about what others think, but rather simply allows a loved one to be who they are—unconditionally, without judgment or reservation.

We are God's hands on this earth. He will guide and direct us; we only need to be willing and listen. This is why our family and friends are gifts to be cherished and tended like a flower garden. How often do we feel overwhelmed by everyday life's demands, only to neglect those closest to us? One simple act of kindness to another can have a "ripple effect" that could change the world.

A huge part of finding happiness is being aware of the many blessings in our lives. Simple basic things, like waking and realizing that you have been given a new day, the face of your beloved, the beautiful blue sky, the laughter of a baby. They were always there, but we were not looking. We can form a mental habit to look at "what's not wrong," rather than dwelling on "what is." In my case, I was losing a treasured son, yet I have three other beautiful children to love and cherish. With practice, counting blessings is a wonderful mind excursion.

The realization that life is constantly changing and transformation is occurring is very enlightening. This is an important concept to come to terms with on our journey. If this were not true, none of us could ever grow. Someday we will all have to say good-bye to everything and everyone we love. As we unfold spiritually, one door closes and another opens. Physical death should not be feared, but instead seen as another part of our spiritual journey back to God.

I still find it strange that a child of mine could have the ability to teach me so much about life. Twenty-nine years ago, when I looked at this tiny baby cradled in my arms, I never could have imagined how much influence he would have over all of us.•

Support Your Transformation

Follow Your Highest Aspirations, Subscribe to Personal Transformation.

As we change ourselves, we change the world.

☑ **Yes,** I want to invest in my future.

☐ 1 year subscription, 5 issues for $19.95

☐ 2 year subscription, 10 issues for $37.95

Name_____

Address_____

City _____ State_____ Zip _____

Country_____

PLEASE ALLOW 4-6 WEEKS FOR DELIVERY OF YOUR FIRST ISSUE. CANADIAN ORDERS ADD $6, ALL OTHER FOREIGN ORDERS ADD $10. PAYMENT IN U.S. FUNDS MUST ACCOMPANY ALL FOREIGN ORDERS. THANK YOU.

Transform Your Life!

S O U L F U L   H E A L I N G

Soul Practice

Q U E S T I O N S

❦

1. What is your relationship to your own wounding: one of compassion, or, like most of us, one of judgment and criticism? How would it be to offer compassion toward your own wounds?
2. Who is a teacher, healer or support person for you in your own healing journey?
3. What makes you laugh? How often do you laugh?
4. Where do you carry a sense of emptiness in your body? How do you try to fill that emptiness: food, shopping, work, relationships?
5. What if love and awakening actually lie in the depths of your own emptiness and fear? How would that change your relationship to, and feelings about, that empty place?
6. What myths have you been told about what forgiveness is? How have these blocked the process of forgiveness?
7. How do you imagine your life would be different if you could practice forgiveness, not just with others, but with yourself?
8. Where do you find yourself in Jacquelyn Small's healing stages? (Be aware that all of us make this journey over and over again throughout our lives!) What do you need in order to move to the next stage?

P R A C T I C E S

1. Write a letter of commitment to yourself about what your commitment to healing means. How much time can you lovingly give yourself to heal? What do you commit to doing? Learning? Being?

2. Rent a movie or read a book that you know will make you laugh. Give yourself permission to laugh out loud. Notice how you feel when the movie is over.

3. Sit down, take a deep breath, close your eyes. Notice where you carry old emptiness in your body. Put your hand there softly. Imagine sending love and compassion to that emptiness through your hand. What happens?

4. Tape the Levine's forgiveness meditation, or have someone you trust read it to you. When you first try this meditation, pick a "small forgiveness." Stephen Levine talks about the magnitude of forgivenesses as one-pound, five-pound, ten-pound or even one-hundred-pound weights. Just as you wouldn't start weight training with one hundred pounds, so it is best not to start "forgiveness training" with one of the biggies. Start small. Don't forget to practice forgiving yourself.

5

Our Lives as
Transformational Stories

If you were to die today, what would be said about you? What would be the story of your life? Assuming that you will live on, there is time to rewrite your story. Do you know what you want your story to be? There is still time to live out the "great story" of your life. There is still opportunity to discover why you are here. Under the right circumstances it takes only a moment of willingness to listen, to know your true story.

This chapter takes you on a tour through the land of story. It will inspire you to tell your stories, especially to yourself. It will tell you how your stories of suffering, stories of healing and stories of what is possible will transform into the "great story" of your life.

YOU ARE YOUR STORIES

You are your stories. You are the product of all the stories you have heard and lived—and of many that you have never heard. They have shaped how you see yourself, the world, and your place in it. Your first great storytellers were home, school, popular culture, and, perhaps, church. Knowing and embracing healthy stories are crucial to living rightly and well. If your present life story is broken or dis-eased, it can be made well. Or, if necessary, it can be replaced by a story that has a plot worth living.

Our greatest desire, greater even than the desire for happiness, is that our lives mean something. This desire for meaning is the originating impulse of story. We tell stories because we hope to find or create significant connections between things. Stories link past, present, and future in a way that tells us where we have been (even before we were born), where we are, and where we could be going.

Our stories teach us that there is a place for us, that we fit. They suggest to us that our lives can have a plot. Stories turn mere chronology, one thing after another, into the purposeful action of plot, and thereby into meaning.

If we discern a plot to our lives, we are more likely to take ourselves and our lives seriously. If nothing is connected, then nothing matters. Stories are the single best way humans have for accounting for our experience. They help us see how choices and events are tied together, why things are and how things could be.

Healthy stories challenge us to be active characters, not passive victims or observers. Both the present and the future are determined by choices, and choice is the essence of character. If we see ourselves as active characters in our own stories, we can exercise our human freedom to choose a present and future for ourselves and for those we love that gives life meaning.

—Daniel Taylor, Ph.D.

Healing Broken Stories

DANIEL TAYLOR, PH. D.

S tories can be broken. The stories we live by sometimes fall apart. They no longer adequately explain our experience or give us enough reason to get up in the morning. Even worse, we sometimes come to doubt there is any story to our lives at all. They seem plotless. We lose any sense of ourselves as characters making significant choices. We cannot imagine a meaningful outcome to events. In such cases, we need to heal our broken stories. The best cure for a broken story is another story.

No story has been more relentlessly battered than that of the Jews. They have survived as a people only because of their commitment to storytelling. Elie Wiesel prefaces his novel, *The Gates to the Forest*, with the following brief story:

> *When the great Rabbi Israel Baal Shem-Tov saw misfortune threatening the Jews, it was his custom to go into a certain part of the forest to meditate. There he would light a fire, say a special prayer, and the miracle would be accomplished, and the misfortune averted.*
>
> *Later, when his disciple, the celebrated Magid of Mezritch, had occasion, for the same reason, to intercede with heaven, he would go to the same place in the forest and say: "Master of the universe, listen! I do not know how to light the fire, but I am still able to say the prayer." And again the miracle would be accomplished.*
>
> *Still later, Rabbi Moshe-Leib of Sasov, in order to save his people once more, would go into the forest and say: "I do not know how to light the fire, I do not know the prayer, but I know the place, and this must be sufficient." It was sufficient, and the miracle was accomplished.*
>
> *Then, it fell to Rabbi Israel of Rizhyn to overcome misfortune. Sitting in his armchair, his head in his hands, he spoke to God: "I am unable to light the fire, and I do not know the prayer; I cannot even find the place in the forest. All I can do is to tell the story, and this must be sufficient." And it was sufficient.*

The right stories can heal our brokenness and cure what ails us. They do so most often by reconnecting us with others who share our story, rescuing us from the sterile cycle of self-absorption, alienation and radical skepticism. When our own ability to narrate our story falters, we can lean on the shared story to sustain us.

Every story implies a community, and community offers us our single best hope for healing broken stories. At its smallest, a story defines a community of two: teller and listener. At its largest, it embraces the entire human community and beyond. Whether small or large, community is healing because it both requires something of us and gives us something back. In story, both teller and listener have responsibilities to the other, responsibility being the fair price we pay for the many benefits of sharing a story with others.

One of the most encouraging truths in a difficult world is that we have the freedom to change our defining stories. Broken stories can be restored, deficient ones replaced, and healthy stories identified and nurtured. If many of our stories are inherited from the various communities of which we are a part, they are also chosen and lived. We can be active participants, not merely passive receivers, in the making and remaking of our story.

Broken or diseased stories are those that fail in any of the crucial areas in which a life story must succeed. They give an inadequate sense of plottedness and meaning to our lives, or of ourselves as characters. Failed stories tend to ignore or undervalue either our freedom or our responsibility. They bind us to explanations of the world that do not correspond with our own experience, or they leave us isolated in a desperate pursuit of individual satisfaction like a dog chasing its tail.

We participate in the creation of the stories by which we live. Although every story we hear has the power to affect us, a handful of core stories determine the general shape of our lives. These are the stories that most directly answer the big questions: who am I, why am I here, who are these others, what is success, what should I do, what will happen when I die? These are our life stories, the ones that organize reality for us, give us our values, and enable us to explain our experience.

We should evaluate these core stories by the highest criteria and act accordingly if they are found wanting. We can heal our stories and choose new ones, for instance, by becoming true, acting characters, rather than mere personalities. Characters are defined by their choices, and their choices are a reflection of their values and understanding of the world. Your most meaningful stories should be chosen, not lived by default.

Many times, the stories you choose *will* be the ones that come from the communities in which you live. There is no particular merit or benefit in rejecting a story simply because it is familiar. But in choosing such stories, rather than passively receiving them, they become your story, and the community story will be different because you are a part of it.

Sometimes, however, our stories are not merely broken or fragmented, they are profoundly flawed. They cannot be healed, only replaced. The same freedom and responsibility that make us characters also give us the possibility of choosing new stories in which to live. One of the clearest indications of a flawed life story is its failure to give one the sense of purpose and conviction necessary to live life with an acceptable degree of optimism and resolve. A failed story no longer encourages the kind of life you feel it is important to live.

Healthy life stories do full justice to our situation, our needs and our nature. They have many qualities, but I would like to suggest four that should mark the stories in which we choose to act as characters. These stories should be truthful, freeing, gracious and hopeful.

A true life story explains the world to us in a way that accounts for the facts of our experience. Inadequate stories require constant stretching, patching, deflecting and suppression. Procrustes is a character from Greek mythology who was less than a perfect host. He invited guests to sleep in a bed but insisted that they fit it perfectly. Anyone who was too short was stretched and made to fit, and anyone too long had overhanging limbs chopped off. Many of us try to live by Procrustean stories that force us to stretch and chop our experience to make it fit.

A truthful life story will not only convincingly account for the facts of our experience, it will be satisfying. It will meet our emotional and intellectual need for meaning and purpose and the sense that our lives have value. Satisfying, however, is not the same as happy. This is one of the distortions in the common American story of success, a good example of a flawed story that at least needs to be supplemented, if not replaced. Enshrined in our "Declaration of Independence" is the quintessentially American idea that we have the inalienable right to pursue happiness. Originally, that probably did not mean much more than the right to private ownership of property (apparently a key to happiness for Americans then, as now). But over the years, we have subtly modified that idea into not simply the right to pursue happiness, but the unquestionable right to be happy, which is not the same.

The American success story tells us we are to achieve this happiness primarily through four avenues: money, power, prestige and pleasure. These are the great themes of countless stories paraded before us in novels, films, self-help books, talk shows, television and advertising. You can be richer, stronger, sexier. You can be envied, on top, out front, desired. You can be confident, gratified, in control, calling the shots, in charge. And, it goes without saying, you will be happy.

Then why aren't we? Why is arguably the richest, most powerful, most envied, most pleasure-soaked society in human history so widely unhappy? We are filled with complaint, frustration, anxiety, hostility and violence. At least, that is what we tell ourselves through the media, day after day. (When was the last time you saw a "study" of anything that concluded that we were healthy and doing well?)

We are unhappy because we are trying to live by a broken story. As attractive as it is in many respects, the American success story simply doesn't tell us the truth. It lies both in suggesting that everyone who works hard enough will have these things, and in suggesting that once you have them, you will finally be happy. It is a testimony to the human appetite for illusion that this story persists in the face of countless counter-stories from disappointed individuals who have followed these paths and found no contentment.

A satisfying story is one that is true not only to how the world is on the outside, but to how we are inside. It is emotionally and spiritually true. We do not have to divide ourselves to live it. We do not have to suppress something we know in our emotions to be true. Such emotional congruence is not a sufficient test by itself, because we know our emotions can support lies, but it is a necessary test. Our spirits will approve our most important stories.

A healthy story is also freeing. Stories that are true conform to reality. Understanding what is real and acting in accordance with it results in freedom—especially the freedom to do things. A bird can fly because it behaves in consort with the aerodynamic laws of nature. It is most free, and most capable, when it aligns itself with the unbreakable laws of how things are. A bird does not lament the restrictive laws of physics; it uses them to soar.

Human beings, on the other hand, too often think they're flying when they're only falling. Our prevailing notion of freedom is "No one can tell me what to do," when it should more often be "Will someone please tell me what to do?" A life story cut off from the stories of others is likely to be both untrue and sterile. Healthy stories free us from excessive self-absorption and "I did it my way" self-centeredness.

Healthy stories free us both from the lies we tell ourselves and from the lies others tell about us. In Alice Walker's *The Color Purple*, Celie is told, directly and indirectly, that she can never be more than a servant to an abusive husband because she is black, female, friendless, stupid and ugly. It is a story she believes until another character, Shug, tells her a different story about herself. Braced up by this new story, Celie sees herself and the world differently, acts differently, and thereby changes her world.

Meaningful freedom is not freedom from something, but freedom to do something. Broken stories trap us in repetitive, destructive acts—or make us passive; healthy ones free us to change ourselves and the world. The latter encourage us to see ourselves as characters with meaningful choices, and motivate us to act accordingly. Nothing is more energizing than the feeling that one has something important to do. Nothing is more enervating than the feeling that nothing is worth doing.

One test, then, of our life story is whether it frees and motivates us to act. It should create for us a world where meaning is possible, and we have a role in bringing it about. Healthy stories are the enemies of passivity, paralysis and cynicism. What, specifically, we do as a result of this freedom is unpredictable. It is more likely to be something small than something big. Most significant acts in the world are small ones. It is the accumulation of small acts, in individuals and in communities, that changes reality.

Another mark of healthy life stories is grace. Grace is getting better than you deserve—or giving better. Grace breaks the one-to-one link between performance and reward. It is essentially a religious idea, growing out of the notion of a creator with a parent's love for the creation. But it can be a powerful force in anyone's life.

Sacred writings are filled with stories of grace. In the Bible, David refuses the opportunity to kill Saul, the man who is trying to kill him; the forgiving father welcomes back the prodigal son; Christ on the cross prays for forgiveness for his crucifiers. The Bible's central story, in fact, is the story of grace.

The giving and receiving of grace should be part of any healthy life story. It is intimately linked to those other qualities of healthy stories—truth and freedom. If the stories I live by are unfettered with falsehood, and if they free me from preoccupation with self so I can act in the world, then I am more likely to be a source of grace to others and, therefore, to receive grace from others.

Grace is the ultimate act of empathy. It is possible on the human level only to the degree that we can imagine ourselves in other people's shoes. Such an act of imagination is a story act. It is being able to see oneself as a character in another's story, and acting in accordance with that imaginative perception in one's own. Grace is more than empathy, but empathy is its starting point. Because I know keenly my own need for receiving better than I deserve, I can imagine your similar need and can use my freedom to fulfill that need.

Grace is therefore a communal act. Only as we feel connected to others will grace flow back and forth. Even the simple, everyday orthodoxy of conversation—"I know how you feel," "That must have hurt," "I would have done the same thing," the nod of the head—are formulas of empathy that may contain flashes of grace.

Last, healthy life stories are hopeful stories. Every story worth living contains the possibility of a desirable outcome. If it is true that we are most drawn to stories of people in trouble, it is also true that our continuing interest depends on the possibility the person will survive that trouble, perhaps even triumph over it. Ultimately, both fatalism and cynicism are boring.

Hope is not mere wishing. It is a reasonable expectation based on past experience. We do not have to bury our heads in the sand to be hopeful; we need only draw reasonable conclusions from the outcome of other stories. If others have made it through circumstances similar to our own, then so might we. If others testify to finding a plot to their lives, then so might we. If others have found a meaningful end to their stories that validates the middle, then so might we. Discovering these aspects of others' stories depends, of course, on hearing them—which brings us back to the importance of community and sharing stories.

Though there is sometimes a tension between the requirement that a healthy life story be hopeful and that it also be truthful, there need be no contradiction. The basis for hope is not naive optimism, but a knowledge of other stories that give evidence that courage, perseverance and faith are at least as strong as evil and misfortune, and often stronger. •

We Heal by
Telling Our Story

RICHARD STONE

Many years ago, I was trapped in Glacier National Park by a fierce blizzard. Wind roared past our camp throughout the night. By morning, the temperature had dropped, and we were stuck in a fog bank that whirled by us and disappeared behind a white curtain. We headed out that day walking head-on into a fifty-mile-an-hour gale with snow and hail pocking our ruddy complexions. Four inches of snow and ice accumulated on the windward side of our packs and clothes in less than ten minutes. I realized that we could die out here and that no one would find us until the next June, when the snows melted.

Huddling together like cattle taking their last stand against a predator, we debated our options and decided to turn back. It was a good thing. The wind whipped harder, and at times I leaned into it with all my weight just to keep both feet on the trail. We struggled to make our way to the few lonesome trees that had guarded our previous night's stay. After setting up the tents, we stripped off our soaking gloves, pants, hats and boots and slipped into our down bags to wait for a break in the weather. Except for a brief dinner of English muffins and peanut butter—and the miserable task of hanging our food out of the bears' reach—we stayed in those bags for nearly twenty hours.

All night, snow pelted the tents' outer protective skin, and wind ricocheted off the mountains, racing with the speed of an avalanche toward our precarious nest in the trees. Occasionally, the sound of thunder, or of a huge boulder tumbling over a cliff, echoed throughout the valley.

Sometime around sunrise, the snow stopped. I decided to venture out. Our packs were barely visible beneath the drifts that had accumulated around the tent. I walked to the pit toilet and was relieved to find our food still hanging from its perch. Not even the bears were willing to brave such a storm. The metal toilet seat was cold, and my legs quivered as goose bumps crept up my ankles to my thighs. It was good to be out of the tent, even if it meant sitting half-naked in the frigid air. On the floor was an old spy novel left behind by a previous occupant. I was too weary to pick it up.

One by one, my friends struggled into the light. With miserable looks in our eyes, and hands and feet hurting from the wet and the cold, we tried desperately to get warm.

Everything was wet. Our spirits were nearly broken. No one wanted to admit it, but this wilderness was just too tough for us.

We hiked out that day. Quietly. Our shoulders were weighed down by the trials of the last twenty-four hours, and the thirteen treacherous miles that day left my muscles screaming and my toes aching.

A JEWEL MADE OF PAIN

I would not wish the above circumstances on anyone, and I would certainly never want to repeat it again. But the very act of telling you this story changes the way I see these events, altering the way I feel. What may have been the most miserable twenty-four hours I have ever spent has been exalted into something worth celebrating. I and my friends survived, living to tell about our brush with disaster, none the worse for wear, and prepared to tackle the wilderness once more.

By telling you about my trip to Glacier, I have taken the stuff of suffering and transformed it into one of the most elemental and important materials of human existence—meaning. By telling the story, I am no longer the victim of circumstances beyond my control. I have wrestled back control by the simple act of description, turning what seems to be a failure in almost every way into a heroic saga of survival. In this manner, even acute suffering can be redeemed.

A few years ago, I heard the story of Arn Chorn, a teenage refugee from the Cambodian war and the horrific slaughter perpetrated by the Khmer Rouge. His journey of healing is a monument to what is possible in each of our lives.

Arn's parents were killed by the Khmer Rouge, who viciously drove city dwellers into the fields to work. Many of the children who survived these forced marches were made to act as human shields for the soldiers. Their life expectancies were, obviously, short.

While in one of the camps, Arn watched as his sister slowly died of dysentery. He had also witnessed many of his other relatives die in this way. When he was forced to leave for another camp, he had no choice but to desert her.

Tearfully, Arn departed, his heart rent with sadness, remorse and guilt. He never saw her again.

It was at this moment when he realized that his fate would be the same if he remained. He fled through the forest to the safety of Thailand. It was the Khmer Rouge's policy to hunt down escapees. If they weren't executed, they would be returned to the camps and watched more vigilantly. The soldiers were not far behind when Arn made it past his last obstacle to freedom—a swiftly flowing river.

While Arn was in a refugee camp, Reverend Peter Pond befriended and eventually adopted him, bringing him to the United States. Even though he now lived in a safe, supportive world filled with material comforts, Arn could find little reason for joy, much less any for continuing his life. His despair was overwhelming.

One day while driving with Arn, a mutual friend, Judith Thompson, asked him to describe the circumstances of his flight from the Khmer Rouge. Until this time, he had not shared with anyone the burden of his decision, made years before. Weeping, he described every step of his escape. With a long history in peer counseling, Judith listened intently and with compassion. During the many weeks that followed, Arn shared his story over and over with Judith, each time revealing a new detail that had been covered by the weight of guilt and shame. With each sharing, Arn experienced a sense of freedom that he had not felt since coming to this country—one that flowed from within.

The powerful transformation Judith witnessed in Arn led her to ask two simple questions that transformed both her life and Arn's—what if other children who had been deeply wounded by war were able to share their experiences with each other? And, what would it be like for children from this country to hear these stories and the details of the abominable conditions that are the by-products of the violent conflicts initiated by adults? Thus was born Children of War, a nonprofit, international effort that brought together children from strife-torn countries around the world. By sharing their stories with each other, and in forums at schools throughout the States, these children were able to make the face of war real for so many of us who are desensitized to violence and conflict. Their pain no longer seemed to be a senseless suffering. It had found meaning and purpose. Now, because of their pain, they could serve the world as witnesses of war. As their despair was "storied," they were able to find a common bond. Alchemically, their stories released them to fully experience the birthright of childhood—joy. We, too, regardless of the nature and depth of our suffering, can rediscover the roots of connection, healing, love and joy by courageously telling our own tales that are filled with grief, pain and distress.

FINDING A PLACE OF WHOLENESS

As our world moves and shakes beneath our feet, we are challenged daily to find new ways of coping with and making sense of it all. Needing to ground ourselves in the realities at hand, while also searching for a perspective that allows us to find purpose in the events, feelings and ideas that surround us, we desperately need tools that can help us keep it all together, giving a sense of wholeness to what would otherwise be a fractured reality.

The narrative structure of story impresses understandable patterns of meaning on experience, no matter how discontinuous an event is with our core beliefs and current view of things. This shows up most vividly in the midst of personal crises.

A friend of mine who works as a chaplain at a local hospital described for me what happens when an unconscious trauma victim is brought into the emergency room. Frequently the patient's identity is unknown, and lifesaving procedures are initiated while a chaplain or social worker attempts to contact the next of kin (if other family members weren't also involved in the accident). But it's not unusual for a parent or sibling to be informed in a more dramatic fashion.

In one case, a mother was driving by the scene of an accident. One of the cars that was mangled looked quite familiar, much like the one belonging to her teenage daughter. As she got closer, she realized that it was a family member's car. Frantically she pulled her vehicle to the shoulder, asking every emergency worker within earshot what had happened. The ambulance had pulled away moments before. She implored those who were first on the scene for details. The shock of the realization practically incapacitated her. She furiously questioned anyone who could give her information: "How did it happen? Who was at fault? In what direction was my daughter's car going? How fast was the other driver going? What condition was she in when they put her in the ambulance? Is she alive? What are the chances she's going to be okay? She is going to be okay, isn't she?"

Before anyone could answer her questions, she pulled back into traffic, racing to catch up with the ambulance. As she entered the emergency room, they were wheeling her daughter into the operating suite. What did she do?

According to my friend, she began talking with whomever she could find, recounting the horrible details of the event, struggling with how this could happen to her beautiful daughter. And she was not satisfied with telling the tale just once. Over and over, she recounted what had happened. She appraised the event from every possible angle.

Each attempt at description represents a quest to digest the horrid consequences of her daughter's accident. Such storytelling can go on for hours, even days. Repeatedly, persons who are traumatized recount the relevant events to anyone with a willing ear. What these people need most, at this time, is generosity of listening. They don't require sedatives, psychoanalysis or even reassurance; it's the patience of someone who is willing to say, "Now, tell me again where you were when the drunk driver ran that stop sign," that gives them the space to begin healing the pain.

This scenario plays itself out daily in emergency rooms throughout the world. It is not specific to gender or age. Universally, human beings will resort to narrative to come to grips with a shattered reality.

In less severe circumstances, the principle also holds true. The only thing missing is the urgency, but the need is there just the same. Representing our world to others through story is innately human, as crucial to our soul's survival as breathing is to the survival of our body. Short-circuit this natural process, and you will witness all forms of disease. It may show up as a physical symptom or as mental distress. More likely, it will appear under the guise of a nameless anxiety, or a general depression that we can't seem to attribute to anything in particular. These are the symptoms of an unstoried life.

Many things in our lives cry out to be storied—unfinished relationships, momentous changes that affect the course of our existence and unjust hurts at the hands of friends and parents. In my experience, the events that need most to be storied are the emotional equivalents of car accidents that could never be spoken about or shared because of fear or shame. The wounds of sexual and physical abuse are prime examples of what could be healed with a minimum of scarring if the victims felt the safety to immediately "story" the event, much as relatives of trauma victims do. But humiliation and fear of retribution prevent the child from speaking his or her truth, and the trauma goes underground, now living outside conscious awareness, emerging in all sorts of dysfunctional ways. If the adult is willing to return to the event, recover the memories, translate them into story form and speak them to a committed listener (in this case, usually a psychotherapist), the event can be redeemed, even transformed alchemically into a jewel made of pain. But it may require years of telling and retelling in conjunction with other healing modalities until the metamorphosis is complete, a new equilibrium is found, and the person once again discovers wholeness within. To weave together the slender threads of a torn life into a firm pattern of meaning that can give even the most pernicious emotional and physical injuries a role of honor in our experience—this is the power of story.•

Living the Mythic Life

J E A N   H O U S T O N,   P H. D.

Because of the acceleration of human experience in our time, each of us, in his or her own way, is becoming a mythic being. We have undergone as many unusual experiences and suffered as many woundings as any mythic character. As in the traditional model of stages along the hero's journey of transformation, we have heard and answered many calls, discovered remarkable allies, crossed and recrossed many thresholds of experience, found ourselves swallowed and regestated in the belly of the whale, entered upon a road of trials and high adventures, died many times to outworn and restrictive aspects of ourselves, and been chronically resurrected.

We have fought monsters of our own and others' making, tried to right wrongs or enhance the condition of life wherever we have found it, and have even discovered a path to the beloved and marriage to the spiritual partner within. Our lives could hardly be called humdrum, but any time they seemed dull, we went out and did something about it. Or perhaps some archetypal force entered in and livened things up for us.

In my travels, I have discovered this phenomenon occurring worldwide. We are all engaged in a mythic experiencing of the life of the soul and, by extension, of the Soul of the World. Indeed marriage to the soul may be the preeminent occurrence in the life of the psyche today. But what is unique about our time is that our lives are not amplified by reflection in the cultural mythic hero or heroine. Our lives are as mythic as theirs. We are direct participants in the story of the Soul of the World. We catch the evolutionary resonance much more directly than we once did, which explains all the new emphasis on personal mythology.

Despite the media dominance of economic and political forms, I feel that the most important event in the present whole system transition is the radical incorporation of mythical and archetypal qualities in our lives. Whenever we study myth, we open the gate to this disclosure. And we can begin to examine our own lives as mythic events—events that tell of the unfolding and uncoding of the Soul of the World.

At this point, the tension between soul and world, inner and outer, public and private begins to disappear as we discover ourselves to be characters in the drama of the world soul, the anima mundi. In this mode, ego structures are seen as only one aspect among multiple aspects of the self. Indeed the most accurate model of human existence reveals innate diversity, both within each individual and among individuals.

The polyphrenic or multiminded self is the healthy self. Spiritually, however, as the psychologist James Hillman reminded us, "the soul's inherent multiplicity demands a theological fantasy of equal differentiation." This means that now those psychospiritual potencies whom we call gods—with the neters of ancient Egypt—need to be seen as polyphrenic, multifaceted images of the One.

In the state of partnership that blends into union, we are digested by God and re-formed by God. And in some sense, God becomes human for us. Meister Eckhart, one of the most powerful conceptual and experiential Christian theologians of the Middle Ages, believed that the mystical union is not the privilege of the few but the very vocation and ultimate realization of humanity. Eckhart, the writer, has God speak to us, saying, "I became man for you. If you do not become God for me, you do me wrong."

In such a statement, our notions of substance and essence begin to shift and vibrate, moving across transpersonal domains. Spirit is infused with matter and matter with spirit. Eckhart believed this entirely because he believed that God is immanent in us all, is in fact our very being. Eckhart said, "If I am to know God directly, I must become completely God, and God I; so that this God and this I become one I."

The "archetype of partnership" is our very reason for being. Marriage to the soul is our raison d'être. Our fears and our limited self-concept keep reducing the sense of the reality and vitality of this union. The quality of our selfhood depends on the presence of that divine image in us, on our communion with this soul, this God-self that we contain. Following from that, it depends on the degree of our own immanence in the archetype of soul or God-self. This relationship can be experienced as the soul's union with its beloved. By becoming immersed in the archetypal and profoundly loving relationship, we can grow toward our true identity in God.•

The Journey for Meaning

SAM KEEN
AND ANNE VALLEY-FOX

What is a myth? Few words have been subject to as much abuse and been as ill-defined as myth. Journalists usually use it to mean a "lie," "fabrication," "illusion," "mistake" or something similar. It is the opposite of what is supposedly a "fact," of what is "objectively" the case and of what is "reality." In this usage myth is at best a silly story and at worst a cynical untruth. Theologians and propagandists often use myth as a way of characterizing religious beliefs and ideologies other than their own.

Such trivialization of the notion of myth reflects those certainties of dogmatic minds, an ignorance of the mythic assumptions that underlie the commonly accepted view of "reality," and a refusal to consider how much our individual and communal lives are shaped by dramatic scenarios and "historical" narratives that are replete with accounts of the struggle between good and evil empires: our godly heroes versus the demonic enemy.

In a strict sense *myth* refers to "an intricate set of interlocking stories, rituals, rites and customs that inform and give the pivotal sense of meaning and direction to a person, family, community or culture." A living myth, like an iceberg, is 10 percent visible and 90 percent beneath the surface of consciousness. While it involves a conscious celebration of certain values, which are always personified in a pantheon of heroes (from the wily Ulysses to the managing Lee Iacocca) and villains (from the betraying Judas to the barbarous Moammar Kadafi), it also includes the unspoken consensus, the habitual way of seeing things, the unquestioned assumptions, the automatic stance. It is differing cultural myths that make cows sacred objects for Hindus and hamburger meals for Methodists or turn dogs into pets for Americans and roasted delicacies for the Chinese.

We are storytelling animals. As our primitive ancestors sat around the fire carving spearheads and eating blackberries they told stories which in time were woven into a tapestry of myth and legend. These tales were the first encyclopedia of human knowledge. They explained where the world came from, why there were people, why snakes have no legs, why corn smut stops birth hemorrhages, why conch shells are sacred, why coyotes howl at night, and why the gods put fire and death on earth. In the dramatic telling, the triumphs of heroes and the antics of fools came alive again. Stories told the people of a tribe who they were, where they had been, where they were going and how to stay friendly with the spirits.

Our modern myths are often unfocused; we don't celebrate our myths enough; they frequently hide like outlaws in the backwoods of the unconscious. For a variety of historical reasons (the emergence of machines, cities, anonymity, money, mass media, standardization, automation) we've lost awareness of storytelling as a way to dramatize and order human existence. But whether we acknowledge them or not, our myths and stories live in our imaginations.

To be a person is to have a story to tell. We become grounded in the present when we color in the outlines of the past and the future. Mythology can add perspective and encouragement to your life. Within each of us there is a tribe with a complete cycle of legends and dances, songs to be sung. We were all born into rich mythical lives: we need only claim the stories that are our birthright.

With a little imagination each person can find within himself a replacement for the myths and stories lost when we ceased living in tribes. A person is a complex being made up of a million individual smells, tastes, memories and hopes. Listen for a few minutes to the voices that run through your mind. Every psyche is a private theater filled with scenes and characters. Listen and you will hear your father, mother, brothers, sisters, children, lovers, friends, enemies, teachers and heroes acting out their dramas on your stage. Hearing the multiple voices within yourself will remind you that you belong to a special clan. Your people still inhabit you. They will help you to celebrate your myths, sing your songs and tell your legends.

The techniques of storytelling and the psychology that underlies them rest on a discovery of the obvious: that what all persons have in common is their uniqueness. Every person has a story to tell. That's what makes a person and defines the journey that person makes through life. There are no autonomous, anonymous, pragmatic individuals—we were all raised by an intimate group that had traditions, values, rites of passage, ceremonies and legends. When we forget our stories, leave our heroes unsung and ignore the rites that mark our passage from one stage of life into another, we feel nameless and empty.

We can rediscover the uniqueness of the person if we reassemble our myths and stories, which have been homogenized into business, education, politics and dissipated in the media. Find the unconscious and make it conscious, find an audience for the untold tales, and you will discover you are already on a rich mythic journey. What most of us lack is only the permission to tell the stories that are our own birthright.

You can't tell who you are unless someone is listening. There are better and easier ways to get an audience than by hiring a psychiatrist. Find a partner to listen and tell your multiple stories, stories of your childhood, your family, your roots. Be all those characters who wander around in your head. Journey back into the past, ahead into your future and out into cosmic time. Discover a few of your many selves.

The emphasis on telling stories amounts to a new way of defining personality and psychology. Psychology ought to be much more concerned with boredom and excitement and less concerned with mental illness and lost and found identity. The dis-ease of the modern psyche is more of a vacuum than a thorn in the flesh. If we are alienated, disgraced, frustrated and bored, it is because of what hasn't happened, because of potentialities we have not explored. Few of us know the fantastic characters, emotions, perceptions and demons that inhabit the theaters that are our minds. We are encouraged to tell a single (true) story, construct a consistent character, fix an identity. We are thus defined more by neglected possibilities than by realized ones. We rehearse and repeat a monotonous monologue while heroes and villains, saints and madmen, ascetics and libertines wait in the wings for a chance to seize center stage and run wild. In this sense, identity is a repetition compulsion, a conspiracy to put a consistent face before the world, to cover up the glorious inconsistency of emotions and desires. The character we develop domesticates the world and leaves us no wilderness to play in. There are many territories of imagination and many strange regions of emotion that we may not enter without throwing our sanity into question. Until we cross some borders, we are likely to remain rational, banal, boring, bored. A major concern of any therapeutic psychology should be to help an individual lose identity.

A psychological proposal is always political, and this one proposes an ideal relationship between the individual and the community. Paradoxically, an individual becomes strongest, most vivid and most open when he discovers the contradictions of his psyche. Each of us harbors the entire range of human possibilities. Every I is a we. We can become authentically public only by first going to the depths of the private. At the heart of the uniqueness of the individual lies the universal. Every person's deepest ecstasies and fears are old as mankind and common as dirt. Thus, the greatest freedom for the individual comes from the love of many stories. The strongest state is the one that keeps the fewest citizens in jails, insane asylums and ghettos.

The only event we can predict with virtual certainty is the one we least like to think about—our own deaths. Death is the doorway to the future, the one fact in a world otherwise governed by probabilities. Before we can fantasize freely about our futures we have to break the death barrier—confront the ambivalent feelings that cluster around our images of the end.

Modern people don't die; they just pass away. Soldiers take care of our killing and undertakers do our burying, preferably discreetly. Classical philosophers insisted that wisdom and happiness were only possible after a person had come to terms with the inevitability of death. Plato defined philosophy as training for dying. If we evade death we avoid the event that sets the definitive limits on our mortality; we cling to the illusion that there's an eternity of time in which to do the things we lack courage to do today. Death disillusions by reminding us that we arise from and return to the earth (humus). It makes us human by confronting us with the fragility of life and the need for decision.

For the human animal there is no purely biological act. Death (like birth or sex) is surrounded with interpretations and explanations. We need to understand what death means and why people should die. Throughout the course of history the myths, images and metaphors used to interpret death reflect a profound ambiguity. It is never clear whether death is friend or enemy, the beginning or the end of life.

Either death is: an end to life, the ultimate enemy, the grim reaper, the castrator. In the Christian tradition, as in many ancient myths, death enters the world as a punishment for transgression against some divine law. Man dies because he ate the forbidden fruit or because he broke a taboo or stole fire from the gods. If there were no enmity between man and the gods, no alienation, there would be no death.

Or death is: a prelude to rebirth, the hidden friend, the womb of life, the lover. In cultures where the feeling for nature remains strong, human life is seen as analogous to the life of plants and death is viewed as one stage in an eternal cosmic cycle. In the winter of his life man dies in order that he may be reborn in the spring. The Hopi Indians symbolize this by burying their dead in the fetal position. In the end we come back to the beginning.

Different psychological realities underlie these two estimates of death. We experience death only as observers. A dying person experiences dying but, presumably, not death. The survivors observe a lifeless body and experience grief, relief, anger and panic. To an observer death seems final. It steals away a unique person whose life can never be restored or repeated. If we have loved the dead person death seems the final enemy of love and life. When we think about our own death we are inundated by the images and fears that surround an imaginary future event. But we confront our feelings about death most directly when we come face to face with any radical change in our lives. Something in us (the ego, the infantile self, the firstborn self) does not believe we can survive fundamental changes in personality structure or life circumstances, and so each crisis in life is shadowed by death. Then when we survive the crisis we realize that change may mean metamorphosis rather than death. The ego dies and a stronger self is born. Then it may come to us that death is only a gateway to wider life, the final trip beyond the prison of the ego.

Speculations and explanations always pale before the reality of death. In the end we have to face it raw. We can escape obsession with death by paying attention to the appeals of living. It is unlived life that makes fear of death persistent and morbid. We might even see our death as a gift to the living: nature decrees that the father dies so the child can inherit his full place in the sun. Even the death of those we love is not a total loss. Death adds the bass notes to the symphony. By our grief for what is missing we know the terrible value of what was once present among us.

Maybe the best we can do is struggle against death as if it were our final enemy, refuse to "go gentle into that good night," affirm the priority of light over darkness. Then, in that penultimate moment (when, it is said, our life flashes before us and we know that it was good), we may allow death to turn its other face toward us and know that it is a friend. Maybe.•

Dying of Perfection

G I L L I A N   R E E S

I will never forget the days when I could barely brush my hair in the morning without getting so tired I felt I was having a nervous breakdown. I had chronic fatigue immune deficiency syndrome (CFIDS), and it was the most frightening experience of my life. It lasted four years.

I was stubborn and didn't want to admit defeat, but when I finally felt like I'd be dead at the end of the year if I didn't do something, I found a Chinese acupuncturist who saved my life—literally, I believe now. He told me I had to exercise in order to get well. What a joke! I could barely get out of bed in the morning. Along with acupuncture and Chinese herbs, he prescribed a daily diet of yoga.

Yoga brought peace and centeredness to my life. Yoga brought an awareness of my body that for years had been off-kilter because of my previous career as a dancer. I had to learn how to practice yoga without needing to be perfect. It was a mistake I'd made more than once before.

In ballet, you learn to ignore the body and its pain, aiming for a perfection that is always just around the corner. Competition, with yourself and others, becomes a way of life. I had never learned differently. With CFIDS I had to.

I had given up dance several years before, after major abdominal surgery and various hip injuries. I started a new career in the frenetic world of entertainment publicity. It was just as competitive as dance, if not more so. I started taking yoga lessons to relieve the stress.

I studied three times a week in a beautiful studio in Hollywood, California. After a few months, my old hip injury hurt so much that the pigeon pose made me cry. Of course, I never told anyone. Say "I hurt" in a ballet class and—well, you'd just never do it. Pain is a given, because it's in pursuit of art.

I remember hearing my yoga instructors, unlike my ballet teachers, say, "Only go as far as you can go," and, "Go at your own pace." I didn't listen.

Yoga became part of my competitive lifestyle. It felt meaningless to me unless my body hurt, I had achieved the perfect pose first, and I was better than everyone else in class. Talk about competitive! My expectations of perfection were unconscionably high. Yoga as a conscious spiritual discipline eluded me, so I gave it up.

My life grew more complex. I worked hard, got a job at NBC, and worked even harder. I started approaching my career the way I used to approach dance. Once again, I became obsessed with perfection and pain.

My life got so complex that I lost all sense of balance. I never rested. I thrived on stress, worked late every night, and didn't take care of my chronic stomach ailments. It was the perfect recipe for CFIDS.

When my doctor suggested yoga as part of my healing, I remembered it as a strong, competitive, painful discipline. But at that point, I would have recited Russian verbs and dyed my hair blue if I thought it would help me get well.

I went to a wonderfully nurturing yoga instructor and struggled through beginner classes with sixty-year-old women who were much sprightlier than I. I felt like a stroke victim learning to walk.

Little by little, I began to create a new relationship with my body, seeing it not as a tool for the perfect arabesque or a tireless vehicle that could give me corporate success, but as part of a much greater whole. I had to feel yoga from the inside out, because my body was too weak to experience it any other way. I began to heal.

After a year, my health vastly improved. I felt human again and infinitely thankful for life. Now that I had progressed to more advanced classes, I couldn't do a class without feeling searing pain in my hips. Had I stopped to listen to my body, I would have heard that my hips weren't the problem. My old nemesis, perfection, was. I was forgetting the lesson that CFIDS had taught me.

Finally, I admitted my "weakness" by telling my new yoga instructor about the hip injuries and my recovery from CFIDS. Asking for help was the hardest part. She showed me how to ease the pain by doing hip-related poses differently and recommended I sign up for a week-long yoga retreat the following Christmas.

In the weeks leading up to the workshop, I argued with myself incessantly. How could I do six hours of yoga a day when I was still healing from CFIDS, and had never taken yoga more than four hours a week? Had CFIDS really given me a different outlook on life or was I just fooling myself by competing in an arena that seemed healthier?

It was clear the first day of the retreat that I was not the best in class. I felt like a wimp. My thighs wobbled like vanilla pudding in earthquake territory. I wasn't the best, or anywhere near it, by the end of the week either.

The instructor specialized in therapeutic yoga. Under his inspired and charismatic tutelage I began to find a new, inner strength that had nothing to do with perfection or competition.

I learned which poses would boost my immune system. I struggled into backbends, and "held" my weakened kidneys in the palms of my hands in shoulder stands. The pain in my hips disappeared and by the fourth day, I felt a long dormant energy pulsating through my body. I felt so good, I didn't care what I looked like. It was a revelation. I made new friends who listened to and supported me. When I boarded the plane to fly back to the states, I cried.

Finally, I was on the road to recovery, not just from CFIDS, but from a lifetime of trying to meet, and beat, unrealistic expectations. Some, other people had set for me. Most of them, I set for myself.

I'm not totally cured. No addict ever is. But I have reached a place where my addiction to perfection is taking a back seat to more important things—like backing off on days when I'm tired, spending more time with friends instead of competing with strangers, and accepting my limitations as I grow older. And like finding the ecstasy of spirit that is there for me—in yoga and in life—every time I stop trying long enough to simply be.•

OUR LIVES AS TRANSFORMATIONAL STORIES

Soul Practice

QUESTIONS

1. How can you see your life as part of the transformational Great Story of life, death and rebirth?

2. What old forms, old broken stories, are asking to die in your life? How may you release them and make room for a new, and greater, story to unfold in your life?

3. If your were to look at the suffering and pain in your life as sacred wounding that allows for the possibility for the Sacred, and new life, to flow in, how would that change your relationship to your suffering, present or past?

4. How might your own wounding open you to be a healer for others in any way?

5. What would it mean for you to move from being a minor actor in the story of your life to being the heroine or hero?

PRACTICES

1. Write down your core story: Why am I here? Who am I? What do I value most, and why? Who are my traveling companions, and why? What does success mean to me, and how do I measure it in my life? What happens to me, and others, when we die? Give yourself at least a month to write this.

   When you are done, read it out loud to yourself. Listen as if you've never heard it before. What is broken in this story? What is healing and empowering? For the pieces that are broken, play with writing new parts that give you life and hope.

   If your story fails to give you a sense of purpose and meaning, how may you release it? This may be a time to seek professional help, for support in finding a new and more life-giving story to tell yourself about your life and history.

2. Find someone with whom you may tell each other your stories. Notice what meaning emerges in the telling that you may have not noticed before. As you listen to the other's story, respectfully listen for unarticulated and unacknowledged meaning in their story as well.

6

The Liberation of Age

People on a spiritual path are familiar with the idea of being in the world but not of it. Being of the world includes being of the society you live in. Modern civilization prizes youth, material wealth and rugged individualism. Its values are embedded in your psyche.

The liberation of age includes letting go of much of your personal history, as well as a great deal of this culture. Obviously, you cannot cling to youth, with its emphasis on appearance and acquisition, and embrace old age, with its peace and wisdom. The years of maturity may be provided for with money, but their wealth comes from an abiding sense of the sacred, the unity of all life and a richness of connection with others. Such wealth, peace and wisdom make possible our giving back to life. The golden years are a time when you can be in the world, but not of it, improving the quality of life around you.

This chapter will help you to value the possibility of freedom and influence the second half of life brings.

THE SECOND HALF OF LIFE

People who identify themselves with their body often find the latter half of life a great burden. Only when you learn to identify yourself with the Soul will the latter half of your life become a great blessing.

Once, when a friend and I were walking at the local shopping district, a young woman reporter stopped me. She apologized for interrupting my walk and said, "Do you mind if I ask you a question?" She cleared her throat. "What would you say is the most unpleasant thing about growing old?"

I wasn't offended. She was a nice young woman; she was just reflecting the assumptions that underlie all our modern attitudes. So I smiled and said, "Now you'd better take down what I say. The latter part of my life is wonderful. In fact, there is no comparison with the first part. All the physical vigor and the running about and the—what do you call it?—the vim and razzle-dazzle of early life, it's all 'sound and fury, signifying nothing.'"

When you have only your physical appearance to depend on, I might have added if I had known her better, there is no escape from the ravages of time. That is why spiritual teachers say, Enjoy your youth, but don't neglect to light the lamp of beauty inside, which will glow brighter with the passage of time.

Our society lives by the rather juvenile theory that beauty and joy are limited to a particular period in life. It's true that children have a marvelous beauty of their own, but every child has to grow up. Teenagers have a certain beauty of their own, but they, too, have to grow up. Similarly, the twenty-somethings and the thirty-somethings will eventually become forty- and fifty-somethings.

When my grandmother, in her sixties, came and sat with us in our ancestral home, she was the center of all attention. Her beauty came entirely from within, a beauty born of the highest feminine qualities. Forgiveness, inward strength, the use of gentle words (which means gentle thoughts), all play a part in making a woman—or a man! Beautiful.

Whatever religion you belong to, whatever country you belong to, everybody responds to this kind of inner beauty. You don't have to advertise. To use one of the great similes from Sri Ramakrishna, you will be like a lotus opening in the rays of the morning sun. The lotus doesn't need to say, "Where are the bees?" The bees are looking for the lotus. All of us, inwardly, are looking for this kind of beauty and love that grows with the passage of time.

—Eknath Easwaran

Coming into Our Own

MARK GERZON

In the second half of life, our old compasses no longer work. The magnetic fields alter. The new compass that we need cannot be held in our hand, only in our heart. We read it not with our mind alone, but with our soul. Now we yearn for wholeness. We yearn to remember the parts of ourselves that we have forgotten, to nourish those we have starved, to express those we have silenced, and to bring into the light those we have cast into the shadows. On this quest for wholeness, we must let go of cliches of adult life, both positive and negative. The standard maps of "growing up" and "growing old" will not serve us well. Using the best information available, each of us must find his own way.

To varying degrees, all of us are trying to break out of what Yale psychiatrist Daniel Levinson, in *The Seasons of a Man's Life*, called the "life structure" that we have built during the first part of our lives. "Every life structure necessarily gives priority to certain aspects of the self," wrote Levinson, "and neglects or minimizes other aspects." No wonder then that the second half is the time when these parts of ourselves that have been neglected, ignored or otherwise suppressed begin to emerge. It is now—or never.

"In this phase of life—between thirty-five and fifty—a significant change in the human psyche is in preparation," concluded Carl Jung, after years of clinical research and reflection. "At first it is not a conscious and striking change. . . . Often it is something like a slow change in a person's character; in another case certain traits may come to light which had disappeared in childhood; or again, inclinations and interests begin to weaken and others arise to take their places."

But what the measured prose of psychiatrists and the carefully calculated statistics of social scientists rarely capture is the experience of inner struggle. These "significant changes" do not occur automatically. In fact, they must often fight against our resistance. In this sense, midlife is a drama more worthy of a playwright than a scholar. We are characters in the play, caught at the opening of the second act, and we do not know what will happen next.

Jung wrote more than fifty years ago that when we begin the second half,

"The elements of the psyche undergo in the course of life a very marked change—so much so, that *we may distinguish between a psychology of the morning of life and a psychology of its afternoon.*" Although my friend Peter Goldmark had never read Jung's words, he wrote these lines of poetry at the age of forty-five:

> *If life is a day, in mine it is after one*
> *And only until dusk will daylight last.*
> *If life is a year, for me August is come.*
> *The young green afternoons of June have passed.*

Just as Jung predicted, Peter had noticed a shift within himself. Noon had passed. He had entered a different part of the day about which he knew very little. But he was aware of crossing the threshold. He was aware of the quest.

Our quest is waiting for us—but only if we listen to these questions. If we ignore our questions and act as if we are still in life's first half, we do so at our own peril. Whoever pretends that the second half of life is no different from the first, wrote Jung, "must pay with damage to his soul." If you don't find the time, the time will find you. Whether you begin your mid-life quest on purpose with your eyes open or against your will with your eyes shut tight, it will one day begin.

Indeed, without your knowing it, it may already have.

We share a quest for wholeness. Have you ever heard of anyone upon their deathbed who said, "If only I had specialized more narrowly in my field?" Have you ever heard of a last will and testament in which the deceased said they wished they had not made love such a high priority; that they had not spent so much time with their children; or that they had not taken such good care of their health? Have you ever heard reports of wise elders who, looking back upon their lives, said they wished they had spent more time in the office, paid more attention to other people's expectations of them, or been more cautious in exploring new parts of themselves?

We never hear such regrets because the second half of life is a quest for wholeness. It turns the tables on the first half. It weighs the balances in favor of integrity. It asks us not to defend who we are but to be open to the mystery of what we have not yet become, the mystery of coming into our own, whoever we may be. It connects us to a quest that goes far back beyond our time, long before the phrase *adult development* was ever coined. Dante opened *The Divine Comedy* with the famous lines:

Midway upon the journey of our life
I found myself within a forest dark,
For the straightforward pathway had been lost. . . .

The quest for wholeness in the second half is ancient and universal. Joseph Campbell defined it well in his classic study of world mythology, *Hero with a Thousand Faces*. He showed that in virtually all the world's myths could be found a shared quest for meaning and transcendence, a "heroic" quest that took place during the years we call adulthood. According to Campbell, the drama of the quest itself was far more than a mere extension of our personal or family psychohistories. It was a joining with the cosmic and timeless tales—what Jean Houston calls "the Larger Story"—that is crystallized in dreams and codified in myth.

"So these old stories live in us?" Bill Moyers asked Campbell during one of their interviews.

"They do indeed," Campbell replied and he went on to outline the challenge of the second half.

As a child, you are brought up in a world of discipline, obedience, and you are dependent on others. *All this has to be transcended when you come to maturity,* so that you can live not in dependency but in self-responsible authority. If you can't cross that threshold you have the basis for neuroses.

Unfortunately, too many of us are locked into the "certain program" of life's first half. Physically, socially, economically, psychologically and spiritually, the agenda of the second half of life varies greatly from the agenda of the first. And yet, lost under the bland generality of "adulthood," we continue to treat each other and ourselves as if nothing has changed. We turn the second half into a "midlife crisis" by pretending that everything is supposed to stay the same—only to discover to our surprise that nothing does stay the same. Possibilities for growth and change in the second half that we never knew existed now emerge.

Unlike the conventional view of the "midlife crisis," the quest does not necessarily begin with a tumultuous upheaval in one's life—an affair, or a red sports car, or a move to a new job. Whether we know it or not (and usually we don't), it often begins with resistance to change. It begins with our pulling against the future and clinging to the past. It begins with our unconsciously saying, "No, not yet!" to what is happening inside us.

Denial is a kind of quest in reverse. We are actually trying *not* to journey. We think our challenge is to stay young and so we pretend that we are still in life's first half, that the transformation isn't taking place. We cling to our youthful selves with all the determination of a shipwrecked sailor gripping a piece of driftwood. Sometimes it requires suffering the loneliness of watching others leave us behind as they set off on new paths. It involves blocking out the sights and sounds and smells that suggest new lands and new possibilities. It demands that we silence our questions, doubts, wonderings and inner yearnings.

The word *midlife* itself for example often produces an adverse reaction. Most people in their thirties and forties (and even many in their fifties) assume that it refers to someone older than themselves. Thirty-five-year-olds think it begins at forty; forty-year-olds think it begins at forty-five; forty-five-year-olds push the entry point back to fifty; and so on throughout our final years. When Katharine Hepburn tells Henry Fonda in the film *On Golden Pond* that they should get together with another "middle-aged" couple like themselves, her cantankerous husband replies, "We're *not* middle-aged. People don't live to be 150!" We resist applying the word *midlife* to ourselves because it acknowledges two interconnected truths: that we may no longer be "young" (whatever that means to us) and that since life has a *mid*point, it must also have an *end*point— and it is not 150!

While in this period of denial, we tend to dismiss these internal signals and wait for them to go away. This is another form of denial: postponement. Postponers accept that they are beginning a journey into a new phase of life but they arm themselves with the illusion of control. They "decide" that their entry into life's second half will begin at a later date. It will happen when they reach a certain age (usually five to ten years ahead). It will happen when they reach a certain income (usually significantly more than they currently earn). It will happen when their children leave home or when they reach some other landmark that like a mirage always recedes into the distance. They dismiss what is happening inside themselves as premature, as if such feelings were permissible only in "old people." (The title of one comedic book expresses this feeling well: *Who Needs Midlife at Your Age?*)

So if you feel you are in this stage of denial, do not immediately assume it is inappropriate. It does not necessarily mean you are being lazy, or obstinate, or otherwise stuck. In fact, you may be working very hard just trying to resist the change you sense is coming. Resistance may be your way of allowing yourself time to prepare for what lies ahead.

Sadly though, denial is not just the first stage of the quest for some people; it is also the last. They sense the possibility of a journey, usually unconsciously, and postpone it indefinitely. They do not feel prepared for such a quest—and who can blame them? None of us is prepared for the unknown. It is frightening, unpredictable, the first step toward losing control. That it is also the first step toward finding our deeper selves, we do not know. Since it preserves the status quo, the incentives for denying, for waiting appear great. Since it involves upheaval and uncertainty, the incentives for moving forward on our quest appear small. Until this changes, we stand still. Sometimes we even regress. We make one last stand, trying to avoid leaving the familiar land of the young and journeying toward the unknown country ahead.

But the time comes when denial no longer works. Looking back on what she called "the most painful year of my life," Jane Fonda reflected, shortly after her divorce, on the choice she had made between denial and moving forward. "You can either pretend," she said, " . . . avoid [the pain], stay real busy, numb yourself through drink or drugs or promiscuity, use your kids as a battlefield, stay angry. . . . Or you can say, if God is having me feel this much pain and suffering, *there's got to be a reason.*"

Indeed there is a reason. But we cannot find it yet. Only one foot has crossed the threshold. We are not in our old world but we are not in the new world either. We are in a gray area, neither here nor there, living in two worlds at once. In this twilight zone, we experience confusion *(fundere,* "to pour"; *com,* "together"). We are con-fused because two worlds are indeed becoming fused: the personality that in the first half of life we grew accustomed to calling "I" and the self that is trying to break through into consciousness in the second half. Finally when the change becomes so massive that we simply can no longer deny it, we awaken as if from a dream. We accept the truth that we are in fact lost. We don't know what is happening to us. Inexplicable exhaustion, mysterious pain, insomnia, uncontrollable crying, profound dissatisfaction at work—whatever our personal symptom may be, we begin to question ourselves, to seek the wound that is not healed, to identify the source of our pain.

Recalling his own quest, Jung called this his "confrontation with the unconscious." Today many contemporary psychologists are shedding new light on the process and naming its various dimensions. Jungian analyst Murray Stein calls it "the return of the repressed." John Bradshaw calls it the "wounded inner child," who is finally demanding to be heard—and healed. Maureen Murdock, speaking of women, calls it "the descent to the goddess," when a woman "meets the dark mother within and reclaims the discarded parts of herself." Robert Bly, speaking of men, calls it "taking the road of ashes" when we feel that our dreams have turned to dust and we are forced to confront "the long bag we drag behind us." Perhaps Connie Zweig, in her prologue to *Meeting the Shadow*, puts it most directly. "At midlife," she wrote, "I met my devils."

But whatever we name the shadow, the fact is that we can't just talk about our anger, pain or hurt anymore. We are now compelled to live it. We can't observe it; we are it. What in the first half of life we decided was not us now comes back to *become* us. Two selves, the I and the not-I, are now pouring together inside us. The question is: What is this new compound, this new self, that will emerge? And at this point, there is no answer—only confusion. The form that it takes usually depends on what parts of yourself you have neglected or minimized— that is, whatever you are least ready for.

For each of us, the parts of ourselves that we have hidden are unique. But they can be summarized by Jung's deceptively simple concept of the *shadow*. We forge our identities in adolescence by highlighting parts of ourselves that Jung called the *persona*. This is what we show the world, what we claim as "me." We define ourselves by keeping the shadow in the dark. As men define their masculinity, they tend to place their feminine side (or anima) in this shadowy underworld, just as women submerge their masculine side (or animus). What may superficially appear to be a "midlife crisis" is the much deeper, long-term psychological process of our shadow seeking the light.

This process is confusing because at least two voices inside us are now claiming to be the I: the old persona, the identity formed in the first half of our lives that is determined to disown these new elements in our psyches, and the awakening shadow, asking—sometimes demanding—to be let in. As the crack widens between who we are and who we are perceived to be, it can be more than confusing. It can be totally disorienting. If we have had the courage to embrace these new parts of ourselves, the alchemy of the second half can combine these two into a new I that is more whole, more wise and more compassionate. But at this point, all we feel is confused.

In this confused and questioning stage of our journey, the Self is barely glimpsed. At this point, we are divided against ourselves. As Ralph Metzner points out, the metaphors abound. "We may be 'shattered' by an experience; we may think we are 'falling apart'; 'coming apart at the seams,' or 'falling to pieces' . . . feel 'torn' between conflicting demands, be 'crushed' by a rejection, 'crumble' under stress, until (the) mind 'snaps.'" It is a time when we speak forlornly about wishing we were "more together," but it is in reality when we feel—and couples do—"split up."

We are likely at this stage of the quest to describe ourselves as torn between alternatives. We may feel torn *between lovers,* unable to decide which to choose, or even wanting both. We may feel torn *between jobs,* one that offers security and prestige and another that offers challenge and uncertainty. We may feel torn *between lifestyles:* for example, an urban existence with all its rewards and stresses and a new life in a rural area with lower income, fewer options but more beauty and peace. Ultimately, we are feeling torn *between selves:* who we have been versus who we are becoming on the quest.

Now suddenly the structure of our lives does not fit us, but we don't know why. Bargains we made, both professional and personal, may suddenly seem unfair. Relationships we chose may suddenly seem unfulfilling. Signs of aging in our faces suddenly seem prominent. A car, home or community that once brought pleasure may now seem utterly inadequate. A lifestyle that seemed satisfying or at least bearable now grates on our nerves and becomes increasingly intolerable. Goals that seemed so clear may now become complex or blurred. Rewards that before seemed destined to bring pleasure now seem empty, not even worth the effort. A life span that only yesterday seemed long now seems inexplicably abbreviated.

When we are confused, many of us act out in ways that reveal the undeveloped (or what Jung called the inferior) sides of ourselves. These emerging parts of ourselves simply do not fit within the confines of the self we constructed in the first half of our lives. Just as teenagers burst the seams of their old clothes, we are bursting at the seams of our old identities. Who we were and how we lived may now feel like prisons to us. We feel (usually unconsciously) a desperate need to escape. At this critical stage, we may speak of being "trapped" in a marriage, "tied down" to a family or job, "stuck" in a rut, "roped in" by certain constraints, or otherwise held captive.

For some, the jail cell is marriage. They feel they must escape from the deadly limitations of their domestic life. For others, it is their job. They feel suffocated, almost incarcerated, by their employment and harbor desperate fantasies of freeing themselves from the Alcatraz of their office. For still others, it may be a physical addiction or psychological obsession, an invisible set of steel bars that prevents them from becoming a free man or woman. In some cases, the prison may be the body itself and the experience of being overweight, ill, in pain or simply unattractive. Given these various forms of imprisonment our *behavior* at this stage not surprisingly resembles that of actual inmates. We are angry and depressed.

At this point, we feel trapped by everything we have done in the first half of our lives. As one executive at a Chicago advertising agency put it, "My past life had such a grip on me that I felt helpless to change things. I felt trapped in my marriage. I felt trapped in my lifestyle. Trapped in my career. Trapped in the high-rise I lived in. Trapped in the high-rise I worked in. Trapped in my skin." For him, these feelings of imprisonment led quickly to a total life change.

When trapped in confusion, we may actually feel as if we are dying, trying to prop up a corpse—an enterprise obviously destined to failure. We may buy our dying youthful persona a new Porsche. We may give it a young lover. We may change the old persona's mask cosmetically, buy new clothes or change hairstyles. But nothing can hide the stench of a dying body or a dying self. If we do not dare to let go and bury the dead, we will be stuck in confusion and mourning. The ghost of the first half of our life will haunt us.

By no means does everyone who begins the quest continue on it. We may be so terrified by the confusion that we try to turn back. We abort our journey. We may revert to the stage of denial, postponing the quest as long as we can. Or we may attempt to make superficial, cosmetic changes on our old persona while avoiding any profound change. We do not want to face the truth that something is rotten in our own home so we call in the building contractor and interior decorator to do some remodeling. Ignoring the deep structural flaws, we add on a bedroom or a lovely deck or some modern skylights in the hope that, once the remodeling is over, life will feel better. Perhaps for a while it does, but not for long. We cannot half-bury a corpse. We cannot partially emerge from our cocoon. Similarly, we cannot *sort of* begin a quest. Either we do or we don't—and the time to decide has arrived.

There is only one way out, and that is *through.* •

The Liberation of Age

MARIA HARRIS, PH. D.

When we claim our freedom and enter the terrain of age, seeking to learn how to proclaim liberty throughout this land to all its inhabitants, a fresh realization grips us. We are confronting an unknown land, a terra incognita. We're exploring it, even creating it, as we go along. We have only the sketchiest of maps.

At the turn of the twentieth century, women's life expectancy was forty-six. The nuances and the fullness of life past fifty weren't major concerns. Only in the years of our own elderhood has life expectancy changed for women, now hovering close to eighty in the United States. Gail Sheehy now admits that as late as 1976, when she wrote her influential book *Passages*, she rarely touched on life beyond fifty. Not only couldn't she imagine herself this old, but most people she interviewed thought of fifty as over the hill.

But even as attention has turned toward the second half of life, more specifically to the years between fifty and one hundred, certain assumptions about age have precluded our asking the right questions. Until now, inquiry into later life has focused on the 5 percent of the over-sixty-five population in nursing homes or the 5 percent of the aging suffering from Alzheimer's, not on ordinary older people. Inquiry has focused not on age in itself, but on age in relation to youth. In fact, the defining characteristic of age has become no longer being young. Youth provides our lens, our angle of vision. A (if not the) guiding question in age has turned out to be, "What does it mean—physically, sexually, psychologically—to leave youth behind?"

For far too long, we elders have been and done what too many students of aging, developmental theorists, or even gerontologists have told us to be and do. We've been taught that age is equivalent to dealing with sickness, loneliness, impairment and decline; and we've bought into the presumption that these conditions constitute the meaning of age. Even as I began writing this book, part of me was surprised to read responses to my questionnaire revealing alive, vital, involved older women who failed to focus on decline and impairment. I wondered whether they were unusual, and concluded they weren't.

In realizing that, I've discovered something I now want to proclaim. From the rooftop of my soul I want to shout, "We've been asking the wrong questions about age." The central questions most fitting for us aren't how to deal with pathologies or inevitable decline and death, although the last two are relevant because the way of all living things is to decline and die. But that's not the meaning of age. Age's central questions are more along the lines of those in the following exercise.

PROBING A NEW SET OF QUESTIONS

Before we explore some more general responses to new questions about age, pause to listen to your own responses. Begin by attending to your breathing, becoming centered and quiet, perhaps using the mantra, "Listen, listen, listen to your heart" for an initial period of three minutes. Then listen to your heart's probing and respond to the following questions:

1. Now that you have entered the land of aging, what freedoms await you?

2. What are some resistances to age once binding you that are now gone?

3. Complete: For me, the best thing about being free to grow old is. . . .

Share your responses with one other person, or write them in your journal, before considering those that follow.

Each person's answers to these questions will differ to some degree. Following are four of my own responses to question one.

We are free to cherish age. That's a mighty course change in an ageist society, so obsessed with youth it's difficult to find the faces of over-fifty (and certainly over-sixty) women in advertising or playing romantic leads against agemates such as Sean Connery or Robert Redford. For those female leads, Hollywood wants women in their thirties—Michelle Pfeiffer or Demi Moore—saying of still-gorgeous women in their forties, fifties or beyond, "We can't use her. She's over the hill."

But as we bid youth a gentle farewell and embrace the freedoms of age, we know we're not over some hill, but in a lush, green valley, full of fresh growth. So we ask, "What does Hollywood know about it?" and turn to age as a source of truth—and strength and power—in our lives, one to be embraced, not feared. We discover that cherishing and befriending age feels right, fits, the way flats do after decades of high heels.

One simple way to cherish our age is to stop creating false images of ourselves by trying to look younger than we are, to abandon "age passing" in favor of proudly exhibiting our actual years. Some of us may add back the years we knocked off our age when we turned fifty; others may forgo makeup. At fifty-eight, I stopped coloring my hair and began greeting the now silver-haired me when I looked in the mirror. When I did, my eyes revealed an older woman at peace with herself and in tune with her inner elder.

Embracing honesty regarding our physical selves allows us to pierce the surface and reach our deeper spiritual selves. Releasing superficial obsessions that may constrict us, we become alert to interior capacities ripe for development, including personal power, honest sexuality and deep contemplation. The fullness of years that "Jubilee" celebrates becomes the basis for a genuinely new spirituality that liberates us even further into wisdom.

We are free to be wise. Sometimes, when I end a workshop, I go around the room and ask women to answer the question, "Who are you becoming?" Last week, when I did that, Alla, in her late fifties, answered, "I'm becoming a wise woman," reminding all of us present that that could be true for us, too.

Becoming wise, like becoming free, takes a long time. Wisdom is a kind of knowledge based on intuition, but the intuition, in turn, comes from living and being in touch with the range of experience long life offers. It's cumulative. But it's physical, too, centered in the body and in blood, birth and pain. It involves acting on hunches, especially the hunch that sometimes the risky action is the right one, the desperate move the only possibility.

Genuine wisdom involves learning from the wisdoms of other forgotten or overlooked people, out of a humility that knows none of us has all the answers. It means learning from the blind how to trust our own fingertips, from women who use wheelchairs how to travel up the ramp, from women of color how to challenge systems that enchain us.

But wisdom also involves admitting that we can make terrible mistakes, have huge gaps in our understanding and always retain the capacity for evil. Whenever I read the entire twenty-fifth chapter of Leviticus, I'm reminded of this. For despite the extraordinary wisdom of Jubilee, there's a dreadful fault line crossing it: the passage that allows some slaves to remain in bondage, as long as they aren't "our" people.

> *As for the male and female slaves whom you may have, it is from the nations around you that you may acquire male and female slaves. You may also acquire them from among the aliens residing with you and from their families that are with you, who have been born in your land and they may be your property. You may keep them as a possession for your children after you, for them to inherit as property. These you may treat as slaves, but as for your fellow Israelites, no one shall rule over the other with harshness. (Lev. 25:44-46)*

I used to be terribly shocked by that, wondering how the first Jubilee people could be so unseeing. I thought of these lines as a scar, a fissure of evil, flawing the wholeness of Jubilee. I still do. But I also suspect that this passage, repudiated in modern times so that the teaching and practice of Jubilee today does extend to enslaved persons, was left there to remind me of terrible omissions in my own life, places of evil I am capable of ignoring.

We are free to let go. A central and recurring theme in Western mystical tradition is detachment, which speaks to the promise of letting go, release and redemption. Although some interpret it as cool distancing from a situation or self-absorbed withdrawal from working toward justice, it is actually a facet of liberation.

Complementing this tradition, the *Bhagavad-Gita* of Hinduism teaches that the detached person is active, but that being active differs here from its usual meaning. A person now acts without looking for the fruits of her actions. Whatever we are called to do or are able to do is now done for its own sake, not for the sake of results or rewards. And although such an attitude doesn't necessarily depend on age, it characterizes later years more than it does youth.

Expressing her own growing detachment, fifty-year-old Anna Mae, who describes herself as "a youngster beginning old age," writes that as she ages, she experiences the power of "a growing freedom and urgency to say what I care about most deeply," coupled with "the desire and will to simplify my life of material and emotional things." The result of that, she adds, is the ability to give "time and space to friends, travel and political involvement." For her, letting go of the habit of saying what's expected and distancing herself from material things enrich her growing into age.

My husband, Gabriel, is a strikingly detached person, a man who is very hard to buy gifts for because "things" don't possess him. A mere fifty-eight, he says detachment means you're willing to wait on life if you must, determined and patient enough to stay at what you feel called to do. Whether your work is designing a cathedral, mopping floors, governing a nation or lying flat on your back in pain, "the human vocation is to stay at our post and do the best we can. And when we've done that," he surmises, the last element in detachment—as it is in the last part of life—is to take no credit but instead "return glory to the Source of all gifts."

We are free to be mature, moral agents. Embracing age, wisdom and detachment leads to a sense of ourselves as mature—grownups at last; as moral—spiritual beings who believe goodness and creativity must triumph over evil and decay; and as agents—human actors who have given up roles such as pretender, little-girl-lost or earth-mother-who-can-fix-all-ills simply to be what we are: human.

Aging means living in the interstices of paradoxes: doing and not-doing, laughing and weeping, living and dying. Freeing ourselves from youth, superficial knowledge and acquisitiveness liberates us to give ourselves to the world. We may have already learned the wonder in a life of continuing thresholds and the quiet grounding achieved when we take time for the hallowing that prepares us for liberation. Now it is time to learn the necessity of the ritual act of proclaiming freedom, one that may begin with our own lives but eventually extends beyond our own personal boundaries.

JUBILEE, A RELATIONAL SPIRITUALITY

It would be a grave error to interpret Jubilee as "proclaiming liberty" simply for ourselves. For those two words are followed by seven more: "throughout the land to all its inhabitants." Claiming personal liberty goes hand in hand with proclaiming it for others. This Jubilee ritual makes it very clear that we who would live its spirituality must reach out beyond ourselves to anyone or anything existing in a condition of bondage, servitude or imprisonment.

An early example of this interpretation occurs in a reading from the Hebrew Bible clearly based on Leviticus. In chapter sixty-one of Isaiah, in a passage beloved to those of many religions and even those of no religion, the prophet-poet writes:

> *The spirit of God is upon me because that God has anointed me; has sent me to bring good news to the oppressed, to bind up the brokenhearted, to proclaim liberty to the captives and release to prisoners, and to proclaim the year of God's favor.*

That "year of God's favor" is the Jubilee year, and here Isaiah affirms that Jubilee prescribes a connected, social and proactive spirituality. The liberty and freedom I want for myself as a Jubilee woman must be earned by doing things that contribute to the freedom of others, things as simple as praying for their freedom and as complicated as joining the Peace Corps, the way Lillian Carter did at sixty-eight. Such activity is a sign the Spirit is upon me also.

The breadth of Jubilee liberty is reiterated in the New Testament in the gospel of Luke. When Jesus returns to Nazareth, where he was raised ("Each of you shall return to your place and to your people, where you were brought up"), and goes to the synagogue to speak to his neighbors, he asks for the scroll containing the book of Isaiah and reads the passage quoted above. Then he adds, referring to Jubilee's relevance to the people gathered in the synagogue, "Today, this scripture is fulfilled in your hearing." The promise of Jubilee cannot be fulfilled in isolation, but only as part of a community.

This meaning of Jubilee as the proclamation of liberty beyond ourselves is alive in modern times. In 1991, for example, missionaries from Panama asked the United States and the World Bank to declare a year of Jubilee in 1992, the five-hundredth anniversary of the voyages of Columbus. But they didn't ask it for themselves. They requested it instead for Central America's poor African American and indigenous peoples, overburdened by crushing and exorbitant debts and referred to globally, as if it were their only identity, as debtor nations. The missionaries saw the relevance of release, forgiveness and amnesty, both beyond themselves and beyond biblical times.

In the United States, the proclamation of liberation from bondage compels us to consider our prisons. We are remarkably ignorant of women's prisons, for example, and the toll prison takes on mothers and children. Unlike in the Bible, where prisoners are not criminals or convicts but prisoners of war, captives, hostages or victims of government oppression, our prisons are too often places of warehousing for many nonviolent offenders who have broken civil laws and who might be better sentenced to community service. Prisons neither rehabilitate nor offer new beginnings.

"Lila served two years for lying about a $167 welfare check. She was offered one year if she would plea-bargain, but she refused, went to trial and got two years," wrote one aging woman prisoner, reporting on this system. Lila still insists she never cashed that check, the reporter continues. "I think it was my cousin done it, but I didn't get that money." Even worse, when her sentence is finished, Lila will still know nothing of budgeting her welfare check, will still not know how to read and write.

The Jubilee woman who tells Lila's story was also an inmate. Jean Harris was finally released in 1993 after serving thirteen years and is now in her seventies. A graduate of both Smith College and New York's Bedford Hills Correctional Facility for Women, she wryly shares Lila's plight with the rest of us, pointing out that we all know people who take $167 tax deductions at lunch and asking whether as taxpayers we have more reason to pay for those lunches than for Lila's check, or Lila's future. In her own Jubilee Time, Jean Harris is devoting herself to women's prison reform and to mothers in prison and their children, modeling the kind of complete Jubilee spirituality to which all of us are called.•

The Challenges of Aging

KATHLEEN WALL, PH. D.
AND GARY FERGUSON

In cultures other than our own, past and present, elders were respected as mediators between the realms of the spirit world and everyday life here on earth. Unlike our society, which tends to devalue age, these cultures value elders because they have the wisdom only age can bring, born from surviving the trials of youth, young adulthood and middle age.

This isn't to suggest that having wrestled with the issues of middle age, we can then coast through the next thirty years in a state of bliss. Our later years have their own tasks or callings. In the last years of life, as Daniel Levinson points out, we have four clear challenges to confront: dealing with loss, coming to terms with ourselves, "generativity" and rediscovering our innocence. It's the reconciliation of these issues that allows people eventually to integrate all the parts of their psyche into a shining whole, to at long last feel as though they are truly living well with the world.

THE FIRST CALLING: DEALING WITH LOSS

Of all the challenges in our later years, none is more demanding, or potentially more significant, than the need to learn to manage loss. As we age, we have to reckon with a decline of health and physical vitality. As we retire from work, we must come to terms with the loss of status and power and maybe even wealth—all of which are highly valued by our culture. This is also the time of course when we're most likely to lose friends and relatives to death. No wonder so many people shake their heads and say, "It's hell to grow old." And yet recent research by Juan Pascual-Leone suggests that mastering the ability to cope with loss in later years may be the key to forging what is commonly referred to as wisdom.

A couple of years ago, Jane, an energetic, intelligent woman in her early sixties, had been suffering with a bad back for nearly six months. She'd gone to a trusted doctor for advice but he could find no organic reason for the problem.

Finally, she and Kathleen decided to try a Gestalt exercise. In a state of quiet, calm reflection, Jane asked her back pain directly what it was there for. As is often the case with such explorations, at first Jane found it difficult to focus; whenever she felt close to getting an answer, some kind of mental or emotional distraction would arise. But she stuck with it and by the third attempt, as she was actually encouraging the pain to intensify—to identify itself—she heard a tiny voice from within.

"Get off my back" were the first words Jane picked up on. "Let life flow. Don't take on so many burdens. Take care of me now so I can be strong again." With new resolve, Jane declared out loud her intention to find ways to put what her pain had told her into practice. This kind of verbal declaration of intent, by the way, is a key part of most rituals. Making such an announcement, especially with another person present, is a wonderful way to anchor your resolve.

First Jane joined a local swimming club, working with an instructor to build a low-stress exercise routine to help strengthen her lower back. Next she found a yoga class that seemed to open her not only to new physical experiences but to spiritual ones as well. In time Jane came to treat these weekly yoga sessions as ritual; just the act of dressing for class for example became a kind of "threshold activity" that quieted her and put her into a state of heightened readiness. By the time the actual exercises began, she was fully able to focus on healing, on making a space for that quiet voice within. "The more I began to see yoga as a healing rite," says Jane, "the more powerful the experience became. At first I wore the same exercise clothes I'd had for years. But then one day I went out and bought a new outfit—a green one—the color of healing. Then on days that I had yoga, I committed to eating only healthy foods—grains, vegetables, yogurt, things like that."

Over time, the yoga ritual became the spark that would light a larger flame of desire for well-being. Today Jane is almost completely without pain. Even more important, she learned how to turn the anguish of a loss—in this case a loss of health—into the kind of inspiration needed to change her entire life. "Find the courage to walk through the cloud," she likes to say, "and you *will* uncover the silver lining."

A somewhat similar situation arose for Ron Horton at a time when he was leading an extremely hectic life as an upper-level advertising executive with a small agency in New York. Although he had never experienced any serious health problems, at age fifty-nine Ron suffered a serious heart attack. Lying at home recuperating, still shaken from his brush with death, Ron began to think hard about his priorities. About a month after his return from the hospital, Ron asked his wife if she would drop him off for a week alone at the family cabin in the Berkshires. It was there, he explained to her, in the peace and quiet of nature that he thought he'd be able to sort out his next move. This was very much a ritual for Ron. He was clearly using exclusive time and exclusive space; there was a fresh, hopeful feeling, he says, in the going away from familiar surroundings. Each day at the cabin, Ron rose at dawn to do the walking his doctor had prescribed. Though he did pack in a few food treats, by and large he existed on heart-healthy cooking. Each evening he wrote in a journal, trying to clarify his priorities in life. Largely as a result of this journaling, Ron reconnected with an old dream he'd had of owning a bookstore, a desire that again seemed to hold special promise and appeal. By the end of the week, he was able to write down several specific steps he could use to build a more balanced and integrated life.

After discussing his plan at length with his family, Ron sat down with his partners at work; happily, they were sympathetic to his need to shed some responsibilities and so worked with him to structure a three-day week. On the evening of the first day he returned to the office, Ron's family threw a surprise party for him. There were balloons, presents, even a cake. And hanging on the dining-room wall was a giant poster made by his family. *The New You!* it said with a wonderful caricature of Ron, flexing his muscles in a bright red sweat suit. "It's still a real effort at times not to turn the things that are supposed to add balance to my life—things like exercise—into some kind of competition," Ron confesses. "But I'm getting there. It takes a long time to change a half-century of habit."

THE SECOND CALLING:
CONFRONTING THE PERSON IN THE MIRROR

A great many myths speak to our need to come to terms with those parts of ourselves we find particularly difficult to acknowledge, the traits we're not particularly proud of. Psychoanalyst Carl Jung talked about this aspect of life in terms of a person's "shadow side," that which lurks beneath the surface, unseen and untended to. Kathleen had a fifty-five-year-old client named Sue, who works as a lawyer in a large San Francisco law firm. When Sue first came to see Kathleen, she was struggling against an old, fierce commitment to being task oriented. She had always strived hard but as of late that striving had left her feeling less and less in touch with a growing need for healthy relationship. At her worst, Sue would bark orders to her husband or chastise her secretary if the woman wasn't meeting her tough performance standards. "Sometimes I get this horrible flash," Sue confided. "There I am standing in my well-ordered world, all alone. Alone because no one can stand being close to me."

One day in her office, Kathleen suggested that Sue do an exercise called the Shadow, which can be difficult at first. This really isn't surprising, considering that most of us have spent a significant portion of our lives trying to ignore or suppress the very thing this exercise is designed to bring forth. After Sue put herself into a relaxed state, Kathleen asked her to let an image of her shadow side begin to emerge. In time she perceived a large, dragon-like creature, which she then tried to draw as best she could using colored markers. Then she went back into a quiet state and asked this "taskmaster," as she called it, what it wanted. Why was it here? How was it protecting her?

It didn't take long for the taskmaster to answer. "If you don't accomplish, you won't be recognized," it said. As she began exploring the source of this advice, Sue came to realize that this was a version of something that her mother used to say to her when she was young. "You can't expect a man to support you," she was told. "You can't trust others to do anything for you. Earn your worth." The positive side to this advice was that it had allowed Sue to lead a life of extraordinary accomplishment. She was able to set goals and then had the discipline to work until she achieved them. But in later life external achievement meant less than it used to; now Sue felt the need to be more empathetic, to learn to be more sensitive and understanding to the people around her.

In the next session, Sue reconnected with her taskmaster, first by spending a few minutes simply looking at her drawing of the dragon and then by re-entering a quiet state. This time though she approached the taskmaster with gratitude; in fact, she thanked it out loud for all it had done for her. She then went on to explain to the taskmaster that the time had come for it to change into something different, that she wanted to transform her drive for success into a commitment to help others. This part of Sue's visualization took a great deal of patience and effort but she continued to work on her own with it several times a week for a couple of months. A year later, Sue retired from her job as a lawyer and began spending more and more time with her two grandnieces.

Soon thereafter she got the idea to set up a local foster grandparent program that continues to do well today.

These inner explorations are not casual exercises but serious rituals. The fact that Sue came to Kathleen's office every week with the express purpose of working on this issue served as a way to thread together her efforts in exclusive time and exclusive space—two key elements of ritual. If you're not working with a therapist, you might consider doing these activities outside your normal environment, perhaps at a friend's house or a hotel, at a campground or a rental cabin.

What symbolic gestures could you use to help transform your shadow into something new, something more appropriate to your life? For example, a rope made into a noose, to symbolize how you have been choking your creative side for fear of rejection, could be fashioned into a hanger for growing a potted plant. A black blindfold, representing an unwillingness to discuss important issues with your significant other, could be bleached white and turned into a talking staff. One woman used a bag of garbage—meant to signify a childhood that had been deadened by abuse—composted it and then used it to grow a small garden. The point of such symbolic action is to communicate to the deeper psyche your desire to transform the angst of a particular problem into the kind of energy needed for new growth. The more people manage to convey desires to their subconscious—which, by the way, is far more versed in symbolism than in words—the more likely it is that aspiration will one day sprout into reality.

THE THIRD CALLING: GENERATIVITY

The last decades of life are about "generativity," which refers to the need to be involved with something larger than yourself—to use such qualities as kindness and compassion to help build bridges of hope for future generations. We see it in the case of Sue, the former career woman who established a foster grandparent program because she wanted to help heal the age divisions in our culture. Other people express their generativity by teaching literacy classes, by becoming mentors for young people going into business, by working on environmental projects, or by volunteering, as Jimmy Carter did, to help build affordable housing for the poor.

The real choice in our later years, said psychoanalyst Erik Erikson, is between being generative and being in despair. We've all known people who seem to lose their zest for life as they grow older, who focus on their aches and pains until they sink into a kind of gloomy despondency. The antidote for such hopelessness is to share something of your higher self with others. What would you like to give to the world? What kind of celebration of life can you offer to those who will follow in the years to come?

THE FOURTH CALLING: THE REDISCOVERY OF INNOCENCE

In China when a man reaches the age of retirement, he dons a red vest. This is meant as a badge of honor, an announcement of his high status in the culture. One of the key effects of this ritual garment is a sign that the man has released his need to behave in a socially sanctioned manner. He is emancipated, free to act more in accordance with his heart than his head. It's a time for living in the land of myth and mystery, a time to build bridges back to the dreams and ideals of his youth.

Another event that has long been considered a catalyst for recapturing the power of the human spirit is menopause. This isn't to suggest that menopause itself is some kind of lark; indeed, for some women it is a painful, extremely unsettling time. But menopause can be thought of as the event that frees a woman to address other issues considered critical to the culture. Rather than tending to the maintenance tasks of everyday living, she can instead direct her powers to providing a base of wisdom and counsel for the society at large. It is a time for a woman to regain (or in some cases to gain for the first time) the sense that her life is really hers, that she is acting out of her own personhood and not just reacting to the demands of others.

In an attempt to reconnect with the power held not so much in menopause itself but in the years that follow, women are crafting new versions of an old ceremony known as croning, a way of welcoming the wisdom of later life. The word *crone*, by the way, which has suffered questionable press for some eight hundred years, is again being placed in a more positive light. The spirit of the crone or wise woman has in fact been known by many names, depending on the culture. The dancing force, the Spider Woman, the mist being and the wild woman are just a few. No matter what you call her though, her essence remains the same. She is perhaps nowhere better described than by Clarissa Pinkola Estes in her fine book, *Women Who Run with the Wolves*. Writing about the essence of the wild woman, Pinkola Estes says:

She is intuition, she is far-seer, she is deep listener, she is loyal heart. She encourages humans to remain multilingual; fluent in the languages of dreams, passion and poetry. She whispers from night dreams, she leaves behind on the terrain of a woman's soul a coarse hair and muddy footprints. . . . She has been lost and half forgotten for a long, long time. She is the source, the light, the night, the dark and daybreak. She is the smell of good mud and the back leg of the fox. The birds which tell us secrets belong to her. She is the voice that says "This way, this way."

CARRYING RITUALS TO LOVED ONES

As our friends and loved ones get older, of course, there is the increased chance that they will need either short-term or extended medical care in hospitals or nursing facilities. Facing health problems is a difficult proposition; and facing them outside of our normal surroundings, far from the comfort of familiar people, sights, sounds and smells makes the task all the more unsettling. Whenever possible, carrying rituals, ceremonies or celebrations to a bedridden loved one is a powerful act. Not only do rituals offer opportunities to reconnect with the values and emotions that bring us joy and comfort, but they reaffirm to an ill person that he or she is still a valued part of the family system—not merely a spectator of life but a participant.

At sixty-five, Martha Sanderling, suffering from cancer, has been in an extended-care facility for two months. While most of her immediate family—two sons and their wives, and three grandchildren—live close by and can see her on a regular basis, her absence from the household has been a terrible loss for everyone. "She's the one who picks the rest of us up when we're down," says her daughter-in-law Julie. "She has the kind of faith that moves mountains." When it came time for Steve and Julie's ten-month-old baby to be baptized, they decided that Martha, though bedridden, should be a part of the event. "Sharing it after the fact with photos just didn't seem good enough," explains Steve. "We wanted her right there in the middle of it."

Permission was granted by the director of the nursing home for the family's parish priest to perform the baptism ceremony in Martha's room. All the members of the immediate family were there as well as several close friends. A floor nurse stood by during the ceremony, in case Martha required any special medical attention. "Seeing the look in her eyes was worth every bit of effort it took to arrange it," says Martha's other son, Jeff. "After the ceremony we placed the baby in her arms and she got this wonderful smile on her face. While the rest of us were standing around talking, I noticed she was looking around the room at each of us, one by one. It was like she was taking stock of all the people she loved."

A wonderful story is told about the Roman statesman Cato, who lived in the years 234–149 B.C. At age eighty with no prior exposure to other languages, Cato set about the monumental task of becoming fluent in Greek. His friends were incredulous. "How can you embark on such a lengthy course of study at your age?" they asked. "It's simple," Cato is said to have replied. "This is the youngest age I have left."•

Creativity and Aging

R O L L O M A Y

In my book *The Courage to Create*, I tried to make the point that all of us have the potential to be creative. I think the later years ought to be the time when we enjoy the creativity that we have. I've always felt that asking people if they are creative or not is a foolish question. The question really ought to be put this way: What is it that you make? What is it that you do? When we think in those terms, then all of us are creative—we all do things, make things. The problem isn't that all of us aren't creative but that some of us are using our creativity more than others. Some of us have developed the courage to use what we have, while others have not. And the stumbling block is fear, simply fear. Let's face it, creative tasks are scary. It takes a throwing of one's self into it. When you throw yourself into something completely, you run the risk of failure. You are alone in the process, and this requires solitude and courage.

One of the problems of living creatively in late life is that it gets harder as you grow old. Thomas Mann once said that writing is something that becomes more difficult the more you do it. This is because one's idea of what's acceptable and what's not becomes more rarefied when one gets older. You have higher standards, you might say. So you have to work harder and harder the older you get, which is the exact opposite of what we've planned for.

But I feel very strongly that creativity keeps us fresh, even though it requires great discipline and struggle. Fresh is the word I use, not young. I don't see becoming young as desirable at all, because young people often don't have the creativity that we have as we grow older. Creativity keeps us fresh; it keeps us alive, keeps us moving forward. You are never fully satisfied; you are always working and reworking your art, your book, your garden, whatever. I don't buy this stuff at all about youth being the happy time. My youth was not, and I don't think other people's youths were so great either. I think the older we get, the fresher we ought to get. We face our fears. We tackle them head on. We have the courage to create.

People in their eighties I've talked with, like B. F. Skinner or Hannah Tillich, have told me that they have only two hours a day in which they can work creatively. The rest of the day they devote to busy work. So you have to plan your days properly and guard your working time—your prime time—very carefully. I stay in my studio each day for four hours, but the last hour and a half isn't worth very much. It was hard for me to accept but what can I do? All I can do is make the most of the creative time I've got. So for two and a half hours I'm moving marvelously; the rest of the time I'm simply fiddling around. But I find joy in fiddling too. I have to accept the fact that I'm not a god. I have to accept my destiny. I have to accept the fact that I can only do creative work for a few hours a day, but that doesn't diminish one iota the joy I get from those two hours. I don't believe in happiness, but I do believe in joy.

I don't seek happiness particularly, but I do seek joy. Joy is the feeling of exhilaration, the buoyancy that comes from creating something you are pleased with. When you are in a state of joy, you don't feel like eating and you don't feel like sex—all of these are put aside and you are in a state of complete excitement. Joy is not limited to the young; it is there for all of us.

As I have said many times over the years, all of us have to take responsibility for our lives. If we want to live joyful lives, we've got to work at it. When I contracted tuberculosis as a young man, I gave myself over to the physicians, did everything they told me to, but I wasn't getting any better. The X rays each month looked worse and worse. Then I realized that I've got to take responsibility for my recovery, that I'm the one who can tell whether I'm getting better or not, whether I'm energetic or whether I need to rest. I began to listen to my body and slowly I got better. I was very poor then; we had three children, and my wife and I had no money. I borrowed whatever I could from my friends, and it was such that I never got out of debt until I was fifty years old. But I still think that period of tuberculosis was the single most important experience in my life. I learned then that not only was I responsible for the disease, but I could stand up, I could fight back, I could creatively tackle my problem.

To this day I believe strongly that overcoming disease is a creative process. One of my lungs from the tuberculosis never came back fully but I now ride my bike twenty-four miles a week, I swim and I climb trees. I had to learn that health is not something that is given to you; it is something you have to achieve, which is why I see it as a creative process. You must learn to be sensitive to your strength, about when you need rest, what you can do, what you can't do, how you must exercise. All of these things are creative processes.

Now I watch my health very closely. For one thing, I meditate. I eat with care. I watch my cholesterol. I make sure that I sleep at least seven and a half hours a night, and I always take a half-hour nap after every lunch. If I stopped these things I would, in two or three months, be a wreck. Those things are necessary for the life I love.

I believe that one lives as long as one has something to contribute. All the creative people that I've known have died once they stopped being creative. Now, I may have the cart before the horse there—they may have stopped their creativity because they sensed that something was being blocked—but I have this prejudice that we live so long as we have something important to say. Once we've said it, we die. Kierkegaard died in his middle forties, but he said what he needed to say. Pascal died in his late fifties, but he said what he needed to say. So I don't know that time is so crucial in this matter of death. Does it make a difference whether you die in your thirties or in your eighties? It seems to me there is an element of eternity and you ought to judge these things not by the number of years somebody lived but by the concept of eternity. One can live an eternal life at thirty or one can live such a life and die at ninety. I hope, incidentally, that I don't get too old. I hope I will die with a heart attack, say, in my late eighties. I'd like to just faint and go out. I don't dread it at all. What there is, if anything, after death I don't know.

One of the saddest things about growing old in America is that we don't honor the old at all. We don't revere older people nearly as much in this society as Indians, Native Americans, other societies have done. Greek society, for example, revered the old. Now, I think this is a sign of the decadence of our age, that we no longer value, no longer see the contribution of, older people. We worship youth, and I think that is the craziest thing I ever heard of. I never want to live my youth over again, and I never met anyone who really did. It's just a figment of one's imagination. But I think that our civilization is now going through a radical decadence and the real question will be, will there be a renaissance or will we blow ourselves up?

I really think creativity is the answer to aging, and by creativity I mean listening to one's own inner voice, to one's own ideas, to one's own aspirations. It may be social work. It may be gardening. It may be building. But it must be something fresh, something new, some idea that takes fire—this is what I'd like to see among older people. When Matisse was in bed and couldn't get up the last year of his life, he found something creative to do. He got himself a pair of scissors and made all these cutouts in paper, and they are fantastically beautiful. I love them very much. I have a reproduction of one in my office, leaning up against one of the walls to remind me of what old people can do in their last years.

When I die, I will surely be unhappy that I haven't done as much reading of Greek mythology as I would have liked. I get so involved when I'm reading Greek myths that I move very, very slowly. I don't turn many pages, but it's a wonderful joy to me. Now, that is what age ought to do for us. Sure, you don't remember names so well, you can't run this or that marathon, your joints are stiffer. . . . All this is certainly true. But at the same time, you have a lot of experience you can call upon, you have a kind of wisdom that leaves out the details and simply goes straight for the important things. This is the meaning of the wisdom of the ages. •

Taking Risks

A N D R E A   S U S A N   G L A S S

I suppose I always had a vague feeling that I would be a late bloomer—a Grandma Moses—because I never knew what I wanted to be when I grew up. Instead of taking clues from the creative ventures that dotted my youth—writing poetry and music, singing, arts and crafts—I bought into the myth of appropriate roles for women of my generation. I would get my teaching credential (because "you can always go back to teaching," my mother advised), get married and raise 2.3 children in a nice house in the suburbs!

In my senior year of college, when I was a student teacher and had my first contact with kids, I discovered I had no rapport with children. I did get married, though never had any children, and I settled into a ho-hum life living in the suburbs, working in an office. I never loved the work, but was a natural organizer, needed the income and didn't think I had any "real" talents.

When my husband decided to go into the retail business, I joined him. After our divorce, I remained in retailing for several more years as I got to use my organizational skills as well as some creativity.

Several years into my second marriage, the next significant career change occurred for me. At the same time my husband and I realized our marriage was on the rocks, I quit my last retail position, exasperated by the dictates and limitations of higher-ups. My creative voice would be stifled no longer. My husband left because he had no intention of supporting me while I tried to find myself. He didn't even know I was lost!

One thing was clear. I would never work for anyone again. I was an artist and an entrepreneur at heart, but alas not a big risk taker. (Although marrying twice was a big risk!) It didn't take long for my now-freed creativity to rear its head—as a "professional organizer."

I organized everything from garages to closets, enjoying the creativity, variety and challenge in each new project. One time, an organizing client needed some bookkeeping done. I said I would do it, and then took a cram course over one weekend with my mother, the bookkeeper. Now that I did bookkeeping, that part of my business began to build as my organizing business declined. It seemed more people had chaos around their finances than their papers. I looked at both as helping people organize their lives, since metaphysically I believed "as within, so without" and vice versa. However, my life was not in such great order, being twice divorced, working back in the office structure and not knowing what I wanted to be when I grew up.

My bookkeeping clients became regulars, which was steady income, but I had again given up my creative voice. About three years ago, I took a part-time job doing office work for my friend's roommate. At first it wasn't too bad, since I worked alone out of his home, made personal phone calls and used the computer and laser printer for some writing I was doing. I had fallen into the security trap as I settled into yet another office job. In order to protect what little was left of my creative voice, I took writing classes. (All through the years I had been a perennial student, taking classes in personal growth, self-esteem, setting goals, business, writing and other subjects of fleeting interest.) As my youthful flair for writing rekindled, wonder of wonder, I started selling articles locally.

When we moved to a real office and grew to fifteen employees, my boss became intolerable, and I barely tolerated it. I hung on for security, though every morning's drive was sheer agony. Several people, including my boss, told me I'd never make it as a writer, and I believed them. Fortunately my parents backed me 100 percent, even helping me out financially, and I usually had a writing group for support.

But the faucet was turned on, and the words and ideas poured out of me in a constant stream. I knew this was what I wanted, what I truly loved. Earlier this year, in a bold move that I imagine came from a combination of anger and frustration, I quit my job. Somehow, my boss talked me into reducing my hours instead of quitting, reminding me that it's tough out there as a writer.

However, when I made my decision to quit, something shifted. I had been visualizing, affirming, imagining and believing that in spite of the odds, I would succeed as a writer, that this was what God had intended for me. I hadn't heard God's voice all that much, because I was too busy "doing" to be still and listen. But I believed that when I discovered what I loved and set my intention to succeed, the universe would open doors. Within a week, I signed my first contract with a literary agent. After years of half-heartedly submitting manuscripts to agents and publishers and collecting a stack of rejections, I got a "Yes!"

A few months later, I quit my job again. This time I meant it—I would never again do work I dislike for someone I don't respect. I didn't know how the money would come, but I knew it would. I knew what I wanted. This time my boss let me go. He knew I meant it. Whatever it was that happened when I made any declaration happened again. Within a few days I got two editing jobs—I now had a way to earn money doing what I loved as I waited for my book deals to close, and for articles to be published. (I still have some long-term bookkeeping clients, so I feel confident I will meet my expenses.)

I expect to be a full-time, self-supporting writer within a year. I know now this is my gift. Yet I never would have discovered it if I hadn't kept taking risks, baby steps though they were, and said "no" to what I didn't want and "yes" to what I wanted. Rediscovering in adulthood the natural talents of my youth has been a miracle for me.•

THE LIBERATION OF AGE

Soul Practice

QUESTIONS

1. What if you were free to cherish, rather than dread, your aging? What would that free you to become and do?
2. Ask yourself Maria Harris's three questions. Make sure to become quiet first, and centered in your own heart:
   Now that you have entered the land of aging, what freedoms await you?
   What are some resistances to age once binding you that are now gone?
   Complete: For me, the best thing about growing old is. . . .
   If you are not yet in the second half of life, imagine yourself to be, and answer the questions.
3. What does it mean to you to embrace wisdom, detachment and mature morality?
4. Contemplate Easwaran's "People who identify themselves with their body often find the latter half of life a burden. Only when you learn to identify yourself with the Self will the latter half of life become a great blessing." What does this mean to you?
5. What are the losses you must acknowledge in your own life as an aging person?
6. As an elder, someone whom in other cultures would be honored for what they had to give back to the culture, what do you have that you can give to your community? What if your community really needed your wisdom and your gifts? How can you put them to use?
7. What parts of yourself have gone unacknowledged or underused in the first half of your life? How may you acknowledge them now, and welcome them into your life?
8. If the second half of life could be thought of and approached as a sacred quest, what might you be questing for?
9. How is creativity seeking to be expressed in your life?

PRACTICES

1. Think of someone you admire who has aged powerfully and gracefully. This person can be a relative, a famous person or a person in literature or the movies. Close your eyes, breathe and relax. Imagine them standing before you, ready to answer any questions you might have about aging powerfully and richly. What would you like to ask them? Imagine asking them. Listen deeply for their responses. When you are done, thank them and gently open your eyes. Record any answers you may have received.
2. If you are not an elder, think of someone in your neighborhood or family or community who is. How may you honor them? You also might interview them about their lives. Ask them what they have learned, what advice they have to give others. They will feel listened to and acknowledged, and you may gain a great deal of wisdom in the process.

7

The Final Transition

We would recognize death more easily if we were less afraid. Paradoxically, if we could accept the inevitability of death, we would value more the preciousness of life. Death lives in our presence, and its occurrence generally brings forth waves of love. Family members reunite and forgive past deeds. Mourners awaken to their own mortality and make lifestyle changes so that they can live with more health, love and meaning.

This chapter explores the benefits of living with an ongoing awareness of death and the healing that death often brings.

IF I HAD ONLY

When I was young and free and my imagination had no limits, I dreamed of changing the world. As I grew older and wiser, I discovered the world would not change, so I shortened my sights somewhat and decided to change only my country.

But it, too, seemed immovable.

As I grew into my twilight years, in one last desperate attempt, I settled for changing only my family, those closest to me, but alas, they would have none of it.

And now as I lie on my deathbed, I suddenly realize: If I had only changed my self first, then by example I would have changed my family.

From their inspiration and encouragement, I would then have been able to better my country and, who knows, I may have even changed the world. These words were written on the tomb in the crypts of Westminister Abbey.

—Virginia Satir

A Year to Live

AN INTERVIEW WITH STEPHEN LEVINE

Your book, *A Year to Live*, is a loving guide for profound healing. Through your own preparations for death, you have given us a year-long program to help us learn to fully live before we die. We are indebted to you and your wife Ondrea's willingness to live deeply into your beingness and to be guides for those on similar paths.

PERSONAL TRANSFORMATION: *What prompted you to live as if you had one year to live, imagining that you would die at the end of the year?*

STEPHEN LEVINE: I was fifty-eight-years-old when I began the year-long experiment. When the Dalai Lama was fifty-eight-years-old, a reporter asked him what he was going to do next with his life. He answered that he was going to prepare for death. The interviewer inquired about his health, and the Dalai Lama replied that he wasn't sick, but that his body was impermanent. When I heard about that conversation, I thought that preparing for death was the natural thing to do.

PT: *How did the one-year-to-live experiment impact your life?*

SL: The year-to-live offered extraordinary insights into the places where I had been numb, and into the still small voice within, which became more pronounced. But the most profound influence was an increase in courage. When you have one year left, fear makes you too small. You better live that life that you're going to be so unhappy to think you are leaving. In twenty years of being with people dying, my wife Ondrea and I have seen miraculous things happen. Relationships untouched for twenty-five years blossom into something you wonder how that person could have lived without. What happens when we find out we only have one year to live? When we know we can't be hurt anymore, that we might die, we feel safe. Why should knowing that we are going to die make us feel safe? It makes us feel unsafe too, but there is this place inside of us that feels safe, that allows us to see what holds back from life, yet says it hates to lose life. How much life we trade off. We trade off more life after we are born than we do after we die.

PT: *You said that during that year you wanted to complete your birth. What do you mean?*

SL: Most people live with one foot in the womb, hopping around the world, never quite coming out. Completing our birth is a process of becoming grounded, putting both feet on the ground. It is taking responsibility for being born, but not responsibility as blame. People say they are responsible for their illness. We are not responsible *for* our illness, we are responsible *to* our illness. We are not responsible *for* our incarnation, we are responsible *to* our incarnation.

Human beings, when not stressed, are utterly beautiful. It is only when we are confused that our hearts shrivel and our minds figure crafty ways out of situations. The rational mind is a completely amoral, problem-solving device. When we relate to life from our minds, we take our feet off the ground. It's like not wanting to touch the floor, fearing that we will be burned. To take birth, we need to put both feet flat on the floor, while recognizing that we're in a world filled with suffering. One-half of all people go to sleep hungry at night. Forty thousand children will starve to death today and tomorrow and the day after. If you have only one foot on the ground, you are unstable, and suffering can push you over. With both feet on the ground, you see that you are not responsible *for* those children dying, but you can respond *to* their dying. It may be tithing some charitable group that feeds, doing hospice volunteer work or strengthening your own practice so that nothing comes out of you that creates more suffering in this terribly suffering world. Birthing is a cleaning up. A lot of people don't want to take off the afterbirth. They want to think they can slip out at any time, that they don't have to take responsibility.

There is absolute joy in completing your birth. Conducting a life review helps the birthing process. Practicing forgiveness and gratitude are aspects of a life review. I went back to images in my head of untoward things I have done in my life. Slowly and gently I approached images that I never wanted to go near again, because I felt shame, guilt and anger. It completes your birth to bring your own life into your heart with mercy. This may not be easy, but it is incredibly fruitful. Most people have a group of thoughts in their head that they are afraid to think around other people, for fear that shame will leak out their ears and be known. We can't live like that. That kind of fear makes us violent and hard to be around. It causes us not to want to put that second foot on the ground.

PT: *You stated that when you were exploring the fear of death, it became clear that the fear of life needed to be investigated first.*

SL: Life has difficulties in it, but the power we have to deal with life, which might never be called on if life weren't difficult at times, is miraculous. Facing life responsibly gives you confidence. The enormous power of the heart, and the power we have to receive the healing we took birth for, is within us all. If life's difficulties weren't jiggling us, we wouldn't spread our legs enough to get our balance.

PT: *Yet we are conditioned to retreat from the unpleasant.*

SL: That's what keeps this world small. That's why forty thousand children will starve to death today.

PT: *Why do we avoid the unpleasant?*

SL: Because it's painful. Aversion to pain is the greatest decreaser of life experience. When you always turn away from difficulties, you're not going to go far. Anyone who has done genuine, long-range spiritual practice knows there are periods that are very difficult. Letting go of our suffering is the hardest work we do.

PT: *You've written that in order to heal, we respond to rather than react to discomfort. We begin to experience discomfort as the pain, not our pain. What's the importance of this?*

SL: It's another way to discuss being responsible *for* and being responsible *to*. When it's *my* cancer, I'm *alone* with *my* cancer. I have nobody, just me and my cancer, and it looks like there is no way out. When I realize it isn't *my* cancer, but *the* cancer, there is space to work on it. *My* depression, *my* cancer, crams me in, like being in a phone booth full of *my* life. You *open* the phone booth and see that everybody is standing outside of their phone booth. It isn't *my* depression, it's *the* depression. When it's *the* cancer, I am in this *flow* of *human-kind*, with all the energy of four or five million other people going through the same thing at this same moment. You connect to something *universal*, which brings peace.

PT: *Is the same true for the dying, rather than my dying?*

SL: Yes. *My* dying is terrible, but on the day *I* die, on the day that everyone dies, roughly 250,000 *other* people will die. The death rate on the planet is about a quarter of a million a day. The death, if I believe in reincarnation, means I've been through this dozens of times before. One friend of mine says, "Can't you take a bad day well?" One of the teachings of being responsible to your life may be learning to take the bad days well.

PT: *How do we become responsible to our death?*

SL: We start relating to it. There is no better way to be responsible to your death than practicing a-year-to-live. Most people who are going to die this year have no idea they will die in less than a year. Even those who have been told they have a serious illness don't know when it will culminate, or if it will go into remission. In the last year of life, people's energies are compromised. Concentration is diminished by medications, pain, fatigue and sleeplessness. Malnutrition may develop. Various conditions arise, that if one is more stable, with both feet on the ground, are easier to go through, for themselves and for the people around them. This year-to-live healing is not just done for you, it helps your world. It's a way of cleaning up the world, in a very nice way. One of the most lovely aspects of the year-to-live was the life review. I went to each person who had been kind to me and thanked them. It took a long time and it was delicious. It broke open my heart. It also balanced the other part of a life review where I dealt with resentments and forgiveness.

PT: *You described the life review as essential to the year-to-live practice. What does it involve?*

SL: The life review consists of practicing gratitude and forgiveness. Start gently, almost casually in the beginning. Let memories come up, and rather than reliving them—tasting that steak, feeling that slap or crying those tears— watch and relate *to* the memories, instead of solely *from* them. Don't push anything away, allow memories, bring them in so they can pass through. A lot of memories are stuck in the mind. It's the same process as dealing with hardness in the belly. We soften, and there is still something hard there, and then that hard thing starts to flow, and we relate *to* it instead of *from* it. We start meeting our memories more softly, just like the hard belly softening the muscles and not pushing, not letting aversion to the past keep you from living in the present.

When I ask men how many have had homosexual experiences, about 20 percent raise their hand, yet about 80 percent have had some homosexual experience. If you can't go to memories of being sexual with someone in day camp, how can you touch the memory about the guy you killed in Vietnam? Or the wife you cheated on? I know people dying with AIDS who had unprotected sex with people after they had AIDS. They are dying in such self-hatred. They did a terrible thing, a stupid, angry thing. However, this is a human being dying. Just as you don't want them to live in the context of their self-hatred and shame, you don't want them to be seen that way in yourself. Forgiveness is very powerful. Had those AIDS patients been practicing a-year-to-live, they may have not been so compulsive in acting out their desires. These are good people. They are lonely and AIDS has them scared and they do something stupid. Everybody has done something they regret. Imagine doing something you regret that you can't take back. Forgiveness acknowledges our human vulnerability. Forgiveness does not condone unskilled actions.

There is no place where forgiveness is inappropriate, although it may take time. People who had terrible things done to them have to have both feet on the ground to be able to forgive. They have to examine their anger, possibly even homicidal rage at the person who hurt them, to get that other foot down on the ground. If you are afraid of anger, you push it out of consciousness, then it pops up and you act on it spontaneously. The more you know that which causes you pain, the less potential it has for causing you pain.

PT: *During a-year-to-live, fear of death is faced. How do we face it?*

SL: Fears arise everyday that are like five- or ten-pound fears. We've become accustomed to these little ones and are able to submerge them with no problem. We think submerging is a sign of our strength, a sign of how far we've gone. It is not. Those fears are opportunities for liberation. They are five- and ten-pound hindrances that we can learn to handle by thorough investigation. You can't investigate pain during bone cancer if you've never done pain meditation before. You can't even investigate pain during a stubbed toe usually. Most people stub their toe and send hatred into it. They are merciless and wish it would be gone. What pain in us most needs is to be *embraced*. We have learned to be *absent*. We feel abandoned by the part of us that could make us feel whole. We scared it off. When you prepare to work with the fear of death, start working with little fears. You step off the curb, a moment of fear. You meet a stranger, a moment of fear. Start with the five- and ten-pound fears because they're workable. We're familiar with them and they don't close our heart. They might tighten our belly a little bit, but we're working with soft belly. Eventually we increase our capacity to work with larger fear. If we went to the gymnasium to pick up the five-hundred-pound weight, the fear of death, we couldn't do it. But we can work out with five- and ten-pound weights. We open to the little angers, fears and doubts, not circumventing them just because we are able to, which decreases aversion to pain and displeasure, and increases our ability to do the work that we were born to do.

PT: *Talk more about the soft-belly practice. How do we soften into fear?*

SL: You start soft belly by physically letting each inward breath that you breathe push the belly out. No more holding the belly. You physically open, letting the muscles soften, letting the tissue soften. In the beginning, you may even push your belly out a little, just to let it know it can go out, that it doesn't have to take half a breath. You start to breathe in to your belly, which is quite a wonderful experience. One foot on the ground may be that we take our breath only into the top third of our body. Eventually, you'll be able to breathe out the bottom of your feet, so to speak, without even trying.

PT: *This opens us to what is in our belly?*

SL: Yes. You practice softening and begin to notice that, although your intention is to soften, there is something hard there. Your heart decides it is time to face that which has caused you to turn away from life. You start allowing thoughts, and they can come and go. You make space around thoughts, moment to moment, every exhale letting go. In the course of this, you find out what letting go means. One of the extraordinary things about soft-belly practice is that it is a physical trigger for the mental state of letting go. People lose their breath when they're watching death or during a moment of anger. That's the time to practice soft belly. Start to look at little angers, doubts and fears. In softening the belly, you let space be there and thoughts and feelings pass through like bubbles. You don't stop anything. Let it all flow. The difference between *my* pain and *the* pain is the *space* it *floats* in.

PT: *This allows us to experience the passing show of consciousness from a place of spaciousness.*

SL: Precisely. Many people have learned soft belly and found it particularly useful in the last year of their life. You can test and verify the benefit of this in your own laboratory, your body. Notice, whenever your belly is hard, which it is almost all the time, what you are holding. You just have to pay attention. I've been doing this practice for forty years, and I still soften my belly one hundred times a day.

PT: *Noting seems essential to this practice.*

SL: Noting is knowing what is happening while it's happening. It is an aid to keep you on the mark. When you open to those five- and ten-pound pains, call them what they are. Note them. If it's an anger feeling in the belly of hardness, notice the mental state. Note what is in the stillness of the deeper mind. Recognize and label, just in passing, not holding. At first it's anger. Then it's frustration, and soon you see desire, frustration, pride, fear, aggression, guilt and shame. You see all those different qualities that make up that single state of mind we call anger. Things become more precise. You go from generalized fear, anger, doubt or hardness in the belly to more subtle reflections, insights and sudden wordless understandings into what is going on. Noting keeps us steady. Particularly when it's a fifty-pound fear. You're afraid your child is on drugs, that your wife is going to leave you or that your parent's X ray is going to reveal cancer. This is the heavier pain of fear. Keep noting to yourself, fear, fear, and going into the sensation, softening. The more familiar you become with any state, the sooner you'll recognize it and the less your natural resistance, your desire to hide, will keep you safe. The closer to its inception you notice, the lighter the weight, and you can exercise more of what seems like free will.

PT: *So we relate to these states rather than being consumed by them?*

SL: Relating *to* our pain instead of *from* our pain is the whole game. Relating *to* our pain is *joyous*. Running *from* our pain is *misery*. If we could contain our pain it would be different. At this state of evolution, human beings cannot contain pain without causing others to suffer. We just can't do it, we are incapable of it. People think that they keep it together by not showing how much pain they're in. They live with the absence of joy, which shows how much pain they actually are in. Joy is a natural state, pain is acquired.

PT: *This is the process of letting go of the suffering around pain. How do you distinguish between pain and suffering?*

SL: Pain is a given. If you have a body and a mind, there is pain. It is an aspect of the law of conservation of matter. Only one thing can occupy any space at one time. When your body walks along and hits a table, the table holds that space and you get hurt. A sensation comes up your arm and your nerve net catches it. If it's small, it goes through the net and we notice it as a distinct sensation. If it's big enough, it gets caught in that net and we experience pain. It is the same with thoughts. We have some idea of who we are, so when another idea comes in, both can't occupy the same space at the same time. Conflicting conditioning results in mental pain.

The pain of being born is a given. Suffering is not a given. *Suffering* is how we *work* with our *pain*. I have seen people who can deal with pain, but are still suffering. Physical pain can intercede in your practice. Pain can make it difficult to be concentrated and stable, to not be frightened or angry. Mental and physical pain attracts grief. Our latent grief comes up. In relating to physical pain, don't wait until it's a three-hundred pounder. Bumping your elbow is an opportunity for liberation. Work with it. It takes you to the edge, but it's just the edge, and when you get there, you'll see that wasn't the edge at all. We can take a lot more than that, unfortunately. Sit with those pains and send mercy into them. See the anger that collects around pain, trying to blame. Grief is separation, and separation comes up to meet injuries, physical or mental. If we want to be free, that's where we have to work. Little pain gives us the opportunity to clear out enormous pain. Suffering is *resistance* to pain. A lot of it is volitional, but some of it isn't, so have mercy on yourself. When working with pain, don't be a tough guy. A tough guy is a weak guy. Toughness is an escape, not an opening.

PT: *Do you differentiate between death and dying?*

SL: Dying is a process of shaking loose of the body. Death is a process of being no longer obstructed by a body. Because we have an idea that we are a body, we limit our understanding and insight. During the year-to-live, you see that you live in this body. You see that your body and your experience float in something bigger, which is why you can feel an inch beyond your skin. Death is the waking dream that we experience sometimes at night, or during insight, or while making love. Death is always present but is obscured by the trappings of having taken form. Death is consciousness, the ongoing flow of object awareness. Objects of awareness are no less real in a dream than they are in the world. Your dream of a tiger is as frightening as a waking experience with a tiger. In fact, your dream of a tiger may be more frightening because real fear comes up. We're not so clever in dreams. Usually our cleverness is sufficient to keep us safe. In dreams we let go and open. My idea is that death is like a waking dream. Those who do lucid dream practice have an advantage. Death is not so different than life. I think that people are going to be surprised. You are not going to have a chocolate soda, as far as it seems. But since most of our experience is mental, an inner experience of what is going on outside, death is not going to be much different.

PT: *Is there a moment of death?*

SL: There is a moment of death when the person standing next to the bed can no longer make contact with the person in the bed. The doctor's instruments no longer measure life in the body. For the individual inside, it's like asking if there is a moment when you fall asleep. There is, but if you're awake in that dream you say, "I'm asleep," and that's the last thought you have. In death it isn't the last thought you have. You recognize that you are in another process. Your philosophy beforehand may define what that process is. I think many people believe they are not dead. They don't think they can be, since they are still conscious. That may be purgatory. There is little more helpful you can do for a friend after they've died than to touch them lovingly, saying, "Whatever you are going through now, you just died, that's all." That may sound stupid, but imagine if it would help. What have you done to help them as much? I think the individual dying notices that something is happening. They notice they are literally getting high. When you look at a person who has just died, you notice they are immobile. The predominance of the solidity element has fallen away. They start to feel like an ocean, like a flow, instead of a boulder. The process is one of letting go. First they let go of the solid elements. Outside, the person can't move, but inside, they are free of solidity. Next you notice that the loved one's circulation system has stopped, their fluids have closed down in their body. You are now certain they are dead because the body is starting to stiffen. Inside, the person feels like fluid and as the fluidity stops, they start to feel like air. As the body hardens, even the air goes away and they become pure energy. It's like an ice cube melting. The edges disappear and there's a pool of water. The pool takes on room temperature which causes it to evaporate. Eventually it goes from a solid cube with defined edges to being invisible because it has become gas and is filling the room equally in all its parts. You may think that is an awful thing to see happen to a body. But remember, when the ice cube evaporates, it remains H_2O. It hasn't changed a bit and neither does human consciousness. It is just contained in a different way, experienced in a different form.

PT: *Who or what dies?*

SL: The *body* dies. I don't think *anybody* dies. It's reverse recycling. With human beings, the container is discarded, and the contents are recycled. The person who is in the body, as a mental structure, goes on, but in a very different way. There have been times when, having the same mind you have now, you have been absolutely joyous, clear and free. The mind you have does not obstruct freedom, how you relate to the mind obstructs freedom. The beneficence of the process of dying is that we're given perspective on our suffering, which shifts from *my* suffering to *the* suffering.

PT: *Are people afraid of death after having a near-death experience?*

SL: I am still afraid of death, and I have been there. Through various means, I occasionally have been beyond the threshold. I know experientially what a few steps into death is. I know that death is perfectly safe. It's like taking off a shoe that is too tight. Even with this knowing, even with seeing some people die as beautifully as saints, the conditioned mind still holds the fear of death. It is fascinating to watch. If even half the mind were evolved enough so that when it received a new piece of truth, it could discard the other half-truth, we would be in better shape. The mind is able to hold conflicting conditioning. The earlier our conditioning, the more deeply rooted it is, and the more difficult it is to balance, to let float. It is so rooted, it holds on to the earth for dear life.

PT: *What insights do near-death experiences provide?*

SL: Near-death experiences, where we see that we are not the body, and that death draws us to a center of love, are great wisdom teachings. They also show that the ignorance we pick up during life doesn't go away easily. When people come back, they say, "I met Buddha or Jesus," or some other image of omnipotence. Few people come back and say, "I saw my true nature, my original face. It was remarkable and reinforcing. I know the healing I was born for, I know what I am made of." People see that luminosity as something different than themselves. This is the ignorance we carry in our life. I had a teacher whose whole practice was letting go of every thought except that he was God. He became enlightened.

PT: *What is the importance of funeral preparations?*

SL: Most people are not prepared for their loved one's death, even if they have been beside their bed for a year. When loved ones die, their absence is momentous. Transitional rituals help acknowledge death. The mind will have things to say for a while around the death. Grief is not just sadness; grief is remorse, guilt, anger, distrust and feelings of abandonment. It is important to be grounded. There is no time that we want to take one foot off the ground more than when we are in grief, and there is no time that it is more dangerous to do so.

Relationships do not end when a person dies. Some other aspect of it deepens and begins. Your relationship isn't over, it is just no longer externalized. The pain involved is the consequence of love. That's what love costs. Some people say the price of love is too high. They will take many incarnations to get by that fear, which is fine. However, there is a point in which fear does not lead our life anymore. We are willing to love even if it is painful at times. I become ecstatic when I talk about what is on the other side of the pain, but it is not right for me to say your pain will go away after a one-year practice, because it may not. It will start to recede in the background and float in something bigger than your pain.

PT: *What else would you like to add?*

SL: I learned from the year-to-live that *love* is the only rational act of a lifetime. Everything else pales in comparison. Things that are motivated by love can still turn out badly in the physical world, but the *intention* for love does not turn out badly, it can only bring a deeper *capacity* for love.•

Understanding the Dying Process

BARBARA HARRIS WHITFIELD

Denial can be harmful when there is a strong possibility that dying is inevitable. If the dying person or her loved ones refuse to accept the most likely outcome, they are missing their last opportunity in this lifetime to share this important final passage.

I was asked to visit a sixty-two-year-old-man who was in the hospital with throat cancer. He told me in a whisper that he was finishing another round of chemotherapy and needed a few more days of inpatient care before he could go home. He said he had not been able to hold food down for weeks at a time and was sometimes being fed through a tube or intravenously.

"I know I'm too young to die," he said so softly that I had to lean in close to his face to hear. "My family doesn't believe I'm dying. They won't listen to me. I tell them I'm dying, and they keep yelling at me, 'You have to fight, Daddy, fight!'"

"How does that make you feel?" I asked.

"I feel like no one hears me," he answered. "I think the cancer is spreading. I can't talk to anyone. No one hears me."

"I hear you, and I'll talk to your family when you want me to." I smiled and made sure we had eye contact. I told him I would return the next day.

I visited every day until he was discharged at the end of the week. Our conversations were always the same, except when his family was there. When they were, he said little. They would ask me to convince their father to fight and regain his strength.

I visited him at home once. My sense was that this man was in prison. He was being kept. He had no voice. He sat in his pajamas and watched the scene of wife and daughters scurrying around—continuously busy with the duties of caring for a catastrophically ill loved one.

The last time I saw him, I witnessed his death. In the hospital, hooked up to tubes, he lay in the bed and looked up at me. "I'm going to die now," he mouthed the words more than he whispered them.

"Your family is in the waiting room. What shall I tell them?" I asked.

"Don't tell them anything. I need to die, and they won't let me." He strained so I could hear his last words to me. "I need to die now."

I sat down quietly next to his bed. I held his hand for a few seconds or minutes, and then I realized that I had to let it go. He needed to leave. Even my touch was keeping him here. His eyes were closed, and I watched the last bit of life leave his face. It was such a peaceful and humble transition.

I checked in at the nurses' station, and they made the necessary call to a resident who came and confirmed he had died. Then I went into the waiting room and told his family. His daughters and wife started to howl. I closed the door. The four women were screaming about their needs, about their loss. I heard anger over his forty-some-year habit of smoking. I heard anger with the doctors and the way they handled his case. I heard anger with the hospital. I waited until the four of them settled down a little and offered my condolences over their loss. I told them I would visit if they wanted me to, and I gave them my card.

I helped them to the door of the hospital, and I never heard from them again.

DENIAL IN A NURSING HOME

I was called to a nursing home to help an eighty-five-year-old woman die. She had been there for three years because of senility and deterioration. Her seven children, ranging in age from fifty-one to sixty-five, sat or stood around her bed. Her husband, still robust for eighty-eight, sat sadly in a chair in the corner.

"My wife has been on her deathbed for over a week now," he told me. "Why did they send for you? There's nothing anyone can do for her. She needs to die."

"May I sit here with you for a little while?" I asked him.

"Yeah," he answered. And he told one of his sons to get me a chair.

I sat with the family for an hour. Each one of the old woman's breaths was loud and labored. Finally, there was a period of about five seconds when she didn't breathe. The daughter who was holding her mother's hand screamed and was then grabbed and pulled back by another sobbing daughter standing behind her. The momentum of this pulled the old woman forward, and she gasped and started to breathe again. I quietly got up and went over to the bed and took the first daughter's hands away from her mother. I held this daughter's hand and rubbed her shoulder.

"We need to let her go now," I said as I looked into the grieving woman's face. "No, I want my mother," she replied and started to cry.

"I know you do. But your mother needs to go now." I was praying silently while I was talking to her. Two other women in the room began to cry along with her. Their father got up, came over and put his arms around the two of them.

"She's right. It's time to let Mama go. I'll be with her again soon, and someday so will you."

The old woman gasped and stopped breathing. A few seconds later, she started to breathe again, and then stopped one more time. I think I was in the room with them for two hours, maybe a little longer, when her breathing finally stopped for the last time. No one pulled on her. No one screamed for her to come back. Her husband stood by her side and said quietly, "I love you. I'll be coming along soon."

By holding back her daughters, her husband and I helped this woman to release. If everyone would have continued calling to her, grabbing her hand or pulling her forward, her dying would have continued much longer. She had to die, regardless of how much her loved ones wanted her to stay.

Sometimes the only thing we can do to assist someone in the dying process is to let go and help the others around us to stand back and let go, too.•

Death and Dying

STEPHAN RECHTSCHAFFEN, M.D.

A ll this time, I thought I was learning to live, when all along I was learning to die." So said Leonardo da Vinci, and we are likely to read his words, smile knowingly, think to ourselves "how wise"—and be glad that they don't really apply to us. We're right: They don't. Most Westerners run from even "talk" of death. True, we cry at movies like *Terms of Endearment* when dying is unrealistically romanticized; we weep at funerals, cheer when the "bad guys" die on television and shudder at newspaper accounts of catastrophes, though we soon get over it. But as for the thought of our own death, while we know in our mind that death is inevitable, we expend untold energy denying it, sensing somewhere in our untrustworthy heart that we are immortal.

We deny death because we are afraid of it. This fear is so deeply ingrained that it, above all other factors, keeps us from being fully in the present. When we are alive, our death exists in the future. If we spend our days worrying about death, we essentially live in the future. In that sense, death robs us of life before we die.

It takes attention to hold off death. We plan. We become anxious. We busy ourselves so we do not have to think about it. And we lose contact with present time and present place where wonder and joy—and not death—exist.

"But I'm not afraid of death," people have told me, "only of some terrible disease like cancer, or some awful injury."

Yes. But probably they are afraid of death, as well. Actually, fear heightens our experience of disease or pain or death, whether it be our own or a loved one's. If we can face calamity directly, then we will experience it as a part of life. When it comes to death, we must recognize that its mystery is unfathomable.

Ram Dass tells of a student who went to a Zen master.

"What can you tell me about death?" the student asked. "Nothing," the other replied. "I'm a Zen master. Not a dead Zen master."

One way to come to the feelings of death is through meditation. Indeed, Philip Kapleau, author of the brilliant *The Wheel of Death*, points out that meditation itself is a "dance" of death, for ultimately death is both the end and the beginning.

I remember with awe an elderly man in my class doing his first meditation. He seemed shaken when it was over, and I asked him why.

"I'm afraid of death," he said.

He had immediately come to a place where he was alone, by himself, facing universal issues. It was remarkable to me that in such a short time he could reach this place that most of us hide from, avoiding any consideration of our true fears. He was overwhelmed, and I empathized with him, having undergone an equivalent experience.

My own fear of dying stems from childhood. When I was eight or nine, my grandfather died, and the words "really" and "forever" buzzed in my head. He was *really* dead; he would be dead *forever*, never to return to spend time with me. I couldn't sleep for months. If death had happened to him, it would happen to me. I would really be dead. I would be gone forever.

Until children understand the concept of time, they cannot conceive of death. Knowledge of death is the prime cause of a child's loss of innocence. Until faced with an understanding of death, children are intrepid daredevils. That is one of the reasons we must watch them so carefully.

It is in the realm of death that the Western concept of linear time is most destructive. In cultures in which people live in circular time, they do not fear death; they look upon it as a blessing. In Bali, for example, funerals are celebrated like births, with equivalent joy and ceremony. For the Balinese, death is simply part of the continuum of birth, life, death and rebirth. As Voltaire said, "After all, it is no more surprising to be born twice than it is to be born once."

The Sufi mystic Jalal ud-Din Rumi, perhaps the greatest of the Persian poets, wrote:

> *I died as a mineral and became a plant,*
> *I died as a plant and rose to animal,*
> *I died as animal and I was a man.*
> *Why should I fear?*
> *Was I less by dying?*

Death is in our lives, and we must recognize that as an unalterable fact. Recently, the six-year-old daughter of a friend was killed on a camping trip in the Adirondack State Park. My friend and his son and daughter had spent an idyllic few days there, close to nature and close to one another.

As they were leaving, they crossed a highway that cut through the park, and the girl was struck by a car traveling sixty miles per hour. She died instantly.

The tragedy was unspeakable; my friend and his son will have to struggle terribly to get through their grief and guilt. But taken objectively, one can see how difficult it is to make a time shift in a world where the slow rhythm of nature clashes with the speed of modern society's most familiar totem, the car.

In the middle of nature, the pace of society intruded in a most horrendous way. (Which is not to say that nature itself can't be cruel, violent, full of death.) Death sometimes has no meaning except that it exists; it can be expected or unexpected, and to live life in fear of death denies life itself.

Death does not exist in the present moment. In the now, there is only life, with its range of emotions and myriad feelings, its universal bounty.

In my time-shifting workshops, I try an exercise. I ask the members to imagine the next six months. It is a time of perfect health and physical well-being; there is plenty of money and, if they choose, they do not have to do another day's work.

At the end of the six months, they will die.

How would they spend those months? I ask. What would their priorities be? I put on a peaceful, beautiful piece of music and let them imagine those six months and their feelings about them.

For most workshop participants, it's an extraordinarily disturbing exercise, and I've been touched by the seriousness and the sadness etched on their faces. Many of them have not come face-to-face with imagined death in so direct a fashion, and their initial reaction is one of shock. Almost always, they take a minute or so before they begin writing, and then they often quickly cross out what they had started to write, pause, think some more and begin to write again, obviously with greater seriousness.

Some start without much depth: "I'd tell my boss off, get good and drunk, and then decide what I'd do"; "I'd have sex with a hundred women, without ever worrying about AIDS"—that sort of thing.

Then the answers get more thoughtful. The most common is, "I'd take a long trip with the person I love, visiting all the places in the world I want to see."

But that, too, gives way to deeper sentiments, and when I go around the group, asking for answers, then I hear about solving relationship problems with a loved one, spending time with the children and not changing anything because life is good. But by far, the most common is, "I'd spend all my time with the people I love."

Yes. Human relationships count most when the prospect of death looms before us, and the exercise clearly points that out. The most dramatic responses are from people who have an estranged relationship with a loved one.

Joe began speaking about his father and how upset he had been about their argument over money; they hadn't spoken for two years. The thought of his imminent death made Joe realize he wanted to heal the rift before dying. So during the exercise, he made amends with his dad. When he shared this with the group, all of a sudden he realized, "Why am I waiting? I need to resolve this now!"

We are all in the process of dying; we just don't know when it will happen. Why not resolve issues and express our love now, before it's too late?

Senator Paul Tsongas once said, "No one on his deathbed ever said, 'I wish I had spent more time at the office,'" and that attitude is reflected here.

It's wonderful that so many people are able to say that they wouldn't do anything differently. Isn't this something we all aspire to? What is more satisfying than contentment?

Long after the participants have gone home, I'll get letters telling me how the exercise forced them to look closely at their lives and, in many cases, made them alter their priorities. What they're doing is mapping out time for themselves, time in the present with the people they love.

Facing death squarely means being squarely in the moment. And the ultimate moments are spent with a loved one, not with a boss.

This, fundamentally, is what our life is about.

Elisabeth Kübler-Ross, in her book *On Death and Dying*, brought this country face-to-face with the fact of death. She told us we did not have to run, could not hide and could approach death with equanimity, even calm.

Even though the book caused a tremendous stir, and several later works by different authors expanded on her themes, only some people listened then, and not enough people are listening now.

Americans see death as a kind of failing or disgrace, like bad breath or body odor. No strong person would die, we seem to say. And so the strong deny it or run in terror, pretending that death is not a fact, not a certainty. At the same time, of course, they do everything possible to prolong life, even when that life is submerged in pain or hopeless senility.

When we deal with the dying, we're adept only at dealing with the business of dying. We build more and more sophisticated instruments of "salvation," an end-care technology that costs billions of dollars to save—what? Lives?

Yes, lives, but surely not the kind of life any of us wishes for.

Partly, I believe, this lust for machines stems from doctors' own fear of death, a kind of subconscious belief that by prolonging life in others, it will prolong their own lives. Too, if they substitute a machine for human contact, then they won't get "infected" by their patients; death will pass them by.

Thus the use of machines obviates for the medical establishment the need for human contact.

This is the most tragic facet of our need to prolong life: the fact that we'll do anything to save the patient, rather than take into account the patient's human needs and desires. I've witnessed dehumanization in hospitals, doctors as callous as prison guards, and all because of their own fear of death.

We tend to praise the "impersonal" physician. If he got involved with all his patients, how could he maintain his objectivity, his sanity? What would his own life be like if he became "emotional" with each of the people under his care?

So we laugh at movies and books that show doctors joking about their patients and about death. But the impersonal physician is limiting his own life, not protecting it, and the laughter I've heard in emergency rooms is hollow.

Many of us have had direct experience of the loss of a loved one and know how difficult it is personally to face the death of someone close. Underlying this discomfort is the fear and pain surrounding our own death, for we know it is inevitable. Our discomfort, like the physicians', comes from our uncertainty about what is in store. At the same time, the more we can directly face the experiences of loss that come into our lives, however unwanted, the better prepared we will be for our own death. If we can feel someone else's physical and/or emotional pain, we will be better able to deal with our own.

Attention to the psychological and emotional needs of the dying is a relatively new phenomenon in American society, particularly for its nonreligious members. The hospice movement, until recently bitterly criticized as "warehousing" the dying, or "despairing" in its attitude, is now seen as the humanitarian effort it has always been.

Many health-care professionals, doctors included, have come to realize that "taking care" of a patient goes well beyond looking to his physical comfort, or prolonging his life.

Joan Halifax, a dear friend and Buddhist shaman, has described the immense *mutual* benefits of simply being with a dying person, with no agenda and no time constraints—just two people coming into the moment. Her work with the dying is an outgrowth of her personal commitment to being mindful. Being with someone who is dying means being stripped of the social niceties that surround our usual interactions.

Ram Dass has described the same phenomenon. He has worked with the dying for many years, and has made society more aware of their concerns. Psychologist Marsha Greenleaf, who counsels the dying both in hospitals and in her office, writes of the vital importance of giving the dying their voice, letting them determine the manner and method of their death according to their psychological needs.

An old friend, Wavy Gravy, has made a career of dressing as a clown and visiting the terminally ill in children's hospitals. To me, this is an act of tremendous courage, but to him it offers enormous spiritual rewards.

In my early years as a doctor, I counseled people that having cancer was an *opportunity* for the patients, since it often forced them to resolve relationships, to bring their affairs in order and to strive for spiritual peace.

In my heart, though, I didn't believe it. I knew it conceptually, but had no firsthand experience myself or with patients.

Then one day I met a woman with cancer, who described herself as "more alive than when I was supposedly healthy." She became closer to her husband than ever before, she told me, and had joyfully reconciled with the rest of her family. "I started living my life in the present," she explained, "in a way that I had never felt before. This disease has helped me fully appreciate what I have in my life." A devoutly religious woman, she accepted her disease as a "blessing," with all its positive implications.

It's true that facing death has the remarkable side effect of bringing one into the present. If we are allowed to keep our humanness, if we entrain with someone who is fully human, too, then dying is indeed an opportunity for fulfillment, perhaps the greatest opportunity of all.•

Death Is a Mirror

DAVID FEINSTEIN
AND PEG ELLIOTT MAYO

The knowledge that death is approaching may have the paradoxical effect of mobilizing a person into a more profound sense of being alive. Two years after a near-fatal heart attack, Abraham Maslow, one of this century's greatest psychologists, spoke of the intervening period as "the postmortem life." Reflecting on how these years were a kind of bonus, an extra gift, he noted that "if you're reconciled with death or even if you are pretty well assured that you will have a good death, a dignified one, then every single moment of every single day is transformed because the pervasive undercurrent—the fear of death—is removed."

In the postmortem life everything gets doubly precious, gets piercingly important. You get stabbed by things, by flowers and by babies and by beautiful things—just the very act of living, of walking and breathing and eating and having friends and chatting. Everything seems to look more beautiful rather than less, and one gets the much-intensified sense of miracles. . . . The confrontation with death and the reprieve from it makes everything look so precious, so sacred, so beautiful that I feel more strongly than ever the impulse to love it, to embrace it and to let myself be overwhelmed by it.

People who, like Maslow, come into peace with the inevitability of death are apt to find that life becomes sweeter. This paradox holds a comforting twist. Even if they don't reach serenity about death until the last few years of life, as did Maslow, or until the last few days (and clinical evidence bears this out), as they do attain it, they attain in retrospect new meaning for the lives they have lived. But why delay in finding peace about death and the renewed vitality that attends it?

ADVERSITY AND THE REBIRTH OF SPIRIT

Charles Cameron was sixty-seven when his world unraveled. Within a six-month period, he discovered that he had diabetes, his company required that he retire (a step he'd wanted to postpone for another three years) and his wife of forty-four years died in a plane crash. He became despairing and suicidal.

Never a religious person, Charles had no emotional, intellectual, or spiritual framework into which he could fit his losses. His life had comprised his work but, as he said later, "not much else." Stripped of his occupation as a sales executive for a pump-manufacturing firm, his humdrum but amicable marriage, and what had seemed good health, he saw no reason to live. It was only at the insistence of his grown son that he grudgingly agreed to enter psychotherapy. Charles said he had "abandoned hope and was just going through my paces to satisfy Danny. I really *wanted* to die, but I was also afraid of dying."

Charles's first task in therapy was to grieve his losses—professional identity, a secure and ordered marriage, and what felt like "the best years of my life—they're all behind me." It took him nearly a year of therapy to see beyond his pained confusion and come to a reluctant awareness that with proper care he might well live another twenty years. Initially, this seemed a gloomy prospect. "All I could imagine was a life of insulin shots, waning strength, dutiful dinner invitations from the kids and television."

At this time Charles was in a serious automobile accident. Six weeks later, we asked him to describe his experience. He said, "I was on my way back from our mountain cabin; I was getting ready to put the place on the market when it happened. I took a curve a little too fast, thinking about Margie and the good times we'd had up there.

"The next thing, I was airborne, and I saw the world tilt. I don't know how long it was but when I came to, I was hanging upside down by the seat belt, and my head hurt like hell. I was cold and it was getting dark. Everything in the car had shifted around and I couldn't undo the buckle. The headlights were on but I couldn't reach the horn. I was more scared than I've ever been in my life.

"I passed out, probably from all the blood rushing to my head, but I didn't pass out completely, if you know what I mean—kind of in and out. Like I knew where I was and that I was probably going to die in this grotesque way but part of me felt sort of separated from it, too. Pretty soon the separated part began to turn away, to disconnect. Then I began to look around. It was a beautiful place—deep woods, river in the canyon and a full moon coming over the ridge. And I noticed it was sort of misty foggy and I was just drifting over the forest floor. I didn't seem to have any substance and the wind was moving me.

"Then came the moment I realized—but deeper than words—that *I am part of it all!* Even though I now believe I had literally died, I knew I didn't want to leave until I made friends with the planet again. I remembered being a kid and reveling in nature and I knew I had to touch that again before I'd be ready to die. And I knew that something was holding it all together—all the pieces. I was irresistibly drawn to finding out more about what that was.

"I came to, still upside down, but I was thinking better. I squirmed around and got the seat belt unfastened. Then I crawled out of the passenger window and up the bank, and the first car along saw me.

"For a week I just basically sat and thought about what had happened. Actually it wasn't *thought*—I sat and absorbed the experience. There never was any doubt about its reality, but what did it mean? Sally [his daughter-in-law] was a big help.

"She's interested in all that 'woo-woo' stuff like the *I Ching*, Tarot and crystals. She told me that she was reading an article in one of her magazines that reminded her of my accident. It talked about a Tarot card called 'the Hanged Man,' and she read a passage to me:

> *The card represents surrender to death and resurrection as the soul leaves the body and then returns. Personality is torn away and a higher power takes over. In the card, a man is pictured hanging upside down, attached to the tree by a snake, a symbol of wisdom. Energy rushes to the head, stimulating greater awareness. In his limited and precarious position, his only task is that of fighting for his life. While he struggles, all of his old realities drop away. He moves into a state of non-ordinary reality where anything is possible, where freedom and enlightenment reside. The boundaries between life and death blur and, if the initiation is successful, the initiate realizes that death is part of life. He then realizes the importance of living life fully and with passion.*

"Blew my mind! These words described exactly my experience hanging there in that car, and they gave form to my deepest inklings about the meaning of the experience. In the following weeks, it was as if the walls fell outward and I could explore ideas and feelings in a new way. A sense of peace came over me that I could not remember having had since I was a boy hiking in the Sierra Nevada. But I also had a sense of urgency. I wanted to drink up the richness of life I saw all around me. I started hiking again, and on every hike I've seen stunning sights I will never forget. I've also been taking much pleasure in reading John Muir's nature journals. The greatest joy comes from my children and particularly I must admit my grandchildren. I was always proud of them but I never slowed down enough to really let myself know them. Now I can enter their world and it is the most extraordinary privilege I've ever had. I can speak with them in their own language and begin to teach them some of the lessons I've garnered in my own life. I hope I will be around long enough to see them into their own marriages and children but even if I'm not, I think I'm planting the best guidance I have right into their foundations."

Coming to the brink of our mortality is usually terrifying. On the one hand, we tend to push away such dreadful proof of our vulnerability as quickly as possible. We cannot, after all, live effectively if we are endlessly focused on the precariousness of life. On the other hand, if we face the underlying anxiety and at the same time learn to accept our mortality, as did Charles Cameron, we invite a rebirth of spirit.

Somewhere in the process, the instinctual terror of death is likely to explode within us. To move through it successfully is to conquer a large measure of the nameless anxiety that we, individually and as a culture, exert so much effort to keep out of our minds. When we have effectively squared off and faced that anxiety, we reclaim our misplaced energy. Less encumbered by nameless fears, we engage life with new vitality. This transformation is, however, a formidable challenge and our culture provides few rites of passage to help us through it.

Personal Rituals and Rites of Passage

"Illness," observed Marcel Proust, "is the most heeded of doctors—to goodness and wisdom we only make promises; we obey pain." And fear. The inner strength and renewed vigor that proved to be the fruits of Charles Cameron's life crisis were harvested within a field of emotional pain. Pain and the fear of pain are certainly among nature's primary markers for guiding behavior and directing growth. Pain is an emphatic critic and teacher, but it is not the only teacher along the way.

Rituals and rites of passage are social inventions that once guided the human spirit on its journey through the world. The culture's wisdom was etched into the mind and body of every person participating in its rituals. Today, the lack of unity and coherence in the culture's mythic guidance allows and in fact forces people to think and act for themselves in ways that were unimaginable in the past. Major shifts in the culture's mythology regarding issues as vital as what it means to be a man, a woman, a parent, a good citizen, a success—are being hammered out on the anvil of individual lives. Even what it means to die, once insistently established by religious canon, is left for each individual to puzzle through. We encounter these challenges without, for the most part, the benefit of sturdy tradition, inspiring myth or vital ritual. Meanwhile we are collectively starving for wise guidance attuned to the unique needs of the day—able to support the emphatic individuality that so strongly characterizes the modern psyche while promoting greater community and connection with the cosmos. Dare we, unschooled and tentative, take on the task of reanimating myth and ritual as integral parts of our own lives?

The following three cases demonstrate the use of psychologically sophisticated rituals. These cases focus on creatively meeting the anguish of bereavement. One of the most important ways we can prepare to accept our own mortality is in the manner by which we come to terms with the deaths of those we love. The rituals illustrated in the following vignettes help the bereaved work through their grief, appreciate the love shared and the gifts gained from the one they have lost, and in the face of death, reflect upon what truly matters in life.

CONTEMPORARY RITUALS FOR FACING LOSS

Imagine the distress as Christmas approaches shortly after the drowning of a family's infant son in their backyard swimming pool. The prospect of having to bear, amidst the surrounding revels of a festive holiday season, the unspeakable grief of having lost their freshest and dearest was anticipated with dread.

Faced with this dilemma, the Cortneys saw their choices as being either to take their three remaining children on a trip in an attempt to "skip" the holiday season altogether or to go ahead with their typical preparations and hope to somehow make it through a "business as usual" holiday. The therapist who was helping the family work through their bereavement, however, encouraged them to consider a third alternative, one that recognized that they were in a process of mourning, that mourning involves specific stages and tasks that may be embraced, and that they could use the holiday season to help themselves move onward in their grief process. They chose to make the holiday a very special "memorial Christmas" for Bobby. Although not an entirely joyous time, it was not entirely somber or at all hopeless. It was alive with authentic feelings, a deepening of bonds and an honoring of a beloved bright child. The holiday turned out to be the essence of nondenial, a conscious, distinct commitment to healing.

The Cortneys identified three aspects of Christmas that focused the family's attention and could be used in honoring the memory of their son: gift giving, caroling and decorating the tree. Throughout these activities, Bobby's picture was prominently displayed.

As the family exchanged gifts, each member, having had time in advance to think about what they would say, spoke of the gift Bobby had been in their lives. The impact of sharing gifts with one another was immeasurably deepened in an atmosphere that poignantly celebrated the preciousness of loved ones. Another family tradition for the Cortneys was to sing Christmas carols. That year they interspersed Bobby's favorite songs, "Itsy-Bitsy Spider" and "Muffin Man," with the traditional carols. To their surprise, they found that laughter broke through their tears, for some the first lightheartedness since Bobby's death. Finally around the tree, they recalled fondly Bobby's first and only Christmas, when he intently observed the family members busily putting up the decorations and then proceeded to hang his own bent-handle spoon on a low branch. For every Christmas from then on, placing Bobby's spoon on the tree was an important part of the celebration.

As you saw with the Cortneys, the social potency of an established holiday can be an element that is worked into family rituals. For Brad and Myra East, dread of the coming Thanksgiving clouded their anticipations. Since their four children had grown and moved away, Thanksgiving was the holiday around which they all gathered in celebration. However, Myra's brother Charlie, the family's favorite uncle, had died the previous June after a bout with lung cancer brought on by thirty-five years of smoking. Aunt Dee, widowed, depressed and disoriented, was hard to be around and, from the time she'd married into the family, had never been anyone's favorite relative anyway.

In late October, Myra, Brad and the adult children discussed over the phone how they might use the upcoming Thanksgiving gathering to ritualize the loss of Uncle Charlie, whose presence had enlivened decades of Thanksgivings. Plans in place, Dee was gently informed that the holiday would be dedicated to Charlie's memory. She was asked to bring his favorite winter hat and other significant memorabilia with her. Despite her protests and trepidations, she was finally persuaded.

The theme of the day was "Thanks, God, for Charlie." Everyone spoke of favorite memories around the table. Later, with the men crashed in front of the television watching football, Charlie's cap sat on top of the set (where it was placed every successive Thanksgiving), keeping him ever present in spirit and sparking memories of his past enthusiasm.

At the end of the day, the Easts put Dee in the center of a hug circle and gave thanks for her (surprising themselves with their sincerity). Then they went to the backyard ceremoniously to plant a persimmon (Charlie's favorite fruit) tree. Under it they buried the old football he had always brought for them to toss around during half-time of the televised games. The fruit of that tree was ever after served as a Thanksgiving treat.

What might, without conscious choice and inventive ritual, have turned into a polite but forced holiday gathering became a memorable and deeply mean-ingful celebration of Charlie's life. Engineering such an outcome often requires courage as well as creativity. One of the bleakest holiday circumstances any of us is likely to face is widowhood in late middle age with children scattered and friends immersed in their own unbroken traditions. Loneliness, loss of purpose and deep sorrow may lead to depression and even suicide.

Marge was sixty-seven when her husband died after thirty-eight years of marriage. Their two adult children were helpful in the beginning but soon returned to their active lives across the state. The first Christmas, Marge visited her daughter but felt alien and confused about her role. Worse, she feared she was a depressing, inconvenient element in their festivities, and whether this was accurate mattered less than her perception.

Resolved to do the next holiday season differently, Marge rose to the chal-lenge of re-visioning her understanding of herself and the holiday season. Her role as the welcoming mother and matron to homecoming family was past. She didn't want to be a "tag-along" in her children's lives, and she began to cultivate a refreshed view of the possibilities.

Marge identified sources of her pleasure around the holidays, including food preparation, decorating and gift giving. She resolved to keep what delighted her as she rethought the holiday experience.

Marge was a skilled watercolor artist, and she set about making small gifts and planning decorations with inventive themes and color combinations. Instead of the traditional turkey and mincemeat pie meal, she developed an original menu using elaborate Greek recipes.

Then, feeling excited, Marge contacted the local college for names of foreign students stranded in a strange country. She invited eight of them, and the party was a roaring success that became a delightful tradition and a source of important relationships for her throughout the year. By the second Christmas, she had twenty guests—all she could squeeze into her home.•

Facing Death

P A U L   C .   R O U D ,   E D. D.

For most people in this culture, coming to terms with death takes at least a lifetime. The fear can be so great and the prospect of peace can seem so remote that many people don't begin the quest until the evidence of their finality overwhelms them. And even when death appears imminent, fears may still make it impossible to confront the meaning of one's own death.

The premise of this discussion is that dealing with death has a profound effect on psychological, spiritual and perhaps even physical well-being. It may seem contradictory, but except in acute medical situations, preparing for death does not conflict with the goal of staying alive. In a personal interview, Sid Baker, medical director of the Gesell Institute of Human Development, explains:

If people are truly in jeopardy, the question comes up whether they are dying or living. In the hospital setting, there is a conflict between helping them do one versus the other. There's a point at which you stick an endotracheal tube down somebody and blow into it and bother them a lot, and there's another point at which you hold their hand and wish them well. And you can't do both at the same time. The whole scene around a resuscitation is so awful compared to the way in which people should be permitted to die.

At least in the nonacute situation, I have resolved this issue for myself. I think that the agenda for dying is to clean up your life: to say things that have been unsaid, to express feelings that have been unexpressed, to finish your emotional business with other human beings. It turns out that is a good recipe for living. In fact, it is the recipe for living.

I may say to a person in jeopardy, "Look, let's face it. You're in trouble here. You've got some metastases, and this is not good news. Here I am a doctor, and I would like you to live, but if you're going to die, there are a few things I'd like to tell you about dying. You may feel that by preparing for death, you're giving up and that you are turning your back on life. But I say, no, the task is the same. If you're going to live, you have to make some changes in yourself that have to do with being more true to yourself. And if you're going to die, you have to go around and talk to some people in ways that are more true to yourself. The paths then lead to the same point."

It's amazing how many people come back and say, "You know, this cancer or this illness has been the best thing ever to happen to me."

Existential psychologists, as well as various Indian gurus, articulate a connection between the individual's fear of death and all other fears. Every human fear is said to be rooted in this primal fear. If one is able to confront his own mortality and free himself from fears of death, all other fears can be eliminated. Some people hold onto their fear of death, believing that they risk death by letting go. However, the fear of death keeps us from living, not from dying.

Whether ill or not, a person's every waking moment is influenced by his or her relationship with death. Many years ago, a physician who counsels both the sick and the well drew a helpful analogy. While we sat in his office, he said, "Imagine that outside the office door is some horrible monster waiting to get you. Consider how you would feel right now in this room." He paused before continuing, "Now imagine that outside this door is paradise. It's beautiful, peaceful and loving beyond your greatest expectations. Consider how you would feel in this room right now." Though the room remained unchanged, even in this fantasy situation my feelings about it fluctuated greatly depending on how I viewed the alternatives waiting for me. The point was made. Our beliefs about death have an immediate impact on our lives.

There is good reason to struggle with this issue. If we believe that some horrible fate is always lurking in the wings, how can life really be enjoyed? But if we live as though death marked the start of some great unknown adventure, we are freed to experience the contentment that comes from living in the moment. Suddenly there is no reason to devote so much life energy to our vigilant but futile attempts to anticipate and control the future.

Intimacy and love are the potential rewards of the dying process. But fear makes us strangers to our own feelings. To "protect" ourselves, we may stay aloof from seriously ill persons and miss the purpose of these difficult human trials. This lost potential will lead to disappointment and loneliness, and it may seem that only death can spare the ordeal of tenuous life. By taking the risk and sharing our pain, anger, fear and love, we experience the comfort and meaning of human connectedness.•

A Core of Love

PAT DUFFY

I can't stand this. I just want to die. My mother spoke the words during the New York winter of seventeen snowstorms. Snow swirled outside the window of her room at the Bronx hospital for advanced cancer patients. My mother would spend the last ten days of her life there.

The hospital counselor had been sent to talk to me during one of my bouts of uncontrollable crying. I'd been staying at the hospital from early morning to late at night, afraid to go to work, afraid to leave, afraid my mother would die, afraid she would die alone.

He entered the hospital Family Room. "Oh, no, not a priest," I thought when I saw him. "I don't want to talk to a priest."

But his words held me. "I've worked with dying patients for many years, and I can tell you that when the end comes, the person chooses the moment. Some want to die with their loved ones in the room. Some wait until they leave. If your mother dies when you're not here, it's because that's the way she wanted it. The main thing is that your mother be at peace about dying. She needs you to tell her it's all right for her to go. You can't save your mother anymore, but you can help her to have a good death."

That night I left the hospital and went back home, and the next day I went back to work. During the days that followed, I taught my classes, then took the express bus to see Mom. I would rush to her room and breathe a sigh of relief when I saw that she was still there waiting for me, still in the world.

It was a great effort for Mom to speak. She was so weak she could barely move. She weighed sixty-five pounds. But she would force the words that mattered to her, "Don't stay too late. It's cold. It's snowing." Her hospital room was warm. Personal items were encouraged. A bulletin board held photos of her grandchildren. A shelf held a small statue of a Buddha from a collection that had belonged to my brother, Jackie, who'd been a lover of Indian art. Next to Jackie's Buddha were lots of cards and snowflake cut-outs from the kids at the local elementary school where Mom had been a schoolteacher for over thirty years. She'd been a great favorite with kids, parents and school staff. She'd been strong, energetic, warm, funny and healthy. Always healthy. "I haven't been to a doctor since the day she was born," she'd tell her friends, pointing to me.

But then Jackie died of colon cancer, discovered at an advanced stage. Jackie was forty-four. "It's not fair," Mom would say, "It's not fair." Now two-and-a half years later, Mom was at the special hospital for cancer patients, dying of colon cancer discovered at an advanced stage.

"Try to drink some apple juice, Mrs. Duffy," the nurse was saying softly to Mom. But the juice ran down the sides of her mouth. Mom could barely swallow. Each day her body was smaller, more consumed by disease. I broke down in tears. "Cry," my mother said to me, "It's good to cry. I could never cry enough."

One Thursday evening toward the end of visiting hours, Mom and I actually laughed. A surreal sight appeared: a white-coated staff attendant was wheeling a minibar through the hospital hallways. The minibar was filled with a great range of wines and liquors. "Like a drink? Like a drink?" the white-coated attendant asked as she wheeled along.

"Mom, I can't believe it. They're serving drinks!" The minibar attendant stopped by the door of my mother's room. "Like a drink?" the attendant asked. "No thanks," I said, looking at the minibar in amazement, "Are you really serving drinks here?"

"Every Thursday night for any visitors who want them or patients allowed them," the attendant said smiling. Then she wheeled on.

In better days, Mom and I had often chosen Thursday for our get-together nights. After work, I'd take the subway from Manhattan to Queens, and Mom would pick me up at the station. Depending on the ups and downs of our respective days, we'd greet each other with smiles or with snaps. But always by the time we arrived at our favorite restaurant, each of us settled with a dinner and a drink, all was well between us.

"Mom!" I laughed. "They serve drinks here on the hospital ward every Thursday night!"

"Have one," Mom said. "Okay, next Thursday we'll have a drink together just before I go. Okay, Mom?" "Okay," she said, "A last drink."

On the tenth day of my mother's stay at the hospital, I arrived in from the snow and the cold.

"If you like, you can stay overnight in your mother's room," the nurses said. After they left us, Mom gathered all her strength and said, "I can't stand this. I want to die."

"I understand, Mom," I said, words and tears rushing together. "I understand how you feel. This is very hard for me, Mom. But I understand how you feel." We held hands.

"I love you so much, Mom. I love you."

"I know you do," she said. "I love you, too."

We continued to say, "I love you," "I love you, too." That was all that was left: a core of love. The core of love that had always been there, beneath everything, at the center of everything, holding us together despite all the inevitable angers, disappointments, misunderstandings that pass between a mother and daughter. Now that the things of this world were disappearing, the core of love was in full view, almost palpable, fully revealed.

A silver-gray light entered the room from the snow-filled sky outside. "One more day," Mom said. "Another day. I don't want to let you go."

"I don't want to let you go either, Mom. Remember, we'll have our drink together tomorrow night. Tomorrow is Thursday."

"Another day," Mom said.

I saw the sores in my mother's mouth that of late had caused her so much pain. The terrible sores caused by thrush. The cancer had left her immune system drained, making her vulnerable to a host of painful afflictions. Treatments were useless. My mother, her body unimaginably weak and sensitive, now experienced all treatments as torments.

Mom became restless. She wanted the covers over her.

But as soon as I pulled the covers up, she wanted them down. Then up, then down. She began to heave and breathe, heave and breathe, wanted the covers up and down.

She fell asleep. I stayed next to her bed, holding her hand. Thoughts swirled inside my head uncontrollably. *What should I do tomorrow morning? Should I go to work? Should I stay? Should I go, should I stay? Yes, I would go to work as usual, as planned. I would come to the hospital after work to see Mom. She would be there waiting for me. It would be Thursday night, and we would have our drink together just like we'd said, wouldn't we?* The whirling thoughts in my mind were echoed by the swirling snows outside the hospital window.

I slept fitfully, waking, sleeping, waking, sleeping until the two states blended together. Outside the window, I saw the swirling snows turn to paper snowflake cut-outs that took the form of an enormous angel gliding by my mother's hospital room. Next, the paper snowflakes took the form of an enormous dove that glided after the angel in graceful procession.

I woke up. It was 4:00 A.M. Mom was breathing, but her eyes were half-closed. I held her hand. For the next hour or two, I watched her breathing get slower and slower until it stopped. We sat together, just the two of us, holding hands.

Perhaps it was 6:30 when a nurse came in. She got another nurse and a doctor who felt Mom's pulse. The doctor, worried and sad, looked at me. "She's gone," he said. "I know," I answered. I put my head on my mother's hand and cried and cried.

A minister came into the room and stood quietly beside me, embarrassed, not wanting to intrude. He asked if I wanted to talk. I said I wanted to be alone with my mother. He left and I stayed with Mom, looking at her face, her opened eyes, holding her hand. I put my forehead on Mom's hand as I held it. I wanted to remember everything we'd said the night before, the core of love, the silvery light.

The minister returned. "Would you like me to say some prayers?" he asked. "Yes," I said. He said prayers, and I listened. When he finished, I thanked him. It was time to go, I knew. I put my hand on Mom's shoulder and pressed it. I said good-bye to the minister. Then I gathered our things together, Mom's and mine, walked down the hall, out the door and through the snowy streets to the bus back home.

EPILOGUE

I'd often wondered at the fact that Mom and I had not had our last drink together. Then in the summer after her death, I had a dream. I'd been out with a friend. It was very late on a warm, summer night. I said to my friend, "I know it's late and it's out of the way, but let's stop by the Buddha Bar for a last drink."

As we approached the Buddha Bar, we saw Jackie's Buddha statue peeking through the window. Then we entered to find my mother behind the bar, serving drinks. "Mom," I said. "You're here."

"Yes," she said, smiling. She looked happy and very peaceful. I sat on a bar stool and we chatted. "Like a drink?" Mom asked. "Let's have a drink." She poured one for each of us.

"Mom," I said, "Now that I know you're here, I can visit you again."

"Yes," Mom said. "Come after work."

Then I woke up. It was Thursday.•

THE FINAL TRANSITION

Soul Practice

QUESTIONS

1. What if you knew you had six months, or one year to live? What would you need to do, say, be, in order to fully "come to birth" during that time? What would your priorities be?
2. What if you were to embrace your impending death compassionately and lovingly rather than turn away and reject it? How would that free you?
3. What fears do you have around dying and death? Name them; just the simple act of naming them makes them lose some of their power over you.
4. What would it mean to you to stop denying your own death? How would that free you to live more fully?
5. If you know someone who is dying, how do you feel in the presence of that person? What fears come up for you? How do you hold yourself back with them? Ask yourself what it would be like to fully show up, open-hearted, in their presence. What do you need to say to them, give them, ask of them, before they die?
6. If someone you know and love is dying, how can they be a teacher for you?
7. How is the recipe for "dying consciously" similar to the recipe for "living consciously"?

P R A C T I C E S

1. Make a life review, whether you are imagining you have a year to live, or know that you are terminally ill. Who and what needs to be forgiven (including yourself)? Whom do you need to make amends to? For what, and whom, are you especially grateful? Whom do you need to thank, and for what? What do you regret, and how can you find some meaning in it and release it? What is unfinished in your life?

2. Practice soft belly: breathe, and allow your belly to soften and relax. Let go of how it looks. Let there be space for anything that arises as you let your belly soften: thoughts, feelings, images. Simply notice them and return to your breathing, and allowing your belly to soften.

3. If someone you love has died, consider designing a ritual or ceremony to honor your grief. Go back and read David Feinstein and Peg Elliott Mayo's article. Write down ideas for honoring the one who has passed on; gather together your community and create a ritual.

8

The Process of
Transformation

Transformation occurs on the inside. It is a movement toward the integration of our being, toward the essence of who we are. It is a private and personal journey. After a certain point, it is a journey we traverse by ourselves. There is no map we can follow all the way home, to the place where we reconnect with our true selves.

There are some who have journeyed ahead of us. They have pointed the way and told us what to look for along the way. They have described the inner terrain with its openings and obstacles. Having been there, they know which qualities are catalysts for our movement, such as a burning desire to know and serve. They help us recognize the spiritual qualities that develop in response to our search, such as kindness and truthfulness.

This chapter discusses the inner landscape of the transformational journey from a variety of viewpoints. As you know, when the student is ready, a teacher appears.

F O R   T H E   W O R L D
T O   B E   T R A N S F O R M E D

The only way the world will be transformed is for the world's inhabitants to make changes in individual levels of consciousness. As we do this, we experience God. God becomes that harmony. Robert Frost said it beautifully: "We all sit around in a circle and suppose, but the secret sits in the center and knows." That center is where I now go when I meditate. I go into that light and I also bring it to me. Like an axle that turns but whose center doesn't move, God is the unmoved secret in the center.

All the Eastern traditions talk about having an inner observer, being able to "die" while you're alive. To be spiritual, to awaken, to be detached means to experience your own death. What does it mean to die while you're alive? It means coming into contact with the part of you that doesn't constitute your humanity. The invisible part of you—the part of you that leaves when you die—is where God resides. And this isn't "mystical"; it's real. You don't have to go to India to discover it; you don't have to wear a loincloth and meditate in a cave.

I find God by giving myself time every day—through prayer, or meditation, or whatever you want to call it—to go into another level of consciousness. I close my eyes and breathe. I center myself and empty my mind and begin to feel the love that is there when I quiet down enough to feel. As I do this, I transcend time and space, and I am in the very presence of God. This, to me, is a direct daily experience of God, and it puts me into a state of harmony and bliss that transcends anything I've ever known.

—Wayne W. Dyer

Finding the Way

JACK KORNFIELD
AND CHRISTINA FELDMAN

Finding the way to authentic awakening presents us with an immense challenge. Naturally enough, we first listen to the voices of external authorities who seem to hold the answers to our questions. It becomes more confusing as we soon discover that the world abounds in a multitude of authorities who gladly and willingly offer us advice, solutions and formulas. Our bookstores overflow with prescriptions on how to be happy, fulfilled and liberated. In the beginning, we may listen and learn from the wisdom of other people's experience. We can be inspired by the example of teachers and sages of past and present.

At some point in the midst of our listening, a number of insights dawn upon us. We see that no single authority holds the hot line to truth, nor is there just one way to awakening. It may also become clear to us that what we hear are simply the different melodies through which the great spiritual traditions have expressed one essential harmony. It is this harmony that is significant and not the manner of its expression. The common elements of all who become wise are that they have learned to listen to this wisdom in their own hearts, to hear the underlying harmony and to travel their own path.

No one can travel our path for us; no one can substitute for us in our quest for awakening. In trusting that wisdom, joy and awakening are our spiritual heritage, we must discover what awakens them in us. No one else can free us from the confusion, fear and attachment that cast shadows of pain on our lives. In accepting this aloneness, we find it is not an aloneness of alienation or withdrawal. We are supported in our spiritual quest by all those of past generations, of all cultures, who applaud and inspire our exploration. Our quest connects us with millions of contemporary companions who seek inner peace and freedom. In the willingness to know our own aloneness, we begin to discover a wisdom and compassion that connects us to all others.

There will be moments when we encounter feelings of despair, doubt and inadequacy. We may wonder how to bridge the apparently uncrossable gap between confusion and clarity, holding and opening, limitation and freedom. In all moments of darkness, we need to remember that we are blessed with humanity's most precious gift—the capacity to be aware. It is a gift to rejoice in; the capacity to be aware is the power to be conscious, to be awake and to transform. It is an immense power, enabling us to penetrate the veils of confusion that limit us, enabling us to connect with and use the inner resources of energy, focus and love that lie dormant.

Exploring what it means to be aware, we learn how to be wholeheartedly present in each moment, present with ourselves, present with all that each moment brings to us. Connecting with the present moment we are able to set aside our anxiety about the future and with what we might gain or lose, have or become. We are able to free ourselves from our preoccupations with the past, our histories, and the burden of our regrets. Our awareness illuminates what is actually here, one moment at a time. And it is in this moment that we are able to learn and to open.

The present moment is the most profound and challenging teacher we will ever meet in our lives. It is a compassionate teacher; it extends to us no judgment, no censure, no measurement of success and failure. The present moment is a mirror, and in its reflection we learn how to see. Learning how to look into this mirror without deluding ourselves is the source of all wisdom. In this mirror we see what contributes to the confusion and discord in our lives and what contributes to harmony and understanding. We see the relationship between pain and its cause on a moment-to-moment level; we see the bond between love and its source. We see what it is that connects us and what it is that alienates us.

In this seeing we begin to learn from our own stories, what delights us and what saddens us. Listening inwardly and learning from our own stories, we see that we are in need not so much of experts to define our way, as of our own clear and direct inner attunement. Our stories reveal our path. In our listening we can understand what we need to let go of and what we need to develop if we are to live in the spirit of peace and freedom.

Our own stories differ only in superficial form and detail from the stories of all beings. There is no living being that does not share our yearning for liberation, to be free from fear and pain. Grief is grief, no matter the heart that endures it. Peace is peace, regardless of the heart that rejoices in it.

How to make our lives an embodiment of wisdom and compassion is the greatest challenge spiritual seekers face. The truths we have come to understand need to find their visible expression in our lives. Our every thought, word or action holds the possibility of being a living expression of clarity and love. It is not enough to be a possessor of wisdom. To believe ourselves to be custodians of truth is to become its opposite, is a direct path to becoming stale, self-righteous or rigid. Ideas and memories do not hold liberating or healing power.

There is no such state as enlightened retirement, where we can live on the bounty of past attainments. Wisdom is alive only as long as it is lived; understanding is liberating only as long as it is applied. A bulging portfolio of spiritual experiences matters little if it does not have the power to sustain us through the inevitable moments of grief, loss and change. Knowledge and achievements matter little if we do not yet know how to touch the heart of another and be touched.

We must be wary, however, of being entranced by idealism. Profound love, compassion, sensitivity and awakening are the possibilities of spirituality that move and attract us. Yet we know that it is easier to love a thousand people in our thoughts than to fully love one person in actuality. It is not difficult to extend boundless acceptance and compassion to those who do not actively challenge us. We acknowledge that it is easy to be armchair philosophers, but then what do we do? Only in the midst of our concrete relationships and day-to-day living can we actually express our wisdom and demonstrate compassion.

We live in undeniable connectedness with all life. Every word we speak, every action we initiate creates a ripple upon this relationship. Understanding this connectedness brings a sacredness to each moment. There is no contact, no perception, no engagement that is inconsequential or insignificant. Each contact is an opportunity for deepening sensitivity and understanding. Our spirituality must touch every area of our lives. We live within our bodies; therefore we are sexual beings, and our sexuality is a vehicle for honoring and respecting the life of all beings. We live in relationship with one another; therefore we are social beings, and every relationship offers us the opportunity to learn how to give and receive with an open heart. We participate consciously or unconsciously in the structures that govern us, and we are political beings by virtue of this participation. Our wisdom empowers us to contribute to the creation of structures that respect the dignity and spirit of all beings. Our spirituality is visible and vital when it embraces every facet of our lives. •

The Heart of Optimism

AN INTERVIEW WITH
JOAN BORYSENKO

In her book *Fire in the Soul* Jean Borysenko shows how a fruitful search for meaning can occur following devastating events. A time of a "Dark Night of the Soul," when we feel torment and despair, can lead to spiritual resurrection. These dark voyages are not easy, they take us through places of suffering. This book is a beacon of light, illuminating the way home.

PERSONAL TRANSFORMATION: *What is spiritual optimism?*

JOAN BORYSENKO: Spiritual optimism is a point of view. The universe is a sacred mystery we are unable to understand. Nonetheless, we need some framework that enables us to grow from our crises and challenges. I believe that the universe is in fact a friendly place. My answer to Einstein's question, "Is the universe a friendly place or not?" is yes. To be spiritually optimistic we have to hold the view that the universe is friendly. Everything happens in order for us or others to grow in wisdom and in love. We need to have this faith, even though in relative reality this world is not safe. Bad things definitely happen to good people.

PT: *How do we develop an optimistic view?*

JB: We live along into it. It is our crises that bring us optimism. Through working with people in physical and psychological crisis, I am aware that when we have a crisis, all our beliefs surface for us to see. It brings up the question, "Why is this bad thing happening to me?" Any time we are in crisis, we have an opportunity to re-examine our beliefs. It's been my experience that when people seek help from family and friends, spiritual traditions, and counseling, they come out of crisis stronger! On the other hand, people who hold to the status quo and who will not engage with their crisis become embittered and miss the opportunity to deeply know who they are.

When I worked as a medical psychologist in a Mind/Body clinic, I watched the ways people answered the question, why me? I saw people let go of helplessness and bitterness. They moved into self-understanding, compassion toward others and connection with the universe. *Fire in the Soul* is a result of watching people struggle with those questions, as well as being healed and struggling with those questions myself.

PT: *You call these times "dark nights of the soul." How do we withstand dark nights and not get lost in pessimism?*

JB: Having a dark night of the soul is not a bad thing. In our culture we focus on the bright side. We have to be optimistic all the time. Life is supposed to be a constant upward progression. If you look at the wisdom of the ancient traditions this is not the case. In many primitive cultures, life involves periods of death and rebirth. That's what initiations are. When a boy becomes a man, he undergoes a manhood ritual that is very difficult, involving physical scourging and emotional isolation. A woman leaving childhood and entering the society of women undergoes a womanhood ritual.

In order to become something new, you have to die. During the process, there is a period that is no-woman's-land or no-man's-land, between what you were and what you have yet to become. That's a dark night of the soul. We need to learn that this is normal. We aren't supposed to know or be in control at every moment. Death and rebirth, and entering into confusion are a natural part of life. We need faith that we grow from these times, and that it is part of our design emotionally and spiritually. Then we don't feel like we are doing or feeling something wrong. Unfortunately, we attempt to abort the process with alcohol or drugs or something that makes us feel better or by ignoring the inner call to be quiet.

PT: *We have to honor this process in a culture that does not.*

JB: Precisely! There is just no room for it.

PT: *In your book you say, "If we have lost our cultural understanding of the value of darkness, we've also lost the priesthood, whose function it was to bring us through these transitions." Please discuss this.*

JB: In our culture, we think that everything should be quickly made right. When people have some sort of a dark night, they often run to a physician. That fascinates me. Seventy-five percent of the time that people go to their family physician they are anxious and lonely. They have illnesses related to stress. They are looking for someone with wisdom to bring them through this time. They are seeking somebody to talk with to help them transform it. It used to be that the healer in a tribe was someone who had not only knowledge of physical healing but also emotional knowledge of people. They knew whether these people were using their gifts in ways that would make them happy and contribute to the whole community. Healers had spiritual sense. Is this person able to open their heart compassionately to themselves and to others? Or are they stuck in bitterness or regret? A healer had many kinds of knowledge.

Now this knowledge is very fragmented. People don't know where to get healing. We've lost that medical priesthood. People go to a physician and get a diagnosis, a label. Psychology, although it can be enormously helpful, generally is a psychology of pathology rather than potential. It, too, has lost its spiritual roots. We have this fragmentation. We need to bring back the priesthood of healers.

PT: *You say that we benefit from the dark night by holding in front of us "first" stories. What do you mean?*

JB: If you look to earlier times, people learned morality from stories. People learned about their connection with one another, the land, and spirituality through storytelling. Stories give us a map of who we are and where we are going. People are hungry to hear stories of life. First stories give maps of transformation, of the phases we go through. We go through evolution because we are human souls, not because we are failures of some sort. We need to transform our endings. First stories do that. Often we get stuck in a story and decide that we're broken or wronged. We don't bring the story through to transformation, where we find the wisdom in the wound and a greater sense of community. Stories show us the way.

PT: *So stories give meaning to our suffering. They offer us possibilities so we can grow and gain wisdom.*

JB: Story makes all the difference, even on a very basic physical level. I wept when I read Victor Frankl's book, *Man's Search for Meaning*, to hear what went on in the concentration camps. Imagine Frankl as a young psychiatrist, coming to grips with the horror of it; arriving with a manuscript, wondering if he could hold on to it, then realizing he could not keep his manuscript and he might not keep his life. His story is essentially that what people told themselves about *why* this horror was happening made all the difference. Those who told themselves the story that it was meaningless gave up hope quickly, and died of the first epidemic that went around or of rapid cardiac death. People who somehow found a way to weave that story into the fabric of life were those most likely to come out.

PT: *How does suffering influence our belief system?*

JB: Suffering brings our belief system fully into view. Often, we're too busy to figure out what we believe. Our beliefs sit there like a pair of sunglasses through which we see the world. We're so used to seeing through those sunglasses that we don't know we're wearing them. Then somebody says, "What's the color of your glasses?" and you respond, "What glasses?" Suffering makes you take a look at the glasses you are wearing. Very often those beliefs have to do with early stories we were told about who we were, who God was and the purpose of human life.

In our country, psychology has been taught that ideas about religion are not our business. These are not ideas you discuss with patients. Clergy deals with religion. Even though I had a mystical interest all my life, I felt that as a psychologist I wasn't supposed to ask my patients about spirituality.

We gave a standard test to people who came to the Mind/Body clinic. One of the questions was, "I think I am being or should be punished by God." I was very embarrassed when I first saw that question and thought, "Punished by God, what a thing to ask someone." The majority of the people actually answered yes to that. I was interested in stress management. What greater stress could a human being have than to think there was some cosmic Peeping Tom looking over your actions, and deciding whether you should be rewarded or punished? I thought I was doing people a disservice unless I addressed those issues.

This is a tremendous issue with people who have AIDS. Many people with AIDS were taught as children that it was sinful to be homosexual. Therefore, AIDS would be punishment for sinning. I told a story in *Fire in the Soul* of a man who had been raised a Southern Baptist. He went to college and left behind that belief in a punitive God but never substituted another belief. When he got AIDS his search started again. When we become sick we generally regress and feel helpless. So his childhood beliefs resurfaced. He had to work through that and it was a very difficult process. He died before he resolved it. It was very sad.

Hopefully most of us do live long enough with our crisis to work through these big questions about the universe, ourselves, the purpose of life and Divine Being. When we do, we find that we are better equipped for the rest of our lives. We develop a more loving and compassionate attitude toward ourselves that is also reflected in our attitude about God.

PT: *In* Fire in the Soul *you say that to use crisis as an opening into this process we need courage. Would you describe the three stages of courage?*

JB: My mother had a particular kind of courage, which was "keep on trucking; no matter what happens, don't look back!" This is instinctual courage. We're a very fortunate generation compared to my mother's. There wasn't much chance in her generation to develop other kinds of courage. If you were in trouble a generation ago, where did you go? Where did you look for help? People didn't go to therapy unless they had a severe mental disorder. There weren't support groups. What did you do with your pain? Very often you buried it underneath, and kept on moving.

PT: *Is that willful courage?*

JB: Yes, and it is very useful. People who don't have willful courage become helpless in times of crisis and are not able to get through it.

The second stage is psychological courage, which comes from examining your life. The recovery movement has introduced many people to psychological courage. In recovery you take a look and say "Wait a minute, what happened to me? What were the wounds of my life? What things happened that led me to be who I am?" This kind of looking allows us to gain wisdom from our situation. We become able to take responsibility for what goes on in our life. The third kind of courage grows out of psychological courage. Once we have begun to look within we become wiser. We develop a knowing perspective.

PT: *We begin to experience Divine Union and know that we are not alone, which reduces fear. Fear feeds on isolation.*

JB: It certainly does. In every moment we have the choice for love or fear. The only way we can get rid of fear is to feel our union with Divine Oneness. Fear leads us to say, "I am uncomfortable feeling isolated from myself and from the ability to have an intimate relationship with others." We begin to look for a deeper relationship to life in general, and eventually this leads into the experience of Divine Union. That is the only time we feel safe.

PT: *Psychological courage seems to be a step toward Divine Union as we begin feeling connected with ourselves and others.*

JB: That is the ancient wisdom of Judaism as restated by Jesus. When asked to summarize his teachings, Jesus said, "This is the spiritual life. Love the Lord Thy God with all Thy heart, with all Thy soul, and with all Thy mind, and love Thy neighbor as Thyself." The question is, how do we learn to do that? We must learn to love ourselves. Then we must learn to love other people, who I think are expressions of ourselves. We're all one big case of Divine multiple personalities. We have to love and understand ourselves. In looking at others we see that we are all some expression of the same thing. I look out into another face and I see myself. We develop compassion, and then recognize what a tremendous experience, what a tremendous gift, life is.

PT: *You say that healing requires reliving and transforming the crisis. How do we do that? And what can help?*

JB: What helps, first of all, is the willful courage to keep on trucking. Willful courage becomes limiting, though, when you refuse to go back and look at the pain so that you can work through it to some new wisdom perspective. Most people are not willing until the pain becomes too much and they get overwhelmed. To heal is to go back and say, "Yes, this is my pain. This was the grief that I felt."

The first step is the willingness to be aware of the places there was pain in our life. It may not be just our childhood. It might be that as adults we inflicted pain upon our loved ones or ourselves and feel guilty. We need not run away. We have to go back and say, "Yes, I am braving this. This situation is the key of my wisdom." Then we can go through our feelings. We work through to the stage where we say, "Yes, I have learned from this."

Once we get to that point, forgiveness comes simply. We feel finished. The issue has no more juice, no energy. We are grateful for the experience. Many people think forgiveness is turning the other cheek and saying "I forgive you." It doesn't work because the grief is still locked in the body. There has not been a conscious transformation of the pain.

PT: *Facing these issues leads us into the dark night. What can help us tolerate this process and hold onto the belief that there is wisdom to be gained?*

JB: When we're going through a period of death and rebirth, and hanging out in that no man's land, we tend to forget about basic things. The body needs to be nourished well. The body needs sleep. The body needs to be out of danger. Nature is a tremendous healer. When people lay on a patch of ground, let the sun beat on them, and the breezes flow around them they feel rejuvenated. Spend some time with nature. We need to move our bodies. People often get sedentary at times like this. Change needs to move through us. We need to exercise. Walk, jog, swim or cycle. Keep the body moving.

It is important to find a way to touch the Divine. For some it is meditation, for others it is prayer. People fail to reach out for the help that is consistently available. I met a woman not too long ago who tried to kill herself. In her near-death experience she got a good reprimand for trying to kill herself and was told that a human life is hard to obtain. She was taken on a tour of many different experiences on the other side. In one of the experiences she saw a room full of people. They looked so alone and disconnected. All around them were beautiful beings trying to minister to them. They didn't feel the presence of those beings. A being of light told the woman that these were people who had died. They didn't realize that they were dead. All they needed to do was ask for help in any way and those beings of light would come to their aid. They could not aid without being asked because it would be a violation of free will.

There is a tremendous amount of help available but we have to learn to ask for it. Learning to ask starts with believing that help is really there. You can pray in your heart for help. There are lots of ways people can do that, depending on the tradition you come out of.

Practically everybody experiences moments daily when they are at one with the Divine. These are moments when you look at something of beauty and are so drawn to it that gratitude or a sense of connection with something larger fills your heart. In that moment you let go of the past, your fears and all the things that separate us. You connect with your own spiritual self, inner self or higher self. You connect with the Whole. You participate with Divine Being.

PT: *Those moments can be with animal, a child or music.*

JB: Yes. You sit down and the cat jumps in your lap. You look into her eyes. Those whiskers twitch and she purrs and you find yourself at peace in your own body. Sometimes people have bigger experiences that last for several minutes.

In a holy moment of meditation you recall such a moment with all your senses. What were you seeing at that time? What were you smelling? Was your body moving? Were you holding something or being held? As you recreate it the feelings come back. You feel peace, gratitude and stillness, and your heart opens. Love becomes a part of the experience and you are in a state of Divine Union. Let the memory fade and then sit quietly in that state. Your attention will wander because it always does when you meditate. At that point you do something to maintain your focus. It could be awareness of breathing or could be repetition of what Thomas Keating refers to as centering prayer.

His definition of centering prayer is similar to what I am talking about with a Holy Moment. He describes center as prayer, immersing yourself in God's presence and entering into that state of being and stillness where you feel connection. He suggests that people pick a prayer word, such as peace, love or Jesus. Instill that word in your mind as you enter God's presence. When I meditate I relive a holy moment first so that I know what it feels like to be in God's presence. Then I use a prayer word to help me stay there.

PT: *It is easier to access help during a crisis if we already have a practice of connecting with the Divine.*

JB: Absolutely!

PT: *When we need comfort we can draw from experience.*

JB: That makes all the difference in the world. When Bill Moyer asked Joseph Campbell, "Do you have faith?" Campbell laughed and said, "I don't need faith, I have experience."

PT: *If we believe that life is a mystery beyond our understanding and that suffering leads us into wholeness, what do we pray for when we call for help?*

JB: There are two kinds of prayer, nondirected and directed. Directed prayer is a request. Please take my cancer away. Please give me a job tomorrow. Research data suggests that directed prayer helps some. It works better than no prayer at all.

But nondirected prayer works even better than directed prayer. The Spindrift Foundation describes nondirected prayers as a pure and holy qualitative consciousness of whoever or whatever is being prayed for. For instance, metaphorically I can look upon myself as a seed. I'm going to grow into a flower. I may not know what the flower is, so I pray simply that my best potential blossoms forth. I think it's best to pray for the very best potential in the situation because we can't know exactly what that is.

Maybe the best potential in a situation is not physical healing, but death in this life. We can't know these things. We pray for the clarity to understand what is best to do in the situation. We pray for healing. We try to heal from our own illusion that we can ever be separate from the Great One. We pray for the removal of negativity, and obstructions of our awareness of the Whole. We don't have to become part of the Whole, we already are.•

Walking the Mystical Path with Practical Feet

ANGELES ARRIEN, PH. D.

R ecently I witnessed a moment of deep soulfulness between two strangers. I was at a bus stop, sitting next to a woman reading a newspaper, but I was totally engrossed in the performance of a fourteen-year-old boy on a skateboard. He had his baseball cap turned around with the bill in back, and he was skating beautifully and very fast. He buzzed by us once, then twice. When he came by a third time, he accidentally knocked the woman's newspaper out of her hands. She said, "Oh, why don't you grow up!"

I watched him glide down to the corner of the block where he stood talking with his buddy. The two of them kept looking back over their shoulders at the woman. She hesitated for a moment, then rolled up her paper, tucked it under her arm, and walked into the street, motioning to him. "Won't you come here?" she called. "I want to talk to you."

Very reluctantly, he skated over to her, turned his cap around with the bill in front, and said, "Yeah?"

She said, "What I meant to say was that I was afraid that I might get hurt. I apologize for what I did say."

His face lit up and he said, "How cool!"

In that moment, I witnessed what is called in Spanish a *milagro pequeño*— small miracle. This small miracle was a holy, healing moment between generations, between two human beings who had just become important strangers to each other. The woman chose to shift the shape of her experience by moving out of reactivity into creativity. This kind of shape shifting is possible when we allow ourselves to speak directly from our souls.

Part of the business of soul, in fact, is to be a shape-shifter. When we are in touch with the deepest undercurrents of our lives, we have no choice but to act honestly, to speak soulfully. Our soul work is, quite simply, to find and remove whatever gets in the way of our being who we are.

In our culture, we don't have many aids to tracking our souls, to keeping in touch with the things that make us who we are and recognizing and eliminating those things that deter us. Indigenous cultures have important information to offer us about maintaining soulfulness in our lives. Just as they have outer tracking devices—for locating such things as food and water—indigenous peoples of the world have internal tracking devices that enable them to integrate their experiences, learn from them and move on.

I have found, among a variety of indigenous cultures, four central tracking devices. We can think of them as four "rivers" that we must learn to navigate in order to keep our souls fed and healthy, in order to keep our true selves alive. One is the river of inspiration. I know I'm still alive if I can be inspired, expanded, and uplifted by events, by beauty, by other people. Another is the river of challenge. I'm still alive if I can bring energy to the experience of being tested and challenged. This river is about being able to accept an invitation to stretch, to move beyond the familiar, to grow.

The third river is the river of surprise. Children love surprises; as adults, unfortunately, we often lose that love. Navigating the river of surprise means being able to be shaken out of our need for control and reawakened to the awe of the unexpected. The last river or tracking device is the river of love. I know I'm still alive if I can be deeply touched and deeply moved by life. If I'm not easily touched by life, my heart has begun to close. Native peoples believe that the heart is the bridge between father sky and mother nature and that, therefore, if we are to stay in contact with both the mystical and the practical in our nature, we must stay healthy and open in our hearts.

The open heart is one that can both give and receive love; an open heart also recognizes that love does not always come to us in the ways we expect. I thought of this recently as I watched a mother and her son, who must have been about seven years old, walking through a public garden. The boy plucked a rose from a bush, brought it to her, and said, "Mommy, you're as pretty as this rose." She took the rose, thanked him, and then said, "Why don't you ever tell Mommy that you love her?"

That mother's heart was closed to the variety of ways that expressions of love might come to her. Perhaps only the actual words would have made sense to her. How sad for both her and her son that she could not hear the "I love you" underneath his statement.

When, whatever the reason, we find ourselves incapable of navigating those four rivers—inspiration, challenge, surprise and love— we have begun to lose touch with our souls. We miss out on the beauty and opportunity of the world; we find ourselves caught in the prison of our own consciousness. And often we don't take soul sickness as seriously as we do sickness in the body. Again, we can look to older cultures to help us find the medicines of soul retrieval.

If you were suffering from the symptoms of soul loss—if you were depressed or dispirited—and went to an indigenous healer or shaman, it is likely that he or she would begin to work with you by asking one of four questions. One of those questions is, "When in your life did you stop singing?" If you can remember a time when you stopped singing, you might remember feeling that you were beginning to lose your voice; you might remember some circumstance or idea or person that made you feel it was no longer safe to give voice to your own truth.

Another question is, "When did you stop dancing?" When you stopped dancing is when you began to lose touch with your body. Children dance spontaneously all the time; they simply respond to music. As adults, we need to ask ourselves when and how it was that we lost that ability to respond; we need to look at how it happened that we stopped dancing.

The third question is, "When did you stop being enchanted with stories?" Stories are the greatest healing and teaching art that we have. Through stories, we transmit values, ethics, traditions, memories and identity. One way to retrieve our souls is to ask ourselves what our favorite stories are, to repeat the ones that we find most healing and comforting, and to remember which ones we especially want to pass on to others.

The last and perhaps most difficult question that an indigenous healer would ask is, "When did you stop being comfortable with the sweet territory of silence?" Silence is recognized by all cultures as that place where we can connect to mystery, where our individual souls reconnect with the soul of the world. In order to allow ourselves adequate contemplation and reflection, we need to be comfortable with silence and solitude.

These four universal healing questions seem simple, yet they hold the keys to many of our soul-sicknesses. Despite all the obvious differences among cultures and peoples, there is not a culture in the world that doesn't sing or dance or tell stories or recognize the mystery in silence. In our culture, silence is often impossible to come by, and this is a tragedy, for silence allows us to replenish ourselves so that we can then give back to the world around us. The lack of generosity that we often experience in the world may be due to the fact that so few of us have adequate solitude within with which to replenish ourselves.

One image I find useful for describing the necessity for replenishing ourselves is that of a well with buckets around it. Our soul—our deep source—is the well. We fill our buckets from that well and then pour out to others what is needed from our buckets. In order to protect that source, we have to be sure that we give from the buckets and not from the well itself and that when those buckets are empty, there is a time for replenishing—a time to refill before we give again. Unfortunately, the frantic pace of our lives often requires that we begin to give not just from the buckets around the well but from the well itself; some of us, I'm afraid, are squeezing the last few drops of liquid from the moss at the bottom. Soul work requires that we give ourselves adequate time for replenishment—time to deepen and integrate, time to come back to the center of our lives.

Meditation is a powerful way to provide our souls with adequate solitude and silence. Though many of us think of meditation as happening in one posture—sitting down, legs crossed—there are actually four universal meditation postures: standing, sitting, lying down and walking. Each of these postures is appropriate for certain kinds of problems or issues.

Standing meditation is useful if you feel victimized or helpless. It can remind you of what it feels like to stand up for yourself, to have literally both feet on the ground. In standing meditation, you can most easily access your authority and power. Sitting meditation gives you access to your own wisdom; sitting is the best posture for suspending judgment, for becoming a fair witness to your own processes. When I feel my self-critic gathering too much strength, I know it is time for sitting meditation.

If are struggling with fear or anger, or any overwhelming emotion, lying-down meditation can help that emotion move more easily through your body. The lying posture is the most healing posture the body can assume; lying down, you can most easily access the nurturing, loving energy within yourself. Walking meditation encourages creative problem solving and helps you to reignite your own creative fire. If I find myself in periods of stagnation or inertia, I re-energize with walking meditation.

Recently I discovered that Albert Einstein arranged his study to accommodate all four of these meditation postures. He had a tall table designed so that he could stand while writing his formulas. He had a favorite chair—an old wingback—to sit on. He kept an army cot in his study, too, so that he could lie down from time to time. And he wore a circular path into the wood floor of that room—just outside the perimeter of a circular rug—from pacing. Though he might not have called it meditation, it is revealing that a man so deeply involved with both science and spirituality structured his work room so that he would have standing, sitting, lying and walking opportunities. On some level, he must have known that each of these postures allowed him to access different kinds of information.

It is becoming more and more important that we not only access such information but bring it into the world. That is our task in this decade. We can no longer continue to support the "either-or" world—the place where we either put all our energy into our own individual paths or into the larger community—but must move into the "both-and" world. Many of us have spent a lot of time doing inner work, in a sense hopping on one leg in the internal world. Our task now is to put the other leg into the outer world, to combine spirit and action. It is absolutely essential that we learn to walk the mystical path with practical feet.

That can be a daunting task. But again, indigenous peoples have wisdom to offer us. In many indigenous cultures you can find some variation on the following rules, which are intended to make living a life very simple. The first rule is, *Show up*. Choose to be present to life. Choosing to be present is the skill of the warrior archetype, an old-fashioned term for leadership abilities. The warrior in us chooses to be present to life.

Once we show up, we can go on with rule number two, which is, *Pay attention* to what has heart and meaning. This rule is associated with the archetype of the healer, the one who recognizes that love is the greatest healing power in the world. When we pay attention to what has heart and meaning, we are opening the arms of love.

When we show up and pay attention to what has heart and meaning, then we can follow the third rule: *Tell the truth* without blame or judgment. This is the path of the visionary, the one who can give voice to what is so. Telling the truth without blame or judgment is not necessarily being "polite," but the truth-teller does consider timing and context as well as delivery. Truth telling collapses our patterns of denial and indulgence, keeps us authentic.

When we are able to tell the truth, we can go to the fourth rule: *Be open to outcome*, but not attached to it. This is associated with the archetype of the teacher who trusts in the unexpected and is able to be detached. Often in the West, we define "detachment" as "not caring," but detachment is really the capacity to care deeply but objectively. If you've taken the other three steps, then the fourth rule should come naturally, if not always easily. If you have shown up, paid attention to what has heart and meaning, and told the truth without blame or judgment, then it should follow naturally that you can be open, but not attached, to outcome.

None of this is necessarily easy to do. But one of the great joys of soul work is that whether we are able to be fully present to life, life keeps calling out to us. No one is immune to the pull of the natural cycles of the universe; no one is immune to love. And because it requires just as much energy, if not more, to stay out of life as it does to be fully engaged in it, why not be engaged? Octavio Paz, a Latin American poet and Nobel Prize winner, realized when he was in his forties just how much of himself he had spent staying away from the deep currents of his life. He wrote this prose poem describing that experience and describing, too, the persistence of the world in spite of it all.

> *After chopping off all the arms that reached out to me; after boarding up all the windows and doors; after filling all the pits with poisoned water; after building my house on the rock of a No inaccessible to flattery and fear; after cutting out my tongue and eating it; after hurling handfuls of silence and monosyllables of scorn at my loves; after forgetting my name and the name of my birthplace and the name of my race; after judging myself and sentencing myself to perpetual waiting and perpetual loneliness, I heard against the stones of my dungeon of syllogisms the humid, tender, insistent onset of spring.*

No matter how we try, soul calls out to us. We may have become so injured in our instincts, so wounded in our souls that our demons threaten to overwhelm us, that we cannot quite hear the call of spring. But spring calls to us anyway. The center of our soul work is ensuring that the good, true and beautiful in our nature is at least as strong as the demons and the monsters; put another way, it is ensuring that my self-worth is at least as strong as my self-critic. That issue is central to all of the indigenous peoples I have studied. If I am living in a way that feeds the good, true and beautiful in my nature—as opposed to feeding the self-critic—then I can heal myself. I can stay in touch with my own deep source, my soul. And I can also be a healing agent in my family, my community, my nation and the world.

I said before that the basis of soul work is really to eliminate everything that gets in the way of my being myself and to feed that which encourages me to be myself. I want to suggest a simple exercise—two simple questions—to help you track that. Each morning, before you step out into the world, ask yourself, "Is my self-worth as strong as my self-critic?" Be sure you can say yes before you go out the door. Then, using your name, say, "Jim, are you Jim?" or "Sally, are you Sally?" and be sure that you can say yes to that, too, before you go out into the world.

All of us carry, within ourselves, an original healing medicine that is not duplicated anywhere else on this earth. If we say yes to those two questions every day, then we can bring our medicine fully into the world. We can, as the woman at the bus stop did, move out of reactivity into creativity. When we live soulfully, each of us can be a shape-shifter; each of us can create holy, healing moments. Each of us can be fully engaged, moment to moment, in the great gift called life.•

Personal Transformation

AN INTERVIEW WITH DEEPAK CHOPRA, M. D. AND RICHARD MOSS, M. D.

RICHARD MOSS: The words "personal transformation" are increasingly used in the community of people seeking psychological and spiritual healing and exploration, but there isn't general agreement on what the words mean. To some people it has to do with personal improvement. To others, like myself, it has to do with a fundamental transformation in the very structure of consciousness. What does personal transformation mean to you?

DEEPAK CHOPRA: I am glad you asked the question like you did, referring to the structure of consciousness. Like many people of my generation, I was exposed to *Vedanta* in India during my growing up years. We were brought up with a vocabulary that laid out a map for the transformation of consciousness. In that sense, what I say in this interview is not original at all.

When you study physics, you've got to learn the vocabulary that physicists use. The same is true if you want to understand the structure of consciousness. People before us have traveled this road; they laid out a map and established a vocabulary. If you understand that vocabulary, you can understand what transformation of consciousness means. This is not the only vocabulary. Many vocabularies can be used to explore maps, and many maps can be used to get to the same place. If I am driving from Boston to New York, I use a road map; if I go by ship, I use another map; if I fly, I use yet another map. The maps explore certain types of territory, but they can all lead to the same destination.

I was brought up to think of transformation of consciousness in a certain sequential manner. I was told that consciousness has different states of awareness. Each state of awareness results in a certain kind of behavior for the human nervous system, and each state of consciousness creates its own physiology. It is not physiology that creates consciousness; rather consciousness uses the nervous system to create its own physiology. As a result of that physiology, your perception of your experience of the physical world is altered. What you behold with your physical eyes is a function of the state of awareness you are in, and as that state of awareness changes what you behold changes. Ken Wilber said, "We can see with the eyes of the flesh or we can see with the eyes of the mind or we can see with the eyes of the soul." Most of us, who have not explored the realms of experience of our consciousness, see with the eyes of the flesh and sometimes with the eyes of the mind, but never with the eyes of the soul. William Blake said so beautifully, "We are led to believe a lie when we see *with* and not *through* the eyes."

In my spiritual indoctrination, from the earliest time of my life, I heard my parents and grandparents use the word *maya* for the artifacts of our perceptual experience. Every time they looked at the world they said, "This is maya." There was a deeper reality, which they referred to as *Brahma*. I became familiar with those words early in life, but it wasn't until many years later that I began to understand they weren't speaking metaphorically: they were speaking literally. As we shift from sleep to dreams to waking states of consciousness, reality shifts. Reality is infinitely flexible and subject to revision. I heard a phrase over and over early in childhood from the great sage Vasishtha, the incarnation of God himself. The great sage Vasishtha told his disciple Rama, "Infinite worlds come and go in the vast expanse of my consciousness; they are like moats of dust, dancing in a beam of light that's shining through a hole in my roof." Those words are beautiful, and I didn't realize until later that they were real; they were not a metaphor for reality. As our consciousness undergoes a structural change, reality shifts because reality is not some external thing. We are specks of awareness that project our own universe and then experience it.

RICHARD MOSS: I am glad that you are talking about the origins of your work and early life. You are articulating a new way of understanding the Vedic and Vedantic tradition. If I take my life in comparison, I don't remember the richness of spirituality in my early life. In my life, and I think this is typical of many Westerners, I didn't understand the lineage of my religion as a phenomenon for expression of consciousness. We don't understand the metaphors in Christianity or Judaism as maps or metaphors for deep states of consciousness. For myself, there was a deep sensitivity bordering on suffering which caused me to seek various disciplines and practices. At the age of thirty, I had a spontaneous experience that you could call a fundamental change of consciousness. For the first time, I began to understand what the teachings from the Judeo-Christian lineage were about. I became hungrily interested in *Vedanta*. I read

Shankara's *Crest Jewel of Discrimination*, and it made sense to me. I read Walt Whitman, and suddenly I was in the state of consciousness of the poet. I was transformed in a way. It seems self involved to discuss this, but it doesn't make sense to readers unless they understand that this isn't theory.

My perception of reality changed. I didn't know that at one level of consciousness you have one body, and when that level of consciousness is changed, you have another body. Yet my body changed, my capacity to perceive changed, my intuition and my energy changed. When a Westerner comes to this lineage of teachings, most of the time we aren't coming because we want to change consciousness, but because we want to be happier, more successful, and want to escape suffering. It is the ego who wants these things, and it is the ego who generates the suffering. There is a fundamental paradox in how people come to spiritual work.

DEEPAK CHOPRA: You are right. You are one of those people who came from the need to alleviate suffering and found that the only way to do that was to go to a level which is beyond the ego, which gives birth to all suffering. Suffering brought you to a spiritual path. In many ways that is more credible than for someone like myself, who was brought up with the spiritual map being talked about all the time.

I, like you, went to medical school. I came to the West and got caught up in the rat race and stresses of a physician's life. It wasn't until I started the practice of meditation that those muffled learnings inside my consciousness from childhood returned and said, "This is what my parents and my grandparents were talking about." I went back to the same books I had seen in my house all the time, such as the *Crest Jewel of Discrimination* and the *Upanishads*. As consciousness began to slowly but definitely unfold these new experiences to me, I looked in books to find confirmation of what I was going through.

I would like to articulate the map I was taught as a child. I was brought up to understand that physiology is a function of our state of consciousness, and reality is an expression of that, as well. The first state of consciousness is deep sleep, which is a dull state of consciousness. Brain waves at that state have a certain pattern. Blood pressure and pulse rate and all the biochemistry of the body are specific to the deep-sleep state of awareness. Even though it is a dull state, it is a state of awareness because you are able to respond to stimulus such as loud noise. The second state of consciousness, as described in *Vedanta*, is the state of dreams in which you have a new kind of functioning in the nervous system. Brain wave patterns, blood pressure and biological functions operate differently in dreams as compared to deep sleep. The third state of consciousness, as described in *Vedanta*, is the ordinary waking state in which we experience the world through our sensory apparatus.

When we dream, the experience of the dream is real. It is after we wake from the dream to the waking state that we realize that what we were experiencing was actually our own state of awareness. The nervous system was translating that state of awareness into the dream. We don't realize in the waking state of awareness that what we experience as the physical world is similarly self-created. The consciousness is expressing itself in a certain way that allows our senses to selectively summon forth the data, out of what is essentially and erratically ambiguous quantum flow, and create the experience of material reality.

What exists out there is an immensity of consciousness and energy and information, or expressions of that consciousness. We selectively summon forth a little bit that our senses respond to, and suddenly we have the experience of objects separated in space and time to form a phenomena. This is not something external out there; it is the projection of our consciousness in the waking state. In the waking state of consciousness we experience the world as real, but it is *maya*. This is an artifact of our sensory experience.

When we wake up from this waking state, we will look at it as if it were another dream. Buddha, on his deathbed said, "This lifetime of ours is as transient as autumn clouds; to watch the birth and death of beings is like looking at the movements of a dance. A lifetime is like a flash of lightning in the sky rushing by, like a current rushing down a steep mountain." You can only see that when you wake up from the waking state of consciousness into the fourth stage, which is the awakened state, also referred to as transcendental consciousness or as a glimpse of the soul. You step out of the internal dialogue, and you witness for the first time.

The awakened state is a nonjudgmental awareness that witnesses everything without being involved in it. There is present, for the first time, a deeper reality of the soul. Walt Whitman, when he first experienced the awakened state, said, "I must not be awake, for everything looks to me as it never did before or else I am awake for the first time and all that was before was just a deep sleep." The fourth stage of consciousness, which we can sometimes glimpse in deep meditation, creates its own physiology, brain-wave patterns, and deep state of restful alertness.

Cosmic consciousness, the fifth state, is the refined state of awareness in which we have the simultaneity of local and nonlocal awareness—local awareness being the experience of the objects of our perception and nonlocal awareness being simultaneously the experience of our own spirit. Local and nonlocal awareness or cosmic consciousness can occur in waking, dreaming and sleeping states. Judeo-Christian traditions refer to this as being *in* this world and not *of* it: you are in *both* places at the *same* time.

Cosmic consciousness is a wonderful experience. I have had it once in a while in long periods of retreat; even though your body is asleep, a part of you witnesses the body's deep sleep. Or your body mind is experiencing the dream state, and a part of you witnesses your body mind having the dream. When you are in the waking state, playing tennis, having a conversation or giving a lecture, a part of you witnesses your body mind going through that process. It is the complete simultaneity of this ever wakeful, eternal, immortal, infinite, unbounded ineffable spirit watching your body mind in the state of dreams, in the state of deep sleep, in the state of wakefulness.

In the experience of cosmic consciousness, there is a sudden appearance of synchronicities or meaningful coincidences because you are connected with the conscious energy field where everything is inseparably connected with everything else.

The sixth state is a further refinement of that. When you behold the object of your perception, you start to pierce the veil of *maya*. For example, you look at a flower, you see the flower as a beautiful red rose, but even as you look, you experience the rainbows and sunshine and earth and water and wind and dust and the void and history of the whole universe. The flower is a microcosm, and as you continue to gaze at it, you see the presence of spirit in the flower. Even the object of your perception begins to contain that witness. The witness here, and the witness there are watching each other. This is referred to in *Vedanta* as Divine consciousness. God says if you can't find God in that flower or rainbow or in the eyes of another being, where are you going to find God, in a book of religion? God is not there. God is life-centered, present-moment awareness where you pierce the veil of *maya*, going beyond this artifact of sensory experience and find a vision of God. No matter where you go, you can't get away from it.

In the divine state of awareness, or unity consciousness, the spirit within me, the observer, and the spirit within the object of my observation, which is that flower, cloud, rainbow or other being, merges, so there is only one spirit. At that moment, I lose complete identity with my personality and with my body, and realize that what I thought of as a person was actually the universal being pretending to be a person. In the state of unity consciousness, I experience the universe as my extended body. I realize that I have a personal body and that I have a universal body, and they are equally mine. I look at that tree, and it is my lungs. I experientially know that the earth is my mother, and the universe is my father, and they are me. Rumi says, "Let the water settle, you will see stars and moons mirrored in your being." *Vedanta* says when you get to that state, you have become immortal because the universe is immortal, and you are experiencing your own immortality. You are no longer this little skin-encapsulated ego: you are a universal being expressing itself locally in space and time.

RICHARD MOSS: In my late twenties, each morning I read one of the *Yoga Sutras of Pantanjali* and then meditated, watching my breathing. Then I again read from the *Yoga Sutras of Pantanjali*. I didn't understand the terminologies, but into my subconscious came powerful images. One month before the major change of my life, a priest friend gave me the gospels. I had not read the gospels for many years. I re-read them and I found myself crying tears of recognition. Yet if I had tried to explain to my rational mind what was being affected, I would not have been able to convey it. When this change in my consciousness came, I found it difficult to pass through. I think this passage may be more difficult when there is no lineage to help you. Suddenly the gospels came to me, and I asked myself, "Who has lived this consciousness?" Strange as it would seem, having been raised as a Jew, it was clear to me that this was the Christ consciousness. Christ lived this. Immediately, inside myself, something eased. I won't say that I relaxed because the stress of the event was awesome for me, but I did know that others had been there before.

The point I want to make is that we can follow a lineage and a teaching, but at a certain place, we enter into mysterious territory that is beyond any teaching, beyond any teacher. These teachings become powerful forces in our subconscious, but we enter something that no longer is attainable by our *effort*. I say this is because most people confuse personal transformation with making a personal *effort* through spiritual practices and psychotherapy. These have profound value and can be helpful, depending on how we define personal transformation. Is it improvement? Is it elimination of certain kinds of negative or destructive patterns of behavior? Or is there something in evolution itself, something given by nature, that the sages talk about, that isn't necessarily the creation of a man's *effort*, but something we can come toward if we meditate or pray sincerely. What I call deep transformation isn't a *willed* process. In fact, it was after I gave up and surrendered inside myself that the real change came, after I realized that my seeking was between me and whatever was real.

DEEPAK CHOPRA: Yes, I agree. Even meditation is never *willed*; it is a process of *surrender*. Most people confuse meditation with concentration, when it is the ability to let go of everything, including concentration. It is the ability to go beyond the thinking process, to transcend it. Exploring those realms of consciousness is a process of total and ultimate surrender. The techniques and the disciplines are tools that help you go to a certain level where you can come to that place of surrender.

Every three months, I take four or five days and go into a silent retreat in some wilderness area, usually a rain forest or desert. About three years ago, I went to the rain forest of Costa Rica to be alone for three days. I didn't take books or writing material because that is not silence; that is having a conversation with the author. After one or two days, I got extremely restless. There was nothing I could do. The restlessness passed, and I experienced a profound silence. The day I was leaving, I went to the airport and stayed at the hotel. There was only one book in the room, the Bible. I read the *Gospel of John* and it was like reading *Vedanta* for me. I was familiar with every word—the word was made into the flesh, I and my father are one, I am in you and you are in me, and greater works than these shall you do. I realized that Christ consciousness is what we are aspiring to and that Christ consciousness is a state of awareness that we go into. Christ wasn't about the crucifixion; he was about the resurrection and redemption. God-realized people are those who have achieved that state of Christ consciousness.

RICHARD MOSS: I find that what limits a person's capacity for love or recognition is what they are afraid to feel. Wherever I go, whomever I talk with, their ability to stay in a marriage, to work consciously, to be without fear and to experience joy depends upon what they have the capacity to feel. I've found in my work you have to address suffering, and the Vedantic tradition suggests that if you use these tools, primarily meditation, you can avoid the necessity of engaging a certain kind of suffering.

DEEPAK CHOPRA: The authors of *Vedanta*, and the great teachers of the *Upanishads* did not have the karmic load that we have. Those problems that are so pertinent to us probably were not important to the great Rishis. Buddha said,

"You know the *Vedantas* very well, but I have to talk to these people who are suffering and how should I do it?" One of the greatest teachings is that if you want to go beyond suffering, you have to experience it. A sutra that I remember well is that nothing should be clung to as *me* or *mine*. A long time ago, I started practicing that in my daily activity, attempting to keep that in my awareness, because reality is the universal being, and the rest is just a kind of a game. Yet, to get to that stage, you have to go through your suffering. If you don't experience it, if you run away from it or avoid it, suffering ultimately manifests the states of hostility, fear, guilt and depression, which are nothing other than not having addressed the suffering when it was taking place. Remembered pain is hostility and anger, anticipated pain is fear and anxiety, pain directed at yourself is guilt. The depletion of energy with all of the above is depression. We have to be intimate with our suffering—express it to ourselves, share it with other people, release our pain and surrender.

RICHARD MOSS: This is the contribution of psychotherapies, even though they don't have a spiritual base. You have laid out this incredible map, but nobody can get to a state of cosmic consciousness if there is more truth in happiness and freedom and less truth in suffering. In other words, you used images of the flower and the sunset, but when you walk through a forest, there is glory in the dead trees lying on the ground as well. The cycle of life and death is part of the truth of life. You were talking about anxiety. Anxiety starts in the mind the moment there is a sense that I exist as a separate self and that I might not get something the separate self thinks it needs.

DEEPAK CHOPRA: In the end, it's all an artifact. That sense of a separate self is really an illusion because there is no separate self. It is easy to understand intellectually that what I call myself is a dynamic bundle of energy that is constantly transforming. I am not the same physical body that I was ten years ago, so I can't be my body. I am not the same mind that I was ten years ago; hopefully it is more mature, so I can't be my mind. I am not my emotional states because those come and go all the time. I am the witness of all that, and the witness of all that is not a person; it is a universal being and I am that universal being. Intellectually I can explain it, but experientially, if somebody meets me on the street and says, "You are a bloody fool," I suddenly start nursing my grievances. That is not me; that's my ego. This whole thing that I call myself is a bundle of memories and dreams and wishes I have created. By referring to myself through objects, I separate myself from my real inheritance, which is that I am a citizen of the cosmos.

RICHARD MOSS: That someone on the street can insult you and you contract is part of the beauty of this world. The creature in us structures our activities to seek pleasure and avoid pain. What structures the average human mind is the pursuit of happiness and fulfillment through jobs, appearance, money, whom we marry and so on. A higher level of consciousness structures the mind through the desire for truth, for true understanding. You can meditate, and you can have glimpses of cosmic consciousness, but you have to turn into this world. You can't say to the world, "Oh, the world is *maya*, it's a lie." You turn to your wife or husband and discover how much pain you can cause in them, and you have to take responsibility for it. Or you feel yourself contract because you lose a job, and you realize that you are identified once again with this separate self. If the first part of the process is ascending to this wonderful state of unitive consciousness, the process is not complete until we bring that into every corner of our human experience—how we raise our children, how we live, how we care for each other. We will be provoked to contract. To the extent that we are insecure we will be provoked into seeking until, we begin to realize, I can't speak for myself because I still contract, but a deep place inside of me realizes that I am not that one who contracts.

DEEPAK CHOPRA: We have to go through it in order to transcend it. And there is no hurry; we have all of eternity to recognize who we really are. What's the big hurry? Whatever we are doing at this moment is from the level of awareness we are in, and in that sense, we all do the best we can. It's okay to desire; it is okay to get insulted. I am reminded of the prayer of St. Augustine in which he says, "Lord give me chastity, give me continence, but not just now."

EPILOGUE TO INTERVIEW BY RICHARD MOSS

It is my feeling that the resurgence of ancient spiritual traditions like Vedanta, Buddhism and Kabbalah have real value for understanding and mastering our human nature. But we need to be discriminating about their limitations for the modern mind and modern situation. For one thing, Vedanta, as well as most meditative or contemplative traditions, were not just divinely inspired activities; they were also doubtless born out of suffering and helplessness. Most of human history was marked by human beings having relatively little empirical knowledge of the outside world and therefore little power to influence it. What was available to be explored that could leverage great power over suffering and toward accepting the general helplessness of early human life in the face of the vicissitudes of nature was the mind.

For the past five hundred years, scientific inquiry has given us unimagined power over nature and our physical circumstances. If the philosophies of India and the East profoundly examined levels of mind, they also encouraged a kind of passivity toward outer life. The contemporary challenge born of our scientific and technological successes is definitely not passivity. On the contrary, it is our helter-skelter rush to exert control over everything that is now leading us to destroy the ecosystem upon which our lives depend.

Against this modern situation, personal transformation becomes the most important work we can do. We must each learn what calls us to such potential for greatness and good, and to such potential for self-destructiveness. Personal transformation is more than a work about individual happiness or individual enlightenment. It is a work about becoming responsive to the evolutionary impulse, a movement from within Life itself that we must understand and obey if we are to continue to exist.

To imagine that Vedanta, even in a modern form, can hold the answers to these challenges is simplistic, naive and maybe dangerous. I think it seduces our egos into imagining that the answers already exist, that they have been attained in the past and all we have to do is follow the map. Of course, even to repeat the inner work that would enable the experiential confirmation of the map Deepak offered is an extremely arduous work. I doubt it can be done, for I believe that true transformation is, after all, a pathless path. In any case, I strongly feel that deep personal transformation must be a work immersed in a wide-ranging, broadly inclusive, contemporary and lived spiritual context and teaching. Crucial to this, I feel, is the birth of a new kind of community of exploration, a new quality of association of sincere individuals. Both Eastern mysticism and Western (or modern) science have the power to lead us to a vision of Oneness, of the interconnected wholeness of ourselves and all things, and we need this. This is the basic root of wisdom, the necessary underpinning for a sane and healthy society. But bringing this vision into the world of social and cultural forms is a lived process that can never be predetermined. To me there is no one tradition, no special practices, no revelations of science that accomplish this. All are important, but every true teacher and every sincere student must reinvent the means anew. The dialogue must never cease, and it must go deeper. The call to transformation must burn forth from more and more nakedly exposed hearts and dedicated lives. •

The Long Way Round

S U E   M O N K   K I D D

When I was a child, a woman named Sweet worked for our family. She cared for my brothers and me as if we were her own. One day, when we were playing at my grandmother's house, we discovered a wheelbarrow full of rainwater. Swimming through it were hundreds of tadpoles.

We raced inside and asked Sweet for three jars. As she was handing them out, my grandmother appeared in the door. "Girls don't catch tadpoles," she said with a laugh. "Sue, you come along with me and I'll teach you to play 'Chopsticks' on the piano." My brothers dashed off to the wheelbarrow, and I ended up at the piano bench.

A few days later, Sweet and I started out on one of our frequent walks to the city park about four blocks from my house. The park was the best of places, and I was anxious to get there. But that day Sweet took my hand and started in the wrong direction. "We're taking the long way round," she told me.

The long way? The words fell like a curse on my ears. Why would we deliberately go the long way? I made a small scene, but Sweet didn't relent. Off we went the long way. Not four blocks, but eight!

We had walked at least six when she stopped beside a ditch swollen with water and tadpoles. She pulled a Mason jar from her pocket, one with nail holes in the lid. "Now aren't you glad we took the long way round? Ain't no tadpoles the short way," she said.

Inside my head I heard my grandmother's words, "Only boys catch tadpoles." Only boys. I hesitated, but Sweet nudged me with the jar. Soon I was elbow-deep in the brown water, chasing after the rich, darting life before me. I was reveling in a new universe and it was one of the grander times of my girlhood. It was the day I learned to challenge the tight, tidy categories of what was expected and possible in my world. Like the tadpoles, I was molting into a new being.

But when I grew up and left home, I began once more to be hammered into tight, tidy spaces of traditional expectation. I learned to conform to roles and wear all sorts of masks that hid my real self. I forgot all about the tadpole experience.

One day I read a poem by Henry David Thoreau, America's solitary walker, entitled "Among the Worst of Men That Ever Lived." The last line of it struck like the bow of a ship hitting a tiny island submerged in my memory. The line read, "We went on to heaven the long way round."

Dear God, I thought, the long way round. The words brought back that long-lost walk to the park, the tadpoles and Sweet's lyrical voice singing to me, "Now aren't you glad we took the long way round? Ain't no tadpoles the short way." The lesson was fresh upon me again: be your true, unfettered, God-given self, regardless of the expectations hammered into you.

It seemed to me that Sweet and Thoreau had touched upon the same genius. Transformations come only as we go the long way round, only as we're willing to walk a different, longer, more arduous, more inward, more prayerful route. When you wait, you're deliberately choosing to take the long way, to go eight blocks instead of four, trusting that there's a transforming discovery lying pooled along the way.

"Nothing can be more useful to a man than a determination not to be hurried," Thoreau wrote at age twenty-five. He decided to turn away from the "lives of quiet desperation" he saw all around him and march to his own "different drummer," to go to heaven the long way round. On February 8, 1857, Thoreau wrote this in his journal, "You think I am impoverishing myself by withdrawing from men, but in my solitude I have woven for myself a silken web or chrysalis, and nymph-like, shall ere long burst forth a more perfect creature."

In his commentary on Thoreau's work, Robert Bly says that "agreeing to a waiting period is part of it." It's part of the process of leaving the petty life, the false life, the old life.

The universe is offering an invitation. A call to waiting. A call to the mysteries of the cocoon. I discovered that in the spiritual life, the long way round is the saving way. It isn't the quick and easy religion we're accustomed to. It's deep and difficult—a way that leads into the vortex of the soul where we touch our innermost transformative powers. But we have to be patient. We have to let go and tap our creative stillness. Most of all, we have to trust that our scarred hearts really do have wings.

The Instant Society

We live in an age of acceleration, in an era so seduced by the instantaneous that we're in grave danger of losing our ability to wait. Life moves at a staggering pace. Computers yield up immediate answers. Pictures develop before our eyes. Satellites beam television signals from practically anywhere, allowing faraway images to appear instantly in our living rooms. Complex life issues are routinely introduced, dealt with and solved in neat thirty-minute segments on television.

Space travel, fax machines, instant coffee, disposable diapers. In ways large and small, we're all encapsulated in a speeding world. We're surrounded by express lanes, express mail, express credit. There aren't just restaurants, but "fast-food" restaurants; not simply markets, but "jiffy" markets. Faster is better. Ask almost anyone.

The modern person tends to live by appointment calendars. I'm embarrassed at how huge my calendar used to be. I had two pages for every day so that I could "design" time the way I wanted—segment it, save it, manage it, stretch it. Since we have designer clothes and designer chocolate, I suppose it's inevitable that we would want designer time, too.

We keep dreaming up ways to conserve time and make it hassle free. I recently saw an exercise bike with a computer attached so that people can get fit while they work; and last week, while thumbing through a catalogue, I noticed a video entitled *Discover Yourself in Less Than Thirty Minutes.*

A study conducted in Pittsburgh timed clerks in major fast-food restaurants to determine which chain served a hamburger, fries and a soft drink the quickest. The winner took forty-six seconds; the loser, a slow three minutes. Apparently such information is important to a society that places its highest premium on the quick and easy.

Quick and easy are magical words with enormous seductive powers. Advertisers know that if they put them on a product it sells better—whether the product is instant potatoes, instant money or instant relief. We're told that we can walk off ten pounds in two weeks, melt off five inches in five days, or just take a pill and do it overnight. We've been lured by promises of getting new glasses in an hour, an oil change in thirty minutes and a pizza in twenty.

Is it any wonder that we're fine-tuned from an early age to seek out the instant fix? We want life to respond like our microwave ovens.

Last week, my daughter plopped down on the den floor in front of the television to do her homework. She held the remote control in one hand and her math book in the other. "I hate math," she said. "It's so hard." Then, in a moment of mischievous whimsy, she aimed the remote at her homework and pressed the fast-forward button. "Wouldn't it be great to just speed up the hard stuff?" she said. Ah, yes. I know that little fantasy well.

SHORTCUT RELIGION

It was inevitable that the lure of the quick and easy would seep into religion. Our churches have filled up with people looking for sudden and painless paths to change and growth—for what Dietrich Bonhoeffer called "cheap grace."

A lot of us have spent our lives in shortcut religion. We haven't been willing to face the fact that while the spiritual journey is joyous and full, it's also long and hard. It asks much—too much sometimes.

Anthony Bloom reminds us that the aim of prayer is nothing less than a "deep change in the whole of our personality." As Thomas Merton says, our commitment is to become "a completely new person." Such extraordinary movements of re-creation don't happen spontaneously or without effort and pain.

When my son was fourteen, he experienced an episode of leg pains that kept him awake at night. The doctor pronounced them as "growing pains." I didn't know such things actually existed. But I sat by Bob's bed in the darkest part of the night and rubbed his shins while he moaned and ached. One night he looked at me and said, "It hurts to grow."

I smiled, unaware then that he was offering me a profound life truth. "But you always said you wanted to be six feet tall," I reminded him.

"Yeah," he muttered, "but I'd like to do it without all this."

He wanted what we all want: a shortcut, some way to bypass the misery and still be six feet tall. To grow up spiritually means having growing pains in the darkest part of the night.

Some Christians (even some churches) have responded to this difficult truth by trying to create shortcuts—promises of easy grace, push-button answers to complicated problems, illusions that we can go to church and work to bring in the kingdom out there in the world without entering the fiery process of bringing it into our own soul.

A woman who used to work at a fast-food restaurant once commented that the people who lined up at her register sometimes reminded her of people lining up in church on Sunday morning. They seemed to be looking for the same thing—a quick and easy way to reduce the hunger inside. "Mac-faith," she called it.

What has happened to our ability to dwell in unknowing, to live inside a question and coexist with the tensions of uncertainty? Where is our willingness to incubate pain and let it birth something new? What has happened to patient unfolding, to endurance? These things are what form the ground of waiting. And if you look carefully, you'll see that they're also the seedbed of creativity and growth—what allows us to do the daring and to break through to newness. As Thomas Merton observed, "The imagination should be allowed a certain amount of time to browse around."

Creativity flourishes not in certainty but in questions. Growth germinates not in tent dwelling but in upheaval. Yet the seduction is always security rather than venturing, instant knowing rather than deliberate waiting.

I once visited a church where the preacher invited people with heartaches and problems to come to the altar. "God will take care of what's bothering you right now," he proclaimed. Not a word about the desert that lies between our wounds and our healing, our questions and our answers, our departure and our arrival. Nothing about the slow, sacred rhythms of spiritual becoming or the spiral of descent and ascent that make up waiting.

When it comes to religion today, we tend to be long on butterflies and short on cocoons. Somehow we're going to have to relearn that the deep things of Life don't come suddenly. It's as if we imagine that all of our spiritual growth potential is dehydrated contents to which we need only add some holy water to make it instantly and easily appear.

I received a letter recently from someone who was feeling impatient about taking the long way round. She wrote, "Pole vaulting is so much more alluring than crawling."

We live in a spiritual environment that tends to emphasize full-blown newness and a sense of "arrival" in the mere time it takes to walk the length of a church aisle. Walking an aisle can be a marvelous thing, as long as we acknowledge that the aisle doesn't end at the altar but goes on winding through life. We seem to have focused so much on exuberant beginnings and victorious endings that we've forgotten about the slow, sometimes tortuous, unraveling of grace that takes place in the "middle places."•

Making Pilgrimage

G R E G G   L E V O Y

My father's favorite game to play with my two brothers and me when we were children was something he called the Alien Game, in which he was a visitor from another planet and we were his guides here on earth. He would point into the sky, for instance, and ask, "What are those formations that move through the atmosphere?" "Clouds!" we'd say with great confidence. "Clouds? What are they made of?" "Water," we'd all say at once. "How does the water get up there?" he'd inquire, "and what holds it up, and why does it move?"

In no time at all, it would become apparent to us earthlings that clouds weren't the only things that were over our heads. Entire afternoons could go by as we pondered the mysteries of water and wind, and how it's possible that we can know so much and understand so little, that we can live with something every day of our lives and never really come to know it.

What the Alien Game taught me—and what I keep trying to remember—is to see with the eyes of a child, who, after all, is in most ways an alien to this world.

In searching out the mystery of our own callings, in trying to find answers to our most basic why-is-the-sky-blue questions of meaning and purpose, we, too, can leave our houses, go out under the clouds, and, with the guilelessness of children, simply ask those questions that seem obvious but often aren't—"Who am I? What matters? What is my gift? What do I need to hear? What on Earth am I doing?" We can also try to approach these questions as if each were an emissary from some Great Unknown, each itself a mystery, and any number of lifetimes insufficient to get us much closer than the outskirts of the thing.

Questioning is at the heart of spiritual journeying, of leaving home for time to go on a retreat, pilgrimage or vision quest, of removing ourselves from the duties and dramas, the relationships and roles that bombard us with messages that may be distracting or irrelevant or even destructive to our emerging sense of self, and that interfere with our asking for responses to our burning questions. In making pilgrimage, we're calling on God rather than the other way around. We're "crying for a vision," as the Sioux holy man

Black Elk called it, the one that may reveal our true vocation, our real name, our purpose; the one that may come as a dream, a fantasy figure, a voice in the head, an animal encounter, an overpowering emotion, a sudden inspiration or surge of creative energy, a chance meeting out at a crossroads. We're practicing the art of following calls because spiritual journeys, like calls, involve a break with everyday life.

"I went to strip away what I had been taught," Georgia O'Keeffe said, describing her retreat to New Mexico from New York City in the 1920s, "to accept as true my own thinking. This was one of the best times of my life. There was no one around to look at what I was doing, no one interested, no one to say anything about it one way or another. I was alone and singularly free."

In taking a walkabout, in leaving home and the distracting fusillade of activities that often keeps us from ourselves, what is in the background becomes foreground, what is overlooked has the chance to get looked over, what is waiting in the wings is given an entrance cue. We ask for a calling and the faith to follow it. We go a'courting. We stand beneath the balcony and croon. We cry out with the longing we feel. We drop our handkerchiefs.

We may or may not get an answer, but what's important is not to cease asking. Perhaps we mispronounced the question, or our timing wasn't right. Perhaps we received an answer and didn't recognize it, or perhaps the answer we heard wasn't the one we wanted to hear, so we ignored it. Maybe we need to travel still further on our journey, around the next turn in the road, over the next pass, into the company of someone we have yet to meet.

Pilgrims, says the theologian Richard Niebuhr, are persons in motion, passing rough territories not their own, seeking . . . completion or clarity; a goal to which only the spirit's compass points the way. Sometimes that motion is religious and sometimes secular. Sometimes we design our own journeys, and sometimes we follow in the paths of those we revere: pacing the garden Jesus paced, sitting beneath the tree where Buddha saw the light, praying in the chapel where Merton prayed, visiting the house where Shakespeare wrote *Romeo and Juliet*, walking the same streets of a village in Mexico or a shtetl in Russia that your own grandfather once walked.

Sometimes we journey with the body, on a long walking meditation or a bicycle trip through the Holy Lands, and sometimes with the mind, as Joseph Campbell did early in his life by holing himself up in a cabin for five years and doing nothing but reading, which the Hindus call ynana yoga, the search for enlightenment through knowledge and the mind. Our approach depends on our primary way of experiencing the spirit. Sometimes we make the journey entirely in private, in solitary retreat or solo vision quest in the wilderness, and other times in crowds, like the great pilgrimages—to Mecca, Benares, Rome, Jerusalem and Compostela in Spain—which resemble enormous migrations.

Simply taking up a bedroll and hitting the road won't generally suffice to alert the forces of enlightenment, however. They require that you do more than just move around. Whether we go to the Ganges or Graceland, maintaining a spirit of observance and self-reflection is key. We must be intent on spending time searching for soul, moving toward something that represents to us an ideal—truth, beauty, love, perspective, strength, serenity, transcendence, sacredness, whatever.

Without this intention, our pilgrimages are only vacations, our vision quests are struck blind, our retreats are not also advances. We're merely tourists and window-shoppers or curio seekers. Perhaps we're even escapees, people in flight rather than in quest. Something like a Law of Spiritual Enthusiasm seems to dictate what sort of response we get to our inquiries, intents and purposes and to highlight the importance of being earnest. The hungrier we are to learn and be guided, the more we're taught and the more we allow ourselves to be taught. We can't fake it, though. The gods and our own souls know when we're being sincere and when we're just smiling and saying cheese.

Spiritual journeying, whether we walk around a holy mountain or sit in a single place on a five-day meditation retreat, is about interior or exterior movement toward *the deep self*. A geographical journey is symbolic of an inner journey for which we long.•

Realizing Your Potential

JERRY LYNCH
AND CHUNGLIANG AL HUANG

According to the *Tao Te Ching*, people who are accepting will ascend; those who are not will descend. A peaceful, accepting frame of mind enables you to adjust to the existing circumstances with success. Resistance to change or the way things are causes hardness, tension, anxiety and stress, all of which obstruct your potential. Rigid tree branches break in a storm; Chinese bamboo bends softly and bounces back unharmed.

Learning acceptance is not easy for anyone. It is a form of self-realization, a huge leap of faith enabling you to come to terms with the way things are, not the way you think they should be. By their very unpredictable nature, sports and exercise are divine teachers affording you the opportunity to test your levels of frustration when circumstances or events change rapidly without warning. For example, many athletes are well prepared and trained, yet they do not live up to their billing. A national-class cyclist, competing in the Olympic trials, talked about feeling helpless as she was struggling with an "off-day" during this important event. "How can I accept that?" she asked. To fight the reality is to further the struggle, which she did. Her anger and fury over the helpless situation further hampered her efforts. When you find yourself having an "off-day" in any arena of performance, it is better to accept the situation, relax and ask yourself: "Since I'm having an off-day, what can I do now; what am I able to do if I can't do it all?" By asking these questions, you take positive action by doing what is possible, and you reduce the stress and anxiety associated with trying to come to terms with the struggle. When things fail to go your way, acceptance and adaptation will help you to function at higher levels and feel better internally during the process.

Many of us also have difficulty accepting injury or illness. Such setbacks halt your physical efforts instantly. Yet, this is where sports and exercise offer the perfect opportunity for inner growth if you choose to use this downtime for reflection and meditation, a time to examine your training program, to ask sacred questions, such as "Where am I? Where am I going? Could I do things better? Am I happy with what I'm doing?" Here is a situation that truly tests what you are made of, whether you are flexible enough to go with the flow.

It's easy to resist acceptance. You may fear that it is synonymous with resignation, a state of predestination where action is useless. Nothing could be further from the truth. Acceptance is truly a sign that you are in tune with a given situation and, knowing who you really are, take positive steps that will help you to optimize your potential. It often means the difference between success or failure. Acceptance is a definite soulful choice, a deeply spiritual act taking you beyond a state of inertness. Accepting "what is" shows an inner strength, one that requires you to assess the situation thoroughly, ascertain what is required in order to function adequately, adapt and then act accordingly. For example, people who inhabit desert regions are not fatalistic about plant life. Given a dry, hot climate, they don't plant flowers that need lots of water; they accept the environment and plant succulents. Accept—adapt—act. It is the action that steers you away from helplessness.

As you begin to get physically fit and well-conditioned, you need to assess the present shape you are in and accept this openly. Once you do accept your physical state, get down to the business of taking appropriate action. Remember that as you take an inventory of what you lack, consider what you have going for you and be sure to emphasize those qualities (physical, mental, spiritual traits) that will help to encourage you and ignite the fires of physical resurgence.

Once you learn the Tao lesson of acceptance in sports and exercise, you are ready to apply it to all of life. The key is to emphasize what you *have* by letting it keep you afloat during the early stages of self-development, rather than focus totally on what you *lack*. You may not be the best speaker or the most knowledgeable teacher at this time, but your innate charisma, charm and caring nature will keep you going until you develop these skills. Notice and nurture what you do have, and you will begin to develop that which you don't. Basically, you need to have the grace and wisdom to accept the aspects of self that you cannot change and to alter those you can. A true champion in sport, as well as a winner in life, does not have it all. One may only use what one does have— repeatedly—and use it well.

LIMITLESS LIMITS

Like the Tao, you are a natural process capable of continual growth and blossoming. In Confucian ethics, the unlimited person is one who constantly reassesses his or her state of being and is willing to do what it takes to improve. When you are in tune with the Tao, you possess the power of continual transformation, from being to becoming. According to Lao-tzu, this process of becoming requires you to be aware of your shortcomings and see yourself as a beginner, totally empty and ready to receive. When you think about it, the beginner has limitless possibilities; the expert has none.

Your power and strength in sports and exercise start with the deep humble sense that you are a beginner with unlimited potential, regardless of how much time you have devoted to your discipline. The concept of being totally empty and willing to learn is a precondition for unlimitedness. In Chinese, we call this empty place "Wu Ji," that which gives you the ability to face your insecurities and flow into the vast sea of potentiality, profound growth and improvement. With the Tao, we are reminded to travel openly on uncharted paths, remain empty and learn to sustain the beginner's mind.

Opening up to the unlimited boundaries of his vast potential was the choice of Keith Foreman. As a freshman "walk-on" on the University of Oregon men's track team, he was told how limited his possibilities were with an elite group of scholarship athletes. Yet Keith saw himself as a beginner with unlimited opportunity to learn, and he took on the challenge of competing with the best. He believed the sky was his only limit. Before he graduated, Keith became only the fifth American runner ever to break the four-minute-mile barrier. Having accomplished this in sport, Keith seized the opportunity to grow spiritually and apply his confidence and strength to other endeavors in life. In his fifties, he continues to push the limitless boundaries of his potential, studying for an advanced doctoral degree and continuing to compete as a national-class athlete.

It's important to understand the difference between two types of limits. There are the "limiting limits," those that are actual, real obstacles defining the boundaries of your potential. For example, in basketball, your lack of height could be a real limiting factor in playing center for the Chicago Bulls; money will determine what you can or cannot afford to buy; without gas, your car won't go; humans can't fly. These are natural limits.

Then there are the "limitless limits," those that we *think* or *imagine* to be limits, yet, with the right shift in consciousness, rarely become limiting factors. Most limitations fall into this category. It has been said that the average human being uses a mere 15 percent of his or her physical and mental potential. We constantly underestimate our capabilities. We even are surrounded by global limited thinking. Consider this situation: after an in-depth study of the bumblebee, the world's best experts in the field of aerodynamics announced that the bee could not fly—it was too heavy, too slow, too small and limited in numerous other ways. Fortunately, the bee couldn't read the final report. Unfortunately, we *can* hear and read, which often works to our disadvantage. Yet, when you refuse to listen, but instead you dig down deep and discover potentials through your physical activity that you never knew existed, you attain a level of spiritual growth that enables you to be open and receptive to what life has to offer when you say "yes" to all possibilities.

Many people have bought into stories of self-limitations. There are those who say "We can't ski, we're too awkward," yet they see a talented skier with no legs; then they hear about the concert guitarist with no arms and reevaluate their limited thinking about playing music. People who argue for their limitations are limited. You need to know that, whatever you imagine your limitations in life to be, if you're willing to trust the enormous capacity for growth that you've been given and take the necessary steps to develop yourself, you will redefine and explore the boundaries of your full potential. The message of the *Tao Te Ching* is clear: trust the power within and use it.

When faced with what you think are limitations, ask close friends for their input, and watch your progress closely so you continue in the direction that contradicts these limits. Maybe they're real, maybe not. But at least you will have tried and discovered the truth.

Remember, too, that some limits can be useful, particularly in sports and physical activities. For example, you have a certain capacity when you begin to work out, and it's good to not strain beyond, in order to avoid injury. The same applies to life: you take advantage of seeing a play or concert because you are aware that it's here for a limited time. Many signs of caution are limits that could save your life. For example, don't exceed the weight limitations for take-off in a plane. It could prove costly.•

Learning to Wait for God

JIM ROSEMERGY

Once we no longer use prayer as a way of trying to convince the Almighty to serve us, we are candidates for a closer walk with God. We say, "Teach us to pray," but the teacher hears us say, "Teach us to wait." Every teacher of spiritual lore knows that the practice of prayer is primarily the art of waiting.

As we embark upon this path, let it be known we do not *achieve* a closer walk with God. We can achieve many things in life, but an experience of the Presence does not come through our efforts. God cannot be scaled the way we climb a mountain. Discipline and persistence are developed in the seeker and skills are learned, but waiting is the primary skill to be mastered. It is like the rising of the sun. We may beg and beseech, burn incense and practice rituals, but these human efforts do not make the sun rise. Basically, we must sit in the dark, face the east and wait. This assures us we will witness the sunrise, but it does not lift the velvet canopy of the night.

Our way of life calls us to use affirmations and denials (statements that affirm what is true or deny what is not true) in pursuit of what is called affirmative prayer. Essentially, statements are formed which we would say if we believed we had received what we wanted. This kind of prayer is based upon Jesus' statement, ". . . whatever you ask in prayer, believe that you have received it, and it will be yours." The prayer of the human being usually considers the "it" to be something tangible we want or at least something which is personal to us. An individual praying the prayer of the human being might say, "The right and perfect place of employment is coming to me now," or "I live the abundant life, for my every need is met."

An extension of this practice of prayer is the idea we have a subconsciousness mind that can be conditioned. The conditioning occurs as we think or say an affirmation and/or denial over and over again. Through this activity, images and beliefs are stored in the subconscious mind. Then through the law, "Thoughts held in mind produce after their kind," these beliefs and images manifest themselves as our life experience. Most people are aware of the nature of seeds planted in the earth, but not everyone is familiar with the fact that thoughts, beliefs and images are seeds which bear fruit in our lives.

WE HAVE THE MIND OF THE CHRIST

These ideas are truth-filled and helpful, but they are still steps along the spiritual path and therefore only partial truths. Several years ago, I was at a prayer retreat and we were given a brief time to relax before one of the meals. I went to my room, not to meditate or pray, but to sit quietly and rest. While I was sitting on my bed, a voice still and small said within me, "Jim, you do not have to condition your subconscious mind anymore."

"Oh," I thought, "why not?"

"Because you have the mind of the Christ." This answer startled me, but it rang true, for I knew it was based on Paul's statement, "But we have the mind of Christ." Obviously, it would be foolhardy to try to condition the Christ Mind. Instead, it needs to be released to do its sacred work and to be an avenue of divine ideas and God thoughts.

Typically, when we decide the subconscious mind must be conditioned, we sing, think or speak a statement (an affirmation or denial) over and over again until it becomes a natural part of our being. However, remember Jesus cautioned us against *vain repetition*, and is it not true the Truth is already written upon our hearts?

Does this mean that our old friends, affirmations and denials, are no longer to be a part of our spiritual journey? Dear friend, they are destined to remain with us and become even more precious. But they are to be used in a different way that makes us more available to Spirit. Those who pray the prayer of the Divine Being know the "it" to be a consciousness of God. The actual practice of affirmative prayer forms statements like, "I am one with God," or "I and the Father are one."

THE HIGH MEADOW

I believe the purpose of affirmations and denials is not solely to condition the subconsciousness mind, but to help release the wonders of the Christ mind within us. Imagine you are climbing a mountain. The summit is an experience of the presence of God. Through human effort, you climb to a high meadow. It is a beautiful place. You can see things you have never seen before. You think you have arrived at your goal, but eventually you realize this is not the summit.

The peak is shrouded in mist. You cannot even see the trailhead that leads to the experience you desire.

At the high meadow, you must wait. No amount of human effort will take you higher. However, a woman is coming to show you the trailhead and to lead you higher. Her name is Grace. Through waiting and God's grace, you are taken into the mist, into the mystery that is the Presence.

In the analogy, we climb to the High Meadow through the use of affirmations and denials. These positive statements, which affirm what is true and say "no" to lies and falsehoods, lift us up in consciousness. Through their use, we do not succumb to negative statements and thinking. We stand our ground and refuse to descend into the valley below and its limitations. During our climb to the High Meadow, there is no conditioning of the subconscious mind. Instead, affirmations and denials are like a lifting wind taking us to a high state of human consciousness that feels good—the High Meadow. We are in a positive state of being, but we have not yet made contact with Spirit. From here we can descend into the valley of negativity, or we can wait for Grace to come and take us higher.

PUTTING ON OUR WINGS

Another image may be helpful in explaining this idea. You are like the great bird soaring near the cliff waiting for the unseen wind to carry you higher. By denying the seeming power of error and speaking the truth, you reach a point where you put on your wings and wait. Suddenly, the wind lifts you higher, and you are in the presence of God. However, before this happens you must learn to soar, to wait.

This is the most difficult part of developing a prayer life. It does not take a person long to know what is true and what is a lie, for such things are written on our hearts. We learn to say the right things quickly, and often can speak an eloquent public "prayer," but there is no experience of the Presence. The reason is there is no waiting. A consciousness of God is not achieved through our efforts. We rise to the apex of human consciousness, put on our wings and wait to be lifted higher.

How often have we spoken our truth, felt a little better, said "amen" and gone about our business, only to have the problem return? The reason this happened is simple: we did not wait. This is why when seekers say, "Teach us to pray," the teacher hears, "Teach us to wait."

LEARNING TO WAIT

The soul that waits walks with God. In human life, there are many skills to learn: listening and communication skills, organizational and leadership skills, and recreational skills. But the skill which invites a spiritual life is waiting. The Bible confirms this idea through a great promise. ". . . but they who wait for the Lord shall renew their strength, they shall mount up with wings like eagles, they shall run and not be weary, they shall walk and not faint." Dear friend, if there is to be a closer walk with God, there must be waiting.

Waiting challenges the typical human being. We are people of action, and resting quietly in prayer seems too passive and unproductive. If God is a great mountain, then let us mount an expedition and scale this great height! This was the reasoning of the people who built and left unfinished the Tower of Babel. The message is clear. The ruins of the tower remind us that God is not achieved through human effort. However, we are not to be passive even though our *action* may appear passive. We can speak our affirmations and denials and ascend the spiritual path to the height of our humanity, but then we must wait. We must become like a child who cannot pass a crevasse in the earth. We must wait for our Father to come, sweep us up into His arms and carry us to the other side.

The challenge of waiting is that the mind wanders. This is *normal* and to be expected. The waiting skills we are to learn gently bring us back to a steady focus upon Spirit, a resting in the everlasting arms. They remind us once more to give the gift of our attention to God. Our first action, once we become aware the mind is wandering, is watching. There is no attempt to refocus the mind. We simply watch. It is as if we are following someone and trying to determine where he is going.

What happens when we watch is illustrated by something that often occurs in the household. A child has asked to have a cookie, but the parent refuses because dinner is only a half an hour away. The child is assured that after supper he can have a cookie. While the meal is cooking, the parent sits in the nearby living room reading the evening newspaper. In a short time, the parent hears the ceramic lid of the cookie jar being removed, and therefore rises quietly and stands at the kitchen door smiling and watching the child stuff a cookie in his mouth while reaching into the jar for another snack. In a brief time, the child feels the "weight of the parent's gaze" and stops taking the treat from the cookie jar.

In our interior lives, we watch the thoughts drifting through the mind. Through unconditional observation, the mind will cease its meandering and come to rest, just as the child ceased reaching for a cookie. It is at this point we resist the temptation to label the stray thought as good or bad. It is essential we not eat of the tree of the knowledge of good or evil. The thought is not good or bad. *It is!* Just as the child is not bad because he reaches for a cookie before supper.•

Creativity and Healing

CANDACE HARTZLER

In late summer 1994, I stood on the jagged edge of a profound healing process. The experience would begin in a creative arts barn tucked into the foothills of the Catskill Mountains in New York. On that warm summer morning, the barn was chock-full of people and activity, and I was terrified. My inner critic was playing yakety-yak games in my head, assuring me I was out of my league.

But I had chosen to spend ten days in a creativity retreat because I had lost a sense of belonging to any league, the human race notwithstanding. Two years prior to the retreat, harsh lessons had begun arriving at heart-breaking speed. A sampler of loss and change prior to the retreat:

- benign lump removed from my left breast
- failed reconciliation with ex-husband
- brother died from a cancerous brain tumor
- another brother diagnosed with brain tumor
- spontaneous hearing loss in left ear

Standing in a corner of the arts barn, watching others dance, play and create, I vaguely recalled memories of the "old" me: bright, capable, liberated, creative. The me standing knock-kneed in the arts barn felt tumbled about by those years of grief and loss.

A woman/child full of fears . . . but nevertheless starving for color in my life, I faked my way through the smiling introductions and quickly moved to another corner of the barn where I began working with bright-colored tissue paper. I chose primary colors: blue, red, yellow. I drew female figures standing forlornly inside large teardrops. I cut, drew, pasted and created. Artistic expression allowed me to be a witness to my feelings—the tears flowed as I drew a child wrapped in the arms of an angel.

The creative urge continued to guide me. Pieces of driftwood stacked haphazardly in another corner of the barn caught my eye. Feeling adrift in my own life, I felt kinship with those dried-out pieces of wood, and by using leather, small stones, lace, beads, buttons and glitter, was able to turn three pieces of colorless wood into magical-looking wands. I connected more deeply to the meaning of "dried-out-turned-magical" through writing. I wrote a fairy tale about a young girl raised among a wolf pack who spent her days picking stones from the wolf pack's fur. She used the gathered stones to embellish twigs she found near the door of the cave. The twigs became magic wands, and the young girl used their power to gain freedom from the wolf pack.

Letting go and releasing became my soul's creative theme over the next ten days as I wept and danced and drummed and played. Authentic body movement intimidated me to the core, but before the prescribed movement exercises, I would counter my fear by repeating lines from one of my favorite angel wall hangings, author unknown: "Angels help you carry the ball, carry your weight, carry a tune, and carry on." I continued to "carry on," engaging with myself and others in the group through use of writing, painting and clay.

Working alongside the eighteen other sojourners in the group, including the loving and creative staff from *The Person-Centered Expressive Therapy Institute*, I learned ways to affirm creativity, courage and the human spirit. The creative process, body movement, collage, painting, drawing, sculpting and writing, served as a midwife—I left the retreat with a rebirthed sense of myself as an empowered creator.

At home, I continued to use creativity as an outlet, making collages out of wood, beads, crystals and ribbon. I drew daily with paper and chalk. I continued to write poems and grew into healing partnership with my authentic, creative child within. I was living again, this time from new depths.

I traveled to California and New York over the next two years, completing four hundred hours of expressive arts training, and the personal became immersed in the professional. I began to facilitate expressive arts groups in my private practice, and offer training workshops for other helping professionals.

Creativity became a tool for spiritual growth and healing. Drawing my shadow, dancing my anger, sculpting my truth helped heal the wounds of change and loss. Today, I travel life paths with a lighter step. I have creative tools for releasing stress and addressing issues—my body no longer needs to manifest the physical symptoms of repressed emotions.

Working with the creative arts has created new dimensions of working and living. Recently, a client I had worked with three years prior to my connection with the arts reappeared in one of my expressive arts groups. She offered bold appraisal: "What's happened to you? You're different, not like the boring teacher-lady you were in those other groups. You dress differently and look happier. . . . Did you get married or something?"

I smiled while handing her paper and pastel chalk for the first group exercise, and then offered a silent prayer of gratitude to the angels of creativity flying ever-so-lowly in the room. •

THE PROCESS OF TRANSFORMATION

Soul Practice

QUESTIONS

1. What is the difference for you between efforting personal transformation, and allowing, or surrendering, to it?
2. What would it mean to practice personal transformation as the long way round, rather than as a weekend workshop or a "do-it-in-twenty-one days" sort of book? How does patience fit into personal transformation?
3. Ask yourself Angeles Arrien's four questions:
   • When in your life did you stop singing?
   • When did you stop dancing?
   • When did you stop being enchanted with stories?
   • When did you stop being comfortable with the sweet territory of silence?
4. When your "soul bucket" is empty, how do you replenish it? Meditation, walking in a forest, holding a baby, painting a picture?
5. How can you practice Arrien's four guidelines: show up; pay attention; tell the truth; be open to outcome?
6. What supports you being aware and fully in the present moment? How can you practice this more consciously?
7. If you knew, down to the very marrow of your soul, that this universe was a friendly place, how would that change your life?
8. Think back on difficult times, or dark nights, in your life. In the big picture, how did they serve your personal transformation?
9. How do you connect with the Divine? Think of as many different ways as you can besides the traditional ones of formal meditation and prayer. Playing with children, sewing, gardening, running, cooking, sitting quietly, dancing, laughing, crying can all be ways of connecting to the Sacred.
10. What would it mean to you to accept yourself, and your life, completely just as they are? How is this different than resignation?

PRACTICES

1. Practice gratitude. Try one of these two ways. The first way is to write down, before you go to sleep, five things/events/people, etc., you were grateful for today. The second way is to write down, once again before bed, one thing, etc., you were grateful for today that you've never acknowledged gratitude for before. This can be a very powerful transformation practice, because it focuses your everyday awareness on noticing new things to be grateful for. You can also practice it if you are in traffic or waiting in line—instead of feeding your frustration, start making lists in your head of everything you're grateful for.

2. Practice "not-knowing." When you don't know something, let others know. See how you feel when you let go of the need to know and understand everything. Make a list of everything you don't know. Allow the list to be a teacher to you. What gifts does "not knowing" hold for you mentally, emotionally, spiritually?

9

Practicing Transformation

Connecting with your spiritual essence is one thing. Being led by your higher self is another. Moment by moment, surrendering your frightened, lonely, ambitious, competitive ego needs to the yearnings of your heart is what the practice of transformation is about. Learning to differentiate between the desires of your personality and the callings of your heart is paramount to transforming your life. Various transformational practices teach you skills so you can listen to your heart, quiet the noisiness of your ego and heal the wounds of your psyche.

The practice of transformation is the ongoing awareness of the workings of your inner life and the ongoing choice to surrender your willfulness to the will of the Divine. Doing so opens you to receive guidance from the highest intelligence.

This chapter will help you to stay on a transformational course, to understand that the practice of transformation is essential for your life to be transformed.

COMMITMENT

If we truly want to have a more extraordinary life, then we must find a more extraordinary place within ourselves to live from. The choice is ours, and it is up to us to make it happen. Although some people may try to sell the easy spiritual trip, there are no angels that are going to come down and wave a magic wand over us, and presto, we're somebody else. All that sort of thing is delusion.

It takes real commitment to walk through the experience of total transformation. The basic practice may be simple, but it is not easy. It takes work, work and more work; it takes practice, practice and more practice.

We start exactly where we are and work from there. The more we practice and find it works, the deeper our commitment will become. This process sets up a powerful self-reinforcing mechanism that allows us to have real intensity and passion for our practice.

Ultimately, such a deep commitment is like a center of gravity within us: it keeps us firmly grounded in the work we need to do to be transformed; it allows us to use that work as a lever to lift ourselves above the tensions in our lives over and over again; it is the base from which we can become truly expansive.

—Swami Chetanananda

Getting Your Ego
Out of the Way

EVELYN AND
PAUL MOSCHETTA

Only your spiritual self has the ability to witness your selfish self and free you from a survival mentality. This is how you get your ego out of the way. Witnessing is being silently aware of what is going on inside you, of all that happens in your mind and through your senses. From the witness stance, you merely want to look, watching the movement of your thoughts, feelings and sensations rising up and passing along on the surface of your consciousness. Witnessing means seeing the workings of your ego self and not acting on them.

You are always talking to yourself. But you rarely, if ever, focus on this inner dialogue as an outside observer. Watch your mind. Observe what goes on inside yourself, the thoughts that pass by, one after another. Then you will get a first-hand view of your ego mind at work.

Witnessing is an alert watchfulness. It is an attitude of watching the watcher. The watcher is your self-centered ego, that part of you which continually makes judgments, conclusions and interpretations of all that it sees and experiences.

Witnessing comes from your spiritual self. It is a special kind of awareness because it is free of any judgments, choices or opinions. It is simply a watching of your inner reactions and responses carefully, without any self-blame or self-glorification. Judging of any kind means that your ego self is back on the scene.

Through witnessing, you get to know your ego self as it really is in each present moment. The neutral observation of witnessing highlights the contradictions between how you see yourself and how you actually behave. Being aware of these differences opens the possibility for change.

When frustrated by little things going wrong, I would get annoyed and cranky. It happens less frequently now because Evelyn and I have spoken about it, and I am very aware of my tendency to react this way. Sometimes it still comes up.

For example, working out of two different offices and having a weekend home in a third location means we live a rather nomadic lifestyle. Recently, Evelyn, after getting ready to start an evening of work, left her travel bag and suitcase on the bedroom floor, blocking a direct path to the bathroom. She turned off the lights before she left. Sometime later, I found myself groping my way toward the bathroom in complete darkness. I stumbled over the bags and almost did a swan dive into the toilet bowl.

Cursing, I got up and turned on the bathroom light. My blaming ego immediately sprang into action: "Goddamn it, how could she be so careless; she never thinks about anything she does. I could have broken my neck because of her. Just wait! I'm going to let her have it but good. I'm going to leave these bags right here so l can show her this mess."

There was a sense of self-righteousness that went along with this inner tantrum. As the thoughts and feelings passed through my mind, my witnessing self observed the whole scenario. I let witnessing take over, allowing me distance from the emotions. In that distance I could consciously choose not to have the angry outburst be my response. A calm feeling took over and instead of waiting to surprise Evelyn with the "evidence" of her misdeed, I moved the bags and later said, "Evelyn, let's both remember not to leave our bags where we can fall over them. I came in before in the dark and tripped. So let's make sure we also always leave the bathroom light on." That was it. No blaming, no judging, no feeling one *up* because I made her one *down*. Just a smooth and easy statement of the facts, which left us still feeling as close and warm as before.

When you can clearly see the facts about a person or situation, right actions will follow. Right actions leave no trace of regret, guilt or shame. Witnessing and right action go together because witnessing helps you to interrupt your tendency to react impulsively with destructive anger, criticism, inappropriate guilt and anxiety. Your spiritual self, because it is not motivated by desire or fear, can see facts clearly. When your self-centered ego is guided by your spiritual self, right action follows.

Only your spiritual self has the ability to witness your selfish self and free you from a survival mentality.

AWARENESS MOMENT TO MOMENT IS KEY

The witnessing attitude is a new way of looking. With a survival mentality, your insecure ego works mostly by analyzing events and situations. As an analyzer it wants to answer a question or solve a problem, to get to the bottom of things, to determine right from wrong, or to reach a decision or draw a conclusion. This way of analyzing is important in the practical side of your life, but it is not very useful in creating intimacy.

So often when couples come to see us for marriage counseling, they spend several sessions acting like lawyers arguing a case. Each partner uses a lot of energy analyzing their situation and making a strong case against the other. They are determined to prove their view of the problem is the correct one. Our effort is to help them understand that there is a better way for them to look at their situation. As long as your analyzing ego is in control, you will tend to see your partner's shortcomings and not your own.

Witnessing is pure "in-the-moment awareness." It happens now, in each new moment, without any analyzing.

When the thinking mind of your ego analyzes a present situation, it is usually looking back at the past or ahead to the future. Witnessing, on the other hand, is pure *in-the-moment* awareness. It happens now, in each new moment, without any analyzing. It is the in-the-moment awareness of witnessing that helps you immediately see your thoughts, feelings and reactions as they begin to arise. For most of us, because analyzing is so common, understanding comes after the fact. For example, we usually become aware of our inner tensions and conflicts after they have firmly taken hold, disguised as a headache, a sudden change in mood or a way of behaving that is uncharacteristically negative and uncooperative.

Through witnessing, when you observe rather than analyze, you begin to see how and when your survival-oriented self shows up and that it has a characteristic pattern or style. Your ego self may consistently appear as meek, apologetic and needing approval. Or it may take the form of smug superiority, sarcasm and conceit. Knowing what your general pattern is helps you be more successful at interrupting your ego self before it makes a mess of things.

ENDING AUTOMATIC PATTERNS

You develop witnessing awareness as you begin to watch for the fears, hurts, angers and anxieties that cause you to get all tied up inside. Gradually you'll learn to observe yourself, to see when and how you cause your own unhappiness. For example, without a witnessing attitude, as soon as you feel the slightest "pinch" of fear, let's say of being controlled or manipulated, you may do something negative as a defense, such as getting nasty, being sarcastic or attacking. These reactions only create more conflict between you and your partner. By witnessing, you *carefully observe* the negative thoughts and feelings that start working inside your mind without acting on them.

Through witnessing, you don't allow your ego self to automatically take over and create more pain. In fact, you see more clearly not only the attack you may or may not have received, but also what you may be doing (if anything) to invite or prolong that hurt or attack. In other words, you become acutely aware of when you are feeling controlled and manipulated and when you are doing the controlling and manipulating.

This kind of self-awareness is new for most of us. Usually, we don't give much attention to what passes through our consciousness. This frequently leaves us feeling overwhelmed, because an unwatched mind has no way of regulating how fast it is going. Giving attention to our mind's flow enables us to begin slowing down our thoughts, feelings and behavior to a more manageable pace. Then in-the-moment awareness is more possible, and we are less likely to go on automatic and repeat patterns that cause us pain and unhappiness.

Through witnessing, you don't allow your ego self to automatically take over and create more pain.

I know that between Paul and myself our selfish selves tend to surface at times of stress. When I feel under pressure, I become anxious and immediately want to eliminate what is causing the stress. I want to move quickly, find a solution, complete the task or solve the problem. For my anxious ego, sooner is much better than later. Often, I fail to see that what I need to ease my stress may be different from what Paul may be needing in the same situation.

Paul needs to move more slowly when under stress. He likes to consider the situation, look it over, think about it and then act. For example, while writing this book, we each dealt with deadlines differently. Each of us worked independently on a topic, and then we came together at an agreed-upon time to collaborate on what we had written. This agreed-upon time was our self-imposed deadline. I always have a strong need to finish on time or, preferably, before the deadline.

Recently, I had finished my writing. Our deadline was Monday morning, and it was now early afternoon on Saturday. Paul said he was going to spend the day getting a haircut, going to the hardware store and then doing some yard work. I saw the anxious ego start thinking, "Why isn't he choosing to use this precious time to work on our chapter? If we worked all day today, maybe we could be finished by tonight. Why is he choosing now to get a haircut and do the yard work? Doesn't he realize our deadline is approaching; we need every spare minute we have. No, I don't want him to spend the day this way. Because of him, we won't finish on time. I must show him, convince him he shouldn't do this; this is foolishness and a waste of important and productive time."

I saw myself begin to be annoyed at him and the situation. Witnessing helped me see that I felt as if I were being controlled, when actually I was about to do the controlling. Seeing all this, I did not try to get Paul to change his plans. I was able to see that he wanted a break from writing, and going out for a while was what he needed to do.

It is your higher self and not your ego that is capable of this kind of observing awareness. The ability of your spiritual self to witness the contents of your consciousness, the continuing movie of your mind, is your saving grace. The detached awareness witnessing enables you to see and break through the automatic thinking, feeling and acting patterns of your ego. These automatic patterns are ways the insecure part of you attempts to control for security. They produce fear and anger. More than anything else, it is fear and anger, stirred up by the ego, that cause distance in a marriage. Interrupting these patterns is essential, and your spiritual self, as witness, makes this possible.•

Beginning Anew

THICH NHAT HANH

You think you can change the world, but do not be too naive. Don't think that the moment you arrive in Vietnam, you will sit down with all the conflicting factions and establish communication immediately. You may be able to give beautiful talks about harmony, but if you are not prepared, you will not be able to put your words into practice. In Vietnam there are already people who can give very good Dharma talks, who can explain how to reconcile and live in harmony. But we should not only talk about it. If we do not practice what we preach, what can we offer anyone?

We must practice harmony of views and harmony of speech. We bring our views together to have a deeper understanding, and we use loving speech to inspire others and not hurt anyone. We practice walking together, eating together, discussing together, so we can realize love and understanding. If older sisters do not hold each other's hands like children of the same mother, how can the younger sisters have faith in the future? If you are able to breathe and smile when your sister says something unkind, that is the beginning of love. You do not have to go someplace else to serve. You can serve right where you are by practicing walking meditation, smiling and shining your eyes of love on others.

We want to go out and share what we have learned. But if we do not practice mindful breathing to untie the knots of pain in ourselves—the knots of anger, sadness, jealousy and irritation—what can we teach others? We must understand and practice the teachings in our daily lives. People need to hear how we have to be able to overcome our own suffering and the irritations in our own heart. When we talk about the Dharma, our words need to have energy. That is not possible if our words come only from ideas, theories or even sutras. We can only teach what we have experienced ourselves.

Eight years ago I organized a retreat for American veterans of the Vietnam War. Many of the men and women at that retreat felt very guilty for what they had done and witnessed, and I knew I had to find a way of beginning anew that could help them transform. One veteran told me that when he was in Vietnam, he rescued a girl who had been wounded and was about to die. He pulled her into his helicopter, but he was not able to save her life. She died looking straight at him, and he has never forgotten her eyes. She had a hammock with her, because as a guerrilla, she slept in the forest at night. When she died, he kept the hammock and would not let it go. Sometimes when we suffer, we have to cling to our suffering. The hammock symbolized all his suffering, all his shame.

During the retreat, the veterans sat in a circle and spoke about their suffering, some for the first time. In a retreat for veterans, a lot of love and support is needed. Some veterans would not do walking meditation, because it reminded them too much of walking in the jungles of Vietnam, where they could step on a mine or walk into an ambush at any time. One man walked far behind the rest of us so that if anything happened he would be able to get away quickly. Veterans live in that kind of psychological environment.

On the last day of the retreat, we held a ceremony for the deceased. Each veteran wrote the names of those he or she knew had died, and placed it on an altar we constructed. I took a willow leaf and used it to sprinkle water on the names and also on the veterans. Then we did walking meditation to the lake and held a ceremony for burning the suffering. That veteran still did not want to give up his hammock, but finally he put it on the fire. It burned, and all the guilt and the suffering in his heart also burned up. We have taken one step, two steps, three steps on the path of transformation. We have to continue on that path.

Another veteran told us that almost everyone in his platoon had been killed by the guerrillas. Those who survived were so angry that they baked cookies with explosives in them and left them alongside the road. When some Vietnamese children saw them, they ate the cookies and the explosives went off. They were rolling around the ground in pain. Their parents tried to save their lives, but there was nothing they could do. That image of the children rolling on the ground, dying because of the explosives in the cookies, was so deeply ingrained on this veteran's heart, that now, twenty years later, he still could not sit in the same room with children. He was living in hell. After he had told this story, I gave him the practice of Beginning Anew.

Beginning Anew is not easy. We have to transform our hearts and our minds in very practical ways. We may feel ashamed, but shame is not enough to change our heart. I said to him, "You killed five or six children that day? Can you save the lives of five or six children today? Children everywhere in the world are dying because of war, malnutrition and disease. You keep thinking about the five or six children that you killed in the past, but what about the children who are dying now? You still have your body, you still have your heart, you can do many things to help children who are dying in the present moment. Please give rise to your mind of love, and in the months and years that are left to you, do the work of helping children." He agreed to do it, and it has helped him transform his guilt.

Beginning Anew is not to ask for forgiveness. Beginning Anew is to change your mind and heart, to transform the ignorance that brought about wrong actions of body, speech and mind, and to help you cultivate your mind of love. Your shame and guilt will disappear, and you will begin to experience the joy of being alive. All wrongdoings arise in the mind. It is through the mind that wrongdoings can disappear.

At Plum Village, we practice a ceremony of Beginning Anew every week. Everyone sits in a circle with a vase of fresh flowers in the center, and we follow our breathing as we wait for the facilitator to begin. The ceremony has three parts: flower watering, expressing regrets, and expressing hurts and difficulties. This practice can prevent feelings of hurt from building up over the weeks and helps make the situation safe for everyone in the community.

We begin with flower watering. When someone is ready to speak, she joins her palms and the others join their palms to show that she has the right to speak. Then she stands, walks slowly to the flower, takes the vase in her hands and returns to her seat. When she speaks, her words reflect the freshness and beauty of the flower that is in her hand. During flower watering, each speaker acknowledges the wholesome, wonderful qualities of the others. It is not flattery; we always speak the truth. Everyone has some strong points that can be seen with awareness. No one can interrupt the person holding the flower. She is allowed as much time as she needs, and everyone else practices deep listening. When she is finished speaking, she stands up and slowly returns the vase to the center of the room.

In the second part of the ceremony, we express regrets for anything we have done to hurt others. It does not take more than one thoughtless phrase to hurt someone. The ceremony of Beginning Anew is an opportunity for us to recall some regret from earlier in the week and undo it. In the third part of the ceremony, we express ways in which others have hurt us. Loving speech is crucial. We want to heal the community, not harm it. We speak frankly, but we do not want to be destructive. Listening meditation is an important part of the practice. When we sit among a circle of friends who are all practicing deep listening, our speech becomes more beautiful and more constructive. We never blame or argue.

Compassionate listening is crucial. We listen with the willingness to relieve the suffering of the other person, not to judge or argue with her. We listen with all our attention. Even if we hear something that is not true, we continue to listen deeply so the other person can express her pain and release the tensions within herself. If we reply to her or correct her, the practice will not bear fruit. We just listen. If we need to tell the other person that her perception was not correct, we can do that a few days later, privately and calmly. Then, at the next Beginning Anew session, she may be the person who rectifies the error, and we will not have to say anything. We close the ceremony with a song or by holding hands with everyone in the circle and breathing for a minute.

After the Beginning Anew ceremony, everyone in the community feels light and relieved, even if we have taken only preliminary steps toward healing. We have confidence that, having begun, we can continue. This practice dates to the time of the Buddha, when communities of monks and nuns practiced Beginning Anew on the eve of every full moon and new moon. Thanks to our practice with veterans and others, we have adapted it for our community. I hope you will practice Beginning Anew in your own family every week.•

Meditation

AYYA KHEMA

One of our human absurdities is the fact that we're constantly thinking about either the future or the past. Those who are young think of the future because they've got more of it. Those who are older think more about the past because for them there is more of that. But in order to experience life, we have to live each moment. Life has not been happening in the past. That's memory. Life is not going to happen in the future. That's planning. The only time we can live is now, this moment, and as absurd as it may seem, we've got to learn that. As human beings with life spans of sixty, seventy or eighty years we have to learn actually to experience living in the present. When we have learned that, we will have eliminated a great many of our problems.

We are all quite able and efficient in looking after our bodies. We wash them at least once a day, probably even more often. We go out with clean clothes. We rest our bodies at night. Everyone has a bed. We wouldn't be able to stand up to the strain of living if we didn't also rest. We have a house where we shelter the body from rain, wind, sun, the heat and the cold. We wouldn't be able to function well otherwise. We feed the body with healthy nourishment, not with anything that we would consider poison. We give it the food we consider good for us and we take exercise. At least we walk. If we didn't, our legs would atrophy and we could no longer use them. Exactly the same has to be done for the mind.

In fact it's even more important because the mind is the master and the body is the servant. The best servant in perfect condition, young, strong and vigorous, having a weak and dissolute master who doesn't know what to do, will not be able to work satisfactorily. The master has to direct the servant. Even when the servant isn't so strong and vigorous, if the master is efficient and wise the household will still be in order.

This mind and body are our household. If this inner household is not in order, no outer household can be in order. The one we live and work in is dependent on the order that we have created in our own inner household. The master, the one in charge, has to be in the best possible condition.

Nothing in the whole universe is comparable to the mind or can take its place. Yet we all take our minds for granted, which is another absurdity. No one takes the body for granted. When the body gets sick, we quickly run to the doctor. When the body gets hungry, we quickly feed it. When the body gets tired, we quickly rest it. But what about the mind? Only the meditator looks after the mind.

Looking after the mind is essential if life is to grow in depth and vision. Otherwise life stays two-dimensional. Most lives are lived in the realities of yesterday and tomorrow, good and bad, I like it and I don't like it, I'll have it and I won't have it, this is mine and this is yours. Only when the mind is trained can we see other dimensions.

The first thing we need to do with the mind is wash it, clean it up, not only once or twice a day as we do for the body but in all our waking moments. In order to do that, we have to learn how. With the body it's very simple, we use soap and water. We learned to do that when we were small. Mind can only be cleansed by mind. What the mind has put in there, the mind can take out. One second of concentration in meditation is one second of purification because, luckily, the mind can only do one thing at a time. Although, as the Buddha said, we can have three thousand mind moments in the blink of an eyelid, we don't usually have that many and we don't have them all at once. Mind moments follow each other in quick succession but only one at a time.

Our mind, that unique tool in all the universe, is the only one we have. If we owned a fine tool we would obviously look after it. We'd polish it and remove any rust. We'd sharpen it, we'd oil it and we'd rest it from time to time. Here we have this marvelous tool with which everything can be accomplished, including enlightenment, and it's up to us to learn to look after it. It won't function properly otherwise.

During meditation we learn to drop from the mind what we don't want to keep. We only want to keep in mind our meditation subject. As we become more and more skilled at it, we start to use the same faculty in our daily lives to help us drop those thoughts that are unwholesome. In this way our meditation practice assists us in daily living and our attention to wholesome thoughts in everyday life helps our meditation practice. The person who becomes master of his or her own thoughts and learns to think what he wants to think is called an Enlightened One.

Please don't be surprised if this letting go of thoughts doesn't work all the time; it will surely function some of the time. It is an immense release and relief when one can think, even for one moment, what one wants to think, because then one has become master of the mind instead of the mind being the master of oneself. Being involved in whatever thoughts arise, unhappy or happy ones, in constant flux and flow is what we learn to drop when we manage to stay on the meditation subject.

Our second step is exercising the mind. An untrained mind is like a wavering, fluctuating mass that runs from one subject to the next and finds it very difficult to stay in one spot. You have probably had the experience when reading a book of coming to the end of a page and, realizing you don't know what you've just read, having to read the whole page over again. The mind has to be pushed to stay in one spot, like doing press-ups, like weight lifting, developing muscles in the mind. Strength can only come from exercising the mind to do exactly what one wants it to do, to stand still when one wants it to stand still.

This also creates power in the mind because it's connected with renunciation, with letting go. All of us have sizeable egos. The "me" and "mine" syndrome and "if you please, I'll keep it and you stay out" attitudes create all the world's problems. We can only be sure that the ego is affirmed when we're thinking, talking, reading, seeing a movie or using the mind in the interests of ego. The great renunciation that arises in meditation is to drop all thoughts. When there's nobody thinking, there's no ego confirmation.

To start with, dropping thoughts will only be possible momentarily, but it is a step in the right direction. The spiritual path is all about letting go. There is nothing to achieve or gain. Although these words are used frequently, they are only ways of expressing ourselves. In reality a spiritual path is a path of renunciation, letting go, constantly dropping all we have built up around ourselves. This incudes possessions, conditioned habits, ideas, beliefs, thinking patterns. It is difficult to stop thinking in meditation because that would be renunciation and it is a moment when the ego doesn't have any support. When it happens for the first time, the mind immediately reacts with, "Oh, what was that?" and—of course—one is thinking again.

To be able to keep the mind in one spot creates mind muscles, gives the mind strength and power.

The body's strength makes it possible to accomplish what we set out to do with the body. The mind's strength makes it possible to do the same with the mind. A strong mind does not suffer from boredom, frustration, depression or unhappiness—it has learned to drop what it doesn't want. Meditation practice has given it the necessary muscles.

The mind, being the most valuable and intricate tool in the universe, also needs a rest. We have been thinking ever since we were very small and innumerable lifetimes before that.

All day we think, all night we dream. There isn't a moment's rest. We may go on holiday but what goes on holiday? The body goes on holiday. It might go to the beach, to the seaside or the mountains or to a different country, but what about the mind? Instead of thinking about the work one has to do at home, one thinks about all the sights, sounds and tastes at the new place. The mind isn't getting a holiday. It just thinks about something else.

If we didn't give the body a rest at night, it wouldn't function very long. Our mind needs a rest, too, but this can't be had through sleeping. The only time the mind can have a real rest is when it stops thinking and starts only experiencing. One of the similes used for the mind is a blank screen on which a continuous film is shown without intermission. Because the film—the thoughts—is continuous, one forgets that there has to be a screen behind on which to project it.

If we stop that film for a moment in meditation we can experience the basic purity of our mind. That is a moment of bliss. A moment that brings the kind of happiness not available anywhere else, through anything else. A happiness that is independent of outer conditions. It's not unconditioned but conditioned only by concentration. It's not dependent upon good food or climate, entertainment or the right relationships, other people or pleasant responses or possessions, all of which are totally unreliable and cannot be depended upon because they are always changing. Concentration is reliable if one keeps practicing.

Once verbalization stops for a moment, not only is there quiet but there is a feeling of contentment. The mind has at last found its home. We wouldn't be very happy if we didn't have a home for this body of ours. We are equally not very happy if we haven't got a home for the mind. That quiet, peaceful space is the mind's home. It can go home and relax just as we do after a day's work when we relax the body in an easy chair and at night in a bed. Now the mind, too, can take it easy. It doesn't have to think. Thinking is suffering, no matter what it is that we think. There is movement in it and because of that there is friction. Everything that moves creates friction.

The moment we relax and rest the mind it gains new strength and also happiness because it knows it can go home at any time. The happiness created at the time of meditation carries through to daily living because the mind knows that nothing has to be taken so seriously that it can't go home again and find peace and quiet.•

God's Will

SRI CHINMOY

God's Will in an individual is progressive, like a muscle developing—strong, stronger, strongest. God's Will is to make an individual feel that there is something abiding, lasting, everlasting. When an individual reaches that stage, he will know God's Will. God's Will we can know from the sense of abiding satisfaction it gives us.

Anything that is eternal, anything that is immortal, anything that is divine, is God's Will. Even though God deals with Eternity, he is not indifferent for one second. For it is from one second, two seconds, three seconds that we enter into Infinity and Eternity. Let us try to feel God's Will in us at every second.

There is a very simple way to know what God's Will is for us as individuals. Every day when we start our day, we build our own world. We make decisions. We feel that things have to be done in a certain way. I have to deal with this person in this way. I have to say this; I have to do this; I have to give this. Everything is I, I, I. If, instead of all this planning, we can make our minds absolutely calm and silent, we can know God's Will. This silence is not the silence of a dead body; it is the dynamic, progressive silence of receptivity. Through total silence and the ever-increasing receptivity of the mind, God's Will can be known.

When the human mind works powerfully, the Divine Will cannot work. God's Will works only when the human mind does not work. When the mind becomes a pure vessel, the Supreme can pour into it his infinite Peace, Light and Bliss.

Right now we do not hear God's Voice. There may be something we hear from within that we feel is God's Voice, but it may be only a voice coming from our subtle physical or subtle vital or from somewhere else. But when we silence the mind, we can hear a silent voice inside the very depth of our heart or above our head, and that is the Voice of God. Once we hear the Voice of God, we cannot make any mistake in our life. If we listen to its dictates all the time, we will go forward, upward and inward constantly.

We are constantly building and breaking our mental house. But instead of making and breaking the house at our sweet will, if we can empty our mind, make it calm and quiet, then God can build his Temple or his Palace in us in his own way. And when he has built his Abode within us, he will say, "I have built this for you and me to reside in together. I have built it, but it is not mine alone. It is also yours. Come in."

The easiest way for us to know God's Will is to become the instrument and not the doer. If we become only the instrument for carrying out God's Plans, God's Will will act in and through us. God does the acting and he is the action. He is everything. We only observe.

> *To easily know what God's Will is,*
> *We have to feed the divine in us*
> *And illumine the human in us.*

How Can I Know God's Will in My Daily Life?

You can know God's Will in your daily life if early in the morning you offer your utmost gratitude to God for what he has already done for you. When you offer your gratitude-heart, then it expands; and when it expands, it becomes one with God's Universal Reality. A gratitude-heart blossoms like a flower. When the flower is fully blossomed, then you appreciate and admire it.

In your case also, when your heart of gratitude blossoms, immediately God is pleased. If you offer gratitude to God for what he has already done for you, then naturally God's sweet Will will operate in and through you. Early in the morning, before you meditate or do anything else, offer as much gratitude as possible; offer your soulful tears just because you have become what you are now. If you do this, eventually you will become infinitely more than what you are now. Gratitude will be able to make you feel what God's Will is. God's Will will act in and through you and God will do everything in and through you, and for you, if you offer gratitude.

How Can I Know What God Wants Me to Do?

You will know easily if you are not attached to the result or elevated by the result. Before you do something, pray to God: "God, if it is Your Will, then please inspire me to do it well." While working, tell God, "God, since I have accepted this work with the feeling that you wanted me to do it, please work in and through me so that I can do it well. From your inspiration, I will be able to know that it is your Will." At the end of the work, whether the result comes as success or as failure, offer it at the Feet of God with the same joy.

How Do I Know If I Am Executing God's Will or I Am Fulfilling My Own Ego?

When you fulfill the demands of the ego, immediately you will feel that you are the lord of the world or that you are going to become the lord of the world. You are bloated with pride, and you feel that the rest of the world is at your feet. Once a desire of yours is fulfilled, immediately you feel, "Oh, my desire is fulfilled: I have become something, and the rest of the world will not achieve what I have." Always there will be a feeling of superiority when the ego is fulfilled.

When you execute the Will of God, the question of superiority or inferiority does not arise. At that time you feel only your oneness. You feel that God has appointed you or that God has accepted you as his chosen instrument, and that he is acting in and through you. No matter what you achieve, even if it is something very grand, extraordinary, unusual, you will not have any sense of personal pride. On the contrary, you will feel extremely grateful to God that he has chosen to fulfill himself in and through you. There will be no pride, but only a feeling of expansion.

To execute God's Will means to achieve something. When you achieve something, you feel an expansion of your consciousness. But when you fulfill the demands of your ego, you feel totally separated from the rest of the world. You are the lord, and the rest of creation is at your feet. In this way you can know the difference between the two.

> Self-giving to God's Will
> Is, without fail,
> A slow-ripening
> But most delicious fruit.

Should We Pray for Something We Want or Should We Just Pray for God's Will to Be Done?

To pray for God's Will to be done is the highest form of prayer. But a beginner finds it almost impossible to pray to God sincerely to fulfill him in God's own way. Early in the morning, a beginner will say to God, "God, I want to be your unconditionally surrendered child." Then, the next moment, when jealousy, insecurity or pride enters into him, his self-offering becomes all conditional. At that time the seeker says, "God, early in the morning I prayed to you so sincerely to fulfill your Will in me, but you did not listen to my prayer. Otherwise, I would have been above jealousy, fear, doubt, anxiety and attachment."

If the seeker prays for something in the morning, and his prayer is not fulfilled in a few hours' time, immediately he becomes discouraged. Then he stops praying and meditating for six months. For a day he offers his sincere prayer, and then for six months he is ready to enjoy ignorance. So when a seeker is just starting out, it is always advisable for him to pray to God for whatever he feels he needs most, whether it is patience, purity, sincerity, humility or peace. Then God will give him peace, light and bliss, which are the precursors of something infinite that is going to come into his inner being.

Once he has received and achieved some peace, light and bliss and has become established to some extent in his inner being, he will have some confidence in God's operation and also in his own life of aspiration.

When one is making very fast progress or is a little advanced, he feels that there is a Reality within himself that is not going to disappoint or desert him. He feels that God is fully aware of what he needs and is eager to supply him with the things that he needs, because God wants to fulfill himself in and through His chosen instrument. At his choice Hour, God will fulfill himself in and through that particular chosen instrument.

When a seeker feels this kind of confidence within himself, that is the time for the seeker to pray, "Let Thy Will be done." At that time he can sincerely say, "God, now I want to please you only in your own way." At that time he will feel that God wants to manifest himself in and through him. He will feel that the moment God makes him perfect, he will be able to serve the divinity in humanity.

If a Member of One's Immediate Family Is Sick, What Is Your Feeling About Praying to God for Healing Power?

Let us say that your mother is sick. Instead of saying, "Cure my mother, cure my mother," if you can say, "I place my mother at the Feet of God," you will be doing the best thing. Your best healing power will be to place your mother at the Feet of God, because he knows what is best.

When you offer your own will to the Will of God, you gain power, and this power will be utilized for God. God himself will tell you how to utilize it. But if you try to heal on your own, in spite of your best intentions, you may stand against the Will of God.

Suppose you pray and meditate to acquire divine power so that you can cure people and help the world. You say, "I want to be a camel and carry the whole burden of the world on my shoulders." But if the camel is not illumined, then how can it help others gain illumination?

You are running toward your goal. If you ask God to give you something, then this is just an additional thing that you have to carry, and it may slow you down. If illumination is your goal, think only of your goal and nothing else.

Again, if a remedy for a disease comes spontaneously from within and you do not have to exercise your mental power or will-power, then there is no question of ego, pride or vanity. If in your meditation, all of a sudden you see inner light and in this light you get a cure for some fatal disease, then naturally you will be able to offer this inner illumination to the world at large. But the best thing is to become illumined first. Then only will you be serving God in his own way. Otherwise at times you will serve God in his own way, and at other times you will be feeding your own ego.

How Can You Tell the Difference Between the Will of God and Wishful Thinking?

In order to know God's Will, one need not be a great spiritual Master or a highly advanced soul. There are very few of these on earth, very few. But one has to be at least a seeker in order to know God's Will. How can one be a real seeker? One can be a true seeker if he feels that he is not only helpless, but also hopeless, meaningless and useless in every way without God. Without God he is nothing, but with God he is everything. He is aspiration. He is realization. He is revelation. He is manifestation. If one has that kind of inner feeling about oneself, then one can be a true seeker overnight.

A sincere seeker tries to meditate devotedly each day. One who meditates devotedly each day will soon have a free access to God's inner Realm and be able to hear the Message of God. Of course, it is easy to say that you have to meditate devotedly, but to actually meditate devotedly may seem as difficult as climbing up Mount Everest. When you start meditating, you have to feel that your very life, your very existence, your very breath, is an offering to the Inner Pilot within you. Only in this way can you meditate devotedly and have a devoted feeling toward God.

During your meditation there comes a time when your mind is absolutely calm and quiet. There is only purity, serenity and profundity in your mind. Purity, sincerity and profundity have one common face, which is called tranquillity. When tranquillity is with them, they are perfect.

When the mind has become calm, quiet, tranquil and vacant, inside your heart you will feel a twinge, or you will feel something very tiny, like a soft bubble. It is a tiny thing, but there in golden letters is written a message. Even if you keep your eyes closed, no harm. Sometimes the message is transferred from the heart to the head, and with your mind you can see that the message has come. But if you have the capacity to go deep within, you will see that the message has already been inscribed in the heart. Just because you cannot see the message there, it has to come to the physical mind to convince you.

Inside the inmost recesses of the heart, where everything is flooded with purity, a message cannot be written by anybody other than God. There no undivine force can enter. This is not true about the mind. In the mind there can always be a mental hallucination, a fabrication or some self-imposed truth that we have created.

But in the inmost recesses of our heart, no disturbing thought, no struggling thought, no strangling thought will ever dare to enter. The depths of our heart are well protected, well shielded by God himself, because God's own Wealth and Treasure is there. He himself is there as a gatekeeper, guarding his Treasure.

When you meditate, please try to feel the necessity of opening your heart fully and closing your physical mind fully. The physical mind is the mind which thinks of your near and dear ones, your friends, the rest of the world. When you bolt the door of your physical mind and open the door of your heart, the mind becomes calm and quiet and the heart becomes all receptivity. When your concentration and meditation are focused on the heart and the heart is receptive, then naturally what the heart treasures, the Message from God, will come to the fore and you will be able to read it and utilize it in your day-to-day life.

Now, it is one thing to hear the Message of God correctly and another thing to listen to it and fulfill it. There are quite a few who can hear God's Message, but in their outer life they cannot execute it. For that, you need faith in yourself, faith that you are not just a child of God, but a chosen child of God. Everybody is God's child, but everybody cannot be God's chosen child because everybody is not consciously aspiring. The chosen are those who really want God here and now, those who feel that they do not exist, cannot exist, without God. Just because you aspire sincerely, you can claim yourself as a chosen child of God.•

Trivial Talk

ERICH FROMM

W hat is trivial? Literally it means "commonplace" (from Latin tri-via = the point where three roads meet); it usually denotes shallow, humdrum, lacking ability or moral qualities. One might also define "trivial" as an attitude that is concerned only with the surface of things, not with their causes or the deeper layers, as an attitude that does not distinguish between what is essential and what is unessential, or one that is prone to reverse the two qualities. We may say, in addition, that triviality results from unaliveness, unresponsiveness, deadness or from any concern that is not related to the central task of man: to be fully born.

Perhaps most trivial talk is a need to talk about oneself; hence, the never-ending subject of health and sickness, children, travel, successes, what one did, and the innumerable daily things that seem to be important. Since one cannot talk about oneself all the time without being thought a bore, one must exchange the privilege by a readiness to listen to others talking about themselves. Private social meetings between individuals (and often, also, meetings of all kinds of associations and groups) are little markets where one exchanges one's need to talk about oneself and one's desire to be listened to for the need of others who seek the same opportunity. Most people respect this arrangement of exchange; those who don't and want to talk more about themselves than they are willing to listen are "cheaters," and they are resented and have to choose inferior company in order to be tolerated.

One can hardly overestimate people's need to talk about themselves and to be listened to. If this need were present only in highly narcissistic people, who are filled only with themselves, it would be easy to understand. But it exists in the average person for reasons that are inherent in our culture. Modern man is a mass man; he is highly "socialized," but he is very lonely. David Riesman has expressed this phenomenon strikingly in the title of his 1961 book *The Lonely Crowd* (New York: Free Press). Modern man is alienated from others and confronted with a dilemma. He is afraid of close contact with another and equally afraid to be alone and have no contact. It is the function of trivial conversation to answer the question, "How do I remain alone without being lonely?"

Talking becomes an addiction. "As long as I talk, I know I exist, that I am not nobody, that I have a past, that I have a job, I have a family. And by talking about all this I affirm myself. However, I need someone to listen. If I were only talking to myself I would go crazy." The listener produces the illusion of a dialogue when in reality there is only a monologue.

Bad company, on the other hand, is not only the company of merely trivial people but of evil, sadistic, destructive, life-hostile people. But why, one might ask, is there a danger in the company of bad people, unless they try to harm one in one form or another?

In order to answer this question it is necessary to recognize a law in human relations. *There is no contact between human beings that does not affect both of them.* No meeting between two people, no conversation between them, except perhaps the most casual one, leaves either one of them unchanged—even though the change may be so minimal as to be unrecognizable except by its cumulative effect when such meetings are frequent.

Even a casual meeting *can* have a considerable impact. Who has not once been touched in his life by the kindness in a face of a person whom he saw only for a minute and never talked to? Who has not experienced the horror that a truly evil face produced in him, even being exposed to it for only a moment? Many will remember such faces and the effects they had on them for many years or for all their lives. Who, after being with a certain person, has not felt cheered up, more alive, in a better mood, or in some cases even possessing new courage and new insights, even though the content of the conversation would not account for this change? On the other hand, many people have had the experience, after being with certain others, of being depressed, tired, hopeless, yet unable to find the *content* of the conversation responsible for the reaction. I am not speaking here of the influence of persons with whom somebody is in love, admires, is afraid of, etc.; obviously *they* can have a strong influence by what they say or how they behave toward a person who is under their spell. What I am talking about is the influence of persons on those who are not bound to them in special ways.

All these considerations lead to the conclusion that it is desirable to avoid trivial and evil company altogether, unless one can assert oneself fully and thus make the other doubt his own position.

Inasmuch as one cannot avoid bad company, one should not be deceived. One should see the insincerity behind the mask of friendliness, the destructiveness behind the mask of eternal complaints about unhappiness, the narcissism behind the charm. One should also not act as if he or she were taken in by the other's deceptive appearance—in order to avoid being forced into a certain dishonesty oneself. One need not speak to them about what one sees, but one should not attempt to convince them that one is blind. The great twelfth-century Jewish philosopher Moses Maimonides, recognizing the effect of bad company, made the drastic proposal, "If you live in a country whose inhabitants are evil, avoid their company. If they try to force you to associate with them, leave the country, even if it means going to the desert."

If other people do not understand our behavior—so what? Their request that we must only do what they understand is an attempt to dictate to us. If this is being "asocial" or "irrational" in their eyes, so be it. Mostly they resent our freedom and our courage to be ourselves. We owe nobody an explanation or an accounting, as long as our acts do not hurt or infringe on them. How many lives have been ruined by this need to "explain," which usually implies that the explanation be "understood," i.e., approved? Let your deeds be judged and from your deeds your real intentions, but know that a free person owes an explanation only to himself—to his reason and his conscience—and to the few who may have a justified claim for explanation.•

Breaking Our Patterns of Overdoing It

B R Y A N   R O B I N S O N,   P H. D.

T ears streamed down my cheeks. Emotionally exhausted and slumped in my seat, all I could do when the flight attendant asked me if I wanted something to eat was wave her away with my hand. I had lost so much weight I looked like a refugee from Dachau. During the takeoff, I didn't care if the plane crashed. Nothing mattered. I was on my way for a sunny week in Jamaica to escape the pain of breaking up a fourteen-year relationship. My life was crumbling under my feet, and there was nothing I could do about it. I felt like half a person. I didn't care if I lived or died. That was the spring of 1983.

I didn't know it at the time but I was living out the critical thinking patterns that I had learned growing up in my family. A few years later I would learn that these patterns had been in my family for three generations.

My grandmother was a compulsive overeater who died from a stroke attributed to her obesity. Her son, my father, was an alcoholic who died from cirrhosis of the liver. I swore I would never be like my "old man." I lived my first thirty years priding myself on the fact that I had "licked" the family disease because I had neither chemical nor food addictions. What I wouldn't discover until midlife was that my family's faulty thinking had been passed down to me and had burrowed itself into the very core of my soul. My general outlook on life was polluted and my relationships eventually became contaminated. I saw myself as a victim of a bad life and a bad relationship.

"Why do all these horrible things keep happening to me?" I whimpered. "Maybe a trip to the Caribbean will ease the heartache."

All I could think about was how to get even with the third person who came between me and my beloved. I carried the hate and resentment as if they were excess luggage. I was so consumed with rage I lay awake until three or four in the morning, plotting and avenging my damaged emotions. Unknowingly all these negative obsessions hurt no one but myself.

My faulty thinking caused me to try everything to cope with my pain, except the things that could help me. I clung to my resentments, saw only misery and despair, blamed everybody else for my hardships and the breakup of my relationship and tried a change of scene to escape my pain. It never occurred to me that there was anything more I could do. My only option, as I saw it, was to react to life, rather than take action. In so doing I disempowered myself by playing the victim. I became cynical, negative and pessimistic—all of which ricocheted, slapped me in the face and multiplied my misery and despair.

Through meditation and affirmations, I was able to let go of my anger and resentment as I lay on the Jamaica beach. I started to notice changes in my life. The nightmares subsided. I felt an inner calm that I had never experienced before, and I slept like a baby for the first time in weeks. I realized that there was something I could do to change my life. I realized that no matter how dismal things appear to be I don't have to be a victim. I learned that I cannot control everything that happens around me, but I can always take charge of what I think, feel and do. This same awareness has helped me get in touch with my overdoing it, to slow down and to take better care of myself because I know I deserve it.

Everyone wants to live a happy life. But why are so many of us miserable so much of the time, constantly searching for serenity and calm with little success? Because we're looking in the wrong place.

An ancient tale about Nasrudin, who lost the key to his house on the way home one night, illustrates this point beautifully.

Nasrudin was down on all fours under the street lamp searching frantically for his key when a stranger came by and asked him what he was looking for. Nasrudin told him he had lost the key to his house. So the stranger, being a kind man, got down on his hands and knees and helped look for it. After hours of searching, the stranger asked, "Are you sure you dropped the key in this spot?" Nasrudin said, "Oh no! I dropped it way over there in that dark alley." Frustrated and angry, the stranger lost his temper, "Then why are you looking for it here?" Nasrudin replied, "Because the light's better here under the street lamp."

Those of us who overdo it are like Nasrudin. Our supercharged lives are stuck in fast forward and focused on the external world. We do not have an internal life. Overdoing it keeps us disconnected from ourselves, subtracts from our human value and prevents us from knowing who we are. We are so defined by what we do we don't know who we are on the inside. The only way out of this dilemma is to redefine ourselves from within.

If unhappiness and discontent are created on the inside, doesn't it make sense that to change our lives we must start there? As we learn to refrain from overdoing it we focus on an *inner* life, not an outer life. Wayne Dyer in his book *You'll See It When You Believe It* puts it this way:

> *We live inside, we think inside, our humanity resides within, yet we spend time ceaselessly looking outside of ourselves for the answers because we fail to illuminate the inside with our thoughts. We resist the principle that thought is everything we are because it seems easier to look outside.*

Once Nasrudin looks in the alley, he will illuminate his life and find his key. Once we look within ourselves, we achieve illumination and discover how to break our patterns of overdoing it.

Twenty-two-year-old Sheila worked for a computer company in New York City. She was bored and weary of the grind of morning rush hours, daily routines and afternoon traffic jams. She had few friends and was generally unhappy with her life. Finally with her mother's encouragement, Sheila decided to go to California to "find herself." After a few months she decided that Los Angeles "was not what it is cracked up to be" so she moved to Seattle.

Unfortunately, moving across the country won't help us find ourselves. We carry our old habits like luggage wherever we go. If we wake up feeling positive and optimistic in Detroit, we wake up feeling positive and optimistic in the Mediterranean. If we wake up anxious and pessimistic in Buffalo, we wake up anxious and pessimistic in the South Pacific.

Those of us who feel incomplete and unfinished often look outside to fill the void. We stuff our lives with projects, computer printouts, deadlines, unhealthy relationships and material possessions. We become addicted to acquiring power and get consumed with making it to the top. We aim for worldly achievements, approval and financial rewards. We become enslaved by greed, competition and material gain as we try to heal our past insecurities and feelings of inadequacy.

We look in the wrong place when we constantly *do* in order to *be*. We are often so busy "getting there," we forget we are already "there" and that there is nowhere else to go. All we really have is ourselves, and discovering the treasure of self is the key. All we need do is look within. It is this inner transformation that improves the quality of our lives.

Overdoing it keeps us stuck in the external world and in the cycle of never feeling good enough. Replacing constant busyness with a rich spiritual life can heal busy habits. Being puts us in touch with our inner world and takes us out of the future and puts us into the present. We discover how to *be* by living in the now and looking within and connecting with our own inner selves. Being allows us to accept and love ourselves unconditionally, *exactly* as we are. Once we face, accept and love ourselves, we no longer have to overdo to feel better about ourselves.

Healing from overdoing it comes from realizing that we cannot control anyone or anything but ourselves and that we can be responsible only for ourselves.

Only through interior change will you find what you have been looking for. It is not out there; it is inside of you. Everything comes from the way you think about yourself. If you want to change your life, change the way you think about yourself first. Everything else follows.

Inner healing occurs only through unconditional love. When you treat yourself as a worthy, loving and competent human being, others begin to treat you that way and the world begins to operate that way for you. Harmony in the world begins with harmony within yourself. You will allow yourself to be led from within once you realize you are your own best guru. That's why "guru" is spelled, "Gee-You-Are-You."

When we put everyone's needs before our own, our needs get pushed to the back burner. Sometimes we resent not having time for ourselves. Self-nurturance is one of the most important qualities we can develop. It has helped me love myself unconditionally, to treat myself with kindness and caring as I would anyone I care about. It has allowed me to approach life with more calm, hope and optimism.

No one can give us free time but ourselves. During quiet, reflective moments we can gain clarity and receive answers to life's challenging problems. Self-nurturance can include listening to soft music, walking barefoot in a summer rainstorm, reading inspirational material, sitting by the ocean watching the waves, meditating in a quiet place or doing something we enjoy that we haven't done in a long time.

The answers within us always come when we put ourselves under the proper conditions. Meditation, prayer, contemplation and mental relaxation all help us receive the answers we need. These activities help us connect with our intuitive parts that guide us from the heart instead of the head—that show us how to *be* instead of *do*. Relying on this "inner knowing" is just as important as using common sense. It's okay to listen to our gut when it says stop, take care or slow down. As we eliminate overdoing it from our lives, we learn to listen with our hearts instead of our heads because this is how the intuitive self speaks to us and guides us.

When we reserve special time for self-nurturance, we send ourselves the message that we are important and worth our own care and attention. We create this time for ourselves by getting up fifteen minutes earlier, going to bed fifteen minutes later or taking fifteen minutes at lunch time. We can always find time for ourselves if we really want it.

The first rule of thumb is to provide ourselves with a mental sanctuary where thoughts and items of doing are not present. We can create this inner place of calm, harmony and contentment anywhere and any time. There is a power within us that brings peace, emotional and physical healing, and serenity. With the help of this power, we can create the best life that we can envision. This power governs the universe and makes trees grow and flowers bloom. With a power this strong we can create the best life possible. We can always go to this inner sanctuary to become refreshed, relaxed and recharged.

HOW DO YOU GET TO THIS SANCTUARY?

Find a quiet place to sit, cross-legged or in a chair for about fifteen minutes. Close your eyes and focus on your breathing. Take a few deep breaths in through your nose and out through your mouth. Let your body relax. Let go of any thoughts that interfere with this process. Feel all the tension in your body slowly drift down your arms and out through your hands and fingertips. Feel all the tension move down your spine, down your legs and out through your feet and toes.

Let your mind rest and your heart be your guide. Your sanctuary can be anywhere and contain anything your heart desires to bring you peace and serenity. As you begin to feel relaxed, create in your mind a safe haven. It can be a void of warm darkness or one of your favorite places at the seashore or in the mountains. Or it can be a place of your own creation where you've never been before. See this place in detail in your mind and create item-by-item all the things around you that will make this *your* sanctuary. This is a place you can return to any time you choose. After you have a clear vision of your sanctuary, spend some time there. Before opening your eyes, make a mental note of it so that you can return to it as often and for as long as you like.•

Divine Spark

PAULA SULLIVAN

As I shook hands with the president, I wondered if anyone else had heard the words echoing in my brain, "This is not what you're looking for." With diploma in hand and a sinking heart, I returned to my seat. Having put off graduate studies and career until our three daughters were in elementary school, I had earned my ticket to success and happiness. Even though the words I heard on graduation night continued to haunt me, I sent out resumes; still, the career position didn't materialize. In the end, I was grateful for a part-time teaching assignment at a community college within walking distance of our home. During the next several years, I came to understand that my hunger was not for a career.

The search for something to fill what felt like a hole in my chest took me to a monastery in a neighboring town. As I stepped onto land once part of the Osage Nation, my heart leaped with joy as I hiked among scrub oaks and pines and inhaled the scent of decaying leaves. This was the beginning of my journey inward, a journey that would take an unexpected turn.

For several years, I spent Wednesdays at this Benedictine Monastery dedicated to dialogue among religions of the East and West. During extended retreat times, I learned to meditate and participated in the common prayer of the community. In discovering Eastern spirituality, studying the writings of contemplatives and mystics, I found the mystic dimension of my own heart.

Noticing the intensity of my spiritual practice, a few close friends worried aloud. Surprised by their comments, I began to wonder about the path I was taking. After some reflection, I realized that my spiritual pursuit was at the expense of my primary relationships with my husband and daughters. In an effort to become more involved in their lives, I went to the monastery less often, yet continued spiritual practice at home. No matter how hard I tried to be involved in the activities of my family, contentment came only during periods of meditation. I couldn't figure out why my spiritual practice seemed to distance me further from my family.

In the midst of my pondering, I won the career lottery as a full-time member of the English faculty at a community college. Even though I had much less time for spiritual pursuits, once established in the workplace I forgot my unhappiness. Now that I was working full-time, I had great concern for the well-being of my family as well as my students. For the next three years I was happier than I had ever been.

When asked to teach creative writing for the first time, I committed to the act of writing on a daily basis. It was then that the internal tremors began. During the summer break, I worked on a novel that seemed to spin out of nowhere; my fingers flew across the keyboard, filling page after page without effort. For weeks I wrote, hours at a time, until I wrote a scene that scared me into silence.

When I returned to the classroom for the fall term, strange sensations filled my body. Often I heard people say they were losing their mind, but I felt I was losing my body. The world as I had known it collapsed within days. A colleague, well into her doctorate in psychology, saw my panic. I had all the symptoms of post-traumatic stress but didn't know why. She handed me the name of a highly regarded therapist and convinced me to call.

In the time it took to set an appointment, I wrestled with God. For ten years I had traveled the transformational journey. It had rough spots, but I was committed to finding the path that would bring my life into balance. Why was everything falling apart? Where was this God I pursued so ardently, this faceless Being I felt drawn to follow? Had I not been a faithful seeker? Lighting a candle, I sat in a darkened room. Just as "This isn't what you're looking for" echoed in my brain a decade before, a new refrain appeared: "Grace builds on Nature." For many months I pondered the meaning of this statement by Thomas Aquinas, a thirteenth-century theologian I had studied in college.

I had stuffed myself with God, but the hole inside was ever widening. Suddenly I realized that all those years of meditation were not wasted. They had strengthened and prepared me to face secrets I had carried a lifetime in the cells of my body. Meditation helped the secrets float to the surface. Now they were ready to come through my voice in the presence of a skilled and compassionate therapist, one able to listen to what family and friends couldn't bear to hear. He empowered me to receive and accept the truth of my childhood as it flowed from my body's memory in a steady stream. Now was the time to heal a childhood covered in denial and fear of losing the mother and father I had nearly sacrificed my *self* to love.

Grace had led me to the monastery, yet it was my human choice to continue the practice of meditation. That practice gave me the resolve necessary to heal my wounded mind and body. Even as a preschooler, I was attracted to anything otherworldly; sublimation had allowed me to block the unspeakable pain lying just beneath the surface of my conscious life. The real work of transformation had finally begun: rediscovering and honoring my human history.

After a year of therapy, I realized and accepted what I did to survive years of abuse. My mind created other personalities that protected me through difficult experiences and times. Now I was ready to learn their histories and mine, to help all of us come into the present rather than remain glued to a shame-filled past. Initially, my greatest resource and steadfast support was my therapist. His unconditional regard for me as a person has helped me choose life and healing when the temptation to do otherwise seemed overwhelming. On many occasions, he worked with my husband and children to help them understand and accept the most difficult times on my journey to wholeness.

On confronting my abusers, I had to accept orphan status. Close friends took on new significance as I began to look at them as my chosen siblings and surrogate parents. My spouse of now thirty years endured frequent and painful tests of our relationship as he supported my desire to heal. It took both of us to commit to the grueling work of integration if our marriage was going to survive. When I felt despair, he nudged me with his faith. When he became weary of the pain my therapy uncovered, my courage inspired him. Our daughters grieved for their mother and themselves in the loss of so many relatives who couldn't bear the telling of the secrets.

In these years of healing, the deep regard my husband and I have for one another and each of our daughters, as well as our individual and family faith in God, sustained each of us. Even in the darkest times, humor became salve for my wounds. As my husband and daughters began to recognize my altered states more easily, their gentle humor often provided a bridge to the present. During these years of "grace building on nature," our daughters met and committed to relationships with sensitive men, full of compassion and humor, adding to our storehouse of Grace.

Early on, writing became a powerful tool in my healing. After only a few months of therapy, I began writing a mythological novel which became the vehicle for integrating the personalities. The writing brought me moments of profound joy and sadness as I processed the experience of childhood. In addition to writing, massage therapy and body work helped me recover a sense of my body as good and worthy of honor rather than shame.

Today, I no longer have to navigate an invisible minefield of other sets of consciousness. Creative energy flows easily into various writing projects and in my teaching. I find great joy in simple things: breathing fresh air, eating good food, singing in the shower. I no longer escape into meditation to find peace; yet periods of meditation continue to be part of my daily life, making me aware of how sacred life is, of the great joy that living in the present moment brings.

While my transformation began with a solely spiritual focus, my wounded mind and body made the spiritual path very difficult. Whole psyches, I have discovered, lead to realms of the Spirit I only dreamed of tapping. Those realms are available, here and now as I work with students, play with my grand-daughter, lunch with friends. When I began to look inward fifteen years ago, the Divine seemed very far away. Today the Divine Spark is as close as the near-est person, blade of grass or sun-filled sky. God is in the recesses of my own heart. I have tasted and digested the meaning of "Grace builds on Nature." •

PRACTICING
TRANSFORMATION

Soul Practice

QUESTIONS

1. What fears do you have about being in solitude? What gifts does it offer you?
2. If you could have a couple of days of solitude right now in your life, what would you use it for: dreaming? planning? creative pursuits? silence and simplicity? working through trauma? self-reflection? rejuvenation?
3. Are you ready to practice knowing God's will in your life? Can you cultivate prayer to ask God's will to be done?
4. How might patience be your ally in the transformational journey? How might you more consciously cultivate it?
5. Do you engage in trivial talk? How might you become more aware of this, and its effects upon you?
6. What, and how, do you overdo? How does overdoing in this way protect you from pain, emptiness or self-reflection? How might you practice self-nurturing and self-reflection instead?

Practices

1. Practice solitude: carve out a couple of days, or even an afternoon, to cultivate solitude, deep company with your own self. Journal about it afterwards if you wish. What were its challenges? Gifts? See if you can consciously practice solitude at least once a month.

2. Do you have a formal meditation practice? If so, are there ways you can commit more deeply to it? If you don't have one, and are interested, check out local bookstores, churches, temples and meditation centers. People also meditate informally through running, walking, gardening, anything that loosens our identification with our thoughts and allows us to drop to a deeper level of connection with our larger Selves and the Sacred. Is this more your way? If so, how can you consciously cultivate it?

3. Before beginning any activity, practice asking God to work through you in that activity. After it is done, offer the activity and its results to God.

4. Cultivate, as Bryan Robinson puts it, an "inner sanctuary." Read his meditation, and commit to doing it every other day for a month. How is your life different after a month of cultivating your inner sanctuary?

5. Practice cultivating your witness, that part of you that can step back and observe yourself and what is happening within you and around you in a compassionate and detached way in the moment.

10

Acting Soulfully in the World

As we change ourselves, we change the world. We change the world in ways small and large, in our spheres of influence, beginning with self and home, extending out into work, community and country.

When we grow in love, we become more compassionate. Our words and deeds inspire and heal. Those whose paths cross with ours are touched with kindness. Kindness begets kindness and everyone involved heals.

As we become more aware of the oneness of all life, we discover that responsibility comes with maturity. We cannot passively respond to injustice and destruction of life. We become agents of peace, human rights and the preservation of life.

Each of us contributes in our own way. Every effort increases the possibility of a more peaceful humanity and the preservation of life on this planet. Growing numbers of people, working together, even though working individually, elevate the consciousness of humanity, so life everywhere can be protected as precious.

This chapter will compel you to take action, in accordance with your inner guidance.

ENTERING THE
TWENTY-FIRST CENTURY

We need to find a way to make use of our suffering, for our good and for the good of others. There has been so much suffering in the twentieth century: two world wars; concentration camps in Europe; the killing fields of Cambodia; refugees from Vietnam, Central America and elsewhere fleeing their countries with no place to land. We need to use the suffering of the twentieth century as compost, so that together we can create flowers for the twenty-first century.

When we see photographs and programs about the atrocities of the Nazis, the gas chambers and the camps, we feel afraid. We may say, "I didn't do it; they did it." But if we had been there, we may have done the same thing, or we may have been too cowardly to stop it, as was the case for so many. We have to put all these things into our compost pile to fertilize the ground. In Germany today, the young people have a kind of complex that they are somehow responsible for the suffering. It is important that these young people and the generation responsible for the war begin anew, and together create a path of mindfulness so that our children in the next century can avoid repeating the same mistakes. The flower of tolerance to see and appreciate cultural diversity is one flower we can cultivate for the children of the twenty-first century. Another flower is the truth of suffering—there has been so much unnecessary suffering in our century. If we are willing to work together and learn together, we can all benefit from the mistakes of our time, and, seeing with the eyes of compassion and understanding, we can offer the next century a beautiful garden and a clear path.

—Thich Nhat Hanh

Taking Responsibility

HENRYK SKOLIMOWSKI

The new story of the universe indirectly tells us that if you understand it, you have to assume responsibility—for your own future, for the future of the planet, for the future of the universe. This last proposition is again so big and awesome that it is overwhelming. So let us express it in different terms. The universe is thinking through us and wants to take responsibility for its own fate through our wills, understanding and care—insofar as we are capable of taking responsibility for things larger than our small egos. Cultivating your own little garden in times of stress, chaos and confusion is a good strategy. But it is an escapist strategy. At this juncture of human history the universe requires more of us, namely that we become active participants in this enormous cosmic story.

Taking responsibility for things larger than your own self is nothing new in the world. It has always been a prerogative of enlightened souls. We simply need to remind ourselves that *to live as a human being is to live in the state of responsibility.* To live in the state of responsibility is the first condition of living in grace. Let us discuss the meaning of responsibility in some depth, for it is quite crucial to our new role as the custodians of the Earth and as redeemers of ourselves.

We cannot live a full human life without exercising our responsibility. *Responsibility, as a peculiar power of human will and spirit, is a crucial vehicle in maintaining our moral autonomy and in repossessing the Earth.*

Responsibility is a subtle concept. It is hard to define; and yet, paradoxically, even harder to live without. Responsibility is one of those subtle, invisible forces—like willpower—for which there is no logical necessity but without which we atrophy. To reiterate, *being human is to live in a state of responsibility.* When we are unable to be responsible or voluntarily give up our responsibility, we are in a sense annihilating our status as human beings.

"Chosen by the gods" are those who possess a sense of responsibility bordering on obsession, like the Buddha or Jesus. "Forsaken by the gods" are those who are void of their sense of responsibility—especially for their own lives.

Great spiritual leaders of humankind, as well as great social and political leaders, are stigmatized with an enhanced sense of responsibility.

The sense of responsibility is not limited to the great of the world; it is known to everybody. For what is the awareness of "the wasted life" if not the recognition that each of us is a carrier of responsibility which goes beyond the boundaries of our little egos and our daily struggles.

Responsibility, seen in the larger cosmic plan, is a late acquisition of evolution. It comes about as consciousness becomes self-consciousness, and furthermore as self-consciousness (in attempting to refine itself) takes upon itself the moral cause: the burden of responsibility for the rest. Responsibility so conceived is a form of altruism. The tendency to escape from responsibility is a purely biological impulse, a self-serving gesture, a form of egoism. Therefore, these two tendencies, the altruistic (accepting the responsibility for all) and egoistic (escaping from it into the shell of our own ego) are continually fighting each other within us. Each of us knows the agony of this fight.

When we observe the lives of great men and women, the lives that are outstanding and fulfilled, we cannot help but notice that they were invariably inspired by an enhanced sense of responsibility. Those who sacrificed themselves in the name of this responsibility did not have the sense of wasting their lives. Their examples are received as noble and inspiring.

The sense of responsibility is now built into our psychic structure as an attribute of human existence and a positive force. The negation of this force is sin because it represents the betrayal of the great evolutionary heritage which brought us about and of which we are always aware, if only dimly.

The smallness or greatness of a person can be measured by the degree of responsibility he or she is capable of exercising for his or her own life, for the lives of others, for everything there is. Infants and the mentally ill are outside the compass of humanity precisely because they are not capable of exercising responsibility, either for their lives or for the lives of others. They are beyond good and evil, beyond sin and virtue, beyond great moral causes that propel the human family in the long run.

Though fundamental to the core of our existence, the very word "responsibility" (particularly within Protestant culture) is dreaded as a heavy burden. However, when seen as enlarging our spiritual domain, responsibility is a force that continually elevates us. "Responsibility" is a word that has wings. We must be prepared to fly on them.

We have now arrived at the context within which to view the idea of responsibility as a theological category, indeed as a pillar supporting our new religious quests. There is no doubt that we have been called upon, in our times, to assume responsibility for the future of our planet and for the future of our lives. God will help us if we help ourselves. What will finally matter is the accumulation of good Karma, good deeds performed together, rather than acts of redemption coming from heaven. *Our sin will be in failing to assume the responsibility that is thrust upon us.* Our redemption will be the act of accepting such a responsibility. We have much to learn from Eastern traditions as far as Karma is concerned. Another term for Karma is responsibility exercised.•

We Can Heal America

AN INTERVIEW WITH
MARIANNE WILLIAMSON

Marianne Williamson is a well-known author, teacher and speaker. She is the best-selling author of *A Return to Love, A Woman's Worth* and *Illuminata*. She is also the author of a children's book, *Emma and Mommy Talk to God*.

PERSONAL TRANSFORMATION: *Your new book,* **The Healing of America,** *stirs our social conscience and disturbs our political apathy. It is a detailed social commentary about how our country has traded the spirit of democracy for materialism. It is also instructive, telling how we can again become a country where equal opportunity, justice and love of life guide social and economic policy. What prompted you to write this book?*

MARIANNE WILLIAMSON: After I wrote *A Return to Love*, I was offered the chance to write another book. I knew then, in 1992, that I wanted to write a book called *The Healing of America*. I ended up writing *A Woman's Worth* and *Illuminata* in between, mainly because it took a long time to study and research for this book.

PT: *The research behind this book makes it a compelling call to action. How do we each discover our own personal call to action?*

MW: Each of us receives direct guidance from the highest wisdom in the universe. All we have to do is ask for it. If each of us would ask, "How might I best use my time, energies and talents to serve the larger world?" we would transform this society and transform the planet. It is not for me or anyone else to tell people what to do. It is up to each of us to do those things that we know in our hearts we should do. For some people, it's getting sober. For some, it's forgiving someone. For others, it is giving service. For all of us, becoming more aware and involved in the social and political issues of our day bears directly on what will happen in this world over the next twenty years.

PT: *You say that our society is organized according to obsolete social principles. What do you mean by that?*

MW: We have allowed ourselves to fall in line behind the gross delusion that economic principles are more important than humanitarian principles. We allow those in power to make balancing the budget more important than balancing the universe. We have witnessed the terrible social disruption that results from placing money before love on such a mass scale. We have allowed this to happen, and it is our responsibility to change it. It's not enough to whine. It's definitely not enough to just tune out and throw up our hands.

PT: *You cite the Declaration of Independence, the Bill of Rights, the Emancipation Proclamation, John F. Kennedy's Inaugural Address and Martin Luther King Jr.'s letter from Birmingham Jail as tablets on which are inscribed our fundamental yearnings and highest hopes. What are these fundamental yearnings?*

MW: Our founders, as children of enlightenment, believed that there is a spirit of goodness within each person and that from that goodness we can derive the wisdom and intelligence to govern our own affairs. Democracy demands an aware mind. Democracy demands depth of intelligence, soul and participation. It's not enough that Jefferson said brilliant things or that King said brilliant things or that Lincoln said brilliant things. If the things they said don't live in our hearts, and the things they said don't spur us to action, then one of the greatest miracles in world history will turn into mere memory.

PT: *You state that the Trail of Tears, the Vietnam War, systemic racism, economic injustice, violence and militarism form a force field, a barrier before our hearts, that prevents us from grasping these tablets. Describe this force field.*

MW: Lack of social and economic justice, and the rage it produces, encroaching militarism, government secrecy and government hypocrisy encourage the average American to think that America is not what it's cracked up to be.

PT: *You indicate that the way we break through this wall that separates us from acting on the principles and the spirit of our founding documents is to begin an archaeological dig into the American psyche. How do we dig?*

MW: President Roosevelt said that to some generations much is given, and from some generations much is expected. He said that his generation had a rendezvous with destiny. Our generation is one to whom much has been given and one from whom much is now expected. We also have a rendezvous with destiny. The question is whether we're going to sleep through the date. When we watch too much television, we're asleep. When we choose to remain ignorant of social and political issues that affect our lives and the lives of our children on a daily basis, we're choosing to remain asleep. When we take antidepressants before trying serious spiritual, psychological and emotional work as an antidote to our despair, we're choosing to sleep. Once you tune in to what is true, once you tune in to what is real, once you tune in to your authentic knowing and your deeper connection to your purpose in the world, you find easily enough what you should do. Until we tune in, we're too disconnected from our own knowing to have any idea what to do next. That's why the social revolution of our time—and we do need a mass social revolution—cannot be organized. It must be initiated by passion. It must be led, as Gandhi said that the Indian Independence Movement was led, by the small, still voice within. The power residing within the individual aligns with the basic tenets of democracy. To retrieve democracy, we have to start practicing democracy. We can't blame others for taking it away, if we, ourselves, abdicate all social responsibility because we are too busy tending to our own gardens.

PT: *Martin Luther King Jr. said, "We need tough minds and tender hearts." What's the relevance of that sage advice now?*

MW: Most Americans fall in one of two categories: tough minds that lack tender hearts, or tender hearts that lack strong critical thinking. Many people with tough minds need to soften their hearts, but many people with tender hearts need to read a book or two. We must have both and be both if we're serious about turning this country around.

PT: *We're exiting the material age and entering what you call an ideational age. Define ideational age.*

MW: Ideas are more powerful than things. We have looked to the external world as the source of our power, and we are coming into an era where we recognize ideas as the source of our power. That is a huge historical transformation.

PT: *Can the tenets of higher consciousness become a major force for social change?*

MW: Everything we do is infused with the energy with which we do it. The first higher consciousness principle to consider is that who we are is as important as what we do. I asked the Dalai Lama, "If enough people meditate, will that save the world?" He answered, "If we wish to save the world, we must have a plan, but unless we meditate, no plan will work." From a higher consciousness perspective, our spiritual work increases our personal power, and thus our effectiveness in the world. Gandhi and King claimed that soul force is more powerful than brute force. Our current dominant political structure defines power in terms of brute force. We have the opportunity, if we're serious about it, to usher in an era in which power derives from soul force. Soul force is neither cheap nor easy to obtain. Many people give lip service to soul force while avoiding its use as a political tool. It's easier to talk about than to practice. In fact, there is a temptation to use spiritual seeking as escapism, an easy opportunity to avoid looking at, dealing with or seeking to transform the suffering of the world. It's an insidious game that the mind plays. We can't resurrect a world whose crucifixion we've ignored.

PT: *How have we drifted away from the first principles of our founding documents?*

MW: Over the last thirty years, opportunity—particularly economic opportunity—has tilted in the direction of the already privileged. The main form of drifting is economic injustice. We give gargantuan subsidies—over $100 billion every year—to wealthy corporations, while our inner cities are filled with millions of people, primarily African Americans, living under social and economic conditions as desperate as those during the worst days of the Great Depression. This country is in major denial regarding critical violations of our own first principles, not to mention the love of God.

PT: *When we take tax money away from nutritional, medical, educational and job training programs for those with the most need, then give tax cuts to the most privileged, we practice economic injustice.*

MW: Martin Luther King Jr. said that when we give money to the poor, people call it a handout; but when we give money to the rich, people call it a subsidy. Why should we be subsidizing the richest companies rather than America's children? We must repudiate the notion that the market alone fuels the social good. It doesn't. And neither does government, by the way. Love does. Americans need to wake up to the fact that seriously disabled children, children who are undereducated, children who receive inadequate care of whatever kind—when cut off from societal compassion—become our main prison population in following years. Our public policies, which perpetuate the disadvantaged state of so many millions of children, are the root cause of crime and most social dysfunction in this country. This is criminally insane, in my opinion.

PT: *Which comes from policies being driven by economics?*

MW: It's not just policies driven by economic principle; it is policies driven by short-term, old paradigm, spiritually bankrupt economic principles. For

those of use who embrace new paradigm thinking, it ultimately makes no economic sense to spend more money on the military than on educating our children. Federally, we spend 22 percent of our budget on the military and 5
percent on education. We're building a B-2 bomber for $1.5 billion—which
the Pentagon doesn't even want—when that money would pay for the annual
salaries of 56,000 elementary school teachers, or 125,000 child care workers.
Public schools throughout the country ask private schools if they could borrow
paper. Schools throughout the country not only don't have enough paper to
write on, many schools in the inner cities don't even have working toilets. It
would cost $112 billion to make the public schools of the United States come
up to minimum building standards. The Democrats suggested $5 million of
seed money to begin the process; the Republicans cut it to zero. Clearly, the
political system, as it now exists, fails to recognize that taking care of our children should be our top priority. According to the laws of metaphysics, this isn't
a matter of opinion. There is one principle that rules the universe—cause and
effect or Karma. What goes around comes around. From a spiritual perspective,
no society as wealthy as ours, that has as many underprivileged children as we
have, has any basis for long-term economic optimism.

　　　PT: *To make the fundamental changes that we are being called to make,
you say that we must be as committed to our spiritual goals as we are to our
political goals. How do we marry the two?*

　　　MW: We marry the two by being awake. When you read that 95,000
children are being cut off from disability payments, saving something like $5
million, but you read that fifty times more than that is going to corporate
welfare, you call your congressman. You write a letter to your local paper.
You write a letter to your senator. Public pressure makes the world go around,
and that's how it should be, particularly in a democracy. Thomas Jefferson
said it is our responsibility to keep the spirit of rebellion alive. Too many of
us who have passionate feelings don't turn those feelings into action; we don't
turn our energy into social force. The most we ever do is to yell at the television set. Taking the energy in our hearts and transforming it into constructive social action is the next step toward our personal and political maturity.
That's the essence of democracy, and it's the essence of the spiritual power
inherent in a democracy. Democracy means that this country will go in whatever direction the people choose for it to go. Right now our democratic rights
are being unraveled for no other reason than that we're not protesting. We

act more like the royalists in the days of the colonies than like our own revolutionary forebears. We are not being attacked directly by the power structure, by taxes and other burdens such as George III imposed on the colonies. Our oppression is not through pain, but through pleasure. The system provides us with so much pleasure—things to buy and toys to play with—that we're on the brink of being consumed by our own consumerism. We are literally stoned on our lovely lifestyles.

PT: *In writing about the marriage of spiritual and political goals, you say that learning to love effectively is the highest form of political training.*

MW: Learning to love is the highest form of political training for two reasons. First of all, our love for people, particularly children on the other side of town, must become a passionate commitment if we're to save this world. Second, we must not allow anger to obstruct our effectiveness. It's our own fault that we have allowed this radical deterioration. We must assume personal responsibility for this, and assert ourselves now. As Gandhi and King made so clear, the only way to eradicate institutionalized forms of injustice is by awakening the conscience of mankind. We must not attack the power structure; we must speak to its conscience. Dr. King used this image: the rich and the poor of America are all on the same boat, and if a hole forms underneath the seat of the poor, we will all go down. If we don't redress the terrible economic inequalities in this country, within five to ten years we're all going to be living in gated communities, shopping in privately guarded entertainment complexes and traveling in police-protected caravans. We already employ in the United States more private police than public police. Other countries find that horrifying, and we should too.

None of this is to say that I'm cynical or pessimistic about the United States, because I'm not. I'm as much of a champion about what's right in this country as anyone is, and I'm as blessed by what's right in this country as anyone is, but we must seek to make opportunity universally accessible here, or this house will fall. In his inaugural address, President Kennedy said, "The free society that doesn't take care of its many who are poor will not be able to save its few who are rich."

PT: *You define economic injustice as, "An internal wounding of the American psyche which is our economic obsessiveness and our moral paralysis in the face of huge amounts of human suffering. Thirty-six million Americans live below the poverty line, a fifth of American children live in poverty, and the* *top 5 percent of our population takes home half of the nation's income. Economic injustice doesn't violate the letter of the law, but it violates the spirit of the law, and it's the consequence of market-based rather than conscious-based policy." You add that we should set morally outstanding goals, such as having the best educated children.*

MW: Definitely. We are supposedly a government of the people, by the people and for the people. We should have the best educated children in the world. Period. Notice that if we make enough money in America, we send our kids to private schools. It didn't used to be that way. Our public education system should reflect our genius, not our shame. We need possibility thinking, not just in our private lives, but in our public life as well.

PT: *So the way we have economic justice is to have morally outstanding economic goals?*

MW: Balancing the budget is important, but balancing our hearts and actions with the laws of God is more important. Love should come before money. I don't believe that God is asking us to balance the budget on the backs of poor children.

PT: *Another facet of healing that you discuss is cultural amends, atoning for our violations against others. What's the value of national atonement in dealing with this country's legacy of slavery?*

MW: Social change occurs most powerfully where conscience has been aroused. An apology for slavery carries with it the potential to shift the national consciousness by touching the national conscience. We need external remedies as well as internal ones, but an apology is a beginning.

PT: *How would we apologize as a nation?*

MW: There are many ways such a ritual could be performed. If we wanted to do it, we could come up with a way. When representative Tony Hall of Ohio submitted a bill in the House of Representatives suggesting that Congress apologize for slavery, there was such an outcry the bill didn't have a chance of going forward. Newt Gingrich called a congressional apology for slavery mere "emotional symbolism." He asked if it would teach one child to read. I say that yes, it would, because it would remove some heavy blocks to our awareness of love. The government recently spent $25 million dollars on a study of adolescents that proved love is by far the most potent positive force in the lives of young people. The word love was actually used in a headline in the *Washington Post*. The world is changing and it doesn't matter what the old order thinks.

Once the ideas are put on the table, something starts to happen. We have to ask, "What is real political power?" I speak in my book about holistic politics. We need to create in politics what we have created in medicine. The holistic model has revolutionized our health-care system because it has revolutionized our mentality. Whereas we used to think that what the doctor said and the medicine he gave us was the core of healing, we now know that a patient's mental, spiritual and emotional involvement is critical to the healing process. We look at politicians the way we used to look at doctors, and we look at legislation the way we used to look at medicine. But in a democracy, what's going on inside the mind and the heart of the average citizen must be a significant factor in correcting, healing and maintaining the system. Without that, democracy is a sham.

Politics, the way the ancient Greeks used the word, did not mean of the *government*; it meant of the *citizen*. The ancient Greeks thought of politics as something more than the purview of governmental leaders and the actions they took. Politics has to do with every individual's involvement with a larger community and the issues that affect us all. When a congressman suggests that we apologize for slavery and Congress strikes it down, that doesn't mean the political power behind the idea is completely lost. Political power is only increased if a critical mass of people sees the idea as a good one. Later on, it will turn into specific action, when the intellectual and emotional soil is fertile. Nothing is more powerful than an idea whose time has come. Our job is to promote the ideas we care about.

PT: *Does one individual's prayer, one individual's letter to a congressman, make a difference?*

MW: Most congressmen receive fewer than a hundred calls on any particular issue. When you read an article about injustice, or whatever bothers you, call the main switchboard at the Capitol in Washington, D.C., 202-224-3121. Ask for your congressman's office and tell them what you think. It's called a constituent call. One call doesn't make that much difference, but a hundred calls make a lot of difference.

PT: *One person, as a part of a critical mass, makes a difference. That's the message of empowerment.*

MW: Absolutely. When you make that call, an amazing thing happens: you feel more powerful. You feel more powerful because you expressed your power. Receiving such calls is not a joke to congressmen. These people do run for election. Unfortunately, in America most people are either turned off to what's happening and are politically resigned, or they merely accept and complain, rather than exercise their own rights and power.

PT: *The critical mass emerges when we take part, in small ways or large ways.*

MW: We should feel that we're part of a broad-based social movement. We should feel absolutely sure, when a headline like 95,000 severely disabled children are being dropped off government assistance rolls, while at least ten times more than that is being given to wealthy corporations, that not only we are on the phone calling our congressmen and senators, but that we know, without a doubt, everybody of like mind is making the same phone call.

Thomas Jefferson said that the forces of tyranny must be put on notice that we are a free and sovereign people and plan to remain so. Social injustice occurs in America mainly because its agents know that we won't complain. They know we're asleep, and they count on our remaining asleep.

PT: *This call to action is a call to participation.*

MW: Absolutely. We retrieve democracy by exercising it. Democracy isn't a static mechanism. To have a democracy, we must use the tools of democracy. As it is now, out of 163 democracies the United States ranks somewhere around 140 in democratic participation. In our last congressional elections, only 40 percent of eligible voters even voted.

PT: *In that sense, the solution isn't overwhelming.*

MW: Exactly! That's what's so incredible. We are to act on spiritual principles—have faith, forgive and act with love. People think there is a more complicated job to perform than there actually is. That's why the story of David and Goliath is so significant. Goliath is much bigger than David, and much older than David, and better armed than David, but David struck him in his third eye. There is one place where the old Goliath order, the giant in our midst, has no defense. Bring love into the process and bring faith to bear upon it. Once you touch the conscience of the giant, the giant is transformed.•

You Can Make a Difference

G E R A L D   G.   J A M P O L S K Y,   M. D.

When I am dead, how will I be remembered? Has my life been so insignificant that I really didn't make a difference? I heard the story of a man who had worked in middle management all his life and then, long before his retirement, died suddenly of a heart attack. A short time later his wife and children moved to another city to live with her parents. Many of the people who had worked with this man went to his funeral, and this experience began to raise questions within them. Many of them realized, "This could happen to me!" One of the things that frightened these people was that not only was this man gone but that after a while it was almost as if he had never been there. One question that all of this raised was, "When I am dead, how will I be remembered? Has my life been so insignificant that I really didn't make a difference?"

These are not easy questions. Many of us avoid asking them because the answers can be painful. For so many of us, the only answers we get feel empty. Perhaps we stop to realize that maybe we will be remembered only because we were a successful salesperson, or that we were always at work on time, or that we got a gold watch when we retired or that we were a good and fair competitor in sports.

It is my impression that most of us don't give a hoot about being remembered for our punctuality or job performance or how successful we were at earning money. When we are tempted to live our lives as robots, caught up in the routine and humdrum business of the world, or when we spend most of our lives competing to see who is best, or who has the most possessions, we may truly feel that our lives are very empty.

I believe that what really matters to most of us are our heart connections, the love we extend to others from our hearts. This is what really makes our lives matter. Many, many years ago, I remember someone saying that living without sharing one's life is a wasted life, and I believe this is true.

As the years pass and we enter that stage of life that some refer to as "old age" or "elderly," there is a temptation to look back on our lives and be disappointed by what we find. And if we look ahead, we see but a few years left, and we may wonder what we have really accomplished. Perhaps we are struck by the feeling that we have had little or no effect on the planet or those who live on it.

How old we are or how many years we have left to live are questions that need not make us feel that our contribution has been small or limited. When it comes to love, there are no big or small gifts. True love is always total and beyond any measurement or comparison.

Recently, my wife and I were having dinner at the home of our dear friends. One of their guests was a most delightful seventy-five-year-old woman by the name of Vivian, who taught me a lot that night about not associating limitations with the aging process.

Vivian was full of zest and vitality. When I asked about her age, she answered with a twinkle in her eye that she was "ageless." It became very clear that night that Vivian keeps her heart young by always having a thirst for new experiences and new knowledge.

Vivian told us that she loves to take classes at the local junior college. When I asked her what she was studying at this time in her life, she told me the following story.

Her sister and she went to the college to sign up for an evening course but found that the course they wished to take was filled. In fact, they were told that every course was filled to capacity except one. When they asked what this course was, they were told that it was a class on how to become a clown.

They laughed and told each other that this would absolutely be the last thing in the world they would be interested in learning. But after further discussion, they looked at each other and said, "Well, as long as we're here, why don't we just go and find out what it's all about?"

They went to the class and were so surprised at how much they loved it that they enrolled that night, and both of them became totally engrossed in the art of becoming a clown. Vivian told how much she enjoyed preparing her "clown self" to bring joy and laughter to others. She said it easily made her forget her own small, insignificant daily problems. She was amazed at what a serious student she became and what hard work it was to learn to be a clown. It took her nearly an hour to create her clown face and put on her costume, and another forty-five minutes to take it off.

Her clown costume is so good that even some of her best friends don't recognize her when she wears it, a fact that Vivian thoroughly enjoys. She says it gives her the freedom to be a totally different person, one who isn't afraid to do and say things that she never knew she was capable of doing and saying.

After graduating from the clown class, Vivian and her sister decided they wanted to be with children and to make them laugh, but they also wanted to spend time bringing more joy and laughter to older people. As a result of their unique spirits, they have become well known in their home state of Illinois, and many newspaper and magazine articles have been written about them.

We were absolutely absorbed with Vivian's story, so she agreed to meet with us again the next day. She shared some articles and photos of herself and her sister dressed as clowns. And do you know what? No one could ever have guessed their ages. They were indeed ageless, just as Vivian had said the night before! Vivian stated that becoming a clown is one of the most wonderful things that could ever have happened to her. It gives her a way to give back in gratitude all the love she has received in her life. She feels so good about herself because she feels useful. It is her unique way of making a difference in people's lives. She knows that each day she brings joy and happiness to people of all ages.

Vivian awakens in me, and I think in almost everyone she meets, the happy, innocent child that each of us has in the center of our hearts. She made it very clear that she lives only in the present and does not worry about the past or the future.

Vivian seems to have known, from the very depth of her being, that the way to heal yourself of irritation, sadness or unhappiness is to do your best to reach out and help others. She is a true messenger of love, of happiness and humor. She vividly demonstrates that when you don't believe there are any limitations or barriers to expressing your potential and being useful, then there truly are none.

YOU ARE NEVER TOO YOUNG

Our society often teaches us that wisdom comes only with age. Another way of looking at the world is to believe that our true perceptions of wisdom have little to do with how old we are, but much to do with how willing we are to see every person we meet, regardless of age, as a teacher of love. This means that a three-year-old has as much to teach us as a ninety-three-year-old. I know that my whole life has changed since I have accepted this premise.

I think that it is extremely important to take a whole new look at what we tell our children. For example, children so often hear us say that you can't do this or you can't do that until you are older and are a grown-up. Some children get the erroneous message that they can't be fully alive and make a difference in this world until they are adults. Nothing could be further from the truth.

In Philadelphia, an eleven-year-old boy by the name of Trevor Ferrell was watching television one night when he saw a story on the news about street people. His heart ached when he saw these people sleeping in the streets on that bitterly cold night. Although it was late, he told his parents that he wanted to go to these people that night and help them. He just knew that there must be something he and his parents could do to help.

His father was pleased that his son was sensitive to the street people's suffering and that he wanted to help, but it was very late and everyone in the house was tired. Trevor, however, still wanted to go. He was not going to believe in any kind of limitation in following what his heart was directing him to do.

Trevor did not let up. Finally his parents agreed to take him to the center of Philadelphia where the television program had shown the street people to be living. Trevor took a single yellow blanket and a pillow from his own bed. While they were driving, he pressed the blanket and pillow against the car heater to warm them.

As they turned a corner in the city, Trevor saw a man sleeping in the street on an iron grating. He called out to his father to stop the car. Then he calmly got out, walked up to the man, knelt down beside him and handed him the blanket.

"Here, sir," he told the man. "Here's a blanket for you." Then Trevor went back to the car and brought the man the pillow. The man's face lit up with one of the biggest smiles Trevor had ever seen.

"Thank you," the man said. "God bless you."

"God bless you," Trevor said.

Trevor and his parents were deeply moved by this experience. The next night and the next they returned, bringing blankets and hot coffee for the street people.

But even this was not enough for Trevor. He kept telling his parents, "There must be something more that we can do." There seemed to be no way that this boy was going to give up his idea of helping the street people. He did not sit down and draw up a logical plan but he did follow his heart.

Trevor began putting posters up all over town, asking for donations to help the street people. The response could not have been more heartwarming. People from everywhere brought warm clothes and blankets and piled them high in Trevor's garage to be taken to the street people. One person even donated a Volkswagen van so that they could take the donations to the people who so desperately needed them.

Over time, Trevor's Campaign, as it was named, was helping to feed and clothe and even provide housing for the homeless people in the inner city. There just seemed to be no stopping the enthusiasm and generosity that people from the community showed once Trevor got it started. A whole change of consciousness began to occur. Everyone began to feel better about themselves. Schoolchildren, business people, even people from high society showed up to volunteer their time.

Even the most complacent and doubtful people began to learn that they too could make a difference. People of all ages turned up to help, not only by giving money but by touching the hearts of the people around them who needed their assistance.

How We Can All Make a Difference Today

Within each of our hearts is an endless list of creative things that we can do to make a difference. This list is revealed to us simply by asking ourselves each day how we might be helpful to others and what we might do to bring more light and love to our planet.

It is possible to start each day letting these two thoughts fill our hearts with compassion and determination, as if our very lives depended on it. I am really talking about a commitment to save our lives and our planet—being very clear that our purpose every day is to help and love others and the vast Universe of which we are all a part.

This means being totally committed to going through each day having the same concerns and interests for others as we have for ourselves. It means focusing our concern beyond our own selfish interests.

Not long ago, I heard Roger Muller, formerly of the United Nations, suggest that we can all start becoming global citizens and peacemakers by simply closing our eyes and visualizing the kind of world we'd like to have.•

Finding Your Life Mission

N A O M I   S T E P H A N ,   P H . D .

L ife is a personal mission. You have a calling that exists only for you and that only you can fulfill. It takes courage and self-love to answer that inner voice, but being faithful to it is the only way to lead a rewarding life. It's also the most natural way to be. As the Zen master said to his student, "Zen is eating when you are eating." Life is living your personal mission.

Your first obligation is to carry out the mission you are meant for, not what your father, mother, mate or friends say you should do. *No one can go through your life, tell you what it is or how to be it, except yourself.* Your mission will begin to take shape within yourself when you listen to your inner wisdom.

We're talking about self-care here: releasing *the need to please others so that you take care of yourself!* Every one of you has an individual mission to fulfill. Each of you has an individual part to play in that process. There are no substitutes for you, no actors standing in the wings to play your role. And there is no need, or time, to meddle in each other's roles!

Your mission is the most important gift you will ever receive and give in your life. It has only one requirement: that you follow the inner voice of your soul. You have no excuses for missing the mark because it's your mark.

The beauty of experiencing your *Life Mission* is that through it, you get in touch with that special spiritual assignment only you are qualified to fulfill.

WHAT IS LIFE MISSION?

Life Mission represents the very essence of who you are. It is your very deepest intention—the heartbeat, core and overall theme that guides your life. It expresses what you are all about. Other words for mission include *calling, quest, sending, destiny* or *assignment.* Mission is the specific path of your soul in this life.

Once you understand that you have a calling, you learn to connect who you are to what you are doing. Everything makes sense because you do it in the light of your mission. Every task takes on a special meaning, subsumed as it is under this highest heading of your life. A mission then provides the vehicle through which the purpose, shape and direction of your soul's path is expressed.

The "I Have a Dream" speech of Dr. Martin Luther King Jr. expressed his mission: namely, that different races of this country could live and play in peace with each other. Everything he did related to that mission, which was, as he put it, to be "a drum major for justice."

Likewise your dream, whatever it may be, illuminates and enlightens your soul's path like a beacon.

WHAT IF I DON'T YET KNOW WHAT MY MISSION IS?

Some fortunate people (for example, Albert Schweitzer or Wolfgang Mozart) knew their mission at an early age and carried it out consciously. If you despair because you haven't yet completely embarked on your mission process, take heart. For many, a realized mission might not begin to blossom until mid-life. Anne Morrow Lindbergh made the transformation from poet to world explorer as a grown woman. John Kennedy achieved his goal of influencing the direction of his country in his forties. Eleanor Roosevelt moved from a subordinate role to a world figure in her later years. And look at Grandma Moses! It is never too late to embark on your mission discovery path.

The important thing here is to seek and then carry out your assignment. Awaken your own discovery process so that you can walk your own journey, just as countless other courageous people have done.

WHY MISSION AND NOT CAREER?

A mission can take various forms: a career, an avocation, a hobby, a pastime, a passion or anything in between. It can be, but is not necessarily, identical with work. The term *Life Mission* refers to who you are and what you do to live out your soul's purpose in life.

A career is only part of what you do. Instead of thinking about your career as the description of who you are, think of it simply as one facet of yourself which—along with your interests, hobbies, relationships, activities and avocations—helps make up your mission. Think of *Life Mission* as the melody, the theme of your life; career, on the other hand, is the musical instrument you play it on. Using different instruments (careers, avocations and the like) you can express your mission in varying and interesting ways, but the melody (mission) stays the same. Thus you have infinite possibilities, infinite variations possible within one basic theme.

Put in another way, work is a description of what you do, but your *Life Mission* is the spiritual and holistic perspective of your life, the meaning of your life. *Life Mission* is therefore a fundamental reflection of who you are.

WHAT ARE SOME EXAMPLES OF LIFE MISSION?

Missions can take various forms, such as the desire to explore the polar ice caps, like Admiral Byrd; to protect consumers, like Ralph Nader; or to be part of a creative duo like Gertrude Stein and Alice B. Toklas.

A mission could be the greening of Los Angeles through planting trees (the goal of an urban organization called Tree People); dealing positively with the death process, as does Elisabeth Kübler-Ross; playing beautiful music on the trumpet, as does Wynton Marsalis; or sheltering injured and sick sea turtles, like Ila Loetscher. A *Life Mission* is therefore an individual role that is beneficial to all life.

Missions can be humble as well as grand. Some humble expressions I have noted are the missions to keep the floors of the local hospital sparkling, to give people the most unusual and unforgettable taxi ride they have ever had, or to make for children the most elaborate and biggest soap bubbles possible.

THE MISSIONARY SPIRIT

Every mission requires courage and commitment. People with a mission are dauntless, tenacious souls. They have answered their inner voice, taken risks and responded when opportunity knocked. Their lives seem to say, "I know who I am and where I want to be, and nothing is going to stand between me and my destiny. I refuse to hold back or to deprive myself of my purpose." To fulfill their calling, mission seekers may have had to battle institutions, government, society, relatives, parents and even mates. They persevere without asking permission from others and accept responsibility for the outcome. And you can do that, too.

FROM MISSION IMPOSSIBLE TO POSSIBLE

In the old TV series *Mission Impossible*, the main character always received an "impossible" assignment to perform. "Your mission, should you choose to accept it . . ." was the stock statement heard each week. The viewers knew the lead character was going to accept that mission and there was never any doubt he would succeed. That's a good message right there. Let's compare that TV series with the concept of mission. *You Get Your Life Mission from Inside Yourself.* Unlike the show's assignment, your assignment comes from within, from your soul. Your first assignment is to discover what has always been there but needs to come into conscious awareness.

"But," you may protest, "I need to pay for my exotic cockatoo, see the kids through school, keep up my standard of living, join the country club." Anything else but, "This is what I need to do." The creative web that you spin, like that of the spider, must come from within. Manifesting your *Life Mission* is like weaving your own special web. There's no other pattern quite like yours.

Your Mission Is Possible. It would be the quintessential cosmic joke for you to want something you couldn't fulfill. If it's your heart's desire, you can *realize* it.

Your Life Mission Is Unique. If you have been conditioned by herd thinking to be a part of the pack, to emphasize sameness and minimize the differences, it's difficult to identify the unique part of yourself.

What is unique about yourself? Statements such as, "I'm a mother of three children," or "I like people," or "I have an aardvark in my backyard" don't count because they refer to something external rather than a special quality within yourself. Focus on a characteristic that has always been inseparable from yourself.

When I asked Jim, a scientist, about his mission, he said he had the unique capacity to know just how things interconnected. At age seven he declared, "The bombing of Hiroshima is bad for people and it will hurt the fish, too!" For him, caring about the planet and making connections between events shaped his unique mission as an environmental caretaker.

Sometimes I Feel Like a Missionless Child

Many people have neglected their mission. They remain, like the man in Kafka's parable "Before the Law," languishing at the entrance gate to their own space.

What might keep you from embracing the thing that is most yours? You may simply need the concepts and tools to gain entry to your mission. Perhaps you're just afraid. Or you might need encouragement. Maybe you feel the years lost will be too painful, that others will disapprove of your decisions or that you'll lose what you've gained if you change course now.

But as the song lyric goes, "So how could you lose what you've never owned?" What do you profit if you've gained the whole world but lost your own mission?

Whatever has kept you off course, you can change now! Denying your destiny is the ultimate self-denial. Remember that:
- There are clues that your mission has always been within yourself.
- Missed missions can—and must—be found.
- You can break through any barriers to your mission.
- Responding to a calling is the true measure of happiness.

There are no shortcuts to figuring out your life, no instant this and immediate that. Look at all the "how-to" books that offer easy solutions and quick fixes. The national passion for alternative ways to get high through drugs, sex or fads is an example of trying to get to the top without doing the work. You reach your peak if you are willing to climb for it.

CLUES TO YOUR MISSION

Everyone likes clues. They provide the most important evidence of your *Life Mission* throughout your life. Here are some vital tips to help get you on the right track with your mission process.

Clue #1: *Look to Your Passion and Enjoyments.* Jean, a real-estate broker, was forever puttering in her garden and helping friends with theirs. She would habitually stop to look at new landscape designs, and she owned a collection of books on interior design. But hard as it is to believe, until Jean observed what she actually liked doing—creating beauty through nature—she didn't recognize the clues! The body always responds to right action and right thought by giving you energy. Look for times when you feel that energy. Most often it will be evident when you are engaged in a passion or enjoyment. When you're on track, you'll catch yourself feeling enthusiastic, moved and alive. Let's look at Brenda's example.

DRAWING ON YOUR SKILLS

A very discerning Southern woman with an investigative bent, Brenda was heading into her forties with a sense of being totally off-base with her mission. A native of Georgia, Brenda loved those old Southern mansions and the sense of history in her environment. She lamented the decay of those buildings whenever she read about it (clue!).

Brenda knew what she was interested in, but she spent considerable time trying to translate it into practical terms. She constantly found reasons that she should not pursue her mission of aesthetic preservation. A French language teacher, she secretly wanted to use her artistic talents to restore and recover art. But she insisted there was no way to express exactly what she wanted because it was so rare.

She told me of an incident on a plane flight in which a fellow passenger described a rather unusual passion. He made underwater drawings of archaeological sites. "Wouldn't you love to do that?" I asked. She literally rose up in her seat, her eyes brightened and she cried, "*Yes!*" Then she slumped back down and sighed, "But there isn't a market for such an unusual thing." For a brief moment, Brenda had experienced a clue of passion.

What would that "water archaeologist" be doing now if he had limited himself with such thinking? The market for your talent needs only one person—why not you?

What are you passionate about? What gives you energy? Include any items from the past. Pay attention to those clues that tell you what *You* want in your mission. Even if the enjoyment is for a fleeting moment, make note of it! Observe what you catch yourself enjoying (it isn't always obvious). Sometimes a passion can stare you in the face and you won't recognize it. By actively being aware of your passions, you can begin to see your mission take shape more clearly.

Get out your mission journal and write down examples. Don't stop to analyze or censor them. Just write down your passions and enjoyments as fast as you can until you can't think of any more. Add any that occur to you over time. After you have a sizable list (say ten or twenty items), look for the clues, common threads and experiences that weave throughout your list.

Do you enjoy physical things? Mental things? Outdoor things? Solitary things? Things involving nature? Animals? Position yourself to encounter more of your passions and enjoyments by seeking out attractive environments where those feelings will be unleashed. If you like animals, for example, go to a zoo. If you like mountains, go hiking. If you like children, go to a playground!

Clue #2: *Monitor Your Aches and Pains.* When you fail to respond to your inner wisdom, you'll feel specific emotional and physical reactions resulting from that neglect. Your mission will nestle somewhere in your body and reveal its presence through aches and pains. Consult your body and let it tell you what the problem is.

Keep track of those aches and pains. When and where do they flare up? Identify any sad experiences you have had and where the pain was located.

What were the circumstances of the experience? How did you react? What caused the pain to stop, if indeed it did?

Clue #3: *Look for Rewards.* You're never punished for pursuing your soul's path. Some form of reward will always occur. Something positive will happen. It might come in the form of a gift, such as a trip to a foreign country from a relative. Or it might be a sudden loan to continue graduate study. I bought new stereo speakers for the first time in seventeen years to encourage and support my reawakening musical self. The first time I listened to these new speakers, I experienced the rush I had felt with the first set. In the next day's mail, I received a check from an unexpected source for the exact amount I had paid for the speakers. Coincidence? Or a reward?

Clue #4: *Analyze Your Fears.* Fear is a friendly reminder that you may be running from the very thing you love. Fear often arises when you refuse to face your mission.

Clue #5: *What Do You Want to Learn?* When you want to find out about something, it shows that a desire is awakened within you. What stimulates your curiosity? Get a college catalog and page through it, picking out five courses you'd take if you didn't have to be concerned about time, money, skills or other restrictions. Write all those items down in your notebook.

Then look for clues about things you want to know more about. Some items on the list may even surprise you. One client's list included astronomy. She realized that she needed to move to a Western state with wide open skies to fulfill her mission of raising people's consciousness about the gentle treatment of animals.

The teacher teaches what the teacher needs to know. Mission and learning mirror each other like reflecting pools. After all, Mozart wanted to learn more about music and Leonardo da Vinci about the human figure (and not vice versa). What you want to learn gives you clues about your mission.

Clue #6: *Who Are Your Heroes?* Think of the books you used to read as a child or the ones your parents read to you. Who are the people, fictitious or real, living or dead, whom you admired? Maybe you kept a scrapbook or clippings on your heroes. Maybe you went back to the city library again and again to reread that one story about Amelia Earhart or the first big-league African American baseball player Jackie Robinson. They will tell you a lot about the person you want to be. The kind of people they were, the situations they found themselves in and the results they got will give you insights into your own directions.•

Nonviolent Seeds

G E R A R D   V A N D E R H A A R

O nce in Damascus when I was strolling along the street called Straight, I watched as a man riding slowly through the crowd on a bicycle with a basket of oranges precariously balanced on the handlebars was bumped by a porter so bent by a heavy burden that he had not seen the cyclist. The burden was dropped, the oranges scattered and a bitter altercation broke out between the two men, surrounded by a circle of onlookers. After an angry exchange of shouted insults, as the bicyclist moved toward the porter with a clenched fist, a tattered little man slipped from the crowd, took the raised fist in his hands and kissed it. A murmur of approval ran through the watchers, the antagonists relaxed, then the people began picking up the oranges and the little man drifted away."

"In Moscow, in what was then the Soviet Union, hundreds of people gathered outside the Parliament during the August 1991 attempted coup. They built barricades of trolley cars, buses, old pieces of metal and box springs—not so much because that would stop the tanks for more than a few minutes, but to enable themselves to enter into dialogue with the attacking soldiers. Mothers and girls gave the soldiers cakes, food, kisses and flowers and asked them not to kill their mothers, sisters and brothers. One friend brought roses and distributed them to the soldiers and gave them a hug, saying, "Don't shoot; be kind to the people."

The little old man in Damascus might have been a Muslim or Jew or Christian. It didn't matter to the crowd what faith he professed. When he moved into the middle of the disturbance, took the upraised fist in his hands and kissed it, he stopped an ugly altercation. His caring act made a big impression on the agitated onlookers. He had sowed nonviolent seeds on the street called Straight. The women who gave cakes and roses to the soldiers at the Parliament building, the Russian White House, during the attempted coup also sowed nonviolent seeds. The soldiers who took these gifts became emotionally unable to fire on the crowd, changing the course of history.

The legend of Johnny Appleseed who wandered through the Midwest in the early years of the nineteenth century, sowing with generous abundance, was based on the life of a real person, John Chapman. As a boy in Massachusetts, he had a habit of wandering away on long trips in search of birds and flowers. In 1801, his wandering took him down the Ohio River, paddling a strange craft of two canoes lashed together and filled with decaying apples. Having brought the apples from the cider presses of western Pennsylvania, John Chapman planted his first apple orchard two miles downriver from Steubenville, Ohio.

After returning to Pennsylvania for more seeds, he continued planting. Besides the apples for which he became famous, John Chapman sowed seeds of many healing herbs, and indigenous peoples of the area considered him a great medicine man. Apple orchards flourished in what had been the wildness of Ohio and Indiana, thanks to the man who became forever known as Johnny Appleseed. The Johnny Appleseed song begins:

> *The Lord's been good to me.*
> *And so I thank the Lord*
> *For giving me the things I need,*
> *The sun and the rain and the apple seed.*
> *The Lord's been good to me.*

Another seed-sowing image comes from the troublesome terrain of Palestine, half a world away from the fertile fields of Ohio.

> *Hear this! A sower went out to sow. And as he sowed, some seed fell on the path, and the birds came and ate it up. Other seed fell on rocky ground where it had little soil. It sprang up at once because the soil was not deep. And when the sun rose, it was scorched and it withered for lack of roots. Some seed fell among thorns, and the thorns grew up and choked it, and it produced no grain. And some seed fell on rich soil and produced fruit. It came up and grew and yielded thirty, sixty, and even a hundredfold* (Mark 4:3-8).

When seed-sowing works, as it did in this parable, it's like magic. The seed multiplies thirty, sixty or even a hundred times. The wondrous power packed in tiny seeds interacts with the nutrients in the soil to produce bushels of apples in Indiana or fields of grain in Galilee.

But before the harvest, the seeds have to be sown. Sometimes that happens by chance, as when the wind blows them. Other times, they're sown scientifically by human beings who know what they're doing. Sowing for a successful harvest takes seeds ripe with potential—and it also takes receptive, fertile soil.

NONVIOLENT SEEDS

The seeds we're looking at here are seeds of nonviolence. They are alive with the gentle power of Gandhi's satyagraha, truth force. They are bursting with the persuasive energy of Martin Luther King Jr.'s soul force. These seeds are rich with reverence for the global ecosystem that nurtures us all. Kept fertile in our minds and hearts, they consist of an alert awareness of a new way of acting, of a different approach to other human beings and to our planet, different from business as usual. The seeds are not different in the sense of a scientific breakthrough or a newly discovered secret of human behavior. But they are different from the familiar pattern of anxious self-concern, of being swept along by the currents of the moment, of carelessly consuming whatever we want from the soil and air and water around us. These old behaviors are what the prophet Hosea called "sowing the wind and reaping the whirlwind."

Instead of self-concern, nonviolent seeds contain compassionate other-concern, such as that shown by the old man in Damascus or the caring women outside the Parliament building in Moscow. Instead of drifting in the currents of the moment, the seeds express a critical awareness of what's going on and a personal perseverance in reaching for truth. They foster what King called a "tough mind," a discerning vision of what needs to be accepted and what needs to be resisted. "The tough mind is sharp and penetrating, breaking through the crust of legends and myths and sifting the true from the false," he wrote. Instead of casual consumption, these seeds generate a prudent and sparing use, trimmed to more spartan needs. Nonviolent seeds nurture a certainty that unchecked exploitation of Earth is poisoning our planet to death. Nonviolent seeds also produce the recognition that returning violence for violence, hatred for hatred only multiplies trouble. As Gandhi said, "An eye for an eye leaves the whole world blind."

FERTILE SOIL

Nonviolent seeds have power to change minds and hearts when the soil on which they're sown is fertile. And it often is, much more often than we might imagine. Gandhi considered nonviolence to be so congruent with human nature that he called it a law of our being. "Nonviolence is the law of our species," he said, "as violence is the law of the brute." He pointed out that the normal pattern of human behavior is nonviolent in the sense that people usually give and take, learn to get along. They routinely make adjustments rather than fight.

> *I claim that even now, though the social structure is not based on a conscious acceptance of nonviolence, all the world over people live and retain their possessions on the sufferance of one another. If they had not done so, only the fewest and the most ferocious would have survived. But such is not the case. Families are bound together by ties of love and so are groups in the so-called civilized society called nations.*

Gandhian nonviolence appeals to something deep in our hearts. People really do hunger for decency, even those whose life experiences have made them hard and aggressive.

The sower of nonviolent seed does not let a tough exterior deter from extending a humane hand—and keep extending it, even when met by rebuffs. Gandhi identified this kind of patience as a form of self-suffering. The key element in nonviolent example, he believed, is the willingness to suffer rather than strike back in retaliation. When others became explicitly aware of the power of nonviolence through the example of those who practiced it, they would be receptive and begin incorporating it in their own lives.

> *Nobody has probably drawn up more petitions or espoused more forlorn causes than I, and I have come to this fundamental conclusion: that if you want something really important to be done you must not merely satisfy the reason, you must move the heart also. The appeal of reason is more to the head but the penetration of the heart comes from suffering. It opens up the inner understanding. Suffering is the badge of the human race, not the sword.*

When our nonviolent seeds fall on the generous and creative side of human nature, they find the fertile soil that, miracle-like, produces the manyfold grain. After sowing them we find—another miracle—that the seeds themselves multiply. Unlike material possessions that diminish by being given away, intangible riches increase when they're shared. If we give away money, we have less of it for ourselves. But when we communicate compassion, when we sidestep an attack and respond with patience, when we live our appreciation of the gifts of nature, we find our nonviolent seeds don't run out—they multiply. We have more of them to give. And those who receive them, when their own ground is fertile, start multiplying them still more.

Just as their increase seems a miracle, the origin of these nonviolent seeds is often a mystery. We don't make them, any more than we make apple seeds. We get them from others, when we're ready for them. Sometimes we have to be well plowed for them to take root in us. And that hurts. But when we're plowed and fertilized and ready, we can receive the seeds gratefully, store them carefully and sow them generously.

SEEDS FOR ALL

We can sow nonviolent seeds in our microcosm, the everyday world in which we live and move and have our being. Every one of our personal interactions can be engaged in with a greater degree of sensitivity, with a conscious effort to avoid words or deeds that hurt, and an equally conscious effort to say and do what will help. "In the end, it is the reality of personal relationships that saves everything," Thomas Merton wrote. One of my favorite stories is the Buddhist Parable of the Tiger:

> There was once a man who was crossing a field and met a tiger. He ran to a great cliff and caught hold of a root and swung over the side of the cliff. But at the bottom of the cliff was another tiger. Soon two little mice came along and began to gnaw on the vine. The man looked in terror at the tiger below. But then he saw a strawberry vine. He picked a strawberry and ate it. How delicious it was!

We often remind each other, in times of stress, to pick a strawberry; it tastes so good. Once in a while we share the Tiger story with others. It never fails to provoke a smile and reduce some of the tension that so often builds up in these pressing times.

We can also sow nonviolent seeds in the macrocosm, the wide world that is our full human habitat. We can engage in community building, in modeling nonviolent conflict resolution, in making others aware of the suffering of migrant laborers. We can stop the nuclear trucks as we earlier stopped the nuclear train. And there might come a time of rare opportunity to exert significant change: ending a famine, averting a genocide, converting to clean energy. The possibilities are limitless. The fields are vast. The seeds are potent. And the results can be awe-inspiring. This is the way a great teacher put it, "A man scatters seed on the ground. Night and day, whether he sleeps or gets up, the seed sprouts and grows, though he does not know how. All by itself the soil produces grain—first the stalk, then the head, then the full kernel in the head." (Mark 4:2-28).

"This," Jesus said, "is what the Kingdom of God is like."•

Taking Care of My Own Needs

JAY JOHNSON

I have called upon prayer and meditation many times over the last few years for assistance and guidance for others in my life who were experiencing physical, emotional, financial and spiritual crises. For months, I had been there for friends and a family member suffering from life-threatening illnesses. My long-term companion, my sponsor in Alcoholics Anonymous and my barber— all three—had heart attacks on the same day. Bypass surgeries and extended hospital stays followed. During the same time period, I received an emergency call that my mother was spitting up blood from a bleeding ulcer.

Most recently, however, it was I who needed help. Following these several months of great stress, I began to experience chest and back pains, numbness in my arms, and two near fainting spells at my job. I called my doctor from work. His nurse reminded me of an appointment scheduled for the following day. I had arranged a series of tests weeks earlier that I had forgotten all about. As I was leaving work to go home, a colleague, who was a healer, approached me. She led me into a quiet office and, after resting her hands on my shoulders for a few minutes, stated that she sensed nothing wrong. She told me to go home, sit or lie down, then to become still and "let it go." She said, "You have the power to manifest these symptoms in your life. You have the power, with God's help, to let them go, as well. And it's okay to cry. It's okay to express your anger."

When I arrived home, I had barely closed my front door when the phone rang. A friend was calling to retell the details and heartbreak of a series of prior broken romances. At first, in my usual manner, I listened attentively but found myself becoming more and more agitated. He was not interested in hearing of my anxieties about my own health. At last I interrupted, stating bluntly that I had to go and hung up the phone.

I moved to my recliner and breathed deeply, visualizing a white sparkling light entering the top of my head, filtering down through my body, and exiting through my feet and hands. At the same time, I pictured the interior of my coronary arteries open and carrying a rich supply of blood with each healthy beat of my heart. As I relaxed, I slipped quickly into a deep meditation. Almost immediately I was filled with such anger that I shook in my seat. Tears flowed down my face and with an audible "whooosh," a great negative energy was released through my feet and was gone.

I fell into a deep sleep and dreamed of being chased by men with knives. I was then led down the street by a man in a long black cape. He took me to a beautiful "safe" house of crystal clarity. A lucid dream, I knew I was at home in my chair sleeping. But at the same time, my awareness of the details around me was remarkable. I could feel the textures of the upholstered furniture and the warm sun shining on my arm through an open window. I could smell coffee brewing in another part of this dream house and could hear the birds in the trees just outside in the lush green garden.

After spending what seemed to be hours examining this beautiful setting, I knew in my dream state that everything was going to be okay. I awoke in my chair and knew that something quite remarkable had happened.

I went to my tests the next morning and passed with flying colors. The symptoms had disappeared completely. My doctor, quite amazed, stated that he could see no signs of my heart attack three years ago and certainly no new damage. Blood levels were all perfect. "Not just acceptable," he said to me, "but remarkable for your history. Whatever you're doing, just keep doing it." With that, he left the examining room as I remained a few moments with my tears of gratitude and thanked God for "my miracle."

When I left the doctor's office, I stopped at a restaurant for lunch. The memory of the dream was still fresh in my mind and emotions. I took special notice of the texture of the wood counter and plastic stools, the smells of cooking, and especially the face of my waitress. Although I had never met her before in my life, she smiled at me like an old friend. As she took my order, the thought occurred to me that perhaps I was still home sleeping in my recliner, and this was all a dream. And perhaps the waitress is also home asleep, and this is all her dream, as well.

It is now a month since this extraordinary experience, and the symptoms have never returned. Some people I have told prefer to dismiss the symptoms as the result of stress and anxiety. They believe there was nothing wrong in the first place. Others simply smile knowingly as if to say, "Of course! If prayer and meditation work for others, why shouldn't they work for you?" I know that I have changed and am grateful to have been given the opportunity to put theory into practice.

I still have many opportunities to help others and to be there just to listen when a friend needs to talk. But I now realize that I must care for myself as well. I am reminded of a preflight announcement on all airlines that goes, "In the event of sudden loss of cabin pressure, oxygen masks will drop down from the ceiling in front of you. Grab the nearest one and place over your nose and face and breathe normally." And the announcement continues, "If you are traveling with a child, place the mask on your face first!" I always thought, "How selfish to think of myself before the child." But now it is obvious to me that if I do not take care of my own needs first, I may not be there to assist others in need.•

ACTING   SOULFULLY
IN   THE   WORLD

Soul Practice

QUESTIONS

1. Ask yourself in your heart, "How might I best use my time, energies and talents to serve the larger world?"
2. How do you abdicate responsibility and choice-making in this democracy?
3. How does your spiritual work increase your power to act soulfully in the world? How can you marry your spiritual practice with right action in the world?
4. What if you really knew that as one person acting you could really make a difference? How would that change things for you?
5. What is your Life Mission, your calling, your soul's purpose for your life? For ideas, turn back to Naomi Stephan's article, "Finding Your Life Mission." How can you begin to realize your Life Mission in small but concrete ways?
6. How do your passions and enjoyments give you clues to your Life Mission?
7. What are your fears around discovering your Life Mission?
8. How might you sow the seeds of nonviolence toward yourself, in your own heart and soul? Toward family and friends? Toward your larger community?
9. What does it mean to be responsible for, and to, your own life? To others? To the planet itself?

P R A C T I C E S

1. Imagine you have died, and you are listening to friends and family still on earth talking about you. How do they remember you, and for what? Write them down. Ask yourself, is this what I wish to be remembered for? If not, write down what you'd like to be remembered for. Brainstorm ways you can live your life so that you will be remembered for the things that mean the most to you.

2. Ask yourself each morning before starting your day, "How might I be helpful to others today? What can I do/say/be today that would bring more light and love to the planet?"

CONTRIBUTORS

Angeles Arrien, Ph.D., is an anthropologist, author, educator and corporate consultant. She conducts workshops on cultural anthropology, psychology and religion.

Jean Shinoda Bolen, M.D., is a Jungian analyst and clinical professor of psychiatry at the University of California, San Francisco. She is author of *Goddesses in Everywoman, Gods in Everyman* and *Close to the Bone.* She lives in Mill Valley, California.

Joan Borysenko is a cell biologist, psychologist and instructor in yoga and meditation. She is author of several books, including *Minding the Body, Mending the Mind; Guilt is the Teacher, Love is the Lesson;* and *Fire in the Soul.*

Swami Chetanananda is abbot of the Nityananda Institute, a spiritual community based in Portland, Oregon. He is author of *The Breath of God, The Logic of Love, Songs from the Center of the Well, Dynamic Stillness* and *Choose to be Happy.*

Sri Chinmoy came to the West from his native India in 1964. He has spent his life spreading the message that all of us will be united as a world family in pursuit of peace. His activities have fostered the growth of individual and global harmony.

Deepak Chopra, M.D., is a writer, lecturer and physician. He is author of sixteen books and thirty tape series, including *Quantum Healing.* He now heads the Chopra Center for Well Being in La Jolla, California, where he lives with his wife, Rita.

Dan Clark is one of today's most popular inspirational speakers. He is the author of *Puppies for Sale and Other Inspirational Tales, Getting High: How to Really Do It* and *Internal Excavations: The Twelve Precepts of Being Fully Alive.* He is also the coauthor of *Chicken Soup for the College Soul* and a frequent contributor to the *Chicken Soup for the Soul* series.

Larry Dossey, M.D., is a physician and former cochair of the panel on Mind/Body Interventions, Office of Alternative Medicine, National Institutes of Health. He is author of *Prayer Is Good Medicine* and *Healing Words.* He lives in Santa Fe, New Mexico.

Wayne W. Dyer is author of eleven books, including *Manifest Your Destiny, Real Magic, Your Sacred Life* and *Your Erroneous Zones.* He lives in Fort Lauderdale, Florida.

Eknath Easwaran is one of the most respected interpreters of spiritual issues in the world. He is founder and director of Blue Mountain Center of Meditation in Tomales, California. He was born and raised in India and has written over a dozen books.

David Feinstein has taught at the Johns Hopkins University School of Medicine and is coauthor of *Personal Mythology: The Psychology of Your Evolving Self.*

Christina Feldman is author of *Women Awake.* She is a Buddhist teacher who leads spiritual retreats worldwide. She lives in South Devon, England.

Gary Ferguson is a freelance journalist and author.

Erich Fromm was author of *To Have Or to Be?, The Art of Loving, The Sane Society, Marx's Concept of Man* and many other classic works.

Shakti Gawain is author of *Creative Visualization, Living in the Light* and *The Path of Transformation*. She and her husband, Jim Burns, live in Mill Valley, California.

Mark Gerzon is author of *The Whole World Is Watching* and the groundbreaking study on gender, *A Choice of Heroes*. He is a speaker, writer, workshop leader and activist.

Connie Goldman, former weekend host for National Public Radio's *All Things Considered* and NPR's arts reporter, has been part of Public Radio for over twenty-five years. She coedited *The Ageless Spirit*, interviews with famous older Americans.

Thich Nhat Hanh is a poet, Zen Master and peacemaker. He is author of thirty books including *Living Buddha, Living Christ; Being Peace* and *Peace Is Every Step*. He lives in Plum Village, a practice center in southwestern France.

Maria Harris has a Ph.D. from Union Theological Seminary in New York. She is author of ten books on religious education and the role of women in the church, as well as the guide, *Dance of the Spirit: The Seven Steps of Woman's Spirituality*.

Jean Houston, Ph.D., is author of many books, including *The Possible Human, The Search for the Beloved* and *A Mythic Life*. A renowned philosopher and teacher, she is codirector of the Foundation of Mind Research in Pomona, New York.

Chungliang Al Huang, an authority on contemporary Taoism, is founder and president of the Living Tao Foundation and director of the Lan Ting Institute in China. He is author of *Embrace Tiger, Return to Mountain* and *Tao: The Watercourse Way*.

Gerald G. Jampolsky, M.D., is author of *Love Is Letting Go of Fear, Teach Only Love, Out of Darkness Into the Light, Good-Bye to Guilt* and coauthor of *Love Is the Answer*. He founded the Center for Attitudinal Healing and works with people with AIDS.

Robert A. Johnson is a lecturer and Jungian analyst. His books include *He, She, We, Ecstasy, Owning Your Own Shadow,* and *The Fisher King and the Handless Maiden*.

Charlotte Davis Kasl is a psychologist, healer, Quaker, social justice activist and author of *Women, Sex and Addiction; Many Roads; One Journey: Moving Beyond the 12 Steps;* and *Finding Joy*. She lives near Missoula, Montana, where she has a therapy practice.

Sam Keen is a noted speaker and author of several bestselling books.

Bradford Keeney, Ph.D., is a psychotherapy teacher, author and speaker.

Ayya Khema is a Buddhist nun. She spends much of her time teaching and writing.

Sue Monk Kidd is author of *God's Joyful Surprise* and is an editor at *Guidepost*.

Jack Kornfield is author of *A Path with Heart* and *Buddha's Little Instruction Book*. He founded and directs the Spirit Rock Meditation Center in Woodacre, California, where he lives.

Ondrea Levine is the wife of Stephen Levine. They lead workshops together.

Stephen Levine is a poet, author and teacher of guided meditation and healing techniques. He is author of *Who Dies? Healing into Life and Death,* and *A Gradual Awakening*. His work encompasses the most painful experiences of the human spectrum.

Gregg Levoy is an adjunct professor of journalism at the University of New Mexico. He conducts workshops and has written on callings and related subjects for the *New York Times, Washington Post, Omni, Vogue* and others. He lives in Tucson, Arizona.

Jerry Lynch is an author, speaker, sports psychologist, coach and national-class athlete. His six books include *Thinking Body, Dancing Mind* (with Chungliang Al Huang), and he is director of the Taosports Center for Excellence in Santa Cruz, California.

Gerald G. May, M.D., is a psychiatrist and author. His books include *Addiction and Grace, Love and Spirituality in the Healing of Addictions* and *Will and Spirit*.

Rollo May, a therapist, is a humanist by temperament. His books include *The Courage to Create, Love and Will, Man's Search for Himself, The Meaning of Anxiety* and *Freedom and Destiny*. Writing, thinking and theorizing dominate his later years.

Evelyn and Paul Moschetta are a husband-and-wife marriage counseling team married twenty-three years. They have been helping other couples solve relationship problems since 1972. They have a clinical practice based in Manhattan and Huntington, New York.

Richard Moss, M.D., is author of *The I That Is We, The Black Butterfly* and *The Second Miracle*. For over twenty years, his work with groups has helped people worldwide transform their lives. He lives in Oakhurst, California, with his wife and children.

Wayne Muller is a therapist and graduate of the Harvard Divinity School. He is founder of Bread for the Journey, an organization serving families and communities in northern New Mexico. He is the author of *Legacy of the Heart*.

Christiane Northrup, M.D., is a holistic physician and member of the Natural Healing Health Advisory Board. In 1986, she and three other practitioners opened Women to Women in Yarmouth, Maine, to address the specific health concerns of women.

John O'Donohue, a Roman Catholic priest, poet and scholar, lectures and gives workshops in America and Europe. The author of *Echoes of Memory*, he lives in Ireland.

Dean Ornish, M.D., is clinical professor of medicine at the School of Medicine at the University of California, San Francisco, and a founder of the Center of Integrative Medicine there. He has written four bestselling books. For more information on Dean Ornish, see his Web site at *www.ornish.com* and *www.ivillage.com*.

Paul Pearsall, Ph.D., is a clinical education psychologist specializing in interactions between the brain, mind, body and immune system. He is author of *Making Miracles* and *The Pleasure Prescription*. He and his wife live in Michigan and Hawaii.

Veronica Ray is author of *Design for Growth: A Twelve Step Program for Adult Children* and the *Moment to Reflect* meditation series.

Stephan Rechtschaffen, M.D., has been a physician and workshop leader on health and personal growth for over twenty years. He is founder of the Omega Institute for Holistic Studies, a center for holistic study of health, culture, spirit and the arts.

Bryan Robinson, Ph.D., is a consultant lecturer and a professor at the University of North Carolina at Charlotte. He is a therapist in private practice and author of *Heal Your Self-Esteem, Work Addiction* and twelve other self-help and psychology books.

Jim Rosemergy is executive vice president of Unity School of Christianity and a Unity minister. His nine books on spiritual living include *Daily Guide to Spiritual Living*.

Paul C. Roud, Ed.D., is a licensed psychologist. Dr. Roud maintains a private practice, specializing in counseling patients who suffer from life-threatening illness. He lives with his wife, Ellen Grobman, and family in Conway, Massachusetts.

Virginia Satir was one of the founders and pioneers of the family therapy movement. She was the author of nine books, including *Peoplemaking, Conjoint Family Therapy, Satir Step by Step* and many others.

Dannel Schwartz is spiritual leader of Temple Shir Shalom in West Bloomfield, Michigan. He is author of *On the Wings of Healing*. He frequently lectures at universities and community centers on spirituality and modern Jewish philosophy.

Bernie Siegel, M.D., is the author of several books including *Peace, Love and Healing* and *Love, Medicine and Miracles*. He started the Exceptional Cancer Patients, a form of therapy that facilitates personal change and healing. He, his wife and family live in New Haven, Connecticut.

Henryk Skolimowski is professor of ecological philosophy at the University of Lodz, Poland, the first such academic position in the world. He has written many books and articles.

Jacquelyn Small is a speaker, workshop leader and consultant on new-paradigm psychology and psychospiritual group work. She is author of *Becoming Naturally Therapeutic, Awakening in Time* and *Transformers*.

Naomi Stephan, Ph.D., is a composer, writer, motivational speaker and educator. She heads her own Life Mission coaching practice offering consultations by telephone, individual Life Mission coaching intensives, as well as creating books and tapes.

Richard Stone founded Story Work Institute. His programs for social workers and hospice and bereavement counselors help the dying and their families explore the life review process. He is author of *Stories: The Family Legacy*, and lives in Maitland, Florida.

Daniel Taylor, Ph.D., is a professor of English at Bethel College. In addition to producing numerous scholarly articles, he has published a poetry collection, *The Treasury of Christian Poetry*, and two books.

Anne Valley-Fox is an educator, writer and author of a book of poems, *Sending the Body Out*.

Gerard Vanderhaar is a professor of religious studies at Christian Brothers University in Memphis, Tennessee. He is a founding member of the M. K. Gandhi Institute for the study of nonviolence.

Kathleen Wall, Ph.D., is a psychologist and director of counseling at San Jose State University. She conducts rituals for individuals and corporations.

Barbara Harris Whitfield is author of *Full Circle: The Near-Death Experience and Beyond, Spiritual Awakenings: Insights of the Near-Death Experience* and *Final Passage: Sharing the Journey as This Life Ends*. She is on the board of the Kundalini Research Network. She and her husband live in Atlanta, Georgia.

Marianne Williamson is an author, teacher and speaker. Her books include *A Return to Love, A Woman's Worth* and *Illuminata*. She is also author of a children's book, *Emma and Mommy Talk to God*. She lives in Detroit, Michigan.

PERMISSIONS

CHAPTER 1   LEARNING TO LIVE

"The Wish to Grow" is from *The Open Moment*, by Swami Chetanananda (English translation). Copyright ©1995 by Rudra Press, P.O. Box 13390, Portland, OR 97213-0390, (800) 394-6868. Reprinted by permission.

"Living in the Fast Lane" is from *Take Your Time: Finding Balance in a Hurried World*, by Eknath Easwaran. Copyright ©1994 by Eknath Easwaran, founder and director of The Blue Mountain Center of Meditation, *www.BMCM.org*. Reprinted by permission.

"Plant What You Love in the Garden of Your Life" is from *How Then Shall We Live?* by Wayne Muller. Copyright ©1996 by Wayne Muller. Used by permission of Bantam Books, a division of Random House, Inc.

"Finding Joy" is from *Finding Joy*, by Dannel Schwartz. Copyright ©1996 by Dannel Schwartz. Reprinted by permission of Jewish Lights Publishing.

"Heart Lessons: Peace, Joy and Happiness" by Bernie Siegel, M.D., is from *Handbook of the Heart*, by Richard Carlson. Copyright ©1996 by Richard Carlson and Benjamin Shield. Reprinted by permission of Little, Brown and Company.

"Joy Is Your Natural Birthright" is from *Finding Joy: 101 Ways to Free Your Spirit and Dance with Life*, by Charlotte Davis Kasl. Copyright ©1995 by Charlotte Davis Kasl. Reprinted by permission of HarperCollins Publishers, Inc.

"Choosing Happiness" is from *Choosing Happiness*, by Veronica Ray. Copyright ©1990 by Hazelden Foundation, Center City, Minnesota. Reprinted by permission.

"Free to Be Present" is reprinted with permission from Delora Ciaccio Ward.

CHAPTER 2   OPENING TO LOVE

"A Brother Like That" by Dan Clark is from *Chicken Soup for the Soul*, by Jack Canfield and Mark Victor Hansen. Copyright ©1993 by Jack Canfield and Mark Victor Hansen. Reprinted by permission of Health Communications, Inc.

"The Awakened Heart" is from *The Awakened Heart* by Gerald G. May, M.D. Copyright ©1991 by Gerald G. May, M.D. Reprinted by permission of HarperCollins Publishers, Inc.

"The Power of Love" is from *The Wings of Joy*, by Sri Chinmoy. Reprinted with the permission of Simon & Schuster, Inc. from *The Wings of Joy* by Sri Chinmoy. Copyright ©1997 by Sri Chinmoy.

"Finding Your Heart of Love" is from *A Home for the Heart*, by Charlotte Davis Kasl. Copyright ©1997 by Charlotte Sophia Kasl. Reprinted by permission of HarperCollins Publishers, Inc.

"Stirring-the-Oatmeal Love" is from *We: Understanding the Psychology of Romantic Love*, by Robert A. Johnson. Copyright ©1983 by Robert A. Johnson. Reprinted by permission of HarperCollins Publishers, Inc.

"The Human Heart" is from *Anam Cara: A Book of Celtic Wisdom*, by John O'Donohue. Copyright ©1997 by John O'Donohue. Reprinted by permission of HarperCollins Publishers, Inc.

"Letting in Love" is from *Everyday Soul*, by Bradford Keeney. Copyright ©1996 by Bradford Keeney. Used by permission of Putnam Berkley, a division of Penguin Putnam, Inc.

"Taking the Step of Unconditional Self-Love" is reprinted with permission from Aline Cook.

CHAPTER 3   HEALING THE BODY

"Your Natural Healing Ability" is reprinted with permission from Christiane Northrup, M.D.

"Illness and the Search for Meaning" is reprinted with permission from Jean Shinoda Bolen, M.D.

"Follow Your Bliss" is from *Peace, Love and Healing*, by Bernie Siegel, M.D. Copyright ©1989 by Bernie Siegel, M.D. Reprinted by permission of HarperCollins Publishers, Inc.

"Miracle Makers" is from *Making Miracles*, by Paul Pearsall. Copyright ©1992 by Paul Pearsall. Reprinted with the permission of Simon & Schuster, Inc.

"Love and Healing" is from *Healing Words*, by Larry Dossey. Copyright ©1993 by Larry Dossey. Reprinted by permission of HarperCollins Publishers, Inc.

"Healing with Love" is reprinted with permission from Dean Ornish, M.D.

"A Clear Voice Rising" is reprinted with permission from Nancy Pasternack.

CHAPTER 4   SOULFUL HEALING

"Awareness" is from *Creating True Prosperity*, by Shakti Gawain. Copyright ©1997 by Shakti Gawain. Reprinted by permission of New World Library.

"Profound Personal Healing" is from *A Path with Heart*, by Jack Kornfield. Copyright ©1993 by Jack Kornfield. Used by permission of Bantam Books, a division of Random House, Inc.

"The Healing Power of Humor" is from *Becoming a Late Bloomer*, by Connie Goldman and Richard Mahler. Copyright ©1995 by Connie Goldman and Richard Mahler. Reprinted by permission of Stillpoint Publishing.

"Find True Healing," is reprinted with permission from Jean Shinoda Bolen, M.D.

"Forgiveness Meditation," by Stephen and Ondrea Levine. Copyright ©1997 by Stephen and Ondrea Levine. Reprinted with permission from Stephen and Ondrea Levine.

"Healing and Moving On" is reprinted with permission from Jacquelyn Small.

"Death of My Son" is reprinted with permission from Carole Schramm.

CHAPTER 5   OUR LIVES AS TRANSFORMATIONAL STORIES

"You Are Your Stories" is from *The Healing Power of Stories*, by Daniel Taylor. Copyright ©1996 by Daniel Taylor. Used by permission of Doubleday, a division of Random House, Inc.

"Healing Broken Stories" is from *The Healing Power of Stories*, by Daniel Taylor. Copyright ©1996 by Daniel Taylor. Used by permission of Doubleday, a division of Random House, Inc.

"We Heal by Telling Our Story" is reprinted from *The Healing Art of Storytelling: A Sacred Journey of Personal Discovery*, by Richard Stone. Copyright ©1996 by Richard Stone. Published by Hyperion.

"Living the Mythic Life" is from *The Passion of Isis and Osiris*, by Jean Houston. Copyright ©1995 by Jean Houston. Reprinted by permission of Ballantine Books, a division of Random House, Inc.

"The Journey for Meaning" is from *Your Mythic Journey*, by Sam Keen and Anne Valley-Fox. Copyright ©1989 by Sam Keen and Anne Valley-Fox. Used by permission of Putnam Berkley, a division of Penguin Putnam, Inc.

"Dying of Perfection," is reprinted with permission from Gillian Rees.

CHAPTER 6   THE LIBERATION OF AGE

"The Second Half of Life" is from *Your Life is Your Message: Finding Harmony with Yourself, Others and the Earth*, by Eknath Easwaran. Copyright ©1992 by Eknath Easwaran, founder and director of The Blue Mountain Center of Meditation, www.BMCM.org. Reprinted by permission.

"Coming into Our Own" is from *Coming Into Our Own* (republished as *Listening to Midlife: Turning Your Crisis into a Quest*, Shambala, 1992) by Mark Gerzon. Copyright ©1992 by Mark Gerzon. Reprinted with permission from Mark Gerzon.

"The Liberation of Age" is from *Jubilee Time*, by Maria Harris. Copyright ©1995 by Maria Harris. Used by permission of Bantam Books, a division of Random House, Inc.

"The Challenges of Aging" is from *Lights of Passage*, by Kathleen Wall, Ph.D. Copyright ©1994 by Kathleen Wall, Ph.D., and Gary Ferguson. Reprinted by permission of HarperCollins Publishers, Inc.

"Creativity and Aging" is from *Ageless Spirit*, by Phillip L. Berman. Copyright ©1990 by Phillip L. Berman. Reprinted by permission of Ballantine Books, a division of Random House, Inc.

"Taking Risks" is reprinted with permission from Andrea Susan Glass.

CHAPTER 7   THE FINAL TRANSITION

"If I Had Only" by Virginia Satir. Used with permission of Avanta The Virginia Satir Network, 2104 SW 152nd St., #2, Burien, WA 98166. All rights reserved.

"A Year to Live" is reprinted with permission from Stephen Levine.

"Understanding the Dying Process" is from *Final Passage*, by Barbara Harris Whitfield. Copyright ©1998 by Barbara Harris Whitfield. Reprinted by permission of Health Communications, Inc.

"Death and Dying" is from *Timeshifting: Creating More Time to Enjoy Your Life*, by Stephan Rechtschaffen, M.D. Copyright ©1996 by Stephan Rechtschaffen. Used by permission of Doubleday, a division of Random House, Inc.

"Death Is a Mirror" is from *Mortal Acts: 18 Empowering Rituals for Confronting Death*, by David Feinstein. Copyright ©1993 by David Feinstein and Peg Elliott Mayo. Reprinted by permission of HarperCollins Publishers, Inc.

"Facing Death" is from *Making Miracles*, by Paul C. Roud. Copyright ©1990 by Paul C. Roud. By permission of Little, Brown and Company.

"A Core of Love" is reprinted with permission from Pat Duffy.

CHAPTER 8   THE PROCESS OF TRANSFORMATION

"For the World to Be Transformed" is from *For the Love of God*, edited by Benjamin Shield and Richard Carlson, Ph.D. Copyright ©1997 by Benjamin Shield and Richard Carlson, Ph.D. Reprinted by permission of New World Library.

"Finding the Way" is from *Soul Food*, by Jack Kornfield. Copyright ©1996 by Jack Kornfield and Christina Feldman. Reprinted by permission of HarperCollins Publishers, Inc.

"The Heart of Optimism" is reprinted with permission from Joan Borysenko.

"Walking the Mystical Path with Practical Feet" originally appeared in *Nourishing the Soul*, edited by Anne Simpkinson and Charles Simpkinson. Copyright ©1995 by Angeles Arrien. Reprinted by permission of Angeles Arrien.

"Personal Transformation," is reprinted with permission from Deepak Chopra, M.D., and Richard Moss, M.D.

"The Long Way Round" is from *When the Heart Waits*, by Sue Monk Kidd. Copyright ©1990 by Sue Monk Kidd. Reprinted by permission of HarperCollins Publishers, Inc.

"Making Pilgrimage" is from *Callings: Finding and Following an Authentic Life*, by Gregg Levoy. Copyright ©1997 by Gregg Levoy. Reprinted by permission of Harmony Books, a division of Crown Publishers.

"Realizing Your Potential" is from *Working Out, Working Within*, by Jerry Lynch and Chungliang Al Huang. Copyright ©1998 by Jerry Lynch and Chungliang Al Huang. Used by permission of Putnam Berkley, a division of Penguin Putnam, Inc.

"Learning to Wait for God" is from *A Closer Walk with God*, by Jim Rosemergy. Copyright ©1991 by Jim Rosemergy. Reprinted by permission of Acropolis Books.

"Creativity and Healing" is reprinted with permission from Candace Hartzler.

CHAPTER 9   PRACTICING TRANSFORMATION

"Commitment" is from *The Open Moment*, by Swami Chetanananda (English translation). Copyright ©1995 by Rudra Press, P.O. Box 13390, Portland, OR 97213-0390, (800) 394-6868. Reprinted by permission.

"Getting Your Ego Out of the Way" is from *The Marriage Spirit*, by Drs. Evelyn and Paul Moschetta. Copyright ©1998 by Evelyn Moschetta and Paul Moschetta. Reprinted with the permission of Simon & Schuster, Inc.

"Beginning Anew" is from *Teachings on Love*, (1997) by Thich Nhat Hanh. Reprinted with permission of Parallax Press, Berkeley, California.

"Meditation" is from *Being Nobody, Going Nowhere*, by Ayya Khema. Copyright ©1987 by Ayya Khema. Reprinted with permission from Wisdom Publications, 199 Elm St., Somerville, MA 02144, U.S.A. To order a full copy of this book, or for a complete Wisdom Publications catalog, please call (800) 272-4050, or visit us at *www.wisdompubs.org*.

"God's Will" is from *God Is*, by Sri Chinmoy. Copyright ©1997 by Sri Chinmoy. Reprinted with permission of Aum Publications.

"Trivial Talk" is from *The Art of Being*, by Erich Fromm. Copyright ©1989 by The Estate of Erich Fromm. Reprinted by permission of The Continuum Publishing Company.

"Breaking Our Patterns of Overdoing It" is from the book *Overdoing It*, by Bryan Robinson. Copyright ©1992 by Bryan Robinson. Reprinted with permission from Bryan Robinson.

"Divine Spark" is from *The Mystery of My Story*, by Paula Sullivan. Copyright ©1994 by Paula Sullivan. Reprinted by permission of Paulist Press.

CHAPTER 10   ACTING SOULFULLY IN THE WORLD

"Entering the Twenty-First Century" is from *Touching Peace: Practicing the Art of Mindful Living*, (1992) by Thich Nhat Hanh. Reprinted with permission of Parallax Press, Berkeley, California.

INDEX

ABOUT THE EDITORS

RICK NURRIESTEARNS has been the publisher of PERSONAL TRANSFORMA-
TION magazine for eight years. He has been involved in publishing transformational books, newsletters and magazines for over seventeen years.

MARY NURRIESTEARNS, L.C.S.W., is a psychotherapist in private practice.
She has twenty-five years of professional experience. Mary has been the editor
of PERSONAL TRANSFORMATION magazine for eight years.

Rick and Mary cocreated and founded PERSONAL TRANSFORMATION magazine, in 1991. They have studied extensively with leading thinkers and trainers
in personal and spiritual transformation. They practice personal transformation in their lives, conduct workshops and speak on personal transformation.
They live in a wooded area near Tulsa, Oklahoma.

MELISSA WEST, M.S., is a psychotherapist, teacher and author. She
co-founded and co-directs LifeQuest, a nonprofit organization dedicated to
contemporary rites of passage. She gives workshops and speaks nationally on
transformation, ritual and rites of passage. She lives in Seattle, Washington.

As your journey of personal and spiritual growth continues, let *PERSONAL TRANSFORMATION* magazine illuminate your way.

PERSONAL TRANSFORMATION magazine is a companion and guide to inform and accompany you on your journey of self-awakening. We will help you develop by connecting you with the many transformational resources available, along with the latest insights on personal and spiritual growth from top experts.